DANTE AND ISLAM

DANTE'S WORLD: HISTORICIZING LITERARY CULTURES OF THE DUE AND TRECENTO

Teodolinda Barolini, series editor

This series publishes innovative and original work of a historicist bent on cultural and literary figures and intellectual currents of thirteenth- and fourteenth-century Italy.

"Dante's World" embraces work on all aspects of the literary cultures thriving on the Italian peninsula in the two centuries straddled by Dante's life. The series treats authors from Giacomo da Lentini and Guido Cavalcanti to Boccaccio and Petrarca. Books in the series consider theological, social, historical, economic, and philological topics and explore gender, rhetoric, and material culture.

Although this series extends well beyond Dante, at its methodological core is an attempt to reverse the essentialism that has been an abiding feature of Dante exegesis. Against that tradition, "Dante's World" brings together a body of critical readings that are historically engaged and hermeneutically complex.

DANTE AND ISLAM

Edited by

JAN M. ZIOLKOWSKI

Fordham University Press New York 2015

Fordham University Press also publishes its books in a variety of electronic formats. Some content that appears in print may not be available in electronic books.

Visit us online at www.fordhampress.com.

Library of Congress Cataloging-in-Publication Data is available from the publisher.

Printed in the United States of America

17 16 15   5 4 3 2 1

First edition

Contents

Images of Muḥammad in Dante

Islam in Dante's Italy

DANTE AND ISLAM

Introduction

JAN M. ZIOLKOWSKI

The title of this collection is not a wild novelty, because since 1921 the wording "Dante and Islam" has been pressed into service repeatedly in various languages as a heading for books, articles, and book reviews.[1] Nonetheless, the phrase may sound jarringly paradoxical, in pairing the poet most emblematic of medieval Christianity with the name of a rival religion. The *Commedia* possesses a stature beyond being merely the foundational and preeminent masterpiece in the canon of Italian literature. It also stands more generally as a centerpiece in Western culture. Among other things, it constitutes a summa of medieval Christian culture and an archetype of Catholic literature.[2] Although Dante could not have foreseen every winding and turning in the subsequent reception of his poem, in *Paradiso* he refers presciently to his work as the "sacrato poema" (*Par.* 23.62 "consecrated poem") and "poema sacro" (*Par.* 25.1 "sacred poem"). Yet the *Commedia* achieves its summa-like (or encyclopedic) qualities in part by incorporating heterogeneous components, some of which render it highly uncanonical for a canonical work.[3] We should not be startled to learn that Dante was already accused of being heterodox and even heretical by some of his near contemporaries.[4]

By exemplifying what is Western, Christian, and Catholic, the *Commedia* exerts in the early twenty-first century a force far beyond what one might expect an early fourteenth-century literary composition still to radiate in a world that is caught up more in the present than in the distant past. For nearly a century controversies have boiled over repeatedly as to what the poem signifies about the perspectives of medieval Christians on Muslims. Nor have the disputes been restricted to what the *Commedia* meant in its own day. Dante's chef d'oeuvre and the iconographic tradition based upon it have also incited powerful reactions from Muslims even in the last few years.

An extreme instance of hostility toward Dante's poem is the arrest in 2002 of alleged Islamic terrorists who were charged with plotting to blow up the Basilica of San Petronio in Bologna so as to destroy a fresco of the Last Judgment (1409) by Giovanni da Modena (flourished 1409–1456), which contains an illustration of Muḥammad being consigned to the flames of Hell that was inspired by Dante's *Inferno*.[5] On an extreme level this conspiracy gives testimony of the outcry that the Italian poet's portrayal of the Muslim Prophet can engender. Less explosively, the Union of Italian Muslims petitioned the pope to request that the offending artwork be concealed because of its insult to Islam. For similar reasons, the group advocated that Dante's poem not be included in the curriculum taught in immigrant areas.[6]

As such episodes demonstrate, the *Commedia* prompts responses that cover a broad swath. On the one hand, it enjoys approbation nowadays as a preeminent work not just of European literature in general but of Christian literature in particular. In this capacity it could be situated at one end of the spectrum by those who view medieval encounters between Christianity and Islam as being the starting points in an ongoing "clash of civilizations."[7] Within a construct that assumes mutual resistance between the cultures associated with the two religions, much could favor the inference that the Latin Christendom exemplified by Dante would not have sought much, at least not knowingly, from Muslims. The West would have incurred debts to the East mainly in specific technical areas, rather than in those more general cultural spheres that would have been likely to manifest themselves in literature.[8]

On the other hand, alternative interpretations of Dante's poem not merely acknowledge but even emphasize—perhaps overemphasize— evidence that speaks on behalf of Islamic influences and that allows for the feasibility of peaceful coexistence between Muslims and Christians. Among such readings, one takes the seemingly contradictory tack of simultaneously admitting that Dante dooms Muḥammad to the torments of Inferno but also of avowing that the *Commedia* formulates "religious pluralism that may rightly be called Islamic"—that "the 'philosophy of religion' that is one of the fundamental components of the *Commedia*—a discourse aiming to foster tolerance for religious and cultural diversity—was in large part a legacy of the Arabo-Islamic philosophical tradition."[9] Other appraisals present Dante as having been not merely resistant to conventional Christianity but receptive and even welcoming to the countervailing enticements of Islam. In effect, they maintain that the Italian poet participated, insofar as his different geographical and cultural position permitted him, in a spirit of pluralism that in studies of medieval Iberia is indicated by the Spanish term *convivencia*.[10]

Convivencia (which could be translated roughly as "coexistence") sums up the peaceful cohabitation that in the right places and times prevailed in the Middle Ages among Christianity, Judaism, and Islam. The word has entered ever more common usage since its introduction by the Spanish philologist and historian Américo Castro (1885–1972) in the 1940s.[11] The coexistence it describes is alleged to have predominated in portions of Muslim-held Spain (known as al-Andalus) and Arabized, Arabicized (if the process was linguistic and cultural rather than ethnic), or Arabicizing (if it was still underway) Spain from about the invasion in 711 to the expulsion of the last Muslims in 1492 (and even beyond if one makes allowance for the Muslim converts to Christianity who were specified by the Spanish adjective *morisco*, meaning "Moor-like, Moorish").[12]

Within these eight hundred years, three particularly noteworthy centuries run from 711 to 1031, while the Umayyad caliphate was installed at Córdoba. The Mozarabs, as are styled the Christians who dwelled under Islamic rule in al-Andalus, adopted ways of life practiced by the Muslims, and these Christians helped to bridge the chasm between the religions and cultures. Taken to an extreme, the concept of *convivencia* could be enlisted to uphold a contrast between a hidebound and almost belligerently backward Latin Christendom and a benign and tolerant Muslim world in which a *pax Islamica*—an Islamic peace—held sway.

Nothing should prevent us from applying the modern Italian cognate *convivenza* to similar effect, to denote comparable conditions of peaceable cohabitation on the southern Italian peninsula and on Sicily, if in fact they obtained there. Muslims not only ruled Sicily for some two hundred years but also abided long afterward as a cultural force under the Normans who supplanted them.[13]

Such evidence can cut—or can be cut—in entirely opposite ways. As the concluding essay in this volume (by David Abulafia) demonstrates, surviving Muslims from Sicily were eventually transported to the mainland and collected in a settlement that endured for decades. Thus the persistence of the Muslim community known as Lucera Saracenorum (Lucera of the Saracens) on the Italian mainland through the end of the thirteenth century could be construed as important confirmation that not only Spain but Italy too had a continuing Muslim presence. Yet the town could be regarded less optimistically as a sort of concentration camp *avant la lettre,* and the dispersal of its inhabitants in 1300 (a date not without significance in the appreciation of Dante's *Commedia,* since it is the year in which the action is supposed to have taken place) bespeaks at least to some degree an antagonism toward Islam on the peninsula.

Lucera Saracenorum constitutes a microcosm of the Muslim foothold in Italy. "Saracens" occupied Sicily and parts of the mainland for most of three centuries, namely, the ninth, tenth, and eleventh. Montecassino, the renowned monastery where Benedict set down his still more famous rule for monastic communal living, had to be abandoned after being sacked and burned by Muslim raiders in 883. In the twelfth, thirteenth, and fourteenth centuries the disruptions of the earlier centuries found compensation, as innovations were enabled thanks to contact with Islamic civilization through the Crusades and Norman Sicily. The Normans inhabited southern Italy cheek by jowl with the Muslims, and they created a dominion over a nearly completely Muslim population. In Sicily the juxtaposition and fusion of cultures led to spectacular outcomes in art, architecture, literature, and other fields. The Palermitan court of King Roger II (1095–1154) intensified a cultural symbiosis between Islam and Christianity that reached its apogee under Frederick II (d. 1250).

Where are we left? Ideological reasons are imaginable that could motivate those who envisage a golden age of yore in which Muslim and Islamophile or at least Muslimophile rulers avoided the hostilities that often arose among Muslims, Jews, and Christians in Europe, the Middle East, and elsewhere. By the same token, it is easy to picture why others could be stimulated to magnify the frictions between Christians and Muslims in the Middle Ages as a means to model—and justify—the conflicts in our own day.

In cultural criticism and literary scholarship Dante's poem holds special relevance, since *Orientalism* (1978), a highly influential book by Edward W. Said (1935–2003), features a brief but pivotal analysis of the *Commedia* as illustrating a midpoint in the progression toward what he calls "the Orientalist vision," a Western stance toward the East in which empirical data about the Orient are disregarded so as to turn "Islam into the very epitome of an outsider against which the whole of European civilization from the Middle Ages was founded."[14] Said's polemic suggests that even long after the formal demise of European empires the academic disciplines once described conventionally as "Oriental studies" have purveyed preconceptions of "the Orient" and "Orientals" and that these academic representations have served the interests of colonial and neocolonial domination in politics, economics, and culture.

In the peculiar physics of the humanities, some actions do have equal and opposite reactions. In this instance Orientalism is reciprocated by Occidentalism, in which Western cultures are distorted and reduced to prejudiced platitudes that are espoused both within and without the West.[15] To date, such stereotyping has garnered far less attention than have the twisted representations to which they correspond, but we need to take care in sidestepping the pitfalls of "the Orientalist vision" not to overcompensate by slipping, consciously or unconsciously, into an Occidentalist vision.

It bears recalling that neither *convivencia* nor Orientalism (or for that matter Occidentalism) is a medieval word: they are modern concepts that have been brought to bear on the Middle Ages, partly (as would be natural) or even wholly in answer to present-day perceptions and preoccupations.[16] To state matters more bluntly, both carry with them the dangers of anachronism and anatopism, from the standpoint of cultural chronology and geography, respectively.[17]

The imperative to rebut Islam and its influence may be seen to have contributed to Dante's decision to frame the *Commedia* as a vision of Hell and Heaven.[18] But such a vague formulation begs a host of questions that spring up in response to the implications of the seemingly straightforward phrase "Dante and Islam." With reference to the first element, does being enshrined as canonically medieval Christian necessarily entail being anti-Islamic, unindebted to Islam, or even untouched by cultures—above all, Arabic and Persian—that since the Middle Ages have been affiliated strongly with Islam? Or, to look from a different vantage point, does being an embodiment of Western culture, as Dante has become, exclude ipso facto responsiveness to non-Western influences?

To turn to the final element in the phrase "Dante and Islam," what exactly did Islam comprehend? In other words, to what extent did the categories of the Arab and Arabic, the one ethnic and the other linguistic, overlap with each other? And what would Dante's conceptions of Islam have been, irrespective of ethnicity or language? He used the word "Arabs" only once (*Par.* 6.49 *Aràbi*), as an ethnic term not for any people contemporary with him but instead for the ancient Carthaginians—the "Arabs" who followed Hannibal across the Alps to invade Roman Italy. And what equivalence was fixed between the Arab/Arabic on the one hand and Islam/Muslim on the other? One certainty is that as we gaze back at the Middle Ages from our own today, we should make no instant equation between Islamic and Arabic or between Christian and Latin, nor should we establish an automatic dichotomy between Islamo-Arabic and Christian-Latin.

As if matters were not already sufficiently embroiled, how did the medieval equivalents of designations such as Berber, Hagarite, Ishmaelite, Moor, and Saracen enter into the picture? Dante's default for referring to Arabs, whether of the Levant, Spain, or Sicily, is the last-mentioned epithet, Saracen (*Saracino*), which serves even more generally to mark Muslims.[19] Whereas in the chansons de geste in Old French the substantive functions as a synonym for pagan, Dante applies it to different effect by coupling it three times with the stock word for Jew or Jewish (*Giudeo*).[20] Dante's own antagonism cannot be questioned when Guido da Montefeltro chides Pope Boniface VIII (1294–1303) for warring on Christians (the Colonna family), describing him as "Lo principe d'i novi Farisei, / avendo guerra presso a Laterano, / e non con Saracin né con Giudei" (*Inf.* 27.85–87 "The Prince of the new Pharisees, having war near the Lateran, and not with Saracens or Jews").[21]

Even ostensibly positive applications of the term, under closer scrutiny, reveal symptoms of being backhanded compliments. Berber women (despite the fact that the unfavorable undertone of "barbarian" probably rang through) are lauded, as are Saracen ones (*Par.* 23.103–5), but less to extol them in their own right than to chastise Florentine ladies by contrast for their shamelessness. Forese Donati (ca. 1260–1296), a friend of Dante, credits Muslim women with being more modest than their Florentine counterparts. Yet the context offers at best mixed flattery, since the drift of the passage is that even barbarians and Saracens (to use Dante's word) surpass in modesty the womanhood of Florence. Likewise, when Dante singles out Italy as being "pitiable even among the Saracens" (*Epist.* 5.5 "iam nunc miseranda Ytalia etiam Saracenis"), he implies not so much that Muslims are extraordinarily compassionate as that the conditions on the peninsula are so wretched as to induce even such aliens to commiserate.

Does Dante offer adequate evidence for us to draw any fine distinctions, or are these questions ones that would engage a philologist today but that would have been irrelevant, inconceivable, or both in the years around 1300? Would we be better off grouping together not only Arab/Arabic and Islam/Muslim but also Arabicizing and Islamicizing? In the last case, we could mull over using a catch-all term, such as "Islamicate."[22]

This collection affords opportunities to achieve many goals, one of which is to facilitate innovative outlooks and to allow for fresh nuances while not overlooking old views or denying obvious realities of the relations between Dante and Islam. The unsettled issues subsumed under this heading have been ramifying in fits and starts for nearly one hundred years, but the preceding century did not come close to exhausting the topics or to guaranteeing any consensus about them. To secure any meaningful new insights into the cause célèbre of Dante and Islam requires investigating generally what effects Islam had on Latin Christendom in the late thirteenth and early fourteenth centuries; what the great Italian poet could have gleaned from other people or texts about Muḥammad and Islam, since much more information was forthcoming than is sometimes realized, as can be gauged from the essay in this collection by José Martínez Gázquez on "Translations of the Qur'an and Other Islamic Texts before Dante (Twelfth and Thirteenth Centuries)"; what of his formation he owed directly or indirectly to Islamic and Islamicate culture (and whether he knew or even could have known that it had come to him via Islamic culture or Muslim learning); which actual Muslims would have resided in Italy during his lifetime; what direct and indirect acquaintance with Islam other Italians contemporary with him may have had, through travels to the Islamic East (or West, since regions of Spain lingered in Muslim hands until 1492), or through contact with Muslims who ventured westward or lived there; and, last but not least, to what degree Dante could have been acquainted specifically with Islamic eschatology.

Although preliminary probings of Dante's perspectives on Muslims, Islamic culture, and related issues antedated the early twentieth century,[23] study of such matters was propelled as never before by a book published in 1919. The volume under scrutiny, *La escatología musulmana en la Divina Comedia* (Muslim Eschatology in the *Divine Comedy*), was first delivered as an inaugural lecture by the Spanish Arabist, Miguel Asín Palacios (1871–1944), on January 26, 1919, upon his election to the Real Academia Española (Spanish Royal Academy [of Sciences]). His central contentions would have stirred unease in some milieus and excitement in others whenever his disquisition came into print, but the subsequent debate reached a singularly contentious pitch because publication took place on the eve of the six-hundredth anniversary of Dante's death (1321–1921).[24]

Among the many consequences of the brouhaha, the phrasing of the title has had a protracted afterlife. When reprinted not ten years after its initial print run, the book was entitled more pithily *Dante y el Islam* (Dante and Islam).[25] The equivalent Italian phrase *Dante e l'Islam* was co-opted as the title when Asín Palacios's magnum opus was finally published in Italy in 1994.[26] The English translation and abridgement was entitled *Islam and the Divine Comedy*, which heightened the polemic force by foregrounding and privileging Islam.[27] "Dante and Islam," whether hallowed or unhallowed by its multiple uses, has been adopted for this collection.

Asín Palacios's argument that Dante was beholden to Muslim sources elicited starkly different reactions, depending upon the field of scholarship to which the given reader or reviewer adhered. After first appearing in 1919, *La escatología musulmana en la Divina Comedia* was received by and large favorably by Orientalists and especially by Arabists, but mostly unenthusiastically or even negatively by Romanists (with the exception mainly of Hispanists). Nowhere was the negativism more widespread and emphatic than among Italian Dantists.[28]

The reception of Asín Palacios's writings has been styled "a scandalous chapter in the history of Dante scholarship."[29] Although the concession that the *Commedia* or any other of Dante's writings may have "Arabesque" properties should not undermine the authenticity of the archetypal and foundational poet in Italian literature, it is understandable how in different times or circumstances the mere acceptance of a possibility that Dante may have been conditioned by Islamic eschatological traditions in his conception of a voyage through an otherworld of Hell and Heaven could have been felt to diminish him. Thus Dantists may have rejected the Spaniard's book with particular vehemence because admission of such indebtedness could have been felt to lessen in one fell swoop the individual genius, Christianity, and Italianness of a poet about whom they had a proprietary sense. Indeed, it has been speculated that the spurning of Asín Palacios's theory has reflected both cultural nationalism and the idolization of Dante that has been styled Dantolatry[30]—that Dantists have disdained the very existence of the theory "as an assault on the sublime author's very Christianity, as well as on his identity as a European and not least as an Italian."[31] On the other side, it has been asserted that Asín Palacios and his supporters were led astray by their own national interests in puffing up the contributions of Spain and Arabic-speaking Islam to Dante's epic project.[32] In this way the uproar is attributed to the opposed patriotisms of philologists and literary scholars, with Italians pitted against Spanish and Muslim.

The day may come when literary anthologies of medieval Italian literature will embrace rather than eschew the full heterogeneity of languages and cultures that were rooted at one time or another on the Italian peninsula. Alongside selections in sundry dialects of Italian would burgeon texts in Medieval Latin, Byzantine Greek, Old Germanic languages, Occitan, Hebrew, and Arabic. A shift to such accommodation would match what has happened in the study of regions such as medieval England and Spain, where in recent years paradigms that had been determined in the nineteenth century by nationalist philologies have been allowed to breathe and to welcome the multiplicities that have been the norm in many stretches of Europe at many times.

All the same, Dantists were by no means altogether unjustified in their reactions to Asín Palacios's foray into Dante studies. The book stood open to criticism, since its hypothesis, for all its brilliance, was overstated. For one, it relied excessively on the notion that Dante drew especially upon the Andalusi mystic Ibn al-'Arabī (1165–1240) and the Syrian poet Al-Ma'arri (973–1057), whose oeuvres even a skilled Arabophone would have had difficulty securing, interpreting, and appreciating in late thirteenth-century Europe—and nothing warrants the supposition in the first place that Dante knew Arabic.[33] Why hypothesize indebtedness on the part of the Italian poet to Arabic sources to which he could not have had access, when Western literature, above all in Latin, abounded in visionary literature of its own?[34]

Consequently, the whole case advanced in Asín Palacios's book was undercut by the nonexistence of a Latin translation that could have mediated apparently recherché Islamic eschatology to Western Christendom in general and to Dante in particular. Yet within a year of Asín Palacios's death in 1944, and just a couple of years after his book had been reprinted in Madrid and Granada with a survey of the discussions that the first edition had provoked, a very plausible missing link in the transmission of Arabic eschatological literature was brought to light. Shortly thereafter, Asín Palacios's hypothesis was possibly confirmed by the publication of medieval texts in Latin and Romance languages (though not Ibn al-ʿArabī's magnum opus, *Futūḥāt al-makkiyya* [The Meccan Openings]), which recount the "night journey" of Muḥammad.

What is the night journey? Islamic tradition holds that one night Muḥammad made a two-stage journey, either a physical voyage or a dream. Although the sura of the Qurʾan known as *al-isrāʾ* refers twice succinctly to the tradition (sura 17.1 and 60) and another sura may allude to it as well (sura 53.1–18), most of the story is conveyed in the traditional writings called the hadith. The first part of the journey is the night journey or *isrāʾ* proper. In it Muḥammad is provided, by the archangel Gabriel, a winged steed named Burāq that he rides from the Kaaba in Mecca to the "farthest mosque," usually understood to be the Temple Mount in Jerusalem. After alighting there and conducting prayer in the presence of other prophets, Muḥammad remounts Burāq and commences the second leg of the night journey, styled the ascension or *miʿrāj*. In this ascent he is taken on a tour of the heavens, where he communes with the earlier prophets and with Allah.[35]

Between 1260 and 1264, the presumptive Arabic original (now lost) of a text about the night journey was translated into Castilian by a Jewish physician named Abraham "Alfaquím" (which corresponds to the Arabic *al-ḥakīm*, "the doctor"). This version of the account incorporates a golden ladder of light that enables Muḥammad to commence his ascent to Heaven. This vivid image has given the surviving texts their names. Abraham's Castilian translation, itself no longer extant, served as the basis for the Latin *Liber scale Machometi* and Old French *Livre de l'eschiele Mahomet* (in both cases, Book of the Ladder of Muḥammad) that were produced by the Italian Bonaventure of Siena, a Tuscan Ghibelline in exile.[36] The Latin version, dated between 1260 and 1264, preceded the Old French, which was itself composed in 1264.

All three translations into Latin and Romance languages were made at the behest of King Alfonso X the Wise of Castile (1262–1284), who in Toledo patronized learning with the help of learned translators from all three religions.[37] In this instance Alfonso would appear (to judge by the prologue to the Old French version) to have been spurred on by a twofold desire, to make accessible the life and teaching of Muḥammad and thereby to ease comparison of what he regarded as the extravagant and fabulous legend of the Prophet with the doctrines of Christ. Thus Alfonso had a polemic motivation that calls to mind the anti-Islamic impulses of Peter the Venerable (ca. 1092–1156), abbot of the Benedictine abbey of Cluny, who roughly a century earlier had orchestrated the translation of the Qur'an and other essential documents of Islamic faith.[38] The collection assembled at Peter's instance is known as the Corpus Toletanum or Corpus Islamolatinum.[39] (The essay in this collection by José Martínez Gázquez on translations of the Qur'an and other Islamic texts is once again relevant.) Consistent with this interpretation, all the testimonies to knowledge of the *Liber scale Machometi* surface in anti-Islamic polemics.[40]

The provenance of the manuscripts points to a wide dissemination outside Spain, since the Latin ones were produced in Brittany (Paris, Bibliothèque nationale de France, MS lat. 6064, thirteenth century) and southern France/Provence (Vatican, Biblioteca Apostolica Vaticana, MS Vat. lat. 4072, early fourteenth century: incomplete), while the Old French text was written in England (Oxford, Bodleian Library, MS Laud Misc. 537, thirteenth century). Beyond the enlightenment that the manuscript transmission brings, both surviving forms of the *Liber scale Machometi* have been shown to have been known in Italy in the fourteenth century.[41] The vectors of the text or of the account it narrated could have been Dominican or Franciscan friars, Jewish merchants, Florentine diplomats (such as Brunetto Latini, who served as ambassador in Spain), or travelers of some other bent.

Why does the potential availability of the *Liber scale Machometi* to Dante matter so greatly? The *Commedia* reveals similarities to Islamic eschatological traditions in both content and structure to such an extent that it is very appealing to see indebtedness on Dante's part. Nowhere does the temptation run stronger than when contemplating Muḥammad's "night voyage." In weighing the implications of the parallels between the "night voyage" and the *Commedia*, it makes sense both to be open to the possibility that the former influenced the latter and to bear in mind a principle that has had to be rediscovered again and again in *Quellenforschung*, to use the German technical word for the assaying of sources and parallels: not all similarities prove borrowing.

Muḥammad's night voyage takes place—no surprise here—at night. Some features of the voyage betray noteworthy parallels to Dante's poem. A guide (Gabriel/Virgil) takes the voyager (Muḥammad/Dante) by the hand, accompanies him to the foot of a hill, and invites him to ascend to the peak, but the voyager is hindered when beasts appear. The Hell the voyager visits lies beneath the city of Jerusalem, and is filled with weeping, wailing, and sounds of woe. Before passing to Paradise, the voyager undergoes threefold ablution. The passage involves a ladder or a flight of stairs. Once in Paradise, the voyager witnesses the springs and rivers, tree of happiness, purifying fire, and overpowering brightness of heavenly luminosity.

Are the likenesses between the *Liber scale Machometi* and the *Commedia* sheerly coincidental, or do they furnish proof that Dante had been exposed somehow to a narration of Muḥammad's night voyage to Hell and Paradise or to Muslim eschatology transmitted through other channels? Enrico Cerulli (1898–1988), one of the two scholars who first published the *Liber scale Machometi* and the one who compared it most minutely against the *Commedia*, concluded that an affirmative answer to the second option cannot be made, although it is conceivable, and that whatever inspirations and narrative details did enter the *Commedia* would have been integrated within a construction that had been composed decisively of elements from classical, biblical, and Christian culture. Thus a battle line was effectively drawn. Asín Palacios, though not yet in possession of the *Liber scale Machometi*, unfolded a very potent hypothesis about the possible indebtedness of the *Commedia* to Arabic sources. His theses were seconded with gusto by the Spanish scholar, José Muñoz Sendino, whose wholly independent study and edition of the *Liber scale Machometi* appeared simultaneously with Cerulli's.[42] Whereas Muñoz Sendino took the *Liber scale Machometi* as incontrovertible proof positive that Asín Palacios's theorem had been correct, Cerulli staked out a far more cautious position.[43]

The circumspection could seem justified, since the *Liber scale Machometi* contains many traits suggestive of the *Commedia*, but no particular phraseology or image that proclaims an indubitably direct connection.[44] Another view would hold that Dante would not have been likely to make an unmistakable allusion in Italian to a Latin text of undistinguished style, and that he would not very well have professed his debt to its content, since it revolved around a personage he scorned as a schismatic at best. In the second Canto of the *Inferno*, Dante acknowledges the trip to the underworld of Aeneas (*Aeneid*, Book 6) and the ecstatic vision of the otherworld described by the Apostle Paul (2 Cor. 12.1–4): "Io non Enëa, io non Paolo sono" (*Inf.* 2.32 "For I am not Aeneas, I am not Paul"). Even if he had come across the *Liber scale Machometi*, he would not have subjoined—and his restraint would not have been dictated by prosody alone—"Anzi, sono io Maometto" ("As a matter of fact, I am Muḥammad") or even "io non Maometto sono" ("I am not Muḥammad").[45] The sources Dante signals belong not to the Islamic but rather to the Western visionary tradition, the richness of which must not be underestimated.

Since many of the polemic reactions to Asín Palacios's book (itself polemic) have had recurrent repercussions in subsequent approaches to the topics it raised, this compendium begins with two articles that offer perspectives on the *status quaestionis* of "Dante and Islam" in the second half of the twentieth century. Taken together, the pieces lend much weight to the notion that the real story to be told is not the presence or absence of an Islamic or Arabic deposit in Dante's writings but instead the reception of *La escatología musulmana en la Divina Comedia* in Dante studies. The controversy has had a life of its own, almost independent of anything that can even be proven about the medieval texts themselves.

The earlier article, by Vicente Cantarino (1925–), has a special relevance, since it was published in 1965 in conjunction with a symposium sponsored by the Dante Society of America.[46] "Dante and Islam: History and Analysis of a Controversy" continues to be heavily cited as a systematic review of the studies that preceded Asín Palacios's as well as of the scholarly reception that his book experienced.[47] The later article, translated here as "Dante and Islamic Culture" from the Italian original by Maria Corti (1915–2002), was presented at a conference in 1999 and printed first in 2001.[48]

Albeit unintentionally, Corti's piece caps work on the topic, not just as the twentieth century reached an end but also as a close came to the period preceding the coordinated 2001 attacks by al-Qaeda terrorists in the United States on the World Trade Center in New York City and on the Pentagon in Washington, D.C., that go under the shorthand of 9/11 and that have further polarized scholars and the general public alike where issues pertaining to the relations between Islam and Christianity as well as between the Near East and the West come into play.[49]

In the politically riven climate of these days, we must guard against succumbing to either extreme in the binarism that pits what could be called Islamophilia (or philislamia) against Islamophobia (or misislamia). Although these contraries—and the words in the second pairing point in the different but related directions of fearing and hating—build upon Islam as their key root, neither assumes profound expertise about Islam in either its modern or medieval guises. Those on both sides may not be able to differentiate a minbar from a minibar or anti-Occidentalism from antioxidants. In addition, a command of Arabic, Hebrew, and other relevant languages, or even a meaningful exposure to such tongues, appears to be rare among those who know medieval European languages. As a result, Westernists might have a practical incentive to overstate the gap between medieval Latins and medieval Arabs, since doing so would exonerate them of the responsibility to grapple with difficult languages. Among the other party, Orientalists (who are likelier to have mastery or at least working knowledge of Latin and Romance languages than Romanists are of Arabic and Hebrew) might enhance the importance of their areas of studies if they demonstrated the obligation of the West to medieval Arabs. Of course, there is no hard-and-fast rule. Not having more than a smattering of a given language does not preclude having romantic feelings about the importance of a culture associated with it: from my undergraduate days I retain a vivid picture of an elderly Hispanist who as he lectured passionately on the contributions of the Arabs to the formation of Spanish culture carefully wrote on the blackboard key Arabic terms—but from left to right.

In any case, the desire of professors to exalt the fields to which they have committed their lives pales beside the pervasive power of politics to dictate what is taught and studied, and how it is taught and studied. The headlines of the early twenty-first century shout out news of ideologies labeled variously as Islamic fundamentalism and Islamic extremism, which are sometimes equated or even linked historically with the national socialism (Nazism, for short) of Adolf Hitler's Germany (1933–1945).[50] Such ideologies, which have been characterized as Islamo-Fascism, lead in turn to attitudes and acts that are roundly condemned in the West. Examples would be (to give only a small sampling) an anti-Westernism and especially an anti-Americanism that manifests itself in violent death and mayhem, an anti-Zionism and anti-Jewishness that invokes the dissolution of Israel and even the eradication of Jews in a new holocaust, and fatwas that call for reprisal, even murder, against authors and other artists who create works regarded as insulting to Islam.

By far the majority of terrorist acts that are reported in the Western media relate to the hypertrophic forms of these ideologies.

Do the horrors of our contemporary world have a bearing on the Middle Ages, or vice versa? If they do relate to each other, then how so? One approach is to elide the differences between medieval Islam and (post)modern Islamic fundamentalism, by arguing that the gulf between the Christian West and the Islamic East existed already in the medieval period or by promoting present-day Islam—or Western culture, as perceived from outside—as being medieval (and not medieval in a favorable sense!) in outlook.[51] If we wish to sit in judgment on the conduct of Christian and Muslim powers in the Middle Ages, then we should omit from our assessment neither the aggressive projection of Christianity against Islam in the Crusades nor the earlier warring sweep—the mother of military jihads—which in the first century of Islam (632–732) propelled the earliest generations of Muslims from their birthplaces on the Arabian peninsula northward through the Levant into Asia Minor and through Persia and westward across northern Africa into Spain. Later conquests added Sicily, Crete, and other Mediterranean islands to Cyprus as Muslim holdings. Many of these lands had been Christian for centuries before the warriors of the new religion made their first incursions.

The contrapuntal move is to sharpen the contrasts between the present and the past, by highlighting the times of harmony among the three main monotheisms in the Middle Ages that tend to be overlooked or ignored amid all the emphasis on current conflicts. This accentuation of pacific phases leads to a focus upon how much more advanced Islamic civilization was than Western Christendom in the Middle Ages and how fruitfully and even peacefully Christians, Muslims, and Jews coexisted in medieval Europe, especially in the Muslim-held or formerly Muslim-held regions of Spain and Sicily.

The world is and has been too intricate a place for the encounters between differing religions and linguistico-ethnic groupings today to be regarded as nothing more than the projections of one strain of past relations into the present. Current events are too complicated—and so is history—for such simplism to serve us well. It is laudable to take a stand against potential evil, and it is also praiseworthy to motivate people to interact on the strength of their shared humanity. In many cases the manifold ambiguities of both the now and the then render very difficult an exclusive choice between the two impulses, and it would be simpler to have a sort of party adherence that would absolve us of the necessity to struggle for answers—but no one ever said that being a responsible historian (or citizen) was supposed to be easy.

With these caveats in mind, let us turn to what should be our point of departure, Dante, and to what we can state as facts. After centuries of having been on the advance, Islam had to contend from the very late eleventh century through the thirteenth with Christian beachheads in the Eastern Mediterranean, in present-day Turkey, Syria, Lebanon, and Israel, and over a much longer stretch of time with the Christian reconquest of al-Andalus, in what is modern-day Spain. In addition, from the thirteenth century on, Islam had to cope with the even graver menace of Mongol encroachments from the east, which reached into its heartlands. However mistaken it would be to caricature the adherents of the two religions as having retreated behind completely impenetrable barriers, the climate was one in which—outside the Iberian peninsula— exchanges decreased rather than increased. In 1291 the Latin kingdoms of Syria and Palestine had been lost to the Mamluks. In contrast, the reconquest (*Reconquista*) of Spain by Latin Christians had made decisive progress and had facilitated the extension of shipping and trade by Europeans throughout the Mediterranean and beyond.[52]

Though many of these adjacencies were drawing to a definitive close in Dante's lifetime, we must recognize that what has been called "the legacy of Islam" was attained not only through cultures that rubbed up against each other simultaneously but also through cultures that succeeded each other and that absorbed elements of each other in the process.

In the Holy Land and Latin Kingdoms of Greece, Crusaders came and went, some for only the duration of short campaigns but others to live their whole lives. In fact, their presence was so extended that even to speak of their coming and going gives a misleading impression of impermanency. The Latin Kingdoms had inhabitants who spent most of their existences, from cradle to grave, in places such as Tyre, and the traffic to and from these locales comprehended pilgrims, merchants, and others, alongside warriors.

Latin Christendom never walled itself off altogether from commerce with Arab Islam, nor did Muslims immure themselves from trade and other exchanges with Christians. Italian communities, among which Venice holds pride of place, had intense mercantile and commercial ties. Missionaries, especially Dominicans and Franciscans, traveled to the East. In this collection the entire essay by Thomas E. Burman on "How an Italian Friar Read His Arabic Qur'an" and pages of others by José Martínez Gázquez, Brenda Deen Schildgen, Maria Esposito Frank, Karla Mallette, and John Tolan are devoted to the Friar Minor Riccoldo of Monte Croce (1242–1320). Riccoldo is a fascinating case in point as a possible channel for transmission of details about Islam to Dante and as an exemplar of the unusual but not unique exchanges that could and did take place.[53]

In 1286–1287, approximately twenty years after entering the Florentine convent of Santa Maria Novella in 1267, Riccoldo set off for Acre with a papal commission to preach. Eventually he traversed the land then known as Palestine to enter Asia Minor, before wending his way to Baghdad via Mosul and Tekrit. Even after the final collapse of the Crusader kingdoms in 1291 Riccoldo remained in Baghdad to study the Qur'an and Islamic theology, but eventually he had to flee. In 1301 he is recorded as being back in Florence. He wrote prolifically about Islam both before and after his return, and in 1315 he was appointed prior of Santa Maria Novella.

Although knowledge of Islam and exposure to Islamic culture flowed into the West through all of these conduits, the chief locus for transmission of cultural awareness was occidental Islam, especially al-Andalus. In Spain Christians and Muslims engaged with one another on a day-to-day basis. Dante traveled hither and yon in Italy, but he never spent time in Muslim lands. He could have heard Arabic words and phrases from those who knew the language, but nothing suggests that he acquired for himself any facility in Arabic that would have enabled him to converse or read. In sum, his picture of Islam and its cultures would have come through his readings and through informants who had had exposure through travels to Spain, Sicily, and other such places with traces (and that last word is often an understatement) of Muslim occupations or even to the Levant.

A further channel of contact warrants mention. In many regions of Latin Christendom the people who are now often designated tout court as Europeans (a concept that did not take shape before around 1600) had no direct interaction with Muslims.[54] The "internal other"—those who stood out by contrast to the prevailing Christianity and ethnicities—comprised individuals who adhered not to Islam but instead to Judaism.[55] Yet since the Jews of medieval Europe were sometimes connected intimately by economic and family bonds to coreligionists in Muslim-held territories such as al-Andalus, they often functioned as intermediaries for Islamic influences. Thus Dante's perspectives on Muslims and Islam cannot and should not be boxed off entirely from his possible encounters with Jews and Jewish culture, even if nineteenth-century assumptions of a fast friendship between him and Immanuel ben Solomon of Rome (known also as Immanuel Romano and Manoello Giudeo, ca. 1265–1331) have often been dismissed as ill founded.[56] The advisability of paying heed to Immanuel and other Jews linked to Dante's Verona is brought home in this collection in the essay entitled "Dante and the Three Religions" by Giorgio Battistoni.

Beyond wondering how Dante could have gained an entry into Islam, specific Muslims, writings by Muslims, the Arabic language, and culture associated with Islam, Arabs, and others likely to have been considered Muslims, we need to isolate which features of "Muslim fashion" and even more encompassingly of an "Islamic way of life" would have been apprehensible to him and other Latin Christians. In this ambit the variegated lexicon of Italian words that derived from Arabic offers useful data to mine.

The Arabic derivatives indicate that interactions with Muslims exposed the Romance-speaking Christians of Italy to many novelties in food and agriculture, textiles and haute couture, entertainment, realms of learning, and technology. The new crops introduced included date palms and citrus fruits, as well as sugar cane for sugar manufacture, and plants such as cotton, hemp, and mulberries, which were used in producing textiles, rope, matting, silk, and paper. Among the foodstuffs would be numbered many spices, in entertainment instruments such as the lute and tambourine and games such as chess, checkers, and backgammon. The learning that streamed from the East through Muslims or at least through Muslim intermediaries encompassed mathematics, science, and medicine. In this collection particular attention is paid to Dante's ultimate indebtedness to Arabic culture in fowling, by Daniela Boccassini in her essay on "Falconry as a Transmutative Art: Dante, Frederick II, and Islam," and other debts along these lines in technical domains such as astronomy and optics could be identified.

The imprint that Arabic left on Dante's language, as on Italian as a whole, is undeniable. These Arabisms, all but one of them lexical rather than syntactic, give further sign of the cultural arenas in which Araboophone Muslims had a command of things and concepts that had been unfamiliar in the West. Arabic words were naturally brought into Dante's Italian to describe offices or functions that were distinctive of ways of life among Arabs. In this category would fall words ranging from "sultan" (*Inf.* 5.60, 27.90 *Soldan*, also at *Par.* 11.101) and "admiral" (*Purg.* 13.154, 30.58 *ammiraglio*) through "assassin" (*Inf.* 19.50 *assessin*) to one characteristically Italian term for boy (*Inf.* 29.77 *ragazzo*). (Although not from a lexical point of view, the essay in this volume on "Mendicants and Muslims in Dante's Florence" by John Tolan deals extensively with the "presenza . . . superba" ["haughty . . . presence"] of the Egyptian sultan to whom Francis of Assisi preaches in Canto 11 of the *Paradiso*.)

In keeping with what has been mentioned already, Dante resorts, wittingly or not, to Arabic derivatives to denote whole bodies of science and know-how, such as "alchemy" (*Inf.* 29.119, 29.137 *alchìmia*), as well as specific terms within them, such as the astronomical "zenith" (*Par.* 29.4 *cenìt*), anatomical "nape" (*Inf.* 32.129 *nuca*), or nautical "south wind" (*Purg.* 28.21 *scilocco*, where modern Italian has *scirocco*). Luxury items, among them gemstones and the colors associated with them (*Inf.* 17.59 *azzurro* "azure"; *Par.* 9.69 *balasso* "ruby"; *Inf.* 30.90 *carati* "carats"; *Purg.* 1.13 *zafiro* "sapphire," also at *Par.* 23.101), and forms of entertainment, such as musical instruments (*Inf.* 30.49 *leuto* "lute") and games (*Par.* 28.93 *scacchi* "chess"; *Purg.* 24.30 *rocco* "staff bearing at the top an ornament like a *rook* in chess"; *Detto d'amore* 456 *alfino* "bishop"; *Purg.* 6.1 *gioco de la zara* "game of dice"). The only Arabic loanword that refers particularly to Islamic religion is "mosque" (*Inf.* 8.70 *meschita*), which arrived via Spanish. The sole example of a calque conceivably based on the Arabic comes when Dante employs the verb *imprimere* to betoken the influence of heavenly bodies upon the earth (*Par.* 17.76–77). But the expression had already figured in Italian before Dante resorted to it.[57]

However preposterous it would be to hypothesize that Dante was conversant in Arabic, more than one passage in the *Commedia* has spurred recurrent speculation that the Italian poet had at least heard enough of the other language to be capable of stressing one proper noun correctly (the name Alì in *Inf.* 28.32)[58] and even of replicating in somewhat garbled form two longer utterances in the language, one pronounced by Pluto (*Inf.* 7.1) and the other by Nimrod (*Inf.* 31.67).[59] But the step would be enormous from accepting the conjecture that Dante could imitate loosely the flow of Semitic languages to convincing oneself on the strength of two lines that he could actually read or speak Arabic.

In any case, Dante's outlook on Islam as a religion is far from identical with his outlook on Islamic culture or on culture mediated through Arabic. A classic article of 1932 averred that "Dante shows much the same view of the Mohammedans as his contemporaries, and it is a low and negligent one,"[60] but his knowledge of Islam and his perspectives on it as a religion are not as typical as this unhesitating declaration presupposes.

Islam shares with Christianity not only the defining feature of being monotheistic but also the claim of descent from an individual, Abraham, who has a place in the Hebrew Bible. Medieval Christians saw their faith as being even more closely related to that of Muslims than to that of Jews, although this recognition heightened rather than diminished the distrust and hostility they felt toward the people they called (among other things) Saracens. The most common or at least popular image of Islam in medieval literary and historical texts was as a polytheistic parody of Christianity that blasphemed the Trinity in its pagan idolatry of Apollo (Apolin in the Old French), Muḥammad (Mahumet), and Termagant (Tervagan).[61] Such is the case, most notably, in the *Chanson de Roland* (Song of Roland).[62] By coincidence, Dante, at once supremely orthodox and unorthodox, lays himself open to the accusation of such polytheism when he invokes the god Apollo in *Paradiso* 1, first as Christ (*Par.* 1.13–15), later as the Holy Spirit (*Par.* 1.19), and finally as God the Father (*Par.* 1.22–24).[63]

The *Commedia* contains unflattering references to Muslims, and Dante demonstrates the ready familiarity with the protagonists and antagonists of the Carolingian cycle narratives that we would expect.[64] All the same, Dante does not retail Islam as the starkly distorted mirroring of Christianity that the *Chanson de Roland* puts forward. Instead, he subscribes to a more learned apprehension of Islam, which misconstrued it not as a discrete religion but instead as a heresy or schism within Christianity itself.[65] In fact, Dante's view of the world was so solidly Christianocentric that he saw each of the two other monotheisms known to him, namely, Judaism and Islam, as being unfulfilled or misfulfilled manifestations of Christianity. Seen from this vantage point, the misrepresentation of Muḥammad as a schismatic did not render him a hostile and dangerous "other" but rather an insider whose sin (truly) was to have ruptured the harmony of a religion and civilization that previously had been unified.[66]

Eventually the perspective that Muḥammad was a heresiarch developed a legendary expression, in a tale (attested no earlier than the end of the thirteenth century) that characterized the Prophet as a cardinal who out of frustration at not being elevated to the papacy resolved to institute a rival religion of his own.[67] Although this legend makes no appearance, at least not explicitly, in the *Commedia*,[68] Islam does not elicit any gentler handling in the *Commedia* as a consequence.

Islam is not mentioned outright at the end of *Purgatorio* 32.130–35, but the description there of a chariot that has its floor broken away by a dragon has been taken by most commentators as referring to the losses Christianity suffered through the growth of Islam.[69] Whether or not this construction of the passage in *Purgatorio* passes muster, other sections in the *Commedia* make clear Dante's conviction that Islam was a corruption of Christianity, conceived deliberately by Muḥammad and entrenched solely owing to gross negligence on the part of the Christian Church and leadership.

Thus in *Paradiso* 15.142–44 Dante volunteers a characterization of Islam in the voice of his great-great-grandfather Cacciaguida, who in the Second Crusade fought alongside Emperor Conrad III (1138–1152) in the Holy Land and whom Dante sets in Heaven among martial leaders, such as Charlemagne and Roland. Cacciaguida places the blame for the very existence of Islam "per colpa d'i pastor" (*Par.* 15.144 "upon a breakdown in pastoral care") within Christianity—in other words, upon shortcomings in the Christian clergy. Nonetheless, the culpability of the Christian clergy in the loss of people—former faithful—to Islam does not make the Muslims any less unsavory, to judge by Cacciaguida's pillorying of them as "quella gente turpa" (*Par.* 15.145 "that execrable race").

Dante presents Islam as a sect, related to Judaism, which stands apart from Christianity (*Inf.* 27.87). In accord with this conception, he lodges Muḥammad in Hell and portrays his punishment as a schismatic. Just five Muslims find a place in the *Commedia*, all of them in the *Inferno* (Cantos 6 and 28), for a total of not even twenty lines: Avicenna (980–1037), Averroës (Ibn Rushd, 1126–1198), Saladin (ca. 1138–1193), Muḥammad (570–632), and ʿAlī (d. 661). Elsewhere in his corpus Dante refers to the ninth-century astronomer and astrologer Jaʾfar Ibn

Muḥammad Abū Ma'shar al-Balkhī (*Conv.* 2.13.22 "Albumasar"); the ninth-century Arab astronomer al-Farghānī (*Conv.* 2.5.16 "Alfagrano"); the late eleventh- and early twelfth-century philosopher, al-Ghazālī Abū Hāmid Muḥammad Ibn Muḥammad al-Ṭūsī (*Conv.* 2.13.5 and 4.21.2 "Algazali"); and the twelfth-century Andalusi astronomer Nūr al-Dīn Ibn Ishāq al-Biṭrūjī (*Conv.* 3.2.5 "Alpetragio," formerly read as "Alfarabio"); as well as to Averroës and Avicenna. Put together, these references point to familiarity with Arabic learning in the physical sciences, mathematics, and philosophy, but none of them hints at any direct acquaintance with Arabic originals. In fact, all of them look to have been mediated through scholastic Latin authors such as Albertus Magnus (the Great, d. 1280) and his student Thomas Aquinas (ca. 1225–1274).

Muḥammad is the only one discussed at any length, in a thirty-eight-line passage; 'Alī merits only two lines, although even that coverage is noteworthy, in view of how much less currency he had in the Middle Ages than Muhummad.[70] As a schismatic who split the body of the Christian Church, Dante's Muḥammad is planted deep in Hell, in the ninth bolgia of the eighth circle. Dante labels those dwelling at this stratum as "seminator di scandalo e di scisma" (*Inf.* 28.35 "sowers of scandal and schism"). Both *scandalo* and *scismo* are Greek derivatives that carry associations relating not to religion in general but to Christianity in particular. To be specific, they presuppose that Muḥammad was a Christian, but a sectarian Christian who caused a schism within the Church.

As is analyzed in this collection in essays by Maria Esposito Frank on "Dante's Muḥammad" and Karla Mallette on "Muḥammad in Hell," Muḥammad is depicted as enduring a bodily mutilation that enacts upon his own person the corporal equivalent to his rending of the Church, one of the most grotesque and ignoble punishments in a poem that is hardly devoid of horrors: he is ripped from the chin down to the anus, with his torso cloven so that his bowels and other digestive organs dangle between his legs (*Inf.* 28.25–36).[71] Then again, it may be a misstatement to characterize Muḥammad as suffering, since in a way he displays a certain proud exhibitionism in splaying his breast with his own hands to show it to the poet.[72] In any event, the correspondence between Muḥammad's alleged sin and the punishment depicted has particular resonance, since the term *contrapasso* ("counter-penalty") appears in the *Commedia* only at the finale of this very canto (*Inf.* 28.142).

It would require almost unimaginable contortions to view the portrayal of Muḥammad and ʿAlī as anything other than a categorical denunciation of Islam, not even as a legitimate faith in its own right but as a degradation of a bona fide religion. Certainly Muslims who have translated Dante have consistently deemed the portrayal of Muḥammad too offensive for inclusion in their versions of the poem. Particularly in Arabic translations of the poem, the passage in the *Inferno* that describes the damnable punishment of the Prophet has been expurgated.[73] All the same, Dante's condemnation of Muḥammad and ʿAlī cannot be equated automatically to categorical rejection of all Muslims. The poet's views of Islam have gained recurrent notoriety in part precisely because he evinces such a positive disposition toward some Muslims: his contempt for the two representatives of Islam as a religion could be felt to find its opposite in his esteem for exemplars of the intellectual achievement and even of the chivalry attained by other Muslims.[74]

Although Dante plunged Muḥammad and ʿAlī deep in the Inferno, we encounter the two only long after having met the threesome of Muslims he set in Limbo: Saladin, Averroës, and Avicenna. (Averroës and Avicenna receive scrutiny in this volume in essays by Brenda Deen Schildgen on "Philosophers, Theologians, and the Islamic Legacy in Dante" and by Gregory B. Stone on "Dante and the *Falasifa*: Religion as Imagination.") Dante does not allocate much space to the three celebrities: Averroës and Saladin merit no more than a full line each, Avicenna just part of one.[75] Thus they seem minimized when measured against the dozen ancient Greeks and Romans who are confined with them in the city of the sages, which is sequestered from Hell proper (or improper) by seven walls. At the same time, the respect that Dante accords them cannot be gainsaid. Although all three were Muslim and Arabic speakers, we need to ponder whether Dante and his coevals in Latin Christendom would have isolated Muslimness as the key or even a key attribute in the identities of the triad. Their religion may matter solely as explaining why they lacked the awareness of the Christian faith that would have saved them from their placement in Limbo. Dante's disposition toward the virtuous pagans (or virtuous unbelievers) is undeniably complex:[76] consider his handling of Virgil, his guide through the underworld. Still, no way lies open for minimizing the fact that Limbo is a part of Hell, just as the canto describing it falls squarely within the *Inferno*. The assertion that "three Muslims rest in a comfortable, almost Paradise-like Limbo along with other virtuous pagans from the classical world" misrepresents Dante's theology.[77] If the threesome receives any special dispensation, it is despite, not because of, their affiliation with what Dante branded as a schism.[78] The only Saracen in Dante's Paradise is Renouard (*Par.* 18.46 "Rinoardo"), not actually a historical figure but instead a literary character (and giant) paired in chansons de geste with the legendary Duke William of Orange (ca. 750–812), who could be awarded a niche among those who fought for Christ solely because he was supposedly converted by William.

In the *Commedia* Saladin, who is also praised in *Convivio* 4.11.14, is placed in Limbo among the righteous unbaptized, albeit set off "solo, in parte" (*Inf.* 4.129 "alone, set apart") from the heroes of ancient Troy and Rome with whom he sojourns.[79] Dante's placement of Saladin in Limbo makes apparent that if the Muslim general had been a Christian, he would have been spared. Although Dante's disposition of Saladin has been taken as speaking to a pervasive sympathy for Islam, we must exercise caution about making generalizations or drawing broad inferences on the basis of a single verse. Dante could have underlined the valor of this Muslim warrior whose forces wrested Jerusalem from the hands of the Crusaders in 1187 so as to bring home the ignobility of many of his contemporary Christians, not to disparage Christianity itself but instead to hint that if even those who cling to a deformed heresy or (to be more accurate) schism could conduct themselves chivalrously, then the truly faithful had even less excuse for their shortcomings. Dante's Hell is replete with backhanded compliments of this brand.

In *Inferno* Avicenna and Averroës are the last two personages identified in Canto 4 (*Inf.* 4.143–44). They appear within a cohort that otherwise comprises individuals who lived before Christ, with the exception of Ovid, Lucan, Seneca, and Saladin. The name of Avicenna is flanked by that of the great physicians Hippocrates and Galen, while at the feet of Aristotle is Averroës, who elaborated the great commentary on the Stagirite. Although the message may be foreign to many twenty-first-century eyes and ears, medieval readers would have shared the assumption underlying these lines that the ancient past and their present were unbroken—that the Muslims belonged on the same cultural continuum as the Christians (or the Jews).

Averroës in particular cannot be labeled simply an Arab. Born in Spain, in Muslim Córdoba, he could qualify as European at least in his geographical origins. But retrojecting a modern-day category of thought, such as European and non-European, is not always the ideal way to assimilate the thinking and writing of the Middle Ages. Although Dante was accused of being an Averroist already six years after his death, he was not faulted for being a crypto-Muslim, for the simple reason that the shortcomings of Averroism were seen to reside in philosophy rather than in religion.[80]

In the case of Averroës and Avicenna, their status as philosophers may have trumped their ethnic and religious affiliations. Avicenna and Averroës entered the Latin cultural tradition as philosophers, where their hegemony was such that it is legitimate to speak of both Latin Avicennism and Latin Averroism.[81] These movements can be seen as two waves related to the problematic reception of Aristotle in medieval Europe, in which first Avicennism and then Averroism challenged the orthodoxy. Ecclesiastics such as Albertus Magnus and Thomas Aquinas managed through their syntheses to keep the new philosophical currents, especially of Averroism, from overwhelming the Church. In so doing, they enabled other churchmen to digest Aristotle as he was mediated through the Arabic-writing thinkers.

Particularly in the *Convivio*, Dante refers to philosophical works which had been composed originally in Arabic but not startlingly he alludes to them exclusively as translated into Latin and—more important—as funneled through Latin Christian thinkers. He evidences a very favorable inclination toward this philosophy. Indeed, he situates Siger of Brabant, a prominent thirteenth-century exponent of Averroism, in the Heaven of the Sun, along with Thomas Aquinas and other teachers (*Par.* 10.136–38), even though Siger had fallen into disrepute in some quarters for his alleged belief that the world was without beginning and end.

The other side of the same coin may be the treatise *De causis*, typically designated as the *Liber de causis* (Book of Causes), which circulated from the 1180s in a Latin translation made by Gerard of Cremona (d. 1187) from an Arabic text (probably ninth century). This is the only Arabic book that Dante can be proven beyond a doubt to have known firsthand in Latin translation. From it he tapped the theory of earthly and mystical love that was central in the *dolce stil novo* (the great thirteenth-century literary movement designated as the "sweet new style") and the metaphysics of light that pervades his conception of Paradise.[82] But it is not a foregone conclusion that Dante would have conceived of this book as Arabic, even less as Muslim, since it was universally accorded to be the work of Aristotle.[83]

To what degree the Aristotelianism that exerted determinative influences upon late medieval and humanistic cultures should be regarded as mainly Greek or instead as at least partially Arabicized is a puzzle still capable of arousing furor. To be more precise, the question is instead to what extent the Arabicized Aristotelianism was Islamicized. The latest expression of the tensions that swirl around this aspect of European and even Western identity can be seen in a recent storm that has earned a reputation as the *affaire Gouguenheim*. This uproar has been stirred by a French book, entitled *Aristote au Mont-Saint-Michel*, written by a professor of medieval history named Sylvain Gouguenheim and published in 2008. Gouguenheim argues that medieval Islam was not hospitable to most of ancient Greek culture, that the Arabs who translated much of Hellenic and Hellenistic thought were Christians, that Greek culture never perished fully in the West whereas it was never really nativized in Islam, and that the large-scale translation of Aristotle in the Middle Ages was launched not from the Arabic in Muslim Spain but rather from the Greek in the Benedictine abbey of Mont Saint-Michel in Normandy.

The paperback that unleashed the tempest has elicited sharply conflicting responses in the popular press in France. For instance, it was greeted warmly in reviews in *Le Figaro* and *Le Monde*, whereas it was criticized searingly in a letter published by *Le Monde* in the cultural magazine *Télérama*.[84] More tellingly, the book instigated a backlash among academics throughout the West with expertise in medieval history and particularly in the role of medieval Islam in the formation of Western culture. The resultant controversy was broadcast to the Anglophone world, especially U.S. expatriates, through a commentary printed in the *International Herald Tribune*.[85]

Beyond the few explicit mentions of Muḥammad and ʿAlī, Muslims (whether identified overtly by their faith or not), and Arabs, the *Commedia* touches on a few Latin Christians who have been tagged as Islamophiles.[86] Although the "quel di Spagna" (*Par.* 19.125 "certain Spaniard") who is described unflatteringly in *Paradiso* 19.124–26 has sometimes been identified with Alfonso X the Wise, the majority opinion holds that the phrase refers to Ferdinand IV, king of Castile and León from 1295 to 1312. Another notable personage aligned with Islam is Frederick II (1194–1250). But though Frederick was acclaimed by some as *stupor mundi* (the "wonder of the world"), in the *Commedia* he is stuck among the heretics, where he undergoes punishment for his hedonism.[87] Dante's damnation of the emperor could rest in part on an awareness of the harem Frederick maintained in a municipality examined closely in the essay by David Abulafia that caps this collection, "The Last Muslims in Italy." Alternatively, he could be familiar with (and disapproving of) the treaty that Frederick reached with Muslims in the Holy Land when he went there in 1228.

Beyond his own missteps, Frederick won fame (or infamy) for his patronage of at least two individuals of questionable intellectual and theological repute, the poet and political figure Pier della Vigna (1190–1249, mentioned but not named in *Inf.* 13.58–69) and the philosopher and scientist Michael Scot (*Inf.* 20.115–17). Nothing conspicuous in the *Commedia* forces the conclusion that Pier was regarded as an Arabicizer or Islamophile: he is condemned in the *Inferno* for being a suicide. For being a magician Michael is lodged in the fourth bolgia of the eighth circle. Michael's engrossment in unsanctioned knowledge, including astrology and alchemy, was not unrelated to his grasp of Arabic, which may have coincided with openness not merely to Aristotelian philosophy as mediated through Arabic translations and commentaries but also to Islam itself.[88] But how much Michael's expertise as an Arabist or what could have been his alleged Islamophilia entered into Dante's unfavorable estimation of him is not readily gauged.

Where are we left in our appraisal of Dante's relation to Islam? If anything has become apparent from these prolegomena, it is that the essays to follow are desperately needed. The enigma cries out to be set in an ampler context than has been attempted in the past. In addition, the topic needs the illumination that can come when those who do not belong to a well-established field join those from within the guild to take a fresh look at an old conundrum. Finally, we must be prepared to test out a variety of solutions as great as the diversity of viewpoints which are now espoused in regard to present-day relations between Western Europe and the Mediterranean expressions of Islam. Christian-Muslim and European-Arab interactions in the here and now run a sweeping gamut, as held true in Dante's lifetime; but the spectrum was not at all the same then as it is nowadays. We must be alert to both all that is the same and all that is different in seeking to frame questions and answers, and we must not allow our hopes or disappointments about the present to mislead us into fabricating from the past something that it was not—into misrepresenting the Middle Ages in the hopes of bettering modernity, postmodernity, or whatever other noun we elect to describe our own epoch.

Distorting a long-gone century so as to correct modern situations that distress us will help no one: the childhood principle that "two wrongs don't make a right" applies at least as well to many human situations as does the *lex talionis* of "an eye for an eye, a tooth for a tooth" (Exod. 21:24, Lev. 24:20, Deut. 19:21). Of course, the trick is always to decide when one is veering into misinterpretation. Not all optimism is to be eschewed, any more than all pessimism. And the past does repeat itself, but usually most readily when both it and the present have been molded so as to permit the resemblance to be evident. Dante, Islam, Christianity, Arab, European, and Italian—these entities have been moving targets since long before the names and terms for them came into everyday parlance.

Before allowing the reader to confront the essays themselves, I would like to render thanks where they are due. At the time of printing in *Dante Studies* 125 (2007) Thomas Kozachek copyedited and indexed with a sure and gracious hand all the essays, and Swift Edgar perused them with a pair of eagle eyes. The editorial board, particularly Richard Lansing, lavished considerable care upon the whole. For this publication as a book all these pages received close ministrations from the team at Fordham University Press. In addition, Michael Boetius Sullivan supplied many of the translations, particularly from the Italian, that were not included in the journal form of this book. In the presentation of Latin texts the so-called consonantal *u* has been standardized to *v*. In general, the changes made from the earlier form have been intended to make the essays more accessible to non-specialist, English-speaking readers. While the essays have not been systematically updated, minor corrections have been made throughout, and a brief bibliographic supplement has been added. Warm appreciation is due to the Dante Society of America, particularly its past presidents Giuseppe Mazzotta and Nancy J. Vickers for their backing of this venture, and its present president, Albert Russell Ascoli, for his permission to reprint.

Approaches to a Controversy

Dante and Islam: History and Analysis
of a Controversy

VICENTE CANTARINO

A me, che morto son, convien menarlo
per lo 'nferno qua giù di giro in giro.
E quest' è ver così com'io ti parlo.

It behooves me, who am dead, to lead him
down here through Hell from circle to circle.
And this is as true as that I speak to you.

—(*Inf.* 28.49–51)

E quello "non è una fandonia come quella che si conta di te."

And this "is not a tale like the one told about you."

—Angelo de Fabrizio, "Il 'Mirag' di Maometto esposto
da un frate salentino del XV secolo" (1907)

The question of Oriental influences on the *Commedia* has been one of the most controversial aspects of Dante scholarship during the last century.[1] The influence of Muslim eschatology on Dante's conception of the otherworld as presented by Miguel Asín Palacios in 1919 and the discovery and publication of the *Liber scale Machometi* (Book of Muḥammad's Ladder) in 1949, containing the Mohammedan legend of the prophet's journey to the infernal regions and his subsequent ascension to Heaven, are the cornerstones in this controversy.

The publications written on the subject since the appearance of Asín Palacios's work, and even before, amount today to a substantial bibliography. Glancing through it, the reader is struck by the extent of the polemic throughout the republic of letters, the passionate tone, and the divergence of opinions. It cannot be denied that this controversy helped scholars to a better understanding of Dante's eschatological background in the conception of his *Commedia,* although it has degenerated, at times, into a crusade to defend the glory of the *altissimo poeta* ("most revered poet") against allegations of Muḥammadan influence.

Even though complete agreement has never been reached and probably never will be, a survey of the controversy should be valuable as an effort to separate issues that are frequently confused and to provide a clear understanding of an important part of the huge Dante bibliography.

Already in the late eighteenth century, the Spanish Jesuit Juan, or Giovanni, Andrés (1740–1817), in a remarkable book on the origin of literature, expressed his opinion that Dante might have been inspired by Arabic traditions in the composition of his *Commedia*.[2] In the nineteenth century, Francesco Cancellieri, Charles Labitte, and Pasquale Villari studied the forerunners of Dante and pointed to Christian legends of the otherworld as sources for the *Commedia*.[3] Alessandro d'Ancona called attention to the similarities between the *Commedia* and Indo-Iranian eschatological legends.[4] Only with Edgar Blochet, at the turn of the century, did the research on Oriental sources gain more ground.[5]

In 1901 Blochet wondered "whether in the *Divine Comedy* and in previous legends pertaining to the same cycle there are traces of this Oriental influence."[6] Blochet believed that the origin of most eschatological legends lay in Indo-Iranian sources, from which they migrated to Christian Europe, where they received form and content.[7] One of these legends was that of the *mi'rāj*, Muhammad's ascension, which "Dante could have heard from one of the knights who entered Jerusalem with the German emperor," for Dante "did not know Arabic."[8] This tradition, however, was considered by Blochet as a remote secondary source: "One must search for his [Dante's] actual sources in the Western versions of the legend, which were disseminated in the Christian world throughout the Middle Ages."[9] By this he meant the Christian legends concerning the otherworld, which he also believed to be derived from Indo-Iranian sources. He points out that some of the episodes in the Christian legends are also found in Arabic eschatology.[10] He had previously studied the Oriental origin of the Greek form of the eschatological legends.[11] The hypothesis of a translation of the Muhammadan legend of the *mi'rāj* did not occur to him, although the idea had been mentioned already by Steinschneider in his studies on the medieval translations. For Blochet, "Dante's achievement consists not so much in having invented the outline of the legend as in having inserted episodes that are unparalleled in any other literature, above all in the Oriental versions of the Legend of the Ascension."[12] The first scientific study of

Muslim eschatology appeared in 1909. Written by Rudolf Leszynsky, it restricts itself to the study, edition, and commentary of the *Kitāb al-zuhd* (Book of Abstinence) by Asad ibn Mūsā al-Umawī (132–212).[13]

Only a few years after Blochet, Marcus Dods published eschatological legends from Egyptian and Babylonian times through the Middle Ages. He introduced some of Jewish origin, but he did not mention any Muslim ones. Dods, unlike Blochet, cautiously stated "that references to the *Divine Comedy* will be made, but they must be taken as quite gratuitous, merely incidental illustrations."[14] He actually credited Dante for having not only composed but also invented the various scenes of the *Commedia*.

In 1905 Francesco Torraca brushed aside Blochet's opinions: "He [Blochet] reasons like this: Dante knew the Western stories of other travels to the otherworld; yet these stories derive from Oriental legend; therefore, it is the first source of the *Divine Comedy*."[15] In his opinion, "Dante has no predecessors, because the *Divine Comedy* does not belong to the shadowy Middle Ages, but to the new, complex, varying, luminescent Italian civilization."[16]

In 1907 De Fabrizio, referring to Blochet's "L'Ascension au ciel" (Ascent to Heaven) and to Alessandro d'Ancona's "La leggenda di Maometto" (The Legend of Muḥammad) took this legend of the *mi'rāj* as the Muslim contribution to Dante's inspiration for the *Commedia*. He based his argument on *Lo specchio della fede* (The Mirror of Faith) by Roberto Caracciolo (1425–1495), in which Muḥammad's ascension is told "very summarily, as if it concerns matters already known to the reader."[17] He believed Caracciolo's text to have been preceded by a long oral tradition: "That the medieval visionaries knew the *mi'rāj* is probable; although we might concede that Dante perhaps knew it, it cannot be confirmed at the current state of studies . . . excluding the hypothesis about a direct, conscious imitation . . . there might remain the possibility of an imperceptible influence which the legend might have had during the composition of the *Commedia*, mingled with other, more important and similar stories, if not absorbed by them."[18]

A few years later, in 1910, Raffaele Ottolenghi turned from Muslim traditions as alleged sources of Dante's eschatology to the traditions of the Spanish Jews, especially in Ibn Gabirol's religious poem *Keter Malkut* (Crown of Royalty).[19] And in 1911 Paolo Amaducci claimed to have found the source of the *Commedia* in Saint Peter Damian's mystical exegesis of Numbers 33.[20]

What Dante scholars thought about the preceding discussions of the possible sources for the *Commedia* can be readily seen in Bruno Nardi's comments on Amaducci's work: "To stir the waters of Dante studies, which for decades illustrious scholars endeavored to purge of disturbing elements and to place it back within the confines of healthy criticism, two volumes suddenly appeared at the end of the winter of 1911—in which Paolo Amaducci made the sensational and somewhat boisterous announcement of having discovered the 'source of the *Divine Comedy.*'"[21]

This "sensational announcement" was quickly forgotten when Asín Palacios's second work on Muslim eschatology appeared in 1919, arousing a great commotion among scholars of Romance and Oriental literatures alike. His *Escatología musulmana y la Divina Comedia* (Muslim Eschatalogy and the Divine Comedy) was not a restatement of former theories. The presentation was new, and so was his emphasis on the Muslim legends of the otherworld, recorded and analyzed with uncommon mastery.[22]

Previously, Asín Palacios had shown Dante to be a follower—through Christian filterings—of the Neoplatonic mysticism of the Cordovan philosopher Ibn Masarra. He had also called attention to the resemblance between the ascent of Dante and Beatrice into Paradise and the ascent of Ibn al-'Arabī, the Murcian mystic.[23] Taking this as a starting point, Asín Palacios asserted that Ibn al-'Arabī's ascension was a mystical-allegorical adaptation of Muḥammad's ascension, the *mi'rāj*. In Muslim lore, the *mi'rāj* was preceded by an *isrā'*, a nocturnal journey of the Prophet, during which he visited the infernal regions of the otherworld. The tradition, widely spread in Muslim writings, was, according to Asín Palacios, the prototype of Dante's journey in the *Commedia*. Having identified this prototype, he turned his attention to medieval Christian legends that antedated Dante. His research "not only confirmed that in Moslem sources there were to be found prototypes of features in the *Commedia*—it further revealed the no less Moslem origin of many of those mediaeval legends themselves."[24]

Asín Palacios adopted the main aspects of Blochet's theory of the Oriental sources.[25] He objected, however, that in Blochet's presentation too little attention was paid to "the nearest influences, constant and stable in the communication between Eastern and Western cultures" and criticized Blochet's lack of documentation.[26]

Asín Palacios's main contributions to this problem were therefore his extensive and well-documented presentation of Muslim eschatology and his emphasis on Spain as the most constant and stable area of communication between the two cultures. The Muslim tradition was not conceived by Asín Palacios as the origin of all human interest in eschatological themes. Nor did he deny the possibility of other ways for the diffusion of Oriental legends. But he emphasized throughout his works the idea of cross-cultural communications that took place in Spain.

The ensuing controversy was caused by implications of Asín Palacios's theory: if accepted, the importance given to Muslim influence required a reinterpretation of the relationship between Christian lore and Muslim lore as well as between medieval Christian folklore and its classical and early Christian models. The militant tone, however, that the controversy assumed was initiated by Asín Palacios's overly confident presentation. For his book is certainly polemical; it tries to convince more than it does to explain. It is therefore hardly surprising that the following dispute had, at times, a tone of violent dissension.

Not everything in Asín Palacios's *Escatología*, however, is written in such a confident tone. His chapter on the transmission of Islamic models to Christian Europe and in particular to Dante is, admittedly, based on assumptions. In the chain of transmission of the legend of the *mi'rāj* to Europe and to Italy, there is a link missing. Asín Palacios tries to solve the problem in three different ways. The first is through Dante's teacher and friend, Brunetto Latini, who during his service as ambassador of Florence to the court of Alfonso X the Wise "was in a position to acquire his knowledge of Arabic at first hand."[27] "Everything thus would seem to bear out the suggestion that the master of Dante Alighieri received more than a merely superficial impression from his visit to Spain, and may well have been the medium through which at least some of the Islamic features apparent in the *Commedia* were transmitted to the disciple."[28] Another way in which Dante could have become aware of the Muslim tradition was through his Jewish friends, such as Emmanuel Ben Salomo or Hillel of Verona.[29] Finally, Dante himself might have had "a certain leaning" toward Islamic culture. Moreover, "if it cannot be proved from Dante's writings that he knew Semitic languages, neither can it be proved that he was ignorant of them."[30] Later, Asín Palacios would say on the same subject "specifically Islamic eschatological ideas and images exist in the *Divine Comedy*, the knowledge of which requires Dante's knowledge of the Arabic language, or of those who translated them."[31] As to the connection between the Muslim models and the Christian legends of the otherworld appearing in Dante's work, Asín Palacios can only offer probable channels. Thus the "missing link" in the transmission became a very important focal point in the later controversy.[32]

The polemic around the *Escatología musulmana* was surveyed and analyzed by Asín Palacios himself a few years later. His replies to the objections (there was not a single case of self-correction) were published in four different journals as "Historia y crítica de una polémica."[33] It contained a comprehensive bibliography of about eighty articles to which Asín Palacios added the short comments of "favorable," "undecided," or "adverse."[34] Of the Dantists, philologists, and other scholars listed, the forces seemed to be rather equally divided. Among the Orientalists, Asín Palacios considered leading authorities like Massignon, Levi della Vida, and Giuseppe Gabrieli as being undecided.[35] The Dantists who did not agree with Asín Palacios—and they were the majority—answered in passionate and often nationalistic tones.

The main objections raised against Asín Palacios can be summarized as follows. First, the Muslim texts are from different sources, authors, geographical areas, and dates. Second, the same analogies can be found in classical, biblical, and early Christian models. Third, the undeniable similarities found between Dantean and Islamic eschatology could be explained in other ways.[36] For example, Christian and Muslim eschatology coincide in many aspects because they developed in parallel—but independently—from remote, pre-Islamic sources. Or they coincide because of a fundamental cultural parallelism or a universal similarity in the way human psychology conceives of the otherworld.

The controversy over the extent of Muslim influence on the works of Dante remained in a deadlock for almost three decades.[37] A survey of the controversy up to the time of Asín Palacios's review reveals two main strands in the discussion. One was the possibility that Dante had known about Muslim legends of the otherworld and about allegorical interpretations of the Muslim eschatology by Muslim mystics. The other was Dante's personal attitude toward Muslim lore and things Arabic in general.

Although it was rejected almost unanimously and without any qualifications by Dante critics, Asín Palacios's theory deeply influenced subsequent research—a fact of which Dante scholars have not always been fully aware.[38] Although the controversy still seemed to be centered mainly on Dante's *Commedia*, strictly speaking, the problem of the "sources" had shifted to that of our basic interpretation of the European Middle Ages. It postulated, namely, a reexamination of our conception of medieval European lore and culture in their relation to the classical and early Christian background, on one side, and to the Muslim contributions and participation in the so-called Western tradition, on the other.

Another aspect of Asín Palacios's theory that has had to be acknowledged by all later investigators is Muslim Spain's undeniable role in the transmission of Arabic lore to the West. In his 1936 article "Dante e l'Oriente" (Dante and the Orient), Leonardo Olschki seems to have had in mind the importance of "the Muslim contribution to the Christian science and philosophy of these centuries."[39] He certainly rejects the claims of those who interpret the Dantean eschatology as "a direct emanation" from the Muslim eschatology as conceived by mystic Sufis and especially Ibn al-'Arabī as well as the exaggerations of those who "overreact to the point of nullification, espousing a Dante who is entirely ignorant of matters of the East and barely interested in them."[40]

However, Olschki evades the main issue in claiming that "in the universal synopsis of the doctrine and history which was present in Dante's mind as a source of meditation and inspiration, the East had a part to play"; for his idea of the Orient and, in his opinion, Dante's in the *Commedia*, is a very vague and romantic one. It is about *l'Asia favolosa* ("the fabulous Asia") of Genghis Khan, "these immense and already inaccessible territories to those in the West" that he is writing.[41] Olschki rightly acknowledges the importance of the Greek and Christian background of Muslim culture: "The teachings of Arabic philosophers were accepted in the West by virtue of their purely speculative content . . . as heirs of this ancient tradition in which the fathers and the doctors of the Church were reconnected by the same origins and the same dialectic. . . . These Arab authors were, therefore, studied and followed in the West by virtue of the spiritual continuity they represented."[42] He also duly stresses the fact that the purely religious aspects as such never took any real part in the cultural exchange: "Muḥammad never had any part; and if Algazali, Averroes, and other authors of the East strove for a substantial, dialectical, allegorical, theological, and mystical harmony with the Qur'an, none of these was able to enter, nor did it penetrate, into Western thought, as it was completely excluded from what was part of the 'law' of Muḥammad and of the moral and religious practice of the Islam."[43] Olschki, however, does not consider another kind of exchange that, while difficult to define, is always present when peoples come in contact. The mutual influence and effects of this exchange—folklore is part of its currency—is only too often disregarded. However, it is precisely at this level of learned, semi-learned, and popular exchange that the problem lies—not in the romantic interest Dante might have had in things Oriental.

In 1944 Ugo Monneret de Villart tried to show that medieval interest in Islam was a Spanish trait, scarcely found in France and to an even lesser degree in Italy, a fact that has been used to refute one of Asín Palacios's premises. One must bear in mind, however, that Monneret de Villart uses "Islam" as a religious term, and the medieval study of Islam that he analyzes is only the purely theological, missionary interest shown by the orders of the time, which was understandably greater in Spain, where the Muslim influence was also greater. He admits, however, the possibility of Dante's having been aware of Muslim eschatology, particularly of the *Kitāb al-miʿrāj* (Book of the Ascension).[44] His findings, therefore, enlightening as they are, cannot be used as arguments in the case of Dante, whose contact with Islam, as pointed out by Asín Palacios, was not on the religious level.

August Rüegg, in his book *Die Jenseitsvorstellungen vor Dante*, published in 1945, presents, as the title of his book indicates, a thorough study of "Concepts of the Otherworld prior to Dante." However, only classic and early Christian visions are investigated.[45] He has, to be sure, a chapter "on the question of Islamic influence on Dante," but his analysis of the Islamic sources is the least convincing in an otherwise excellent study.[46]

With regard to the problem of the similarities between the Christian and Muslim legends of the otherworld, he finds it "natural that the Middle Ages, in both Arabic and Germanic cultures, have largely similar characteristics, since they grew from the same tradition, although they have a more Roman-Germanic-Celtic coloring to the north of the Mediterranean, and a more Oriental-Greek one to the south."[47] Rüegg does not ask whether Dante knew the Muslim eschatological legends. Moreover, he wrongly attributes to Asín Palacios the claims that all Muslim forerunners of Dante are direct sources for his *Commedia*. Hence his argument that in such a case "we would be forced to assume that Dante had freely at his disposal an entire library of writings of Arabic mystics, philosophers, and poets, originating from various centuries."[48] He also brings up the argument of the "missing link" in the transmission: "If Dante had found conveniently in one text all of these models, thus amassed and arranged as they appear in Asín, then one would almost have to consider a Muslim source."[49] Rüegg obviously demands of the Arabic source a similarity that he hardly expects from Christian models.

In 1949 an Italian and a Spanish scholar, Enrico Cerulli and José Muñoz Sendino, working independently and unaware of each other's research, published the Latin and French versions of a Hispano-Arabic book containing the legend of Muḥammad's journey to the infernal regions and his ascension to the heavens.[50] The book, called *Liber scale Machometi*—or *Libro della scala* and *Livre de l'eschiele Mahomet* in the Italian and Old French versions—was translated at the order of Alfonso X by the Jewish physician Abraham Alfaquím into Romance and by Bonaventura of Siena into Latin.

Besides the edition of the texts, Cerulli adds in his book a thorough study of the diffusion of the *Liber scale Machometi* in the West, including quotations from Muslim eschatology used by medieval authors. In the last chapter, "Dante e l'Islam" (Dante and Islam), he examines Asín Palacios's statements in the light of the *Liber scale Machometi*. Cerulli does not attempt a restatement of Asín Palacios's theories; rather, he conscientiously and with moderation tries simply to analyze the similarities and parallels between the *Liber scale Machometi* and the *Commedia*.

Nevertheless the *Liber scale Machometi* caused the controversy to flare up again. In spite of the objections made against Cerulli's edition from the linguistic point of view, by Levi della Vida and by Groult, the *Liber scale Machometi* was hailed as the "missing link."[51]

As Levi della Vida notes in his 1949 review of Muñoz's and Cerulli's editions, "Nowadays it is no longer possible to harbor any doubt that the Book of the Ladder was made available to the Latin West in two if not three versions; that it was unknown to Dante seems highly improbable. Asín's thesis concerning not just the possibility, but also the reality of relations between Dante and Islamic eschatology is thus definitively confirmed."[52] In 1954 Francesco Gabrieli wrote in *Diogenes*, "Cultural nationalism—or, as I prefer to interpret it, mental laziness put together with diffidence and the lack of positive proof—can no longer deny that the brilliant hypothesis of thirty years ago has at last a splendid confirmation, at least in the intuition on which it was based."[53]

Bruno Nardi, on the other hand, in his 1955 article "Pretese fonti della *Divina Commedia*" (Purported Sources of the *Divine Comedy*), heatedly rejects the above-mentioned statements—"Since it seems that someone has forgotten the old principle of reasoning: *a posse ad esse non datur illatio* ('a conclusion cannot be drawn from the possible to the actual')"—and requests more positive proof: "Such a statement cannot be made until after careful and thorough comparative analysis, for which many materials have been adduced, but to me it seems that this has not yet been done as it ought to have been."[54]

Since the publication of Cerulli's book the controversy had already been focused on the comparative analysis that Nardi requested. Cerulli himself had already reduced considerably the number and extent of the similarities between the Muslim eschatology and the *Commedia*. His relatively moderate tone and offering of fewer points of similarity were frequently referred to as a retreat from Asín Palacios's first position, but wrongly so, for the similarities and coincidences pointed out by Asín Palacios were still valid, and so were the objections concerning the diffusion of the Muslim traditions throughout Christian Europe. Cerulli's approach was different and so, therefore, were his conclusions. He simply compares the *Commedia* with the Muslim eschatology as it appears in the *Liber scale Machometi*, this book being the only literary source so far discovered that could have been known by Dante.

Beyond the assertion that Dante did not copy directly from the Muslim legend as found in the *Liber scale Machometi*, Cerulli's study resulted in very little agreement among scholars. Levi della Vida, for example, says "the *Book of the Ladder* . . . has furnished some important elements to the *Divine Comedy*, whether in the general design or in particular details."[55] Manfredi Porena, on the other hand, says, "as for the relationship between the *Book of the Ladder* and the *Divine Comedy*, the only thing that seems nearly certain to me, is that in Dante there are no imitations, nor even any certain echoes or reminiscences of the Muslim book."[56] The diametrical opposition expressed in these two comments is characteristic of the divergence of opinion among commentators after the publication of the *Liber scale Machometi*.[57]

Clearly it is no longer a matter of the similarities found in both traditions, Christian and Muslim, but of those found in the two works, Dante's *Commedia* and the anonymous *Liber scale Machometi*. Dantists frequently require the relationship between the *Commedia* and the *Liber* to be proved by similarities that can only be explained as reflections of the influence of the *Liber*. Indeed they require not only a similarity but a faithful copy, and this they rightly say is not to be found. Umberto Bosco says in this respect, "here we must admit that each of these analogies can legitimately be questioned; each, perhaps, can be explained by a common source or shared underlying human experience. But their entirety remains impressive."[58] This entirety has not yet been studied.

It should be pointed out (Levi della Vida had already mentioned this fact) that the *Liber scale Machometi*, if considered as the only source for Dante's acquaintance with Muslim eschatology, necessarily confines Asín Palacios's arguments from a general Muslim influence to the influence of this book. In this respect, the nature of the book seems to be the greatest objection against Asín Palacios's theories, because, in the *Liber scale Machometi*, there is nothing of the mystical and allegorical interpretation of the legend as we find in Ibn Masarra or Ibn al-'Arabī. Nor is there anything of the doctrine of light that was Asín Palacios's starting point in his search for the Muslim sources of the *Comedy*.

This observation, however, cannot be used as a definite refutation of Asín Palacios's theory. On the contrary, the diffusion of the Mohammedan legend in Christian Europe has been proved by literary documents, namely, the *Liber scale Machometi*. To reject a priori any other contacts between Christian and Muslim lore, through literary or oral channels, would be to adopt a position that can hardly be considered reasonable.[59] For we know now that toward the end of the twelfth century, there was written an allegorical and philosophical treatise on the soul's journey into the otherworld.[60] It was composed in either Sicily or Catalonia, and shows obvious and deep influence of Avicenna's philosophy and also of Ibn Gabirol, proving that by the beginning of the Duecento (i.e., the thirteenth century) such philosophical allegories of Arabic descent were known in Christian Europe.

It is generally accepted that Dante was not particularly inclined toward things Arabic as such. But it must be emphasized that Dante lived, worked, and composed his *Commedia* in a world where Arabic thought was omnipresent in learned circles. Dante admittedly drew on a Latin translation of an Arabic book, the *Liber de causis* (Book of Causes), for fundamental elements of his theory of earthly and mystical love and the metaphysics of light that permeates his vision of Paradise.[61] The *Libro della scala* shows that this was also the case with the eschatological themes of Muḥammad's legend. We must admit this fact in spite of the apologetical and missionary efforts of the Church. In fact, this importance given to things Arabic aroused the Church's missionary zeal against them, with the consequent creation of an image of Islam as the "vilissima religio" ("vilest religion").[62] From this perspective an evaluation of things Arabic can still be made.

The most impressive a priori argument against any influence of Muslim eschatology is the contrast between Mohammedan and Dantean attitudes. This, however, should not be overemphasized, since there are many parallel cases of borrowing and even of translation with radical changes in spirit and form during the Middle Ages.

In his 1951 article "Mohammedan Eschatology," Olschki correctly points out that Muslim eschatology drew from Jewish, Christian, and Parsi sources. He also points to the Christian-Mozarabic influence on the development of Mohammedan eschatology in the Middle Ages, which "seems to have been an accomplishment mainly of Spanish Moors living in a Christian and Mozarabic environment, therefore longer and more directly influenced by Christian and Biblical trends and motifs than the coreligionists of Asia."[63] This influence was undoubtedly present, but seeing Mohammedan eschatology as "an accomplishment of Spanish Moors" needs further qualification. His final assertion also needs qualification: "A sober and critical comparison of the two texts shows that Mohammedan eschatology as displayed in the *Book of the Ladder* contributes nothing in any appreciable way to the structural and episodic scaffold of the *Divina Commedia* or to our historical and interpretive understanding of the poem."[64] If we agree that Dante's masterpiece is not an isolated monument, which can be studied independently of the circumstances that formed Dante's world, then Asín Palacios's theories and the *Liber scale Machometi* are undoubtedly contributions to our understanding of the poem.

Silverstein's 1952 article "Dante and the Legend of the Mi'raj" drew attention especially to the problem of the relationship of the eschatological legends in the twelfth century to their classical and early Christian sources. He, in short, rejects Asín Palacios's opinion concerning Muslim influence on them and stresses the continuous tradition and growth of the legends throughout the early Middle Ages. But at the same time, one cannot help noticing Silverstein's efforts to present Asín

Palacios's ideas in the most extreme way: "These traditions, Night Journey and Ascension, according to him [Asín Palacios] provided a major source of matters and ideas for the *Divina Commedia* and to a large extent directly; but where not directly, then through their previous use (Asín's word for some instances is 'plagiarism') by other Christian visions in the Middle Ages."[65]

The arguments with which Silverstein demonstrates the continuous evolution of the Christian legends are certainly convincing. Yet the polemical tone of his expositions is also unmistakable. Returning to Dante's case, he seems less convincing as he canvasses the whole Christian field in search of examples that might strengthen his arguments: "In the ninth-century vision of Charles the Fat the incident also appears in a form particularly suitable to Dante, who might readily have borrowed it thence, transformed by a memory of the Classical centaurs for Inferno, Canto 12."[66] In his discussion of the *Liber scale Machometi*, Silverstein uses the more reserved approach of Cerulli's exposition as an argument against both Cerulli and Asín Palacios; this also is inappropriate, at least insofar as Cerulli's arguments are of a different nature from those of Asín Palacios, as shown above. It is therefore surprising to find in the summarizing paragraph the following remark: "No one will wish to claim that it [Silverstein's survey of traditional Christian visions precursory to Dante] has proved the absence of Muslim influence among them. On the contrary, some evidence suggests that such influence may indeed have operated at certain points, and to deny this possibility, even probability, would be as intemperate as it was on Asín's part to believe that nearly everything in the tradition came from Islam."[67] "Certainly," he further states, "the presence in Western texts of certain motifs which the Italian poet used need not mean that he got them from a Christian work rather than a Muslim text which, by means of a translation, he could read."[68]

Bruno Nardi's 1955 article "Pretese fonti della *Divina Commedia*" (Purported sources of the *Divine Comedy*) makes no new contribution to the controversy. It shows rather to what extent the controversy has ceased to be a problem that can be restricted solely to the study of Dante's sources. The controversy has become a problem to be solved only with a reinterpretation of our understanding of the European Middle Ages as a time in which Arabic and Jewish cultural elements as well are given the place they deserve as components of the so-called Western tradition. In this light the "influence" of a specific work on any particular author is only an episode. Considering the state of the controversy at this point, the conclusion at which Richard Lemay arrived in his 1963 article on Dante comes as a surprise: "If Dante knew Arabic, is it not true that the problem of his borrowings from Arabic literary sources would then become much simpler? Dante had the means of reading whatever he wanted or interested him: whether he busied himself with the Risālat al-Ghufrān of Abū al-'Alā' al-Ma'arri [not Ma'āri!] or various great mystic works of Ibn al-'Arabī of Murcia, famous works among the Arabs and widespread through the cultural realm of Islam, his known inspirations, and especially the numerous parallel passages between these works and the *Divine Comedy*, demonstrated by Asín Palacios, would have nothing to surprise us!"[69] Obviously the author is not aware of the preceding controversy. "If Dante had known Arabic all this could be explained very easily." Unfortunately, Dante's knowledge of Arabic has not been proved in any way; moreover, to explain things easily is beside the point.

Dante and Islamic Culture

MARIA CORTI†

iven the stimulating proximity and well-known contacts between the Catholic and Islamic worlds during the Middle Ages and
during Dante's own lifetime, a particular methodological rigor is needed
to evaluate Arabic philosophical, mystical, and eschatological texts as
sources for Dante's writing.

At the end of the thirteenth century, the relations between these
two worlds grew closer in intriguing ways after a lively period in
which Arabic works were translated into Latin. A great expansion of
two large cultural centers—Sicily and Toledo (with its renowned
Toledan school of translators)—also took place at this time. Sicily and
Toledo were, not coincidentally, dominated by two exceptional political figures of the Duecento: Frederick II, king of Sicily and emperor
(1194–1250), and Alfonso X the Wise, king of Castile and León (1221–
1284), who ascended to the throne in 1252, two years after the death
of Frederick II. Both were linked from their infancy to the Islamic
world and were therefore influenced by Islamic culture in their linguistic and cultural upbringing. History has given to both of these
rulers great credit for cultural exchanges between the two worlds,
as Michele Amari (1806–1889) and Francesco Gabrieli (1904–1996)
highlighted.

Naturally, Dante did not know Arabic; thus the mediation of Latin
or Old French was indispensable for him, and the observation of Ernst
Robert Curtius (1886–1956) on this topic is still pertinent for Dante
scholars and for Arab scholars interested in Dante: "Before Dante scholarship lies the great task of methodically studying Dante's relation to the
Latin Middle Ages."[1] To study that relationship means also investigating

the methods of Dante's approach to the Arabic-Latin historical and cultural context of his time.

Three methodological possibilities arise. The first is that processes of interdiscursivity existed during Dante's era. That is to say, there was circulation between the cultural worlds through which a fact, a piece of information, a technical term, and so forth, could become part of a common heritage precisely as a consequence of interpretation through interdiscursivity. In such a case, it is impossible (not to say dangerous) to single out a direct source for a shared trope. The second possibility is when there are phenomena that can be termed intertextual, by which it can occur that a text *x* offers a structural model to a text *y*, as it were, a model by analogy. This analogical relationship does not mean text *x* is necessarily the source of *y*—that the author of *y* had read or had at hand the text of *x*: the author might have read a summary that gave the structure of the work or had heard an oral summary, as at times happened in several works mentioned by Miguel Asín Palacios (1871–1944).[2] The third possibility is that an Arabic text is, in a scholar's opinion, the direct source of one of Dante's works. In this case, the literary derivation from the Arabic text must be supported on the grounds of literary history: a translation of the Arabic text into Latin or Old French or a familiarity with it in Dante's literary context. Then one must prove that a correspondence is not merely thematic but rather formal; furthermore, the correspondence must be extensive enough not to be coincidental but isomorphic by design.[3]

From these methodological premises, I would like to offer (within the limited scope of this paper) some examples of these three possible connections between Dante's *De vulgari eloquentia*, *Convivio*, or *Commedia* and one or more Arabic texts. I will begin with two examples—quite different in terms of their relative weight but both visible in the Ulysses episode in *Inferno* 26—of Arabic influences that are traceable to the historical reality of interdiscursivity. Dante writes of the passage through the Pillars of Hercules:

> Io e' compagni eravam vecchi e tardi
> quando venimmo a quella foce stretta
> dov'Ercule segnò li suoi riguardi
> acciò che l'uom più oltre non si metta
>
> I and my companions were old and slow
> when we came to that narrow outlet

where Hercules set up his markers
for men to heed and never pass beyond
(*Inf.* 26.106–9)

As I have shown elsewhere,[4] the taboo on passing through the Pillars of Hercules is absent from Greek and Latin tradition; the most ancient references go back to Arab and Spanish geographies, again confirming the striking relationship between the Christian and Arab worlds at the outset.[5] Guido delle Colonne, in his thirteenth-century *Historia destructionis Troiae* (History of the Destruction of Troy), clearly states that this prohibition is Arabic in origin: "Dicitur Sarracenica lingua *Saphy*" ("It is called *Saphy* in the Arabic tongue"),[6] using a term that is found again in the form *Saufì* in the anonymous *Mare amoroso* (Sea of Love):

E mai non finirei d'andar per mare
infin ch'i' mi vedrei oltre quel braccio
che fie chiamato il braccio di Saufì
c'ha scritto in su la man "Nimo ci passi,"
per ciò che di qua mai non torna chi di là passa

And I shall never cease to wander over the sea
until I see for myself that arm
that has been called the arm of *Saphy*,
that has written on its hand "None shall pass,"
through which the one who passes never returns.[7]

This instance of one text recalling another has been quoted because of the importance of the statue of Muḥammad, which announced the prohibition against going forward by pointing his left arm in the direction of the strait, a gesture that according to Arab geographers meant "Return to the place from which you have come," or in other words, "Do not go forward."[8] Various interdiscursive historical facts relating to the Arabic noun *Saphy* are thus behind the verses of the Ulysses episode. However, to search for a direct source would here be senseless.

The second interdiscursive case is more ambiguous and invites more speculation. The noted Italianist Mario Fubini (1900–1977) wrote a wonderful essay on the episode of Ulysses as a sublime product of Dante's pure imagination.[9] Certainly the narration of the rash, Promethean, and fascinating event is the work of Dante's own genius.[10] To be precise, however, it should be noted that the theme of Ulysses's shipwreck, related in the prophecy of Tiresias in Book 11 of the *Odyssey* ("thanatos ex halos," "death by water," that is, by the sea) is not Dante's invention; rather, it gives signs of itself as a centuries-old topos in drama, already appearing as such in Aeschylus and Sophocles.[11] Although it is tempting to view the inherently fascinating qualities of the text as entirely original, we must ask, is it all purely Dante's invention?

Three aspects of the story are notable upon first reading it: the connection between the character and the Pillars of Hercules; the sea voyage from Campania to the Pillars; and the shipwreck. These first two develop through interdiscursive topoi. The first, besides having within it an echo of the *saphy*, or prohibition, reminds us of Strabo (60 BCE–20 CE), who in the third book of the *Geographica* (Geography), dedicated to Iberia, describes (relating to the Greek sources of Posidonius of Rhodes, Artemidorus of Ephesus, and Asclepiades of Myrleia) the city of Odysseia, with its temple of Athena, on the mountainous slopes above the Straits of Gibraltar. A great Byzantine writer of the twelfth century, Eustathius of Thessalonica, also speaks of an Odysseia in Turdetania, above the Pillars of Hercules, in his commentaries on the *Odyssey* and on Dionysius's *Periegesis* (Voyage). And we should not forget that Servius in his commentary to Vergil (*Aen.* 6.107) writes that Ulysses would have arrived at the most distant part of the ocean.

If, therefore, the theme of Ulysses's voyage beyond the Pillars of Hercules already existed in classical and Byzantine cultures, we can add to it the theme of the *via Heracleia*—the route by sea that traces the Mediterranean islands from Cumae, in Campania (Dante's Gaeta, "prima che sì Enëa la nomasse" "before Aeneas had so named it" [*Inf.* 26.93]), to the Pillars of Hercules. An interesting point made by Ramón Menéndez Pidal is that this maritime passage was also used by Arab geographers and traders, as it was the least dangerous in regard to the winds.[12]

We now arrive at our third theme, shipwreck, which offers dramatic evidence of itself over the centuries. Strabo, in the *Geographica*, lingers over one of his sources, Asclepiades of Myrleia (modern Murdanya).[13] Asclepiades, who came from Myrleia on the Bosphorus to Odysseia in order to teach Greek grammar there, began to make his way around the area, writing his *Periegesis*. In this text, Asclepiades notes that in the temple dedicated to Athena (the protective goddess of Ulysses) at Odysseia, one could see affixed to the walls shields and spurs from Ulysses's ship, souvenirs of a failed undertaking. It is likely that a faint ghost of this shipwreck theme survives in the Arabic-Spanish prohibition against passing through the Pillars—the prohibition that Ulysses calls into question while in Dante's company. In fact, in the vernacular translation of the *Historia destructionis Troiae* we read "quello luogo ove le predette colonne d'Ercole sono fitte, s'appella in lingua Saracina *Saphis*, ed è il luogo ove più oltre non si puote ire per tornare" ("that place where the aforesaid Pillars of Hercules are erected is called in the Saracen tongue *Saphis*, and it is the place beyond which one may never pass in order to return again").[14] "Per tornare" alludes to a punitive shipwreck that awaits those who would risk such a venture, and we find this again in the first Canto of *Purgatorio* (*Pur.* 1.131–32 "che mai non vide navicar sue acque / omo, che di tornar sia poscia esperto" "that never saw any man navigate its waters / who afterwards had experience of return"). To the myth of the shipwreck one can also add the myth of a long and unpredictable journey, since the failed expedition of the brothers Vandino and Ugolino Vivaldi, Genoese explorers who voyaged beyond the Straits of Gibraltar in 1291, gave rise to a certain amazement and fear.

This theme of the Arabic *Saphy*, then, followed by the punitive shipwreck, is conveyed by the Arabic tradition, as highlighted by many events: the construction of the gilded statue of Muḥammad with its menacing gesture; the Norse tradition by which the Bay of Cadiz is known as *Karlsá* ("water of the man," i.e., of the statue); and the Norwegian account of the voyage of Saint Olaf, who arrived from the outside at the Pillars of Hercules by sea along the coast of France, only to have to turn back owing to the injunction of the statue of Muḥammad (in the dream).[15] It is upon this exciting theme and the traditional fear of a long voyage "per l'alto mare aperto" (*Inf.* 26.100 "on the deep open sea") that Dante constructs the allegorical significance of Ulysses's shipwreck which is contrasted through references to his own text to the beginnings of the three canticles.[16]

Equally significant is a comparison with *Purgatorio* 1.130–33:

Venimmo poi in sul lito diserto
che mai non vide navicar sue acque
omo, che di tornar sia poscia esperto.
Quivi mi cinse sì com' altrui piacque

Then we came onto the desert shore,
that never saw any man navigate its waters

who afterwards had experience of return.
There, even as pleased another, he girded me.

This is a further example of self-referentiality in the Ulysses episode, with an even more conspicuous indication in the repetition of "com' altrui piacque" ("as pleased another"), which indicates two extraordinary experiences, one negative and one positive. God himself sends Ulysses's boat to the bottom of the sea (*Inf.* 26.141 "e la prora ire in giù, com'altrui piacque" "and plunged the prow below, as pleased another") as punishment for his presumptuous *curiositas* (curiosity), whereas Dante is encircled by "l'umile pianta" (*Purg.* 1.135 "the humble plant"), symbolizing the humility of the quest.

The Ulyssean theme of the voyage opens the first two canticles, and it is also found in the third, at the moment of the ascension into the heavens. In Canto 2 of *Paradiso*, the "piccioletta barca" (*Par.* 2.1 "little bark") corresponds to the "compagna picciola" ("small company") of *Inferno* 26; then, the phrase of Ulysses, "ma misi me per l'alto mare aperto" (*Inf.* 26.100 "But I set out on the deep open sea"), corresponds to "tornate a riveder li vostri liti: / non vi mettete in pelago" (*Par.* 2.4–5 "turn back again to see little shores: / Do not commit yourselves to the ocean"), where "pelago" indicates "l'alto mare aperto." Both Ulysses and Dante the pilgrim take to waters that "già mai non si corse" (*Par.* 2.7 "were never coursed before"), Ulysses by violating *saphy* (here meaning "prohibition"), Dante by a privilege granted by Minerva, Apollo, and the Muses.

The desire to know for the sake of knowing brings the shipwreck and the mad flight, while the Dantesque "sete del deïforme"—the thirst for God's form (*Par.* 2.20)—guides Beatrice and Dante upward on their journey-flight. In both cases the metaphoric sea closes up according to the untroubled laws of nature, as at *Inferno* 26.142 ("infin che 'l mar fu sopra noi richiuso" "until the sea closed over us") and *Paradiso* 2.15 ("dinanzi a l'acqua che ritorna eguale" "ahead of the water that turns smooth again"). Dante infuses the three situations with an even more precise allegorical significance (which I do not examine here) that signals an exemplum of the intellectual voyage, making Ulysses—as first put forth by Jurij Lotman (1922–1993)—"the original double of Dante,"[17] the negative hero of a journey that is undertaken in Dante's time by those who wish to be *sapientes mundi*, the radical Aristotelians, who Augustine would have said to be shipwrecked before reaching *ad philosophiae portum* (*De beata vita* 1.1 "the harbor of philosophy"). We are thus looking at Dante's brilliant transformation of the topos of the intellectual shipwreck. Indeed, Benvenuto da Imola noticed that Dante has told the story of Ulysses "propter aliquod propositum ostendendum" ("so as to make evident some purpose").

A curious and in some ways ambiguous piece of evidence is worth noting, which is handed down in an as yet unedited thirteenth-century text concerning Trojan material, part of the *Tercera parte* (Third Part) of the *General estoria* (General History) of Alfonso X.[18] According to this history, Ulysses,[19] having founded the city of Ulixbona (Lisbon) and having been struck by a sense of longing and nostalgia for his dear wife Penelope and his son Telemachus, whom he had not seen for twenty-five years, told his men to prepare themselves for the trip back to their native land. They left with favorable winds and arrived at Ithaca, having avoided the enchantress Circe. One night, Ulysses had in a dream a strange vision, in which a beautiful woman appeared to him with the signs of death that boded sadness and lamentation to him. Ulysses says that the woman's hand showed him "the scabbard of a lance that had impressed upon it two fishes of the sea, which is salty water, and she then curtly blocked my view."

It is not clear how to elucidate the elements in this vision of death in the Castilian text nor how to interpret them, like the seers consulted by Ulysses, as news of patricide. For us, the important detail is that the imaginative process created through the long journey of Ulysses continued to construct itself around the theme of *curiositas*/death. The Castilian tale lies outside discussions of Dante's sources, but, like other discoveries found in the fantastic texts of the geographers of that age, it does not allow us to refute categorically the possibility that from behind such interdiscursivity there could one day emerge a precise source. No specific source has emerged: it is only within the realm of possibility—the paths of reading are as infinite as those of Providence itself.

I would like to move from the first process of relations between two cultures, namely, interdiscursivity, to the interaction between two or more texts, which is to say intertextuality. Here I will consider the episode recounting the Tower of Babel in *De vulgari eloquentia* 2.8.6–7, which is clearly constructed upon Genesis 2:34, around the two periods of construction (the ascent) and confusion (the descent). In the first, Dante not only describes the activities of a thirteenth-century construction site but he also lists several *officia* (offices) and *ministeria* (ministries), using a structure offered him by *Aeneid* 1.423–25 (the construction of Carthage).

It is the second phase of the story, Dante's description of the confusion of languages as a social reality, which is interesting for our purposes. It is through social commerce that the members of professional groupings, those who belong to a certain *status* or guild, are able to understand one another: for them "eadem lingua remansit" (*DVE* 1.7.7 "a common language remained"). It is not the same for individuals. Nimrod, the great inventor, is alone in speaking a language that is otherwise unknown to mankind (*Inf.* 31.80–81). This version of the *confusio linguarum* (confusion of languages), which renders it as an *allegoria in factis* (allegory of reality—historical allegory) of the medieval city (particularly Florence, whose citizens in Dante's *Epistle* 6 are defined as "alteri Babilonii" "other Babylonians"), is not seen in Petrus Comestor, Vincent of Beauvais, or even in the numerous texts used by Arno Borst in *Der Turmbau von Babel* (The Tower of Babel).[20]

There is, however, such a version of the tale in Alfonso X's *General estoria*, 1.43b.24. As shown by Hans-Josef Niederehe, Alfonso begins by elaborating on the versions of Comestor and Vincent of Beauvais, amplifying them with a spate of construction images. These images center on the inability to communicate among individuals,[21] as one calls for pitch and is given water, while another calls for water and is given tools.

In writing an essay on the Tower of Babel in 1978,[22] I asked myself whether Dante knew this text or had heard someone speak of it or whether the two texts had a common, but still unknown, Latin source. Here I would favor the significant intermediation between Arabic-Castilian culture and Florentine culture by Brunetto Latini. Brunetto was not only in Toledo as a Florentine ambassador in 1261, but he also remained in contact with Spain during the time of the French (that is, until 1266) as a personal friend of Alfonso X and of several translators of the Toledan school. The notion of what I call Brunetto's European importance is gaining ground, thanks in large part to Spanish Romance philologists, as I have tried to demonstrate.[23] Proof of the movement of ideas, first from the Toledo school to Brunetto and then through a period of Arabic culture onward to Dante, is doubtlessly provided by the *Convivio*.

The philosophical basis needed to understand Dante's cultural activity in the *Convivio* is Aristotle's *Nicomachean Ethics*. Which Latin translation did Dante use in order to read this work? There was an excellent translation from the Greek by Robert Grosseteste called either *Translatio Lincolniensis* (The Translation of Lincoln, as the author was the bishop of Lincoln) or *Liber ethicorum* (Book of Ethics). This text was used by Albert the Great as well as by Thomas Aquinas. However, Dante did not use this text, except when it is conveyed through Albert the Great's commentary. Rather, he used as a rule a translation from Arabic, the *Translatio Alexandrina* (Translation of Alexandria), also known as the *Summa Alexandrinorum* (Epitome of the Alexandrians). This text is the Latin translation of an Arabic-Alexandrian compendium, attributed in the manuscripts as *ab Hermanno Teutonico* (by Herman the German). Herman, of the Toledan school, finished his translation on April 8, 1244. In Toledo it was at times common to use Jews as mediators for Arabic texts, but Herman consulted only Arabs in completing his translations, as can be inferred from several particular linguistic characteristics, including proper names.[24]

It was Brunetto Latini who brought the *Translatio Alexandrina* to Dante's attention. He had the Latin text in his possession in Toledo (according to various testimonies), and he used it in his *Tresor* (Treasury). Dante, following Brunetto's lead, regularly used the Arabic text in the first and fourth essays of the *Convivio*, and at times he looked directly to the French of the *Tresor*, as I have shown.[25] Brunetto was inspired to write the *Tresor* itself, as an encyclopedia of knowledge, by the *Setenario* (The Septenary) of Alfonso X, a work interwoven with Arabic-Castilian elements that was actually begun by Alfonso's father, Ferdinand III, and explicitly driven by the word *tesoro* ("treasure") in the text.[26] The *Convivio* thus offers a brilliant example of intertextuality between a Greek text by Aristotle, an Arabic compendium, its translation into Latin, the French *Tresor* by Brunetto, and the *Convivio*, in which both the Latin translation of the Arabic text and the French translation in the *Tresor* would be translated into Italian.

One thing to consider here is that a relationship of genre among texts can also reveal something else—something that surpasses the idea of a source. It can illuminate the text from a new angle, a point of view that has a different orientation. It is not by chance that before "intertextuality" gained currency one finds Lotman's phrase "cultural textuality." This term presupposes that the text is a reality not only organized through the signs of a language but also one that situates itself at various levels of a culture with possible temporal and spatial expansions available to it. The distance between the "text of departure" (*Nicoma-chean Ethics*) and the "texts of arrival" (the Arabic compendium, *Tresor*, *Convivio*) becomes more stimulating when intertextuality is involved, whether from the viewpoint of history or from the viewpoint of literature.

I would now like to consider our third possibility—a true Arabic source for the *Commedia*. To begin, it should be noted that many themes found in the three canticles of the *Commedia* correspond to Arabic texts, which are not, however, direct sources. These include the voyages of Muḥammad into the afterlife (Inferno and Paradise—in Islam there is no Purgatory); the hierarchy of the heavens and the structure of the infernal circles; the concept of *contrapasso* ("counter-penalty") in the punishment of sinners and the materiality of some of these punishments; the earthly desires of the dead (themes discussed by Avicenna[27] and al-Ghazali [1058–1111] that are later taken up by Giles of Rome and the Oxford school, which is alluded to in *Purgatorio* 25.105–8); Jacob's ladder as a pathway to the heavens; the metaphysics of light; gigantic animals and ruined trees; along with other motifs and themes found, for example, in the *Escatología musulmana* of Asín Palacios.[28]

These thematic correspondences, given their broadly diffused presence, cannot be constrained within a discourse of direct sources but only of possible intertextuality, unless it can also be verified using the conditions listed above of a text translated into Latin or Old French, a historical context that can justify Dante's knowledge of the work, and similarities that are not only thematic but also formal and wide-ranging enough not to be coincidental but instead to be isomorphic. With this in mind one can point without any doubt to the *Liber scale Machometi* (or with the variation of the third word as *Mahometti*, as it is called in the Parisian codex, Bibliothèque nationale de France, MS lat. 6064), as a source for such features as the city of Dis and the Malebolge in Hell as represented in Dante's *Inferno*. This text, ultimately of Arabic origin, was discovered not, as is often written, by Enrico Cerulli, but rather by Ugo Monneret de Villard.[29] I believe it is also possible to confirm that in the *Paradiso* there are analogical intertextual relationships, which will be shown later.

The first question is obvious: How did Dante come to know the *Liber scale Machometi* (Book of the Ladder of Muḥammad)? Clues are not in short supply. The text, which was composed in Arabic in the eighth century, was first translated into Castilian, the primary language according to the directives in place at the Toledo school of Alfonso X.[30] It was translated by a Jew named Abraham Alfaquím, Alfonso's physician. Still at the Toledo school, Bonaventura of Siena translated the *Liber* from Castilian into Latin and Old French in 1264. Bonaventura was one of the exiled Tuscans who had taken refuge at Alfonso's court, where he acted as notary. During his time there he also became acquainted with Brunetto Latini, who arrived in Toledo between 1259 and 1260. Antoine Cabaton writes, "It is absolutely impossible that, at this half Arabic, half Christian court . . . Brunetto Latini neither saw nor came to know the translators of Toledo: that in his travels from Toledo to Seville, where the king resided alternately, he did not question them."[31] Our earlier discussion on Brunetto's *Tresor* seems to have strong confirmation. It is also natural to think that Brunetto would have passed these bits of knowledge on to Dante.

We know[32] that in one category of codices this text was included as a pendant to the Collectio Toletana, a famous collection of Islamic texts that were translated and disseminated throughout Europe thanks to the promptings of Peter the Venerable, abbot of Cluny.[33] In this context it is not at all strange that the *Liber scale Machometi* was referenced by Fazio degli Uberti in his *Dittamondo* (Words of the World, 1350–60), a fact already noted by Alessandro d'Ancona (1835–1914) and subsequently by Cerulli.[34] There was also an ample summary of the *Liber* in Castilian that was attributed to Saint Pedro Pascual, an ecclesiastic of the Mercedarian order. In the library of the Università Cattolica of Milan there is a *Bibliografia Mercedaria* (Bibliography of the Mercedarians), in the second volume of which there is a discussion of this summary with the title of *Libro del parayso y del infierno* (Book of Heaven and Hell), which was given between 1288 and 1292 by Pascual to Pope Nicholas IV—predecessor of Boniface VIII. Having read this text, I was able to deduce that it was not definitely a source for Dante,[35] although it could have been for the fifteenth-century Salentine monk Roberto Caracciolo, author of *Lo specchio della fede* (The Mirror of Faith).

Reading the *Liber scale Machometi* in Latin, one is convinced that it was a direct source for Dante because of its descriptions of the Muslim Hell, which must have struck Dante for their bloody and violent concreteness. From the Paradise of the *Liber*, however, Dante appears to have been more selective in adapting certain elements, as there is a hyperrealistic aspect to life in the heavens in the *Liber* (castles for the blessed, litters, beautiful women, and so forth) that is completely foreign to Dantesque (and Christian) ideology.

Let us begin with the Hell of the *Liber*, which reveals correspondences with Dante's vision that are not only thematic but also specifically formal, wide-ranging, and isomorphic; that is to say, the similarities are realized within the same formal or semantic structure in each text. We see, for example, the parallel between the *habitatio dyaboli* (dwelling place of the devil) and the City of Dis. This begins from the description of a gigantic enchained demon, which will then pass into the *Commedia* as the giant Ephialtes: compare "cathenis ferreis ligaverunt unam manuum ante et alteram retro" (*Liber* par. 149 "they bound one of his hands in front and the other in back with iron chains") with "el tenea socinto/dinanzi l'altro e dietro il braccio destro,/d'una catena" (*Inf.* 31.86–88 "he had his right arm shackled behind/and the other in front,/by a chain").

Arriving at the *habitatio dyaboli*, we see in the *Liber* (par. 150) that the dwelling place of the devil is a *castrum* (the *fortezza* of *Inf.* 9.108); it is girded by the *valla* (Dante's "alte fosse/che *vallan* quella terra sconsolata" "the deep trenches/that are the moats of that doleful city" at *Inf.* 8.77–78). There are then "muri, turres, moenia et domus omnes" ("walls, towers, battlements, and whole houses") that are "de igne valde nigro, qui ardet continuo in se ipso" ("of entirely black fire, which burns constantly within itself"). At *Inferno* 8.70–75, Dante speaks of the (strangely Arabic) "meschite" ("mosques") "*vermiglie* come se di *foco* uscite/fossero" ("red as if they had come out of the fire"), adding "Il *foco* etterno/ch'entro l'affoca le dimostra rosse" ("The eternal fire/that blazes there within makes them show red"), and, at line 78, "Le mura mi parean che *ferro* fosse" ("The walls seemed to me to be of iron")—an image perhaps prompted by the black fire of the *Liber*. In this *castrum* there is "quaedam porta, per quam vadit homo ad infernum magnum" ("a certain door, through which one goes to the great inferno"). We should also remember that Phlegyas cries "usciteci . . . qui è l'intrata" (*Inf.* 8.81 "Out with you here! This is the entrance"). Further, the *Liber* says that the doors through which the demons enter and exit are seven in number; in his turn Dante writes "chiuser le porte que' nostri avversari" (*Inf.* 8.115 "These our adversaries shut the gates").

The seventh, eighth, and ninth bolgias of the *Commedia* have significant thematic and formal similarities with the fourth and fifth terraces of the *Liber* as well as with a final listing of sins that begins with the "seminatori di discordia," the sowers of discord. In Dante's seventh bolgia, there are thieves who, as everyone knows, turn into serpents before being quickly turned back into men so that the punishment can continue. The same occurs in the *Liber* (par. 140), where it is said that God makes the damned return to human form in order to punish them all over again. Paragraph 143 explains that serpents have a venom that immediately burns the damned, reducing them to ashes ("destrueret et reduceret in cinerem"). Compare Dante's description of Vanni Fucci:

> Né O sì tosto mai né I si scrisse,
> com'el *s'accese e arse, e cener tutto*
> convenne che cascando divenisse

> Never was *o* or *i* written so quickly
> as he caught fire and burned, and turned
> completely into ashes as he fell.
>   (*Inf.* 24.100–2)

It seems to me that the Islamic text should be added to the list of sources headed by Lucan (cited for the serpents of Libya at *De bello civili* 9.711–14, 9.719–21]). Staying with the topic of the thief-serpent duo, Dante adds:

> Poi *s'appiccar, come di calda cera*
> *fossero stati*, e mischiar lor colore,
> né l'un né l'altro già parea quel ch'era

> Then, as if they were made of hot wax,
> they stuck together and mixed their colors,
> and neither the one nor the other appeared as before.
>   (*Inf.* 25.61–63)

The *Liber*, having described the fusion of man and serpent, concludes: "ita quod ipsi liquefiunt, prout liquefit ante faciem ignis cera" (*Liber* par. 142 "just as wax melts before a flame, so [it is] that they turn liquid"). Dante grabs this idea and with a striking flight of the imagination transforms it into lofty poetry.

In Dante's eighth bolgia, which houses the fraudulent, we see "di tante fiamme tutta risplendea / l'ottava bolgia" (*Inf.* 26.31–32 "with so many flames / the eighth pit was all agleam"). In the *Liber*, the same thing occurs in the fifth region, but here the flame is generated by a piece of brimstone that is aflame and attached to the neck of the damned: "Lapis et peccator faciunt in simul flammam unam" (*Liber* par. 146 "the stone and sinner produce at one and the same time one flame"), which Dante seems to have used with the aid of a metaphor, "e ogne fiamma un peccatore invola" (*Inf.* 26.42 "and each steals away a sinner"). The *Liber* later specifies that, according to the Qu'ran (sura 14.51), "cooperiuntur igne facies peccatorum" (*Liber* par. 146 "the faces of sinners are covered by fire"), which could be related to a line in Dante, "catun si *fascia* di quel ch'elli è inceso" (*Inf.* 26.48 "each swathes himself with that which burns him").

Our final example, which is possibly the most suggestive of Dante's playful project of reformulation, is seen in the ninth bolgia with the sowers of discord. Dante seems to be amusing himself in *Inferno* 28 as he puts into Muḥammad's mouth the words that are spoken by Gabriel in the *Liber*. Gabriel speaks to Muḥammad about those "qui verba seminant ut mittant discordiam inter gentes" (*Liber* par. 199 "who sow words to cause discord among people"). The appearance of the metaphor of *seminare* (to sow) is certainly not a casual coincidence (compare *Inf.* 28.35 "*seminator* di scandolo e di scisma," "sowers of scandal and of schism"). As often occurs, a certain feature, such as a metaphor, is able to generate thematic and formal patterns through Dante's exceptional imagination. In the *Liber*, sinners find their lips being cut off or their tongues being pulled out with fiery pincers ("forcipibus igneis"); in Dante's eighth bolgia, there is a veritable pandemic of slashing and cutting. Yet there is even more. Immediately afterward in the *Liber*, Muḥammad reflects on the *contrapasso* principle: "Vidi peccatores omnes qui, prout erant singulorum peccata, ita diverso modo suppliciis torquebantur" (*Liber* par. 201 "I saw all the sinners who, just as their sins were individuals', so in varying fashion they were tortured by punishments"). It is unlikely to be a coincidence then that in the ninth bolgia, at the conclusion of the canto, Dante has Bertran de Born (ca. 1150–1215) say, "Così si osserva in me lo *contrapasso*" (*Inf.* 28.142 "This is the retribution observed in me"), the only example of Dante's use of this particular word.

There is no contradiction in the fact that above it was also posited that the idea of the *contrapasso* was also among the intertextual connections found in Asín Palacios's *Escatología musulmana*. The example given here, from the *Liber* (that is, a particular source that abounds in correspondences), shows that the Arabic text will indicate the direction of the research, either on the path of intertextuality or on the more gainful path of the direct source.

The relationship between the Muslim Paradise of the *Liber* and the Christian Heaven of the *Commedia* is more complex than what we have seen above. Dante was attracted by several particular types of intellectual speculation on the metaphysics of light that were current during his time. And in the examination of the metaphysics of light, he entered into a sort of intellectual competition with these speculations, generating new relationships between the spheres of his own creativity and those of the mystics. Thomas Aquinas had already considered the ideas of the Arab mystics particularly important and declared them as such. Dante offers in the third treatise of the *Convivio* more proof that he used Bartolomeo da Bologna's philosophical-theological writings on light, presented in six parts with the title *Tractatus de luce* (Treatise on Light). Bartolomeo was a friar and professor who succeeded Matteo d'Acquasparta in the school of theology in the second half of the thirteenth century and was *magister Provinciae Bononiensis* (master of the Province of Bologna) from 1285 to 1289. Among other things, this *Tractatus*, which was certainly used by Dante for its semantic distinctions in terms of light (*lux, lumen, radius, splendor*), is filled with citations of Arabic works—Avicenna, Averroës, Albacen, Alfarabi, and others.[36]

Concordances of Dante's *Paradiso* reveal seventy-three instances of *luce*, sixty-nine of *lume*, and seventeen of *splendore*, all corresponding to the precepts laid out in the *Tractatus de luce*. It is certain that the lyric inspiration of the *Liber scale Machometi* and Dante's *Paradiso* did not filter through from Bartolomeo da Bologna's treatise. However, it must be recognized that the viewpoint of intertextuality provides for us another type of expertise that results in an elaboration of the situation, providing new implications and possibilities. This viewpoint does not exclude that the eight Heavens of the *Liber* could have offered analogical models for three basic situations that deal with the presence of light in the heavenly afterlife, situations that are connected to one another both in the *Liber* and in the *Commedia*.

The first situation could be described as a potentiality of the metaphysics of light, through which God, in the *Liber*, is light, referred to as *claritas*; light, or *claritas*, is blessedness, and as such it connotes the figures and objects of paradise by defining their celestial nature, which is splendor and blessedness. In the *Liber* we read, "Claritas ibi existens tanta est et tam magna quam claritas solis talis est respectu claritatis illius qualis est claritas unius stelle respectu claritatis solaris" ("the brightness present there is so great and powerful that the brightness of the sun in comparison with its brightness is as the brightness of a star in comparison with the brightness of the sun");[37] Abraham "erat eciam totus claritatis circumvolutus vestibus, que plus quam sol in estate splendore lucebant" ("was entirely enveloped in clothes of brightness, which shone with splendor more than the sun does in summer").[38] As a leitmotif, the pure *claritas* reappears as it envelops the angels and the blessed. We find an analogous spirit and a similar meaning for light in Dante, for example in the first hundred lines of *Paradiso* 26: something here seems to go beyond the typical concordance between Islamic and Christian mysticism that has been investigated by specialists in the field.[39] It seems really to be intertextuality.

The second situation is that the divine force of *claritas* results for a mortal in loss of sight. In the *Liber*, upon the appearance of God, Muhammad exclaims: "Et tunc Deus abstulit visum ab oculis et ipsum reddidit ita cordi quod eum corde vidi, oculis autem minime" (*Liber* par. 125 "And then God took sight from my eyes and restored it to my heart, so that I saw him with my heart but not at all with my eyes"). This blindness recurs with Dante: "lo viso spento" (*Par.* 26.1 "my quenched sight"), and "la vista in te smarrita e non defunta" (*Par.* 26.9 "the sight in you is confounded, not destroyed"). The idea of the substitution of the heart for the eyes is similar:

> . . . quasi tutta cessa
> mia visïone, e ancor mi distilla
> nel core il dolce che nacque da essa

> . . . my vision almost
> wholly fades away, yet in my heart
> the sweetness born of it is still distilled.
>   (*Par.* 33.61–63)

The notion expressed in paragraph 4 of the *Liber* in regard to the "indirect" vision also seems to point to a possible influence on Dante's metaphysics of light: the eyes of man can grasp the splendor of divine light, but only indirectly. That is to say, the eyes must fall on things or figures that are illuminated by this light, as a *lumen secundarium* (*Liber* par. 377 "secondary light"). This phenomenon is perceptible in the continuous reflection of God's light as seen through Beatrice's eyes, fixed upon Dante.

Francesco Mazzoni examined the reflective eyes of Beatrice in a *Lectura Dantis Scaligera* (1963). In *Paradiso* 18.8–12, the poet claims to renounce any further description of the light that he sees reflected in Beatrice's eyes because his mind (that is, his memory) is not capable of relating such an ineffable experience without divine intervention. The drama of human inadequacy and divine ineffability is certainly present in the *Liber scale Machometi*, but we should not forget that there is also another certain mystic source used by Dante, namely, Richard of Saint Victor's *Benjamin Major*.[40]

The third situation connected with the *claritas* of the *Liber* is the circular movement of the luminous angelic spheres, which in turn produces music and song. Dante describes this sound as the "dolce sinfonia di paradiso" (*Par.* 21.59 "the sweet symphony of Paradise"). These spheres are described between God and the angels of the curtains and circles in the eighth heaven of the *Liber*: "Et circa eosdem circulos erat angelorum multitudo quam maxima qui dicuntur Cherubin" (*Liber* par. 48 "And around the same spheres was the very great host of angels who are called Cherubim"). Only God knows their number, the *Liber* continues. The cherubim "laudabant Deum et nihil aliud faciebant. . . . Eundo et veniendo numquam Deum laudare cessabant" (*Liber* par. 49 "praised God and did nothing else. . . . Coming and going they never ceased to praise God"). They also sing in the seventh heaven, where, according to Muḥammad, "nullus eorum assimilatur alii, neque in forma neque in loquela neque in aliquo membrorum" (*Liber* par. 58 "none of them is like another, either in shape, speech, or any of the limbs")—comparable to Dante's description of "più di mille angeli festanti, / ciascuno distinto di fulgore e d'arte" (*Par.* 31.131–32 "more than a thousand angels making festival / each one distinct in effulgence and in ministry").

As for the circles created between God and the angels, the "circulata melodia" ("circulating melody") of the archangel Gabriel also comes to mind, as he, in *Paradiso* 23, moves about the Virgin Mary, singing, "io sono amore angelico, che giro" ("I am the angelic love that whirls"); he will continue to circle the Virgin until she finally ascends to the Empyrean. Consider too the flames that encircled Peter Damian:

> A questa voce vid'io più fiammelle
> di grado in grado scendere e girarsi,
> e ogne giro le facea più belle

At these words I saw more flamelets
from step to step descending and whirling
and each whirl made them more beautiful.

(*Par.* 21.136–38)

We could also point to the "semicirculi" ("semicircles") seen in Canto 32. I have discussed elsewhere other features that strongly connect the *Liber* and the *Commedia*.[41] To conclude, I will limit myself to a few examples of structural features of the *Liber* that allow Dante to construct an analogical model (that is thus intertextual), notwithstanding the abyss that separates the two texts and their authors. At the beginning of Muḥammad's journey, three voices attempt to stop him, recalling Dante's own three beasts. Muḥammad goes up a ladder from the earth to the Heaven of the Moon, which is full of luminous angels, the same ladder belonging to Jacob that brings Dante from the seventh terrace to the earthly Paradise and which seems to Dante "d'angeli sì carca" (*Par.* 22.72 "laden with angels"). There are also several intriguing similarities between paragraphs 96–109 of the *Liber* and Dante's earthly Paradise—a great garden with an enormous tree, from whose roots spring two rivers. The blessed drink of one of these rivers and are purified; they drink of the other and receive the grace of God. Notwithstanding the biblical resonances of these two rivers,[42] the reader thinks of the Lethe and the Eunoe.

There is also a procession in the *Liber* (par. 102) with camels covered with coats that seem to be of red and white silk. They have golden chains about their necks, with precious stones that shimmer like candles. Upon their arrival, God on his throne reveals his face: "Discoperuit pulcherrimam faciem suam . . . et se ostendit eis" (*Liber* par. 13 "He uncovered his most beautiful face . . . and showed himself to them"). This brings to mind Beatrice's raising of her white veil to reveal herself in the *Purgatorio*: "quando nell'aere aperto ti solvesti" (*Purg.* 31.145 "when in the free air you did disclose yourself").

This list could be longer, but every list is only a means subordinated to a goal; it is best to eschew the excessive boldness of the scholar who wishes to catch a glimpse of the splendor of a direct source in the *Liber scale Machometi*. But the text certainly generated flashes within Dante's imagination, leaps of fantasy, and playful poetics such as calling the houses of the city of Dis "meschite"—the same name given to the temples of the Saracens. To be a complete and direct source, as some would like, does not seem to be the proper end for the popularizing *Liber scale Machometi*. Rather, Dante knew many texts and was able to blend them together within the framework of his singular imagination, giving to each its proper role in the creative process. In order to preserve and be faithful to this creative drive, scholars must continue to create for themselves doubts, distinctions, and clarifying principles.

Translated by Kyle M. Hall

Dante and Knowledge of the Qur'an

Translations of the Qur'an and Other Islamic Texts before Dante (Twelfth and Thirteenth Centuries)

JOSÉ MARTÍNEZ GÁZQUEZ

I n the face of Islam's rapid westward expansion the Christian world maintained an attitude of hostility and ignorance, favoring the rise of a complex network of legends and derogatory distortions that deformed reality and cast the Prophet Muḥammad as Christianity's greatest and most powerful enemy. In its rapid spread through east and north Africa and early arrival in Spain, Islam had stolen from the Church entire communities that had previously been Christian. Muḥammad and his followers were considered to be the very incarnation of Satan and his demons—the incarnation of the Antichrist, as Peter the Venerable bluntly declares:

> And this [heresy], undoubtedly conceived in another age through a scheme of the devil, was first spread by Arius and later promoted by that Satan, namely, Muḥammad, and truly will be brought to fulfillment by the Antichrist entirely according to the devil's effort.[1]

This attitude explains the persistence throughout the Middle Ages of derogatory legends about Muḥammad as well as the profound ignorance in which the better part of Christian Europe remained with respect to Islamic doctrine.

This context frames Dante's position regarding the presence of Muslim characters in the *Commedia*. Among these characters are Muḥammad and his son-in-law 'Alī, both of whom Dante places in the ninth bolgia of the eighth circle, where are found "seminator di scandalo e di scisma" (*Inf.* 28.35 "sowers of scandal and schism"); such a conception is entirely consonant with the vagaries and dim references surrounding Islam in the Middle Ages.

The same vague attitude of derogatory zeal appears in the multiple *Vitae Mahometi* (Lives of Muḥammad), possibly known to Dante, which were written over the course of the Middle Ages. These vitae present Muḥammad as a necromancer, an impostor who seduced a simple people, or a libertine driven by lust.[2] In other cases they saw Muḥammad as a person who, having been brought up in the Christian faith, renounced this faith and preached a heresy derived from Christianity.[3] A multitude of biographies of the Prophet that echo fallacies of this sort found their way into apologetic writings as well as vernacular literatures. As an example from Dante's immediate environment, the Florentine Andrea Lancia, a contemporary writer credited with the authorship of *L'ottimo commento alla Commedia* (The Best Commentary on the *Commedia*), presents Muḥammad as a cardinal aspiring to the papacy.[4]

By the mid-twelfth century, however, the Christian world—or at least the most learned of the clergy and principally the Cluniacs—disposed of a group of texts translated into Latin. These texts were produced in Spain in 1143 by Robert of Ketton and a team of translators paid by Peter the Venerable. Among these texts were a *Vita Mahometis* (Life of Muḥammad), the *Liber generationis Mahometis* (Book on the Birth of Muḥammad), and, finally, the *Alchoran, id est, collectio preceptorum*, the first translation of the Qur'an. These translations were followed in 1210 by a second Latin rendering of the Qur'an and one of an Islamic theological text, the *Libellus Habentometi de unione Dei* (Ibn Tūmart's Tractate on the Oneness of God), both by Mark of Toledo, canon of the cathedral of that city.[5]

The figure of Peter the Venerable and a journey made by him to the Iberian Peninsula in 1142 had a special influence on the first translations.[6] While in the kingdoms of Castile and León, Peter had the opportunity to visit the monasteries being constructed along the Ebro River, which formed the boundary line with Muslim territories, and to witness the reality of contact between Christians and Muslims. Moreover, he was able to meet scholars involved in Latin translations of Arabic works on astronomy, astrology, mathematics, and medicine. In this setting Peter conceived the idea of translating a collection of Islamic texts that included the Qur'an itself and was known as the *Corpus Toletanum* or *Islamolatinum*.[7] The express end of this project was to acquire a closer knowledge of Islam so as to oppose the enemy faith not only militarily but also with the intellectual arms of a direct knowledge of its sources. Furthermore, Peter hoped to accomplish the refutation of the doctrines of Islam, a feat not previously attempted by Christians in the heart of the Church and one that passionately interested him:

> Whence my heart lit up inside me, and a fire began to burn in my reflections. I was filled with indignation that Latin Christians were ignorant of the cause of such a great disaster, and that their own ignorance could not incite them to resistance, for there was no one to respond, because there was no one who understood.[8]

Peter the Venerable, Robert of Ketton, and Robert's Team of Translators

This broad conception of the battle against Islam stimulated Peter the Venerable, during his journey through Hispanic territory, to form a team of translators in a city located along the Ebro River, probably Tarazona or Tudela. The team included Robert of Ketton, who would tackle putting the Qur'an itself into Latin, and Herman of Carinthia, a translator who produced in León a rendering of the *Liber generationis Mahumeti* as well as a synopsis of Islamic doctrine that went by the title *Doctrina Mahumeti*. Also among this group were a Muslim by the name of Muḥammad, Peter of Toledo, and Peter of Poitiers, the personal secretary of the Abbot of Cluny.

The Corpus Islamolatinum has been transmitted entirely or partially in approximately thirty manuscripts. The oldest of these, Paris, Bibliothèque de l'Arsenal, MS 1162, dates from the last third of the twelfth century and is judged by Marie-Térèse d'Alverny to be contemporaneous with the life of the translator.[9] It contains the following texts:

> Summa totius heresis ac diabolice secte Sarracenorum
> Epistula domni Petri abbatis ad domnum Bernardum Clare Vallis
>   abbatem
> Fabulae Sarracenorum cum iubendi religio . . . [Robert of Ketton's
>   prologue to the Chronica mendosa]
> Chronica mendosa et ridicula Sarracenorum
> Liber de generatione Mahumet et nutritura eius
> Item doctrina Mahumet
> Prephacio Roberti translatoris [in Alchoran]
> Apologia Al-Kindi[10]

Epistula domini Petri Venerabilis Cluniacensis abbatis ad dominum
   Bernardum Clareuallis abbatem de impia secta Mahumet
   pseudopropheta

The translation of this group of Islamic texts into Latin represented
an advance in Western Christendom's knowledge of Islam, the significance of which probably not even Peter the Venerable was able to
perceive. James Kritzeck has highlighted the importance that the ac-
quisition of direct sources of knowledge of Islam had for the religious,
social, and intellectual history of Western Christianity.[11] Such documents allowed for the refutation of Islamic doctrine and were essential
in disputes and controversies between Christians and Muslims. The
effort behind the translation of Islamic works into Latin and the reception of these texts contributed to the emergence in Europe of a new,
more objective and grounded point of view regarding the doctrine and
work of Muḥammad.

After Bernard of Clairvaux's probable refusal to attempt a refutation of Islam, this project, framed by a broad perspective on the interests of the Church and shaped by Peter's general frustration at the
Christian attitude toward Islam, allowed him to follow through with a
duty that his circumstances imposed on him. He hoped that his efforts
would result in the conversion of Muslims and support the faith of
Christians by helping them to avoid falling into the infernal abyss of
that religion:

> I will err in no way if in plain sight I have done my duty and, as I
> have said, kept for God what is his. This work could not, certainly
> could not at all, once taken up for God, remain unfinished, if only it
> could help the converts, thwart the enemies, strengthen our own
> people, or at least make good on the 'Peace to men of good will'
> [Luke 2:14] promised to the writer of these words.[12]

In this endeavor Peter the Venerable took as his model Saint Augustine and other Church Fathers, lamenting that, whereas all the other
heresies had had someone to refute them properly, the same had not
been done with Islam. So, taking up the most effective arms available—
including intellectual ones—in the struggle against Islam,[13] and avail-
ing himself of the texts translated into Latin on his own initiative, he
accomplished his mission by composing the *Liber contra sectam siue
haeresim Sarracenorum* (Book against the Sect or Heresy of the Sara-

cens).[14] Despite the fact that he directly approached the sources of Islam in this work, there persists for Peter some doubt and uncertainty as to how to classify this religion. Moreover, it remains uncertain whether Islam is a heresy derived from Christianity:

> Plainly, I had for writing this reason, which many and great fathers had. They could not suffer any rift, even a small one, in the Christian faith, nor did they tolerate against pure doctrine the perverse evil of heretics of any sort. They took care not to remain silent when they were obliged to speak, being advised—what is more, being entirely conscious—that, in the subtle balance of judgment before God, they would be held no less responsible for a vain silence or, what is more important, a harmful silence, than for a careless or blameworthy word. Thus with letters, thus with books, thus with various profound treatises they gagged "the sinful mouth of those who speak" and, with the Spirit of God speaking through them, they prostrated, stomped on, and destroyed, according to the apostles, "all the haughtiness of Satan arisen against the science of God."[15]

Like many other Christian scholars, Robert of Ketton, a Cluniac monk from England, was attracted by the richness of Arabic science. In 1142 Robert found himself in Spain, on the banks of the Ebro, with the intention of translating texts on astronomy and geometry. While there, he met Peter the Venerable and, momentarily leaving aside the scientific texts, acceded to the latter's requests. With the assistance of the aforementioned team of translators, he produced the first translation of the Qur'an as well as renderings of other Islamic texts previously unknown to Latin Christianity.

In the prologue to his rendering of the Qur'an, the translator wrote a dedication to Peter the Venerable in which we find clues that explain everything related to his manner of work and the criteria relevant to the execution of his translation. He shows himself aware of the ignorance of Islam among Christians and shows that this ignorance, denounced by the Abbot of Cluny, leads to serious harm:

> But all of Latin Christendom until now imprisoned—I will not say by the ruinous misfortunes of ignorance or of negligence—has not only suffered an ignorance of their enemies' cause but has also declined to dislodge it.[16]

He wants to bring forth his work in order to arrive at the construction of the refutation of Islam to be undertaken by Peter the Venerable.

The desired result would be an attractive, comfortable edifice, well founded and indissoluble, from which nothing would be eliminated. The text would remain unaltered, the only exception being that which would contribute to its intelligibility:

> Therefore I have brought stones and lumber [i.e. I have translated], so that afterward your most beautiful and comfortable edifice may rise up well-established and indestructible, without summarizing anything, without altering anything appreciable, except that which could aid comprehension.[17]

The very right that supports the Christians in their confrontation with Muslims justifies in the translator an attitude of attack and forthright hostility. Robert of Ketton believed that his work's principal utility should be to serve Peter the Venerable's planned refutation of Islam by contributing materials that corroborated the Christians' position and gave them sharper and more powerful weapons:

> Consequently, as you destroy the enemy camp and even its shelter, drying up its well, since you are the best part of the world's right hand, the hardest flint of religions, the generous hand of charity, the law demands that you confirm the protection of your own people and diligently sharpen your spears, in order that its source may flow with greater force. And may you build more amply and capably the bulwark of its charity.[18]

Robert of Ketton's Latin translation presents more or less important discrepancies with respect to controversial points of Islamic doctrine and adopts various solutions that depart from the content and original form of the Qur'an. The division of the suras in the Latin text does not correspond to the accepted division in the original text, given that the translation includes 123 in comparison to the 114 of the Qur'an. Probably following a Qur'an arranged for liturgical reading, he subdivided the first, more extensive suras in succinct fragments, which are also related to the Qur'anic divisions of the 'ushr (a decade or group of ten verses: *haxra,* as Robert writes it) and *hizb* (half a *juz'*, one of thirty twenty-page sections of the Qur'an: *hisbi,* in his text).[19] To these new suras he attributed individual titles, whose content, most often slanted and probably drawn from prejudices against Muslim doctrine and customs, sought the final disqualification of Muḥammad and his doctrine.[20] In this way he shows his interest in emphasizing the Satanic inspiration of Muḥammad and what are, by his judgment, the latter's numerous lies and twisted interpretations of Jewish and Christian doctrines. Thus, for example:

> Azoara [XVII] [[Seventh]]. Being stirred by the evil spirit, he interweaves here endless fables of Adam and Eve, Beelzebub, certain unknown prophets, and Moses, without ceasing to reiterate the customary incoherencies, lunacies, and extremely stupid words.[21]

He also went so far as to suppress some Qur'anic verses in their entirety. This method is employed throughout the text. Sometimes the content of the suppressed verses is conveyed by paraphrasing two or more verses in a phrase with a vague sense. The translation constantly undermines Muḥammad's claim that the Qur'an is a work revealed by God, containing the very word of God.

Peter the Venerable's refutation of Islam, being based on a direct knowledge of Islamic sources, shows a certain consideration toward Muslims. But his negative judgment of Islam and Muḥammad does not diminish in intensity, and he holds to his purpose with the forcefulness with which the Church Fathers refuted all the previous heresies. Thus Peter's endeavor prepared a series of weapons that, based on a greater knowledge of Islamic sources, would help Christians to preserve their faith and, insofar as it was possible, to guard against Islamic doctrines.

Mark of Toledo's Alchoranus Latinus and Libellus Habentometi

The archbishop Rodrigo Jiménez de Rada, together with Mauricio, canon and archdeacon of the cathedral of Toledo and bishop-elect of Burgos, charged Mark of Toledo with the second translation of the Qur'an into Latin around the year 1210. In 1230 Mark would also translate, at Mauricio's request, a compendium of Islamic theology, the *Libellus Habentometi de unione Dei*, which comprehends a series of the professions of faith of Ibn Tūmart (Latinized as Habentometus), the mahdi of the Almohads, on the unity of God.

It must be emphasized that both translations were done in a brief period of time, one before and one immediately after the battle of Las Navas de Tolosa, which took place in Jaen on July 12, 1212. This event represents the definitive turning point in the defeat in al-Andalus of the Almohads, among whom Ibn Tūmart was a central figure. Jiménez de Rada had preached in favor of a crusade against the Almohads and personally fought in the battle. Mauricio and Mark also contributed to this victory.

In the prologue to his translation of the Qur'an, Mark fails to mention not only the existence of the first translation but also his predecessor Robert of Ketton and the group of texts that had been compiled in the *Corpus Islamolatinum* at the initiative of the Abbott of Cluny. Jiménez de Rada and Mauricio also seem unaware of the prior rendering, given that they commissioned the translation and considered it a necessary tool for their fight against the Muslims.

Mark introduces in the prologue to his translation an anthology of legends that denigrate the figure of Muḥammad, highlighting as they do his supposed vices and the tricks he allegedly used in the propagation of his doctrine among ignorant communities. This legendary biography of Muḥammad, which brings together the derogatory commonplaces accumulated by Christians over the course of five centuries, describes him as a charlatan and necromancer who used magic tricks and chicanery in order to seduce simple people:

> And when by means of fantastic illusions he was, like a magician, leading astray uncultivated people, calling himself at times God's emissary and at others God's prophet, and explaining to them lessons that he made up.[22]

He constantly highlights Jiménez de Rada's preoccupation with the upholding and preservation of the faith of the Christians who were in contact with Spanish Muslims. Clearly, Rodrigo worried about the proselytizing of the followers of Muḥammad, who so quickly had spread their religion and had subdued so many Christian communities. Similarly, he maintains his conviction that it was intolerable that Muslims had converted Christian temples to mosques and had substituted the holy offices, celebrated by Christian bishops to the sound of bells, with calls to prayer that, pronounced from towers transformed into minarets, deafened the ears of the Christian faithful:

> It happens that as a punishment for their sins, he himself as well as his successors subjugated to their heresy almost all peoples, from the North to the Mediterranean Sea and from the Indies to the regions of the West. They did so at times through deceptive preaching, at others through military defeat. Alas, they not only subdued these regions, some of which had already received the faith of Jesus Christ,

but also occupied certain regions of Hispania through the betrayal of their partisans. In many places where many priests formerly offered divine obedience to God, loathsome and criminal men now make supplications to Muḥammad, and the churches that had previously been consecrated by the hands of bishops have now been reconverted into profane temples.[23]

This perception was experienced in a much closer and more painful way by the Christians of the Iberian Peninsula and propelled them to an intensification of the armed fight for control over the land. They placed in this idea their hopes of recovering the ancient political and religious identity of the Hispano-Visigothic community, which they tied to the memory of all that previously constituted the kingdom of Hispania. The Christians of the Peninsula desired to link themselves with this kingdom as a natural and just continuation of the Christian kingdoms that antedated the arrival of the Muslims.[24]

Mauricio shared this concern. Moreover, he intended to help some Saracens who had been dissuaded from the detestable precepts of Muḥammad to approach the Catholic faith. Thus both patrons persuaded Mark to put forth the effort of translating the Qur'an, "the book in which are contained sacrilegious projects and impious precepts" ("liber in quo sacrilega continebantur instituta et enormia precepta"), in the hope that knowledge of it would be salutary and act as an instrument for the upholding of the Christian faith. These circumstances prompted the humble canon of the cathedral of Toledo to accept the imperious demands of his patrons and to satisfy them to the best of his ability by carrying through with the translation in accord with the exigencies of Christian orthodoxy.

Consequently, Mark translated the Qur'an in order that the Christians of the Hispanic world who were unable to participate in the armed struggle against the Muslims could take up intellectual arms—knowledge that would allow them both to show the falsity and imposture of Islamic doctrines and to make plain the degradation of their founder, Muḥammad, by drawing attention to the supposed vices and tricks he used in propagating his doctrine among ignorant communities.

But I, Mark, humble canon of the same [cathedral], wishing to obey the just vows and desires of both in this beneficial work, dedicated myself wholeheartedly to it. In order to help in carrying out their vow and desire, I translated the book of Muḥammad from Arabic to

Latin in accordance with their request and the interests of the Christian faith.[25]

Mark of Toledo also translated a work on the unity of God. This text represents the most important piece of Islamic theology written by Ibn Tūmart. In this translation Mark reaffirms the reasons for which he had translated the Qur'an three years earlier, highlighting his intention to give Christians, through the knowledge of both works, the means to fight against the Saracens by impugning their doctrines.

He sums up the presentation of Muḥammad as a character who was dishonest in his doctrine, confused in his exposition of it, shameless with his words, and contrary to the truths of the doctrine of Christ as well to the better part of the Old Testament, with which Muḥammad shows very little agreement:

> That Muḥammad is proved to have been dishonest in his teachings, confused in his words, shameless in his statements, and contrary in his deeds to the New Law of Christ himself, as in many things to the Old Testament, in agreement with few.[26]

He concludes in the prologue that, in short, he translated the Qur'an and the *Libellus Habentometi* so that Catholics, by examining both Islamic texts, would find secret means to impugn them:

> But I, Mark, the deacon and canon of Toledo, who translated the book of Muḥammad, rendered the little book of Ibn Tūmart from Arabic into Latin. This second translation was done at a later date and at the request of the teacher Mauricio, archdeacon of Toledo and bishop-elect of Burgos. The hidden road to attacking lies open to Catholic men who inspect each of these two books of the Moors.[27]

Several of these copies have been preserved in Italy and could certainly have circulated through Florence in the time of Dante. Elsewhere in this collection, Thomas Burman proves that Riccoldo da Monte di Croce (1243–1320), a contemporary and countryman of Dante, could have read and had in mind the second translation of the Qur'an by Mark of Toledo as well as other texts, such as the *Liber denudationis* (The Book of Denuding), in the glosses that appear in Paris, Bibliothèque nationale de France, MS Arabe 384.[28] Literal citations meant to help a potential Christian reader with the meaning of the original Qur'anic text appear in many of these glosses. He also employs the same text of the Latin Qur'an of Mark of Toledo in the commentaries and analyses put forth in the work *Contra sectam Sarracenorum* (Against the Sect of the Saracens), which the Florentine Dominican composed in order to refute the doctrines of Islam and to denigrate the life and work of Muḥammad.

The same could have occurred with other Muslim works known and translated in Spain, such as Muḥammad's voyage to the world beyond, the *Liber scale Machometi* (Book of the Ladder of Muḥammad), translated by Bonaventure of Siena around 1263 in the court of Alfonso X. Brunetto Latini, ambassador of the Republic of Florence during the years 1259–60, had lived in the same court, soliciting aid against the King Manfred and the Ghibellines, at a time when the Wise King still aspired to the throne of the Holy Empire. An intense exchange of scientific, literary, and religious texts belonging to the three cultures took place around the figure of the monarch. Brunetto Latini had the opportunity to familiarize himself with these texts and reflects this contact with them amply in his *Tresor* (Treasury).[29] Among these texts were the translations of the Qur'an and others concerning Muḥammad and Islamic theology. Being Dante's teacher, Brunetto could have made Dante aware of these texts upon returning to Italy.[30] All of these works circulated in the cultural milieu of the late thirteenth and early fourteenth centuries and constitute the body of information of which Dante could have made use in composing the *Commedia*.[31]

Translated by Andrew Gray

How an Italian Friar Read His Arabic Qur'an

THOMAS E. BURMAN

That no one has undertaken any serious study of Paris, Bibliothèque nationale de France, MS Arabe 384, is a sign of how far the discipline of medieval studies is from exploring even the most remarkable sources surviving from the Middle Ages. This manuscript, a handsome though hardly ornate copy of the Qur'an in Arabic, apparently produced in Egypt or Syria in the late twelfth or early thirteenth centuries, has been part of what is now France's national library since 1622 and has been well cataloged since late in the nineteenth century. The remarkable fact—which will preoccupy us here—that it has dozens of marginal notes in medieval Latin, written, according to a nineteenth-century scholar, by a "Roman Catholic cleric who possessed a perfect knowledge of the Qur'an and of the Arabic Language" has been known just as long.[1] Indeed, François Déroche has recently reiterated this point in his excellent catalog of Arabic manuscripts at the Bibliothèque nationale, making clear that there are actually *two* Latin hands to be found in the margins, both dating from the late thirteenth or early fourteenth centuries.[2] By any interpretation, this Qur'an manuscript is an important, perhaps even seminal, source for understanding how Latin Christian scholars interacted with the holy book of Islam. Yet references to it in studies on these topics can be counted on one hand.[3]

What follows are the results of my initial examination of this precious manuscript. I have focused here on the question that struck me the first time I looked at this Arabic Qur'an and its Latin marginalia ten years ago: who *were* these medieval Latin scholars who had such an advanced knowledge of the Qur'an and the Arabic language? As it happens, my initial guess a decade ago that one of those hands had to be that of the learned and widely traveled Dominican Friar, Riccoldo da Monte di Croce (fl. 1267–1316), has proved correct, though the identity of the other hand remains elusive.[4] After demonstrating that Riccoldo is the author of the second and much more abundant set of notes, and that he was consulting MS Arabe 384 extensively as he wrote his widely read *Contra legem Saracenorum* (Against the Religion of the Muslims), I will discuss what these notes tell us about how he read the Qur'an. Among other things, we will see that while he could read Islam's scriptures perfectly well in Arabic, he frequently read them alongside an earlier Christian apologetic work entitled *Liber denudationis sive ostensionis aut patefaciens* (The Book of Denuding or Exposing, or The Discloser), written by an Andalusī Christian, as well as in conjunction with Mark of Toledo's Latin Qur'an translation of the early thirteenth century. What we see in all this is not only the dependence of this learned Dominican on ideas and texts of Spanish origin but also the intriguing paradox of a learned scholar with direct experience of Islam and profound knowledge of the Arabic language who nevertheless carefully filters his expertise through a long-enduring tradition of Christian Qur'an reading. Pondering this filtering process opens up, I suggest in conclusion, some interesting new questions that scholars might ask about the medieval tradition of arguing about religion that was so very much alive in Dante's lifetime and among his own countrymen.

The two sets of Latin notes on this Qur'an manuscript are easily distinguishable. One set is written in a larger hand, the same hand that added foliation to this codex, and that also wrote on folios 1v and 2r a list of Qur'anic teachings, much like the lists of Qur'anic errors that can be found in contemporary Latin translations of the Qur'an.[5] The second, more extensive, set of notes, written in a smaller script, appear to have been added at some point afterward, for in a few places the location of these notes with respect to nearby notes in the larger hand can only be explained if they were written later. This is particularly evident in the list of Qur'anic teachings at the beginning of the manuscript, where the smaller hand adds material wherever room can be found among the statements written in the larger hand.[6]

While there are other possible authors of one or the other set of notes—his older confreres Ramón Martí and William of Tripoli, for example, or Ramón Llull, all of whom knew Arabic well[7]—Riccoldo da Monte di Croce is as likely a candidate as any. A Dominican scholar and missionary with an extensive knowledge of Arabic who sojourned, moreover, for a number of years in Baghdad and elsewhere in the Middle East, he wrote four works dealing with the Middle East and Islam, including the *Contra legem Saracenorum*, perhaps the most widely read treatise against Islam in the later Middle Ages.[8]

Several kinds of evidence indicate that he was, in fact, the author of the second and more extensive set of notes and that he was reading this particular copy of the Qur'an before and during the composition of his *Contra legem Saracenorum*.[9] First of all, both Riccoldo's famous anti-Islamic treatise and this Arabic Qur'an manuscript, MS Arabe 384, are closely connected in the seemingly insignificant issue of how Qur'anic suras are cited. While the sura titles have become much more regularized in the modern period, many suras traveled under more than one name in the Middle Ages.[10] On several occasions Riccoldo cites a Qur'anic sura in *Contra legem Saracenorum* using one of the less common titles, and in all these cases that I have found, the relevant sura bears that same unusual title in MS Arabe 384. Sura 98, for example, usually known as "al-Bayanah" (The Proof), is referred to as "Lam yakūn" (its incipit, meaning "They are not") in this manuscript. When Riccoldo cites this sura, he uses an abbreviated version of this same uncommon title, "lem," and we will come across other examples below.[11]

Second, if the overlap in sura titles suggests that Riccoldo may have been reading this manuscript while he wrote *Contra legem Saracenorum*, the striking parallels in content between this second set of marginal notes in MS Arabe 384 and the text of *Contra legem Saracenorum* argue even more strongly for Riccoldo's consultation of this Arabic Qur'an and his authorship of these many notes. A large percentage of the notes consist simply of Latin translations of the Qur'anic verses beside which they have been written, and in many cases Riccoldo quotes these very verses in the same or very similar Latin translations in *Contra legem Saracenorum*. For example, here is the somewhat awkward translation of the first part of verse 4:48 in the margin of this Arabic Qur'an manuscript: "Deus non parcit si quis dat ei participem" ("God is not restrained if someone gives a partner to him"). When Riccoldo quotes this verse in chapter 15 of the *Contra legem Saracenorum*, his translation is identical. There are many other examples, as we will see in what follows.[12]

Third, MS Arabe 384 contains a lengthy note—squeezed on to one of the folios that contain the errors of the Qur'an drawn up by the ear-

lier reader—which is probably an initial sketch of the ninth chapter of
Contra legem Saracenorum. This note begins with the words "This book
[i.e., the Qur'an] is against the holy apostles because it says that they
were Muslims and imitators of Muḥammad," and goes on to list how it
also inveighs against the Gospel writers, holy prophets, patriarchs, the
Blessed Virgin, the Son of God, the Holy Spirit, God the Father, God
in general ("simpliciter"), and, in addition, speaks untruths about demons, each of these assertions defended briefly by evidence from the
Qur'an, often cited by sura number and folio of the manuscript itself.[13]
Chapter 9 of *Contra legem Saracenorum* embodies the same argument,
asserting that the principal errors of the Qur'an can be reduced to ten
types that Riccoldo listed at the beginning of the chapter (after which he
elaborates on each sequentially): "It speaks false things about itself, about
Christians, about Jews, about the apostles, about the patriarchs, about
demons, about angels, about the Virgin Mary, about Christ, and
about God."[14] The overlap between this list and the note in MS Arabe
384 is not exact, but the parallels are clear. The overlap between the
respective arguments in favor of these assertions is even more striking.
The note demonstrating that the Qur'an speaks against the patriarchs,
for example, points out that sura 2 says "that Abraham was a Muslim,
and also Jacob and his sons." In *Contra legem Saracenorum*, Riccoldo
says much the same thing, but more fully and correctly: "Concerning
the patriarchs, Muḥammad says the same thing. He says in many
places in the Qur'an that Abraham, Isaac and Jacob and their sons
were Muslims."[15] An addendum to this lengthy note in MS Arabe
384 observes that "likewise also [the Qur'an] says that God and his
angels greeted Muḥammad and prayed for him," citing sura 33 explicitly. In his treatise Riccoldo points out that "Muḥammad says in the
surah *Elehzab* [i.e., *al-aḥzāb*, sura 33] that God and his angels pray for
Muḥammad," Riccoldo reworking here his earlier translation of the
tricky verb *yuṣallūna* ("they prayed," "they greeted," "they called down
blessings upon").[16] This and much else in this note suggest that it is an
initial outline of *Contra legem Saracenorum*, chapter 9.

Finally, we know in fact what Riccoldo's handwriting looked like
from other manuscripts, and it is identical to that found in these notes.
J.-M. Mérigoux, the modern editor of Riccoldo's *Contra legem Saracenorum*, has pointed out that marginal annotations in a manuscript now
in Florence are certainly in Riccoldo's own hand. This Florentine manuscript contains a copy of *Contra legem Saracenorum*, and while the

text of that work was not copied by Riccoldo, it is certain that the annotations on it were made by Riccoldo himself.[17] Adding all this evidence together it becomes inescapably clear that the second set of Latin
notes in this Arabic Qur'an manuscript are the work of the widely traveled Dominican scholar and missionary, Riccoldo da Monte di Croce.

There is, not surprisingly, much to be learned about how Riccoldo
interacted with the Qur'anic text by looking not only at these notes
but at their relationship to *Contra legem Saracenorum*. For one thing,
we find confirmation of just how learned in the Arabic language of
the Qur'an Riccoldo was. His careful translations, paraphrases, and
intriguing observations in the margins of MS Arabe 384 certainly are
those of "a Roman Catholic cleric who possessed" perhaps not "a perfect knowledge of the Qur'an and of the Arabic Language"[18] but
something surprisingly close to it. His translations generally show a
thorough knowledge of Arabic and real concern to get things right.
Indeed, in more than one place we find evidence of Riccoldo reworking and clarifying his translations as he moved from the Qur'anic
translations in the notes on MS Arabe 384 to his quotation of the
same verse in *Contra legem Saracenorum*. For example, he translates
part of 59:21 in the margin of MS Arabe 384 as follows: "Et si misissemus hunc alcoranum super montem, videres eum pre timore Dei
scissum" ("And if we had sent this Qur'an upon a mountain, you would
have seen it split apart on account of the fear of God"). When he
quotes the same verse in his treatise, he gives us a carefully improved
version. It follows the Arabic word order more closely and adds words
here and there for clarity, "unum," for example, to indicate that the
word "montem" ("mountain") is indefinite in the Arabic original ("ja-
bal"): "Si misissemus hunc Alchoranum super *unum* montem, videres
eum conscissum pre devotione et timore Dei" ("If we had sent this
Qur'an upon a mountain, you would have seen it split apart on account
of the devotion and fear of God").[19] Indeed, there is a great deal of evidence of Riccoldo continuously returning to the Qur'an manuscript
as he wrote, consulting both his marginal translations and the original Arabic itself, and making adjustments and improvements to his
initial versions of Qur'anic verses.[20]

Riccoldo made a substantial number of marginal translations that
have no direct relevance to anti-Islamic polemic and apologetic.[21] For
example, he provides the first few, and sometimes all, of the verses of
many of the later suras apparently just to get a sense of their contents

and not because they have any Christian polemical or apologetic use-fulness).[22] But in many cases the translated passages in the margins of MS Arabe 384—even those that Riccoldo did not go on to use in his *Contra legem Saracenorum*—have obvious relevance to the medieval Christian argument with the Qur'an and Islam generally. That he trans-lates and paraphrases parts of 2:187 is a typical example, since Chris-tian polemicists frequently quoted this verse, which tells Muslims that they may eat and drink during the nighttime hours of Ramadan, since it seemed to them evident proof of the laxity of the Muslim fast.[23] Likewise Riccoldo translated part of 22:78, "Habraham nominavit vos Saracenos" ("Abraham named you Muslims"), in the margins of his Arabic Qur'an because the Qur'anic assertion that Abraham and his sons called themselves Muslims was likewise a favorite target of Chris-tian attacks on the Qur'an.[24] Riccoldo used neither of these transla-tions in his treatise, but they and many other examples are clear evidence of the extent to which he read Islam's holy book looking particularly and zealously for the parts that could be used most effectively to attack Islam and defend Christianity.

But while Riccoldo left an abundance of evidence in the margins of MS Arabe 384 of his direct, learned, and generally polemical engage-ment with the Arabic text of the Qur'an, there is also plenty of evi-dence that he read Islam's holy book alongside of, and indeed often through the lens of, other texts. At one point, at least, Riccoldo actu-ally incorporated information that he learned from a Qur'anic com-mentary or Muslim informant. After providing a translation of 2:189, a verse stipulating that "it is not righteous that you enter the houses from their backs . . . so enter the houses by their gates," Riccoldo writes, "The gloss: that is, do not have sex with your women in the disallowed rump."[25] Though several interpretations of this verse showed up in the Muslim commentaries, al-Qurṭubī observed that this passage was read by some as a metaphor for "having sex with women, a command to come to them from in front and not from behind." Al-Qurṭubī clearly objects to this interpretation, quoting the earlier Andalusī commenta-tor Ibn 'Aṭīyah who remarked that it is "far-fetched, altering the mode of speaking (in this passage)."[26] Here is a case, then, where Riccoldo, like other Latin Qur'an readers, came across a Muslim interpretation of a Qur'anic verse that was, in Christian eyes, especially damaging to Islam, and he used it as a weapon against Islam, rather than invok-ing other, far less sensational views.[27] But it is also clearly a case of

Riccoldo reading the Arabic Qur'an through the lens of an Arabic commentary.

Intriguingly, in addition to reading the Qur'an through a Muslim commentary, Riccoldo also read the Arabic Qur'an through the medium of comments made by the earlier annotator of this Qur'an manuscript. In the *Contra legem Saracenorum* Riccoldo quoted verse 21:91, which tells how God breathed his spirit into the Virgin Mary, for this was the sort of passage that Christian apologists frequently cited to show that the Qur'an actually teaches the doctrine of the Trinity. Yet the close Latin translation here, "insufflavimus in eam de spiritu nostro" ("we have breathed into her from our spirit"), can be found in the margins of MS Arabe 384, though not in Riccoldo's hand, but rather in the earlier set of notes on this codex.[28] In some places Riccoldo both follows and modifies the Latin versions of the earlier annotator, as when he quotes verse 5:110 in a Latin version that appears in a marginal translation in the earlier hand, with Riccoldo, however, filling out the ellipses that appear there.[29]

While Riccoldo was an excellent Arabist, he nevertheless also read the Arabic Qur'an alongside the early thirteenth-century Latin version of Mark of Toledo. A literal translation that followed the Arabic word order, this Latin Qur'an lent itself to this purpose, and we know of other medieval and early modern scholars reading it in conjunction with the original Arabic Qur'an.[30] Thus at 17:88—a verse often quoted by Christian polemicists that asserted that if humans and jinn worked together to fashion a "Qur'an" like this one, they would not be able to— Riccoldo jotted down Mark of Toledo's version in the margin of MS Arabe 384 but inserted his own quite different translation of the same verse in *Contra legem Saracenorum*, this latter version deriving, perhaps, from the incomplete Latin translation that he says he was working on previously.[31] We find Riccoldo drawing on Mark's translation here and there throughout the Qur'an, especially in the later suras. The nonpolemical translations of parts of the later, short suras, for example, generally derive from Mark's version. At least once he quotes Mark's translation right beside his own work. Above, I noted that he included a commentary's gloss after providing a translation of 2:189. The Latin version of the verse in this case is from Mark's translation. Yet just before this note, he carefully inserted his own translation of 2:187.[32] Mark of Toledo's Latin Qur'an, much less read than Robert of Ketton's earlier Latin paraphrase of the Qur'an, clearly lay close to hand as Riccoldo worked his way through his Arabic Qur'an.

What is most striking about the evidence presented so far is the extent to which it seems to demonstrate how sure-footed Riccoldo was in his Christian reading of the Qur'an. This widely traveled Dominican seems to know exactly what passages to focus on, precisely which verses are useful for attacking Islam and defending Christianity. He confidently seizes on just the sort of verses that had been used by Christian apologists and polemicists against Islam for at least one hundred fifty years in Latin Christendom and at least four hundred years among Arab Christian writers. Indeed, he seems to give every indication, as he worked his way through this handsome copy of the Qur'an, that he had assimilated the age-old tradition of Christian Qur'an reading long before he ever got his hands on this Arabic Qur'an and began writing *Contra legem Saracenorum*.

But in point of fact, even as he was jotting notes in his Arabic Qur'an, and writing against Islam in his treatise, Riccoldo was still actively absorbing that enduring Christian way of reading the Qur'an, and this too is evident from his marginal notes and the content of his treatise. As Mérigoux has shown, Riccoldo frequently read the Qur'an through the lens of still another earlier text as he wrote his widely read treatise, the learned but obscure anti-Islamic tract *Liber denudationis sive ostensionis aut patefaciens* (The Book of Denuding or Exposing, or The Discloser). Originally an Arabic work, written probably by a Mozarabic Christian in Andalusia, it survives, as far as we know, only in a Latin translation, itself preserved in a single manuscript now at the Bibliothèque nationale in Paris. As Mérigoux has demonstrated, this treatise is the most important source for *Contra legem Saracenorum,* and its methods often shaped Riccoldo's views decisively.[33] Probably written originally between 1010 and 1132, the Latin translation was produced at an unknown date before Riccoldo came across it. Riccoldo quotes or paraphrases this Latinized Arab-Christian work, often extensively, though without attribution.

Indeed Riccoldo derives some of his Qur'anic quotations directly from *Liber denudationis* rather than from his direct reading of his Arabic Qur'an or Mark of Toledo's Latin version. In the sixth chapter of *Contra legem Saracenorum*, Riccoldo discusses the ways in which the Qur'an contradicts itself. Near the end he points out that if Muḥammad only knew Arabic, he could not have been a prophet to all peoples, for "in the Chapter of the Prophets he says that God said to him: 'We have not sent you except to all peoples.' But how will he go to all peoples in seventy languages who does not know how to recite his message other than in the Arabic language?" These lines abridge a somewhat longer passage in *Liber denudationis*, and this explains the fact that while Riccoldo says he is quoting from sura 21, he is actually quoting 34:28. The source passage in *Liber denudationis* actually quotes *two* Qur'anic verses, 21:107 and 34:28, but when he abridged the longer passage, Riccoldo wrote the sura title of the former verse while skipping to the actual words of the latter.[34] Since Riccoldo did not translate this latter verse in the margin of his Arabic Qur'an,[35] and since the wording of the verse actually quoted (34:28) in *Contra legem Saracenorum* is identical to what we find in *Liber denudationis*, it is clear that our Italian friar was not, in fact, reading the Qur'an directly at all here, but quoting it through that earlier anonymous treatise—and not even very accurately.

But his reading of the Qur'an through *Liber denudationis* is often much less passive (and sloppy) than this. In fact there is striking evidence that Riccoldo was often reading that earlier treatise and his Arabic Qur'an side by side, thinking through the Qur'an as he read *Liber denudationis*, but also, and more interestingly, thinking through *Liber denudationis* as he read the Qur'an. In the fourth chapter of *Contra legem Saracenorum*, for example, Riccoldo incorporates a much longer passage from *Liber denudationis* that refutes one of the miracles—the splitting of the moon—which Muslims frequently attributed to Muḥammad in the Middle Ages. A number of slightly different hadiths relate this miracle story, explaining that while Muḥammad was sitting one night outside Mecca with his followers they asked him to perform a miracle, so he pointed at the moon and it split in two. These hadiths were then typically quoted in Qur'anic commentaries to explain the rather obscure first verse of sura 54: "The hour approached and the moon was divided."[36] *Liber denudationis* retells these events, basing itself on one of these well-known hadiths and quoting 54:1 directly. When he incorporates the passage from *Liber denudationis* into his own treatise, Riccoldo changes words here and there and once again abridges, but only slightly. One of these small changes, however, is quite interesting: Riccoldo's quotation of the translation of the relevant Qur'anic verse itself—"The hour approached and the moon was divided." The author of *Liber denudationis* gave us "Apropinquavit hora et *partita* est luna" ("The hour approached and the moon was *divided*"), while Riccoldo has written "Apropinquauit hora et *fracta* est luna" ("The hour approached and the moon was *broken*").[37] Remarkably enough, if we look back at Riccoldo's Arabic Qur'an, we find in the margin next to this verse exactly the same translation as he used in *Contra legem Saracenorum*: "Apropinquavit hora et *fracta* est luna."[38] While largely relying, then, on *Liber denudationis* for the content of this account of Muḥammad's miracle, Riccoldo insisted on using his own translation of 54:1 as it appears in the margins of his own Arabic Qur'an rather than the translation found in the earlier treatise from which he was borrowing so enthusiastically. Here, therefore, we are able to watch Riccoldo reading both the *Liber denudationis* and Arabic Qur'an simultaneously.

Similar examples occur elsewhere. When arguing in chapter 8 of his *Contra legem Saracenorum* that religion of Islam is "irrational," Riccoldo observed that Muḥammad "spoke the opinion, in the Qur'an in the chapter *Elmeteharrem*, which means 'prohibition' or 'anathema,' which goes as follows: 'O Prophet, why do you prohibit what God allows you [that] you seek to please your wives? God has now established a law for you that you might dissolve your oaths.'" This whole passage is based closely on a section of the seventh chapter of *Liber denudationis*. Once again Riccoldo changes the translation of the verse itself while leaving the rest of the text much the same. But the most striking difference is in another small detail. *Liber denudationis* refers to the sura in question (66) as *Eltahrim*, his Romanization of the common Arabic title of this sura, "al-Taḥrīm" (Prohibition). While most of the language of the passage, therefore, other than parts of the Qur'anic verse, follows *Liber denudationis* closely, Riccoldo refers to the sura by another name, "al-Mutaḥarrim" (the Prohibited), a less common alternative name. It should come as no surprise by now that this is just what this sura is called in his Arabic Qur'an.[39]

The large number of parallels between Riccoldo's *Contra legem Saracenorum* and *Liber denudationis* indicate that this older, originally Arabic, treatise was, like the Arabic Qur'an, often at his side as he wrote. The evidence we have just seen makes clear that from time to time he consulted them both at the same time—*Liber denudationis* informing his thinking, and shaping how he read the Qur'an and the Qur'an clarifying and correcting what he found in *Liber denudationis*.

This interactive reading of the two texts even left its mark on Riccoldo's Arabic Qur'an ·manuscript itself. At 2:221, where the Qur'an instructs Muslims not to wed female idolaters until they believe and that they "should not give [their] daughters to male idolaters in marriage until they believe," Riccoldo wrote in the margin of his Qur'an, "Hic videtur concedere sogdomiam [sic]" ("Here he appears to allow sodomy").[40] This is a tendentious misreading of the key verb *ankaḥa* (to give in marriage) as its cognate, *nakaḥa* (to marry, have sex with). Here Riccoldo was clearly guided (or at least encouraged) into this misreading by *Liber denudationis*, which, in its tenth chapter translates these verses in a similarly tendentious way: "Do not have sex with males who associate [something created with God] until they believe" ("Nec etiam cognoscatis masculos participantes donec credant"), and then sums up the situation with virtually the same phrase that Riccoldo wrote in the margin of his Arabic Qur'an: "Hic satis concedit sodomiam" ("Here he effectively allows sodomy").[41] This suggests that.Riccoldo came across this distorting way of reading this verse in *Liber denudationis* first, then sought out the passage in his Arabic Qur'an, which he proceeded to read in a similarly distorted way, adding a brief note on this verse in his Arabic Qur'an that was actually derived from *Liber denudationis*. And there is one more step: having learned from *Liber denudationis* that this verse (2:221) could be read as if it condoned sodomy, Riccoldo then went on to use this verse in just this way in *Contra legem Saracenorum*: "Likewise in the chapter of the Cow, he allows ["concedit"] sodomy as much with a male as with a female, for he says to Muslims that they should not pollute themselves with male infidels until they believe [compare 2:221]." Once again, having borrowed a polemical argument and specific terminology from *Liber denudationis*, Riccoldo prefers to use his own translation of the verse in question, though his version is even more tendentious.[42] But what is most striking in this complex act of moving his attentions from *Liber denudationis* to his Arabic Qur'an and then to the writing of his *Contra legem Saracenorum* is the way in which that obscure, originally Arab-Christian work informed both his Qur'an reading and his polemical writing.

There is doubtless much more that can be learned about how Riccoldo da Monte di Croce interacted with his Arabic Qur'an from his remarkable annotations in MS Arabe 384, and from the text—his *Contra legem Saracenorum*—that they informed. But even these preliminary findings allow us to draw some valuable conclusions. First, not only did the anonymous *Liber denudationis* inform his thinking about the Qur'an and Islam but still another text from Spain, Mark of Toledo's Latin Qur'an, played a key role in his Qur'an reading. (This is an important finding as well, by the way, for the reception history of Mark's version—something about which we know very little.) Mérigoux has proposed that Riccoldo quoted Mark's version once in *Contra legem Saracenorum*, but it is clear that he actually turned to that literal translation extensively as he read Islam's holy text. An Italian friar of great knowledge and experience of Islam, gained in his travels in the Middle East, Riccoldo nevertheless turned to the Iberian tradition of making sense of Islam that was so influential in Europe throughout the Middle Ages. It is probably right, moreover, to see Riccoldo's older confrere, Ramón Martí, as the go-between. I have argued elsewhere that Ramón knew *Liber denudationis* in its original Arabic version. Mark's translation of 1210–11, moreover, would certainly have been available in Spain two generations later, when Ramón was engaged in Qur'an study. There is, moreover, some evidence that he was the author of the first set of notes in MS Arabe 384.[43] In this manuscript's marginalia, then, we can see written out not only the extensive influence of Spanish anti-Islamic thought elsewhere in Europe, but also possible evidence of scholarly interaction between two of medieval Europe's most knowledgeable interpreters of the Qur'an and Islam.

In the importance of these Spanish texts to Riccoldo's study of Islam's holy book, we see, secondly and more importantly, an intriguing paradox that runs throughout Riccoldo's reading of his Arabic Qur'an. On the one hand, Riccoldo reveals himself in these notes and in his composition of *Contra legem Saracenorum* as a scholar very much in control of his subject. He is an expert in Arabic who rarely stumbles in translation, who is completely at home with the vocabulary, morphology, and syntax of a language very different from either his mother tongue or Latin. He insists, moreover, on bringing his linguistic mastery to bear on his principal source, checking the Qur'anic translations in the *Liber denudationis* against the Arabic original, and often preferring his own Latin versions of the verses in question, all the while following that treatise's arguments with little hesitation. Furthermore, his ability actually to find in his Arabic copy of the Qur'an the suras which *Liber denudationis* cites under different titles argues for a knowledge of Qur'anic arcana—that suras are known by alternative titles and, moreover, what those titles are—that cannot fail to impress us. Riccoldo is, moreover, innovative in his anti-Islamic thinking, his ninth chapter, initially sketched out, as we saw, in a note on MS Arabe 384, having no close parallels of which I know in Latin polemical literature.

On the other hand, we find that even as Riccoldo is writing *Contra legem Saracenorum*, he is still striving to understand and build on a much older tradition of anti-Islamic writing deeply rooted in Arab-Christian thought, and he is still, moreover, turning to Qur'anic study aids, such as Mark of Toledo's translation, to help him make his way through the text of that difficult book.

This paradox is a dynamic one. Riccoldo relies both on his great learning and familiarity with Islam as well as traditional sources as he reads the Qur'an and writes against it, but these two approaches actually play off each other. Riccoldo's Arabic learning allows him to alter *Liber denudationis*' Qur'an translations and sura titles; *Liber denudationis*' Christian interpretations of the Qur'an influence him as he reads his Arabic Qur'an. In Riccoldo's Qur'an study and his polemical writing in *Contra legem Saracenorum*, therefore, we see the dual process of reading Islam's holy book through a tradition of interpretation and reading this tradition of interpretation through detailed knowledge of that holy book.

We are used to reading the extensive medieval literature of religious disputation as it appears to us in finished products: treatises against one or another religion, imagined literary dialogues between members of two or three religious communities, carefully edited summaries of actual religious disputations. In these texts, religious disputants generally have the appearance of unchanging types whose positions and beliefs are static and seemingly inborn. The interactive process that we glimpse in Riccoldo's Qur'an reading and anti-Islamic writing provides us with a very different picture. Here we see time-consuming consultation of earlier works and philological sophistication in handling the Qur'an. We see the physical Qur'an itself used as a notebook on which to sketch out polemical ideas. We see, in short, an engaged, serious intellectual working through difficult problems. Even if we find his work distasteful, he is no longer a tedious type; he is now an energetic, many-sided human. Modern scholars of medieval religious polemic, apologetic, and disputation have generally focused on questions either of fact—who had what accurate knowledge of another religion? when? how?—or functionality—how does a text (mis)represent the religiously other in ways that allow communal boundaries or political hegemony to be maintained? In watching Riccoldo read his Arabic Qur'an, I suggest, we may have an opportunity to move beyond these two (admittedly fruitful) lines of inquiry, for it strikes me that there is more of interest here than can be grasped by asking about levels of knowledge and mechanisms of social control. Explaining why Riccoldo went to the trouble of changing "partita est luna" to "fracta est luna," or why he carefully copied Mark of Toledo's Latin versions of the beginning of many suras into his own Arabic Qur'an requires that we ask new questions—about how, for example, religious disputation fits in with other intellectual trends and learned practices of reading, or about the *purpose* of performing this intricate evaluation of the Qur'an (and simultaneous evaluation of the traditional Christian way of reading the Qur'an) rather than focusing on its end products—questions that will very likely deepen our understanding of the medieval fondness for arguing about each other's holy texts.

*Images of Islamic Philosophy
and Learning in Dante*

Philosophers, Theologians, and the Islamic Legacy in Dante: *Inferno* 4 versus *Paradiso* 4

BRENDA DEEN SCHILDGEN

I n this essay I argue that the first *dubbi* (*Par.* 4.8 "doubts")[1] that Beatrice answers for Dante in *Paradiso* 4 relate two issues that constitute a retrospective consideration of *Inferno* 4 and a recanting of some earlier philosophic positions found in the *Convivio*. These issues are the poet's relationship to the learned traditions and poetic practices of ancient Greek and medieval Arab philosophy. Whereas in the *Convivio* Dante had attempted to accommodate the differences about the relative influence of heavenly bodies on the human soul as outlined by ancient Greek and medieval Arabic philosophers, by the time of the *Commedia* he had clearly rejected this more pluralist position in favor of Christian revelation. Following the Christian synthesis developed by Thomas Aquinas, in which Christ is the means to unite nature and the transcendent, he endorses orthodox Christian views on the nature of the soul and the freedom of the will against the legacy of the Greeks and the Arabs.

In *Paradiso* 4, Beatrice directly acknowledges the role of poetry in expressing theological understanding, and thereby offers a key to interpreting what Dante sees before him. She rejects what to her are errors in the Greek and Arabic philosophical legacy, positions that emerged as a result of the study of Aristotle by Islamic thinkers from the eleventh century onward. But her endorsement of allegory to discuss theology finds explicit parallels in Islamic practices. Thus while Dante distances himself from Greek and Arabic philosophy, his use of allegory to express his theological beliefs reveals certain affinities with Sufism, that is, Islamic mysticism, although not exclusively, for these poetic practices also find parallels in Western allegorical practices.[2]

As is well known, the recovery of Aristotle in the West posed serious intellectual challenges to academic and theological practices and
understanding, as it had earlier to Islamic thinkers. The commentary
by Averroës (d. 1198) on Aristotle's *De anima* (On the Soul) introduced
ideas into Western intellectual circles that attracted significant ecclesiastical attention in the thirteenth century[3]—so much attention in fact
that a papal interdiction at the University of Paris in 1277 forbade their
being taught. Siger of Brabant (*Par.* 10.136), among others, expounded
the concepts of Aristotle and his commentators. In his *Quaestiones in
tertium De anima* (Questions on the Third Part of *On the Soul*), *De
anima intellectiva* (On the Intelligible Soul), and *De aeternitate mundi*
(On the Eternity of the World), for example, Siger had promoted the
heretical view that the soul was a separate entity, and that like the
world, it was immortal and eternal, that is, preexisting the body into
which it was born.[4] Aristotelian rationalism, through the medium of
the Arab commentators, challenged theological methodologies and
orthodox teachings in both the Islamic medieval world and the Latin
West, provoking a clash between philosophers and theologians. Throughout the *Commedia*, but especially in *Paradiso*, Dante's incarnational
poetry attempts a theological and aesthetic reconciliation of the opposing group of thinkers.

In the *Convivio*, Dante appears to align himself with the philosophical traditions of both the Arabs and the Greeks.[5] When he mentions Beatrice, "quella viva Beatrice beata," for the last time in *Convivio*
(2.7.7 "that Beatrice of blessed life"), in fact, he enlists all the philosophers (Aristotle, the Stoics, Cicero), the gentiles, and the followers of
diverse laws—Jews, Saracens, and Tartars—who find agreement in de-
nouncing as wrong and pernicious the beliefs that the afterlife does not
exist and that something eternal does not reside in us (*Conv.* 2.8.8–16).
Later (*Conv.* 4.21.2–3), citing Avicenna, al-Ghazālī, Plato, and Pythagoras as his authorities on the nature of the soul,[6] he writes:

> Veramente per diversi filosofi de la differenza de le nostre anime fue
> diversamente ragionata: ché Avicenna e Algazel volsero che esse da
> loro e per loro principio fossero nobili e vili; e Plato e altri volsero che
> esse precedessero da le stelle, e fossero nobili e più e meno secondo la
> nobilitade de la stella. Pittagora volse che tutte fossero d'una
> nobilitade, non solamente le umane, ma con le umane quelle de li
> animali bruti e de le piante, e le forme de le minere; e disse che tutta
> la differenza è de le corpora e de le forme. Se ciascuno fosse a

difendere la sua oppinione, potrebbe essere che la veritade si vedrebbe essere in tutte.

Truly, various philosophers have argued differently about the difference of our souls: for Avicenna and al-Ghazālī maintained that they were in and of themselves noble or vile from the beginning; and Plato and others maintained that they proceeded from the stars and that they were more or less noble according to the nobility of the star. Pythagoras maintained that all were of a single nobility, not merely the human souls, but together with the human souls those of brute animals and of plants, and the forms of minerals; and he said that the only difference lay between their matter and their form. If each were to defend his own opinion, the truth might appear to be in all of them.[7]

Several points in this passage illustrate Dante's relationship to Greek philosophy and its preservation, commentary, and further development by the Arab philosophers and Sufis. First, he does not separate classical Greek learning from Arab learning: for example, he names Avicenna (980–1037) and the Sufi al-Ghazālī (1058–1111) alongside the Greeks.[8] Second, he clearly considers them all thinkers who, in a debate, could point to the common truths in their ideas, even though in *Convivio* 4.8, with due reverence for the philosopher, Dante reformulates Aristotle's system of knowledge to bring it into accord with the Christian dispensation, which demonstrates that Aristotelianism, uninformed by revelation, is ultimately blind.[9] Third, here he presents the classical philosophers' ideas about the soul and the role of the heavenly bodies in their predilections as somehow all capable of being reconciled.

First addressed in *Purgatorio* 4, this debate recurs in *Paradiso* 4, but by the time Dante writes *Paradiso*, he emphatically endorses Christian views on the question of the soul (tripartite, that is, vegetative, sensitive, and intellective—the last of these being specifically human)[10] and its destiny, whereas in the *Convivio* he is less emphatic.[11] In fact, as a palinode for parts of the *Convivio* and as a retrospective gaze on *Inferno* 4, *Paradiso* 4 addresses why Plato, Aristotle, Avicenna, and Averroës find themselves in Limbo. Dante had not condemned Averroës and Avicenna for any personal sins, but in a radical intellectual and theological gesture, he had placed them among the virtuous pagans in Limbo, together with Socrates, Plato, and Aristotle (*Inf.* 4.143–44, 129).

Averroës, in fact, "che 'l gran comento feo" (*Inf.* 4.144 "who was the great commentator"),[12] received special attention for his intellectual achievement. But in *Paradiso* 4, Beatrice's answer to Dante's question about whether the soul returns to the stars, as Plato had expounded in the *Timaeus*, corrects the *Convivio*'s failure to distinguish between the various thinkers on the topic of the human soul:

> Ancor di dubitar ti dà cagione
> parer tornarsi l'anime a le stelle,
> secondo la sentenza di Platone.

> Further, that the souls appear to return to the stars,
> in accordance with Plato's teaching,
> gives you occasion for doubt.
>
> (*Par.* 4.22–24)

The answer comes twenty-five lines later, after a related question about the apparent hierarchical tiers in Heaven (*Par.* 4.25–48) has been addressed:

> Quel che Timeo de l'anime argomenta
>   non è simile a ciò che qui si vede,
>   però che, come dice, par che senta.
> Dice che l'alma a la sua stella riede,
>   credendo quella quindi esser decisa
>   quando natura per forma la diede.

> What Timaeus argues about the souls
> is not like this which is seen here, for
> seemingly he holds what he says for truth.
> He says the soul returns to its own star,
> believing it to have been severed
> thence when nature gave it for a form.
>
> (*Par.* 4.49–54)

Here Beatrice specifically states that Plato's view of the soul returning to its star of origin is wrong, as Dante can see (*Par.* 4.50 "che qui si vede"). Still, she is willing to concede that if Plato had meant that some influence emanates from the stars, there might then after all be some truth in his views:

> E forse sua sentenza è d'altra guisa
>   che la voce non suona, ed esser puote
>   con intenzion da non esser derisa.

S'elli intende tornare a queste ruote
    l'onor de la influenza e 'l biasmo, forse
    in alcun vero suo arco percuote.

But perhaps his opinion is other
than his words sound, and may be
of a meaning not to be derided.
If he means that the honor of
their influence and the blame returns
to these wheels, perhaps his bow hits some truth.

(*Par.* 4.55–60)

But beyond this small concession, Beatrice holds that the Platonic view
(found in numerous other ancient and Arab philosophers, according to
Dante) once led "almost all the world" (*Par.* 4.62) into error. Clearly
excepting the Jews, Dante here looks back to Limbo to attempt to explain why the virtuous pagans remained there following the Crucifix-
ion and why the ancient Jews were liberated. As in *Purgatorio* 16, in a
direct refutation of Averroistic ideas, Marco Lombardo responds to
Dante's *dubbio* ("doubt") about the influence of the stars on the freedom of the will:

. . . "Frate,
    lo mondo è cieco, e tu vien ben da lui.
Voi che vivete ogne cagion recate
    pur suso al cielo, pur come se tutto
    movesse seco di necessitate.
Se così fosse, in voi fora distrutto
    libero arbitrio, e non fora giustizia
    per ben letizia, e per male aver lutto."

. . . "Brother,
the world is blind, and truly you come from it!
You who are living refer every cause upward
to the heavens alone, as if they of necessity
moved all things with them.
If this were so, free will would be
destroyed in you, and there would be no justice
in happiness for good, or grief for evil.

(*Purg.* 16.65–72)

Marco's correction amounts to the poet's recantation of positions held in
the *Convivio* regarding philosophic pluralism and a sharp delimitation

of the philosophies of Plato, Avicenna, and Averroës, whose positions lacked the theological revelation that Dante receives through Beatrice. The doctrine of free will also undermines the notion that the stars could direct human souls. In stating the Christian view of the freedom of the soul, Dante suggests one reason why the ancient philosophers and their Arab followers might be domiciled in Limbo.[13]

Also in *Paradiso* 4 Dante addresses the issue of "allegorical" representation of divine realities when Beatrice explains to him that the appearances in Heaven have been adapted for his intellect. She likens this process to the pattern of the sacred text that attributes human traits to the divinity:

> "Così parlar conviensi al vostro ingegno,
>   però che solo da sensato apprende
>   ciò che fa poscia d'intelletto degno.
> Per questo la Scrittura condescende
>   a vostra facultate, e piedi e mano
>   attribuisce a Dio e altro intende."

> "It is needful to speak thus to your faculty,
> since only through sense perception
> does it apprehend that which
> it afterwards makes fit for the intellect.
> For this reason Scripture condescends
> to your capacity, and attributes hands and feet
> to God, having other meaning."
>   (*Par.* 4.40–45)

In this passage, Dante has Beatrice show how poetry functions to express the inexpressible. Specifically she explains how allegory uses "literal" language and images because they can communicate to his senses what later apprehension may convey to his intellect. To explain why Dante, through his deluded understanding, sees souls hierarchically arranged in specific heavens even though they are really all in the Empyrean, Beatrice singles out the venomous notion that there is inequality in Heaven. Of course, this idea does find a place in the Greco-Arab philosophic traditions because they assign greater privilege to the superior intellect. This difference between the Greco-Arab philosophical position and the orthodox Christian belief also constitutes yet another retrospective look back at the philosophers who inhabit Limbo and why they might be housed there. The allegorical mode, Beatrice explains, suits his intellect because for Dante to see the souls, they must represent their spiritual state concretely, so that he can apprehend them through his senses.[14] Citing the authority of the Bible, which employs metaphoric language to speak about divine things, Beatrice here also elaborates the poetic system of *Paradiso*. In linking poetry to theology as the means to express the inexpressible while also connecting Dante's poem with the semiotic system of the sacred text itself,[15] Beatrice also suggests that theological truth can only be mediated through poetic language.

The corrections here (the place of souls in the heavens, the influence of the stars, and the soul's trajectory) embrace an acceptance of fundamental and central tenets of Christian orthodoxy in which Dante's poem resides: that the soul and body are unified; that because the soul is beyond all finite influence, it is free and will survive after death rather than return to some form of a Neoplatonic Ur-soul; and that the human will is free. Dante appears to have used Canto 4 in all three canticles to examine the issue of the nature of the soul as deliberated on by ancient Greek and Arabic philosophers: in *Purgatorio* 4, the poet specifically identifies the Platonic idea of multiple souls (in a hierarchical order) within one human as "quello error" ("that error"):

> Quando per dilettanze o ver per doglie,
>   che alcuna virtù nostra comprenda,
>   l'anima bene ad essa si raccoglie,
> par ch'a nulla potenza più intenda;
>   e questo è contra quello error che crede
>   ch'un'anima sovr' altra in noi s'accenda.

> When through impression of pleasure, or of pain,
> which some one of our faculties receives,
> the soul is wholly centered thereon,
> it seems that it gives heed to no other of its powers;
> and this is contrary to that error which holds
> that one soul above another is kindled within us.
>
> (*Purg.* 4.1–6)

Like Aristotle in Book 3 of *De anima*, Dante, following Thomas Aquinas, believed that the soul constituted a unity that was dependent on the body in this world and without which the soul could not survive. Averroës had taken the extreme position that the soul and body were so inextricably tied that the soul could not survive death.[16]

On the issue of allegory, earlier in his career, Dante had elaborated on the allegorical system he was applying to interpret *Convivio*'s first canzone:

> questa sposizione conviene essere litterale e allegorica. E a ciò dare a intendere, si vuol sapere che le scritture si possono intendere e deonsi esponere massimamente per Quattro sensi. L'uno si chiama litterale . . . L'altro si chiama allegorico, e questo e quello che si nasconde sotto 'l manto di queste favole, ed è una veritade ascosa sotto bella menzogna . . . Lo terzo senso si chiama morale, e questo è quello che li lettori deono intentamente andare appostando per le scritture ad utilitade di loro e di loro discenti . . . Lo quarto senso si chiama anagogico, cioè sovrasenso; e questo è quando spiritualmente si spone una scrittura, la quale ancora [che sia vera] eziandio nel senso litterale, per le cose significate significa delle superne cose dell'etternal Gloria.

> this exposition must be literal and allegorical. And to convey its meaning, one must know that the Scriptures can be understood and must be expounded mainly through four senses. The first is called literal . . . The second is called allegorical, and this one hides under the cloak of fables, and is a truth hiding beneath a beautiful lie . . . The third is called moral, and this is the one that lectors ought to seek for intently throughout the Scriptures, for their own profit and that of that of their pupils . . . The fourth sense is called anagogical, that is to say, beyond the senses; and this is when Scripture is expounded spiritually, which, though it is also true in the literal sense, through the signified things it signifies supernal matters of the eternal Glory. (*Conv.* 2.1.2–15)

However, the system of allegory that Dante lays out here radically differs from that which Beatrice explains in *Paradiso* 4. Here, Dante explains that the literal is a "bella menzogna" ("beautiful lie") that covers diverse other meanings that can be unveiled through interpretation. Beatrice asserts in *Paradiso* 4, however, that because of the limits of human language to reveal divine truths, metaphoric language must substitute for its referent. She also implies that the limits of the human intellect itself make revelation, exemplified by her own mediation of truth, necessary to enable him to understand divine truth. Here too Dante is correcting or adding to what he had said about interpretive reading practices in the *Convivio*. The difference is between a rather prosaic theory in the *Convivio* about how allegory functions, and the acceptance in *Paradiso* that the ineffable cannot be put into words, "Trasumanar significar *per verba/* non si poria" (*Par.* 1.70–71 "The passing beyond humanity may not be set forth *in words*" [my emphasis]).

However, more is at stake here than straightening out the *Convivio*'s philosophical and poetic missteps (as well as the limitations of ancient Greek and Arabic philosophy); for Dante, through Beatrice's answers to his quandaries, approaches the heart of the debate about the relationship between philosophy and faith, and what poetry offers to this debate.[17] In the Heaven of the Sun, where the poet sees the theologians he admires, in a further elaboration of the ideas raised in *Paradiso* 4, Dante implies the interdependence of faith and reason, thus linking Dominic and Francis (the Dominicans and Franciscans), "principi . . . che quinci e quindi" (*Par.* 11.35–36 "princes . . . who on this side and that"). Furthermore, when interrogated on faith by Saint Peter in *Paradiso* 24, Dante makes the point that it is through scripture (and thus metaphoric language) as the foundation of logic that faith is unfolded.[18] Here faith is not sidelined in favor of reason, nor reason undermined, but both are necessary components of the visionary understanding that scripture reveals.

Turning to the Islamic tradition on allegory, we see some important parallels with Christian theologians and with Dante. The difference in the application of allegorical methods of the philosophers and Sufis in Islamic culture parallels the interpretive strategies of Albertus Magnus and Bonaventure in a pattern that differentiates between those under the influence of the Aristotelian recovery and those worried about its implications to orthodox theological understanding. In a previously published essay, I discussed how the Islamic commentary tradition on the *mi'rāj* (Book of the Ladder) reveals the diverse applications of allegorical reading strategies in the Islamic (High) Middle Ages (ca. 950–1150).[19] More particularly, I argued that the *mi'rāj* and its commentary tradition highlight a division in interpretive methods between the philosophers (*falasifa*) and the Sufis, a philosophical debate that was also occurring among theologians in the later Latin Middle Ages.[20]

The *mi'rāj* tradition can be considered a commentary on or expansion of sura 17.1 in the Qur'an, in which with God speaking, Muhammad is described as going by night from the sacred temple (Mecca) to the farther temple (Jerusalem).[21] Widely dispersed in many different versions, the *mi'rāj* is a combination of both the night journey and the vision of Heaven. In this vision, one night as Muhammad was sleeping in Mecca, the angel Gabriel awakened him and lifted him onto an exotic mount, a winged animal named Burāq.[22] Accompanied by Gabriel, Muḥammad traveled through the seven Heavens, saw the marvels of Heaven and punishments of Hell, met all the former prophets, and, climbing the heavenly ladder, encountered God. Multiple versions of the *mi'rāj* are extant.[23] Besides various Arabic, Persian, and Latin versions, Old French and Castilian versions still survive. Closer to Dante is the *Contra legem Saracenorum* (Against the Law of the Saracens) which includes a version of the *mi'rāj* and a commentary on it written by Frate Riccoldo da Monte di Croce (1234–1320), a Florentine who had entered the Dominican order in 1267 and who lectured at Santa Maria Novella intermittently until he left for Asia in 1288, where he became a scholar of Islam. Riccoldo returned to Florence from Baghdad, where he lived for eight years, and from the Holy Land in 1300, so it is likely that Dante encountered him, especially since the poet frequented the Dominican *studium* (college) at Santa Maria Novella.[24] Riccoldo's works also include an *Itinerarium* (Itinerary) that was translated into Italian in the fourteenth century,[25] the *Confutatio Alcorani* (Refutation of the Qur'an), the *Libellus contra errores Judaeorum* (Pamphlet against the Errors of the Jews), as well as his major work, *Contra legem Saracenorum*, all of which circulated in Florence in the fourteenth century.[26] In his commentary on the *mi'rāj*,[27] Riccoldo calls the "vision of Muḥammad" ridiculous. The *mi'rāj* has many parallels with Dante's *Commedia*, and as a consequence, particularly since a Latin version was circulating, Dante's poem has often been linked with the earlier Islamic work.[28]

For some Islamic writers, such as Ibn Ṭufayl, the *mi'rāj* was literally true. For the Sufis, like al-Ghazālī, it was a model for ecstatic experience. For the philosophers, such as Avicenna, it became a text to be rationalized. A version, attributed to Avicenna and written in Persian, allegorized the journey narrative and all that the pilgrim had seen to bring out its philosophical implications. Called "the first Scholastic," Avicenna's achievement as a philosopher and his influence on later philosophical developments cannot be overestimated. The recipient of the Hellenistic synthesis of Neoplatonism and Aristotelianism, Avicenna's discipline, energy, and intellectual force created the Aristotelian system as method and as philosophy, as it was understood for the next five hundred years both in the Latin West and Islam.[29]

Avicenna's text tells of Muḥammad's ascent into Heaven, but the commentary that is the central purpose of the work uses allegory to accommodate the literal level of the text when it does not make sense according to rational apprehension. He writes, "A friend of ours has continually inquired about the meaning of the Ascension, desiring it explained in a rational way."[30] Thus by making the text a philosophical allegory he diminishes the text's visionary mode expressed in its literal words in favor of the philosophical meaning he finds hidden beneath the surface.

In rationalizing the visionary metaphorical level of the text, Avicenna follows the classical dichotomy between poetry and philosophy that was first articulated by Plato. Avicenna, sweeping away the literal level, writes, "If a person thinks that a human body reaches a place where the intellect reaches, it is impossible. Because the intellect reaches through intelligibles; it does not reach through duration or instrument, nor does it go by means of time." As for "journeys," "destinations are of two types, either intelligible or sensible. The conveyor of the sensible is the senses; the conveyor of intelligibles is the intellect."[31] For Avicenna, Burāq, the creature on which Muḥammad is seated, is "the Active Intelligence," the means by which an intellectual journey can be made. According to his interpretation of the ascent of the ladder, "The true sources of universal concepts . . . are the translunar Higher Principles, that is, the celestial Intelligences, beginning with the 'Active Intelligence' ascending through the other celestial Intelligences, and culminating with the Necessary Existent."[32] The angel Gabriel, his guide, the angel of Revelation, leads Muḥammad through Heaven. Burāq ("Active Intelligence") and Gabriel ("Revelation") make it possible for the pilgrim to transcend time and space intellectually.

Discussing the historical reality of Muḥammad's night journey, Avicenna concludes that "Since the conditions of the Ascension of our prophet, upon whom be peace, are not in the sensible world, it is known that he did not go in the body, because the body cannot traverse a long distance in one moment. Hence it is not a corporeal ascension, because the goal was not sensual. Rather, the ascension was spiritual, because the goal was intellectual" (124). Thus, for Avicenna the meaning of the quotation from the *mi'rāj*, "that night when Muḥammad was sleeping," becomes simply an explanation for the fact that "at night humans are freer, for bodily occupations and sensual impediments are suspended" (125).

In contrast to Dante's physical journey to the otherworld, where his body radically distinguishes him from the disembodied souls he encounters, Avicenna separates the mind from body through allegory to interpret the journey as intellectual. Avicenna writes of Burāq, or "Active Intelligence," that it reaches the Intelligences before the world of the sensible and corruption; it is the mount that helps the one who is traveling intellectually and spiritually; of its dimensions, he says, "it is greater than the human intellect and lesser than the First Intelligence" (127), "First Intelligence" being the term he uses for God. Reaching the mosque (that is, coming from Mecca to Jerusalem) is reaching the brain. For Avicenna, the ladder is the means to go from "external senses" to internal senses (130), guided by the "internal faculties." This ascent can happen only when the five senses are properly disciplined (130). Muḥammad's ascent up the ladder through the various heavens is explained in terms of Ptolemaic astronomy and astrology. Avicenna gives power to the planets over human activities in contrast to Beatrice, who corrects Dante's mistaken views on this issue. Thus Mercury has two kinds of influence, auspicious and sinister, whereas Venus rules over joy and mirth (131). The sun "rules over the conditions of kings and great men" (131), but Mars "rules over the conditions of the bloodthirsty and sinful," Jupiter "over folk of rectitude, piety and knowledge" (132), whereas Saturn is again sinister and auspicious but perfectly so (132). Avicenna glosses the description of the throne of God and the encounter with God as follows: "Divine, holy Presence is free of body, substance, and accident, which exist in these worlds. It is above these categories. By necessity, it neither needs nor is connected to place, time, locality, how much, how, where, when, activity and passiveness, and the like" (135). Finally, to apprehend the intelligible is Paradise; therefore, the internal journey, if it achieves this end, reaches eternity: "The journey was intellectual. He [Muḥammad] went by thought. His intellect perceived the order of existents until the necessary Existent. When cognition was complete he returned to himself," that is, to his bed in Mecca. In contrast to the *mi'rāj* text itself, Avicenna's allegorical reading is clearly intended for "rationalists." Awarding a privileged position to rational thinking, Avicenna argues in his conclusion that only rationalists should read his commentary because "sensual-minded outsiders" could not understand its meaning: "It is not possible to show the inner meanings of these words to one of the ignorant masses. Only a rationalist is permitted to enjoy the inner meaning of these words" (138). Constructing an intellectual (and implied social) hierarchy for encountering the divine, Avicenna's allegory represents the very kind of error for which Beatrice chastises Dante in *Paradiso* 4.

Avicenna's interpretive strategy is completely consonant with his discussion of the metaphoric mode in his commentary on Aristotle's *Poetics*, in which he distinguishes poetry from logic, arguing that the imaginative trait of poetry is the only feature that interests the logician: "It is the [proper] concern of the logician to examine poetry with regard to its being imaginative. The imaginative is the speech to which the soul yields, accepting or rejecting matters without pondering, reasoning or choice. In brief, it responds psychologically rather than ratiocinatively, whether the utterance is demonstrative or not" (*Poetics* Intro. 2).[33] For Avicenna, metaphor is equivalent to imaginative syllogism,[34] a tool of the logical system that he makes the foundation stone of his intellectual project. In discussing how language should be used for imitation, Avicenna writes, "It is not proper to imitate that which is not possible, even though the impossibility is neither apparent nor famous. The best subject matter for [imitation] is morals and opinions." He favors morals and opinions because they belong mutually to the domains of the logician, rhetorician, and poet and are ruled by probability or possibility.[35] Avicenna's commentary on the *Poetics* of Aristotle reveals his position on metaphoric discourse, while his commentary on the *mi'rāj* demonstrates how this approach can be applied to a text. The *mi'rāj* is understood as logic hidden behind a visionary literary surface. In both works, he confers a privileged status on the rational to remake the poetic surface into philosophical meaning, and in the commentary on the *mi'rāj* he applies allegory to achieve these ends.

Sufi commentary on the *mi'rāj* represents another strand for understanding Muhammad's ascent as it provides the metaphoric model for Sufi mystical journeys.[36] Whether as dream or rapture, the Sufi interpretation describes the mystical approach to God. Since any Sufi can make the journey to God, the hierarchical journey upward becomes one of discipline and simultaneous reconciliation of faith and intellect, for the seeker must travel from the self by "not fostering the desires and lusts of the body which soon distract the soul from gaining any furtherance in its aspiration to God."[37] The ladder of ascent must be ruled by an intellectual and ascetic rigor, as al-Ghazālī writes in *Freedom and Fulfillment*: "I brought my mind to bear on the way of the Sufis. I knew that their particular way is consummated only by knowledge and activity [by the union of theory and practice]. The aim of their knowledge is to lop off obstacles present in the soul and to rid oneself of its reprehensible habits and vicious qualities in order to attain thereby a heart empty of all save God and adorned with the constant remembrance of God."[38] In *The Incoherence of the Philosophers*, which takes up many philosophical speculations of his time, al-Ghazālī confronts the philosophers, particularly Avicenna, to argue about their interpretation of the resurrection of the body, which, like the rationalization of the *mi'rāj* text, sought to understand resurrection as a philosophical problem. For al-Ghazālī, the tie between rational philosophical traditions and Sufism was central to a healthy religious life.[39] On allegory, like Beatrice in *Paradiso* 4, al-Ghazālī explains that the law is revealed in parables to accommodate the understanding of humanity, but he nevertheless insists that "what has come down to us describing Paradise and the fire and the detailing these states has acquired a degree [of explicit statement] that does not [render it] subject to metaphorical interpretation." On the other hand, paralleling Dante, he insists that it is impossible to attribute "place, direction, visage, physical hand, physical eye, the possibility of transfer, and rest to God . . . Metaphorical interpretation [here] is obligatory through rational proofs. What he has promised in the hereafter, however, is not impossible in terms of the power of God."[40] Thus al-Ghazālī separates what can from what cannot be subjected to allegory: that which pertains to the nature and appearance of God (allegory) versus the literal, the afterlife, and the physical resurrection of the body and soul (not allegorical).

In contrast to the philosophical approach of Avicenna, for the Sufis, the Prophet's ascension signifies that his soul was loosed from the fetters of phenomenal being, and his spirit lost consciousness of all degrees and stations, and his natural powers were annihilated, not of his own will, but through his inspired longing for God.[41] Avicenna's commentary on the *mi'rāj* reveals an intellectual disdain for the visionary rendering of "eternal things." He focused on the metaphoric transformative journey that he understood as philosophical, and he achieved this interpretation through allegorizing the text so as to make it consonant with reason, that is, understandable through the intellect.

Two thirteenth-century Latin theologians responded differently to the "rationalist" challenge posed by the recovery of Aristotle, and their responses parallel those found in Avicenna and the Sufis, respectively. The responses emphasize how the recovery of Aristotle provoked intellectual challenges in both the Islamic and the Christian worlds of the twelfth and thirteenth centuries. In terms of parallelisms, the works of Albertus Magnus and Bonaventure reveal interpretive practices similar to those found in Avicenna and al-Ghazālī. Like the Sufis, Bonaventure uses the ladder metaphor, whose origin for both Christians and Muslims is Jacob's Ladder (Gen. 28:12–13), to describe the mystical encounter with God. Describing his desire for peace, Bonaventure begins his *Itinerarium mentis in Deum* (Journey of the Mind toward God) with an interpretation of the meaning of Francis's vision of a winged seraph in the form of the crucified Christ. Clearly troubled about how to understand the saint's vision, Bonaventure, like al-Ghazālī speaking of Muḥammad's ascent, interprets the seraph's six wings in a mystical-allegorical fashion as the six levels, or steps, of illumination by which the soul may be ecstatically elevated to God. Enriching his commentary with numerous biblical references, Bonaventure shares al-Ghazālī's effort to reconcile philosophical and mystical apprehension. His text rests on a hierarchy that arranges intellectual activities from observing, speculating, reading, and even knowing to Christian attributes of joy, love, humility, and union with God. It is not through the rational path alone, but through humility, love, and joy that the mind can ascend to God. The steps to God are through his vestiges (or signs in the world of nature that provide the opportunity for meditative discoveries)—some are within, some outside, some timeless, and some temporal. But to enter into the truth of God humans must go beyond the temporal to the eternal.[42] Like the Sufi mystics who see Muḥammad's night journey as a symbolic/spiritual model to be emulated, Bonaventure interprets Francis's vision as providing the symbolic/allegorical pattern for the journey into the mind of God. He writes on the mystical ecstasy in which the human's affection encounters God that we enter into peace by passing the six considerations. Like the six steps of the true throne of Solomon, where the true man of peace resides we find the interior Jerusalem. This is neither the historical city nor the historical temple of Solomon, but the place of the inner vision of peace that Jerusalem symbolizes. The steps to reach this goal are like the six wings of Francis's seraph (*Itinerarium* 6). Here too we find parallels with Avicenna and al-Ghazālī, for whom Jerusalem represents allegorically the goal and end of the journey, whether intellectual or mystical.

Albertus Magnus offers an interesting counterpoint to Bonaventure. Albertus took the Aristotelian challenge in his stride as he set about writing his commentary on the Apocalypse of John,[43] which is particularly interesting in the context of the Islamic allegorical readings of the *mi'rāj*. Like the *mi'rāj*, the symbolic dimension of the Apocalypse of John, another visionary text, invites allegorical intervention.[44] To compare his approach to those of Bonaventure's and the Arabic philosophers, I will examine how Albertus allegorizes the vision of heavenly worship at Apocalypse 4:3: "Et iris erat in circuitu sedis similis visioni zmaragdinae" ("And a rainbow just like an emerald was around the throne"). He writes that the rainbow is a sign of Christ through whom mankind is reconciled to God (here represented by the throne). He seeks to explain the visionary elements of Apocalypse 4:5— "Et septem lampades ardentes ante thronum quae sunt septem spiritus Dei" ("And seven flaming torches, the seven spirits of God were burning before the throne of God")—through a theologically informed allegorical reading of the text. He glosses the passage as follows: "The seven flaming torches, the gifts of the Holy Spirit, are burning with love of God." Like Avicenna, Albertus is interested in rationalizing the text under discussion, in other words, in eliminating the visionary elements of the literal level to discover the theological (or philosophical, as in Avicenna) meaning within. But Albertus, in contrast to Avicenna, does not apply an allegorical interpretive strategy to philosophize the text; rather, he accepts the visionary elements as symbolic, using them to explicate theological positions that conform to orthodox beliefs. For Albertus, theology becomes the intellectual discipline that aids him in interpreting the biblical text. He clarifies, and in a sense bypasses, the visionary aspects of the text by allegorizing them. Bonaventure, on the contrary, like the Sufis, uses biblical metaphor to expand on his own mystical theology, in which the contemplative ladder to God makes reason a necessary but lower step on the ladder.

For some time scholars have recognized that by the late Middle Ages the uses of allegory had been transformed. Here, of course, as the above examples make clear, I am not using the term *allegory* as a literary mode to denote a single didactic moral purpose underlying the literal meaning of any text, as did Bernard F. Huppé and D. W. Robertson, Jr., in the 1960s.[45] Indeed, Erich Auerbach's excursus on how Dante's figural imagination uses allegory to turn the poem's characters into "*figurae* of the fulfilled truth that the poem reveals,"[46] does not exactly apply here. Also inappropriate is Lee Patterson's idea that allegory was transformed from a "radically depersonalized and transcendentalizing" form, as in Prudentius or the *Roman de la Rose* (Romance of the Rose), to the dramatic subjective representation of later medieval writers.[47] Likewise, Hans Robert Jauss's catalog of allegorical genres does not apply.[48]

Rather, although linked to the glossing tradition of biblical commentary—inspired by the symbolic and just plain difficult elements of the sacred text itself—for Albertus, Bonaventure, and Dante, allegory is a reading (and writing) strategy designed to convey theological insight or understanding. For Albertus, allegory is a reading strategy to make the visionary elements of the text into rational theology; for Bonaventure, allegory is the literary means to unveil the visionary images, making the words themselves the symbolic means to unfold the mystical journey. Jauss's and Auerbach's understanding of allegory can and have been applied to the *Commedia*, for its discursive allegories are moral, political/historical, social, and theological. But in *Paradiso* 4, Beatrice seems to be saying that allegory is the only means to accommodate the visionary mode of *Paradiso* because of the insufficiency of our intellect and of language itself, which must compromise with our sensual imagination.

In *Paradiso* 4, Dante addresses two concerns of his poem. First, in straightening out his intellectual understanding, he must come to terms with how classical (i.e., Greek and Arab) learning differs from Christian revelation. Second, in figuring Paradise, he must confront the inadequacy of language to make this grand leap (*Par.* 23.61).[49] As al-Ghazālī did for Islam, Dante provides a poetic theology—for through the mediation of Beatrice, Dante offers a great synthesis of all of the schools of thought in the service of Christian truth.[50] The limitations of the philosophical schools represented in Limbo are once more revealed, as is Dante's inability to see Paradise as it really is or to describe it for us.

In considering "Dante and Islam," one might want to ask how all of this directly addresses the questions often posed about the Italian poet's use of Islamic learning and texts and his general attitude toward Islam. On the political front, as I have argued, although it cannot be denied that Dante (like Thomas Aquinas) condemned Muḥammad and ʿAlī as schismatic (*Inf.* 28),[51] he did not endorse crusade politics, a papal and mostly French sponsored inner-European policy from 1096 onward. Dante's political focus was on Europe and its multiple corruptions (whether ecclesiastical, political, or social), against which he raged throughout the *Commedia*. Europe's political and religious schisms and their consequences to civic and moral life, not the schisms within Islam, as he understood them, were what brought him near despair.[52]

On Dante's intellectual indebtedness to Islamic learning, I concur with Cerulli and Miguel Asín Palacios, and therefore do not doubt that he knew and used Arabic learning and textual resources. (Indeed, since al-Ghazālī's theology is much closer to Dante's than either Averroës's or Avicenna's, even though it lacks the Christian Trinitarian and incarnational element, one might wonder why al-Ghazālī does not appear in the *Commedia*.) However, more productive perhaps in understanding the poet's relationship to this inherited learning is to highlight the parallelisms between the two geographically and culturally contiguous cultures—they shared the same Greek legacy and often shared the same lands. Discovering how individual authors made use of this legacy during this time of intellectual ferment in the wake of the rediscovery of Aristotle perhaps yields greater understanding than just a recognition that it exists. For example, in Bonaventure's deploying allegory to focus on the spiritual implications of the texts he interprets and Albertus's using allegory to reach the rationalized theological meaning veiled by the visionary surface, we see a parallelism with the rationalizing approach of Avicenna and the spiritualizing approach of al-Ghazālī. The rationalizing approach to knowledge of divine things led to fierce confrontations within Christianity and Islam, respectively, as the inherent danger of heresy or apostasy emerged. It was anxiety about this danger from the recovery of Aristotle that prompted much of al-Ghazālī's and Bonaventure's theological work. This discussion of the approaches to classical learning in the Islamic and Christian cultures of the period provides yet another avenue for understanding what was at stake in the religious and intellectual controversies of the twelfth and thirteenth centuries for both Islam and Christianity. Although Dante may have embraced the philosophic schools when he abandoned Beatrice for Lady Philosophy in the *Convivio*, by the time he was writing *Paradiso* he had sharpened the intellectual distinctions between Greek and Arabic philosophy and Christian revelation informed by theology. He allows Beatrice to invalidate the venomous Platonic and Avicennan ideas that the soul returns to its origins and that the stars possess complete power over human behavior. Finally, like al-Ghazālī and other Sufi writers, rather than explaining visionary elements away as in the rationalist approach, Dante shows that metaphoric language, as a kind of incarnational linguistics, is his chosen, and perhaps only, means to integrate philosophy and theology, or reason and faith.

Dante and the *Falasifa*:
Religion as Imagination

GREGORY B. STONE

Every law [i.e., religion] comes about from revelation and has intellect mixed with it.

—Averroës, *The Incoherence of the Incoherence*

In Canto 26 of *Paradiso*, in the third and final of the three "examinations" on the theological virtues that Dante must pass in order to attain the credentials requisite for continuing higher in his journey toward God, he is questioned by John the Evangelist on the topic of love. John asks Dante to identify the goal toward which his soul aims—in other words, the object of his love: "dì ove s'appunta / l'anima tua" (*Par.* 26.7–8 "declare the aim on which your soul is set").[1] Dante answers, in brief, that his chief love is for the highest good, the source and cause of all other goods (*Par.* 26.28–36). After endorsing this answer, John then asks Dante to tell who directed him toward loving the highest good: "dicer convienti / chi drizzò l'arco tuo a tal berzaglio" (*Par.* 26.24 "you must tell who directed your bow at such a target"). Dante replies that he learned his lessons concerning love from both philosophy (*Par.* 26.25 "filosofici argomenti") and scripture (*Par.* 26.26 "autorità"). Expanding on this thought in a series of three parallel three-line stanzas known as *terzine,* Dante attributes his proper understanding of love to his reading Aristotle (*Par.* 26.37–39), Moses (*Par.* 26.40–42), and John the Evangelist himself (*Par.* 26.43–45). One and the same ethical truth—that the chief object of our love ought to be the highest good—is taught, apparently with equal effectiveness, by a pagan philosopher, a Jewish prophet, and a Christian evangelist.[2] John confirms Dante's response, granting his assent to the notion that right love is taught by both philosophy and by religious revelations:

E io udi': "Per intelletto umano
e per autoritadi a lui concorde
d'i tuoi amori a Dio guarda il sovrano.

And I heard: "Through human reasoning
and through authorities concordant with it,
of all your loves, keep that of God the highest.
(*Par.* 26.46–48)

The relation between philosophy and scripture is one of concord, harmony, and equivalence. There is no notion here that revelation provides a necessary something that cannot be learned by "human intellect" alone. (In this aspect as in many others, the examination on love administered by John differs sharply from that on faith administered by Peter in Canto 24.)[3] John even hints slightly at the priority of philosophy to scripture. He says that certain scriptural authorities agree with human intellect—as if reason is the standard by which the scriptures (on this question of love, at least) are measured. Human intellect is singular, whereas the authorities are plural. Some authorities may accord with reason, others not; the right ones are those that do. If John had reversed the terms here and said, "In accord with the Bible and with those philosophers concordant with it, the highest of your loves is directed to God," the implication would differ: various formulations of human reason would be measured by how well they match up with the truth of revelation.

If human intellect is indeed the standard by which scriptures are gauged, then one who has attained a right understanding of love, from no matter what source, has no need for any scriptures (again, when the question at stake is love). This seems to be the thrust of Dante's remarking that the Good (*Par.* 26.16 "lo ben") is the "Alpha and Omega of all the writing / that love reads to me" (*Par.* 26.17–18 "Alfa e O è di quanta scrittura / mi legge Amore"). These verses are interesting semiotically: Alpha and O, insofar as they are meant to indicate the letters of the alphabet, the signifiers of a written text, are replaced by (or rather, they simply *are*) the signified content, the rational meaning, the intelligible universal. This is a strange kind of *scrittura* (or scripture): a text without signifiers, a pure content without form, a kernel with no shell. Scripture as a tangible artifact, as actual words on actual pages, disappears as something superfluous. The Good is the Alpha and Omega, the beginning and end, the origin and goal of love, and one who knows this does not need it further revealed in writing. Reading such-and-such scripture is unnecessary for one whose love is rightly directed toward the Good. And perhaps the wise human can dispense with scriptures, or, as Judah Halevi's Philosopher says in the *Book of Kuzari*, can choose whichever religion he pleases.[4]

My point is not to insist on the possible heterodoxy of this episode in *Paradiso* 26; rather, it is to suggest that the question concerning the relation between *intelletto* and *scrittura* remains an open one, even near the end of Dante's itinerary. This episode's reaffirmation of the value of *filosofici argomenti* manifests a more general truth: that Dante designed the *Commedia* to speak to different levels of audience, one of which comprises philosophers.[5] Dante does not leave philosophy behind at some point in the poem; nor does he invite philosophers to follow him by relinquishing their faith in philosophy. It is not the intellectuals, but rather the non-intellectuals, who are left behind at the beginning of *Paradiso*, when Dante warns most readers that they ought not to read the *Commedia*'s final canticle (*Par.* 2.1–6).[6] There is no threshold moment in the *Commedia*'s trajectory when philosophy is surpassed by revelation, and—as I shall discuss at the end of this essay—the distinction between Vergil and Beatrice is not (at least not for philosophical readers) a distinction between reason and faith. A philosophical interpretation remains available, for those readers inclined to interpret philosophically, all the way to the end of *Paradiso*. Thus the poem's most important theological moment—the vision of God in the closing verses of *Paradiso* 33—is also its most important philosophical moment: it is the conjunction of the individual human's soul with the active intellect, the philosopher's ultimate felicity (indeed, "salvation") as variously understood by Avicenna, Averroës, Albertus Magnus, and by Dante's best friend, Guido Cavalcanti—and well beyond into Renaissance Europe.[7] Dante's great poem, which he conceives as belonging to the genre of prophetic revelation, is (as Averroës says concerning revelation) "mixed with intellect" from beginning to end.

For the past several decades, the consensus among American Dantists has been that Dante means the *Commedia*, in part, as corrective to and indeed penance for his excessive flirtation with philosophy in the *Convivio*. Dante's return to Beatrice following his dalliance with Lady Philosophy has been interpreted as his rededication to the Christian faith, following a period during which he had strayed into the dark wood of radical Aristotelianism. In this view, the *Commedia* follows Aquinas in affirming the value of philosophy while emphasizing its limits and in insisting that the attainment that matters most of all, true felicity, lies beyond philosophy's grasp: the higher reaches of Dante's *itinerarium mentis in deum* ("path of the mind toward God") can only be attained through the Christian faith, Biblical revelation, and God's grace.[8]

This theological approach is not incorrect: it does correspond to one of the *Commedia*'s hermeneutic levels, and thus it has produced innumerable valuable readings of the poem. But it does not tell the whole story of Dante's view of the relation between philosophy and religion. One way in which we may see a more complete picture is through studying the *falasifa* ("philosophers," from the Arab-Islamic term *falsafa*, "philosophy"), for whom the question of the relation between revelation and reason is always pressing.

The *falasifa* are, strictly speaking, the rationalist philosophers of the classical Islamic tradition—figures such as al-Fārābī (known in the West as Alfarabius), Ibn Sīnā (Avicenna), Ibn Bājja (Avempace), Ibn Ṭufayl (Abubacer), and Ibn Rushd (Averroës). But—as indicated by the fact that each of these was well enough known in the West to earn a Latin name—this tradition should not be conceived as restricted to the Islamic world, where, it is fair to say, *falsafa* came to an end following the death of Averroës in 1198. Rather, this tradition was assimilated and developed—to a greater or lesser extent and with varying emphases—by numerous important Jewish and Christian philosophers in late medieval and Renaissance Europe.

The great twelfth-century Jewish philosopher Maimonides (Averroës's contemporary and fellow native Andalusian) is rightly to be ranked among the *falasifa*, not so much because he wrote his monumental *Guide for the Perplexed* in Arabic, but because the core of his philosophy is fundamentally al-Farabian.[9] Although Maimonides emigrated from Spain at the age of twenty-five and eventually settled in Egypt, he left an enormous legacy in Europe. But his numerous followers among his coreligionists, such as Gersonides (1288–1344 CE, also known as Levi ben Gershon) and Moses of Narbonne (1300–1362 CE), who were active in Provence, Italy, and Catalonia, did not simply rely upon studying their illustrious predecessor; rather, they mastered the tradition of *falsafa* and, although they wrote in Hebrew, therefore must be counted among the *falasifa*.[10]

The massive and undeniable influence in the Latin West of Avicenna and Averroës (both of whom Dante honors with a place in Limbo) extends beyond the mere provision of access, with commentary, to most of Aristotle's works (Averroës) or the virtual domination of the curriculum in psychology and medicine (Avicenna). More importantly, if less conspicuously, these two offered an intellectualist understanding of the afterlife (grounded in al-Fārābī's *On the Intellect*) that provided an alternative conception of the means to the attainment of felicity than that offered by the Christian faith—an alternative that proved appealing to some intellectuals of Christendom.[11] This group includes not just the famous leaders of Parisian Averroism in the 1270s, Boethius of Dacia and Siger of Brabant, but lesser-known yet more knowledgeable figures, such as Dante's contemporary Jean de Jandun.[12] Dante's poetic mentor, Guido Cavalcanti, was an adept in *falsafa*, and his whole lyric corpus revolves around the possibility that the human mind might conjoin with intellect—in other words, the possibility of attaining the intellectual felicity that Albertus Magnus called the *fiducia philosophantis*, the "faith [firm hope] of the philosopher."[13] Albertus is himself an interesting case: although he may well not have considered himself to belong to this tradition, he nonetheless understood its essentials and incorporated them in such a way that he could almost be classed as a *falasifa* himself.[14] Petrarch's vitriolic rant against his Averroist contemporaries testifies to the fact that *falsafa* was still very much a live tradition in the decades following Dante's death.[15] The issues raised by Islamic Aristotelianism remained preeminent concerns that extended well beyond the confines of the schools: even Boccaccio, an author who at first glance seems to have little to do with philosophy, was preoccupied with them in many of his works.[16] This tradition (by now so assimilated as to be identical to a certain significant strain of "European" philosophy) lived on through the sixteenth century, firmly established in Venice and especially Padua, where Averroës seems to have been taken more seriously than Aquinas.[17]

To posit a relation between Dante and the *falasifa*, then, is not to imagine the Italian poet as having to look back and outside to some alien body of thought remote in time and place; it is not to suggest that he was motivated by some antiquarian curiosity or some inclination for the exotic. It is, rather, to insist that the legacy of *falsafa* was a living, organic element of Dante's native intellectual environment.

In general, *falsafa* was the project of remaining faithful to both Aristotle (as well as, in some cases, to Plato as seen through the lens of Neoplatonism) and to one's religion—usually by regarding religion as representing philosophy symbolically or as perfecting it by doing some things (rhetorical and political things) that philosophy cannot do by itself. In the view of the *falasifa*, scriptural discourse uses sense imagery—concrete particulars, which are primarily meant for the masses of ordinary folk. Insofar as these concrete images are meant for the masses, they offer lessons pertaining to practical wisdom, right and wrong actions, and ethics. Insofar as some of scripture's images symbolize theoretical and metaphysical truths, they have a double function: they veil these truths from the masses (who would not be pleased, to say the least, were they to be told the true understanding of the afterlife), while also confirming for philosophers what they know through philosophy.[18] To ordinary folk, scripture gives a foundation for right *praxis*, while only giving harmlessly broad principles (e.g., that there *is* an afterlife) concerning true *theoria*, or indeed while withholding *theoria* and discouraging interest in metaphysical truth. To philosophers, scripture gives the same foundation for right *praxis* that it gives to the masses, but it also proves its divine provenance (thus gaining the philosopher's assent to its practical commands)—its status as prophetic revelation—by containing symbols that, properly interpreted, agree perfectly with Aristotle and Plato.[19]

Al-Fārābī (ca. 870–ca. 950 CE), known in the classical Islamic philosophical tradition as the "Second Teacher" (second only to Aristotle himself), ascribed to the view that each religion is a sort of language: just as (he would have argued) different languages all name one and the same set of universal things, so do different religions name the same set of universals. He thus views Islam as one of many religious languages that differ from one another in speech but not in rational content. Muḥammad provided an Arabic vocabulary in order to signify the universal truths of philosophy for Muslims in a manner appropriate for their particular historical situation. That which philosophers know as the First Cause is named "Allah" in the Qur'an. When the Qur'an speaks of the "Spirit of Holiness" or the "Angel of Revelation," it names that which philosophers know as the Active Intellect. References to darkness and light in scripture refer to the philosophical notions, respectively, of matter and form. The Islamic *imam*, for al-Fārābī, signifies the Platonic philosopher-king. That which Islam terms *wahy* (revelation) means, as Richard Walzer puts it, "the highest human knowledge which only the metaphysician is able to attain."[20]

When one encounters this method of translating the letter of scripture into philosophical terms, it indicates fairly well that one is in the orbit of the *falasifa*. When in the *Convivio* Dante remarks that the term *angeli* (angels) is a vulgarization used by the common folk for those substances, separate from matter, that are rightly understood by philosophers as "intelligences," he is engaging in *falsafa*—and is in fact repeating Avicenna, as mediated through Albertus Magnus.[21] When, also in the *Convivio*, Dante interprets (in a manner that is, one must admit, extremely forced) "Galilee" to mean *speculazione* (i.e., theoretical intellection)—and when he goes so far as to interpret Christ to mean the same, he is allegorizing in the manner of al-Fārābī (and, especially, in the manner of Averroës).[22] And lest one get the impression that Dante's practicing this hermeneutic in the *Convivio* is an error for which he repents in *Commedia*, we should add the following: when Beatrice, in *Paradiso* 28, presents Pseudo-Dionysius the Areopagite's *De caelesti hierarchia* (On the Celestial Hierarchy) in such a way that this theological vocabulary concerning the ranks of angels (cherubim, seraphim, thrones, etc.) is shown to be perfectly concordant with Avicenna's *Metaphysics*, she teaches in the manner of the *falasifa*. But there *is* in fact a difference with respect to the *Convivio*: now it is not a matter of a "vulgar" versus a "true" understanding (the vulgar, after all, have been left behind in *Paradiso* 2); rather, it is a matter of two alternative registers. Beatrice offers theological vocabulary for theologians, philosophical vocabulary for philosophers—but in both cases she is referring to one and the same theoretical, metaphysical, and theological reality.[23]

In his *Decisive Treatise, Determining What the Connection is Between Religion and Philosophy*, Averroës insists that there is no discrepancy between the truths of revealed scripture, properly understood, and the truths of Aristotle's philosophy. The rational content of Islamic scripture, like that of the other religious laws (foremost in his mind, of course, are Judaism and Christianity) is Aristotle's philosophy: religion, in its authentic teaching concerning the way things really are, is fully compatible with Greek rationalism:

> Since this Law [i.e., Islam] is true and calls to the reflection leading to cognizance of the truth, we, the Muslim community, know firmly that demonstrative reflection [i.e., philosophy] does not lead to differing with what is set down in the Law. For truth does not oppose truth; rather, it agrees with and bears witness to it.[24]

But Averroës's view does not amount to an indifference to religion—and certainly not to any opposition to religion; nor does he deny that

Islam is superior to the other monotheisms. He does not long for the day when everyone will be taught to understand Aristotle. (Following Avicenna, Averroës insists that philosophers should share their knowledge only with other philosophers and that they should not even suggest to non-philosophers that religion's truth content is philosophical.[25]) On the contrary, Averroës affirms that religion is in the final analysis superior to philosophy. While religion and philosophy are, as vehicles of rational truth, purely equal (since philosophically acute interpreters will see that the truth of religion is identical to the truth of philosophy), nonetheless religion has a "something extra" that philosophy lacks: a rhetorical, practical level that uses moral imperatives and institutes legislation for the sake of peace, justice, and a felicitous social order. Religions prescribe laws and institute practices that are beneficial for the political health of the community. Philosophy, which can only be mastered after great training and by those possessing uncommon intellect, will only ever be understood by a very few, and thus it can never serve as a society's primary practical and ethical guiding discourse. Religion's positive moral and political effects are rarely if ever achieved by philosophy. A prophet (such as Muḥammad) performs two tasks. Like the philosopher, he presents the truth concerning the way things really are. But he also, in his role as "lawgiver," does something that normally exceeds the philosopher's capacity: he inspires human communities to organize themselves in ways conducive to peace and justice. Thus Averroës tells us that, while every prophet is a philosopher (since the rational content of every virtuous religion is one and the same universal rational truth), not every philosopher is a prophet.[26] Although grudgingly admitting that a religion of pure intellect is conceivable, Averroës insists that such a religion would be deficient, lacking the rhetorical force and practical guidance that can be provided by authority alone.[27] The exemplary philosopher should not abandon his religion and should not aim to destroy or demystify the very notion of religion; rather, he should do his best to see that his religion is put to positive social use.[28]

Averroës not only affirms the necessity of religion in general and its superiority to a law of pure intellect, but he also affirms the superiority of Islam.[29] In *The Incoherence of the Incoherence* he says that one ought to "choose the most virtuous [religion] in his time—even when all of them are true, according to him."[30] But one might ask, if all religions are equally true, how can one of them be "more virtuous" [i.e., better] than others? The answer is that a religion is not deemed better because it is "more true" (in fact the truth content of all virtuous religions is identical) but rather because, in a given time and place, it *works* better to organize the laws, practices, and ethical attitudes of a community. Since a religion amounts to a universal rational truth (common to all religions but accessible only to philosophically acute interpreters) as well as practical prescriptions (accessible to and obligatory for all members of a community), what makes for distinctions and rankings among religions lies entirely on the practical, "lawgiving" side of things. Some prophets have given laws that are better—that work better—than others (in certain concrete historical situations).

Among the best examples of the attitude on the relation between philosophy and religion shared by many of the *falasifa* is the charming philosophical novella *Hayy Ibn Yaqzān* ("Alive" Son of "Awake"), written by Averroës's mentor, the twelfth-century Andalusian Muslim philosopher and scholar Ibn Ṭufayl. The tale's protagonist, Ḥayy Ibn Yaqẓān, is born on "a certain equatorial island, lying off the coast of India, where human beings come into being without father or mother."[31] As the product of spontaneous generation, Ḥayy's thoughts and, eventually, his philosophical system develop wholly from his relations with his natural environment (he is raised by a doe, for whom he feels the strongest possible filial love and whose death is the traumatic experience that initiates his philosophical questioning). Ḥayy's mature and full-blown philosophical system represents the truth at which a naturally gifted human mind will autonomously arrive, without the influence or coercion of human family, society, and culture. At stake is a thought experiment meant to answer the question that is nicely formulated by Lenn Goodman, an English translator of the tale: "What discoveries would be made by the isolated soul freed from prejudice and unimpeded by dogma and tradition?"[32]

For our purposes, the specifics of Ḥayy's naturally attained philosophy (which, in its highest stage, tends toward mysticism) are unimportant, since the real force of the story has less to do with the positive doctrines of Ḥayy's thought than with the relations between his thought and that of others. Near the end, we see that the whole novella has been a preparation for the crucial, brief final episodes. Near Ḥayy's island is "a second island, in which had settled the followers of a certain true religion, based on the teachings of a certain ancient prophet— God's blessings on all such prophets."[33] Among the inhabitants of this second island is a young man named Absāl, a devout follower of the island's religion, one who has studied and meditated on its writings so that he has come to see its literal teachings as "symbols, concrete images of things."[34] Seeking solitude conducive to religious contemplation, Absāl travels to Ḥayy's island, thinking it uninhabited. The two soon become fast friends, and in the course of their conversations Ḥayy teaches Absāl his philosophy, while Absāl gives Ḥayy an account of his religion. As a result, Absāl comes to see that the veiled or symbolic meaning of his religion is nothing other than Ḥayy's philosophy: "Absāl had no doubt that all the traditions of his religion about God, His angels, bibles and prophets, Judgment Day, Heaven and Hell were symbolic representations of these things that Ḥayy Ibn Yaqzān had seen for himself. The eyes of his heart were unclosed. His mind caught fire. Reason and tradition were at one within him. All the paths of exegesis lay open before him. All his old religious puzzlings were solved; all the obscurities, clear."[35]

The true essence of Islam (for the identity of the second island's traditional religion is barely disguised) is expressed abstractly, without images or metaphors, by Ḥayy's philosophical system. But as the tale comes to an end, and Absāl brings Ḥayy back to Absāl's island so that he might teach its inhabitants the truth concerning the scriptures, it is clear that not even those "nearest to intelligence," let alone the masses, will ever accept the philosophical understanding of religious doctrine:

> But the moment Ḥayy rose the slightest bit above the literal or began to portray things against which they were prejudiced, they recoiled in horror from his ideas and closed their minds. . . . The more he taught, the more repugnance they felt, despite the fact that these were men who loved the good and sincerely yearned for the Truth. Their inborn infirmity simply would not allow them to seek Him as Ḥayy did, to grasp the true essence of His being and see Him in His own terms. They wanted to know Him in some human way. In the end Ḥayy despaired of helping them and gave up his hopes that they would accept his teaching.[36]

The tale ends on a pessimistic, or at least quietistic, note. Ḥayy and Absāl return to Ḥayy's island, reconciled to the fact that philosophy has no role to play in society, which is better left in the hands of traditional religion. Although the religion of the masses is not—on the literal level—true, it nonetheless has a positive, utilitarian, policing function:

"The sole benefit most people could derive from religion was for this world, in that it helped them lead decent lives without others encroaching on what belonged to them."[37]

The question concerning Dante's relation to Arabic rationalism is a large one that can be approached from several angles. In what follows I will primarily consider just one topic: the importance of the philosophers' notion of prophetic imagination for our understanding of *Purgatorio*. The point is not to give a full account of either the religious imagination as conceived by Islamic Aristotelianism or of Dante's understanding of imagination; rather, it is to give an example of the kind of fruitful encounters that can arise by reading Dante as if he were one of the *falasifa*.[38]

In numerous respects, *Purgatorio* is the canticle of the imagination. Many of the most memorable figures whom Dante meets are imaginative artists of one sort or another, such as musicians, painters, and poets. *Purgatorio* is punctuated by Dante's three conspicuous dreams (in Cantos 9, 19, and 27), whereas *Inferno* or *Paradiso* contain none. Dante dreams in *Purgatorio* and nowhere else precisely because this is the canticle of imagination, and dreams are a privileged locus for the exercise of the faculty of imagination. (As Averroës says, echoing a view shared by all the philosophers, "It is therefore manifest . . . that of all the faculties of the soul, it is the imaginative faculty that dreams are primarily related to.")[39] Dante confirms that imagination is among *Purgatorio*'s foremost concerns by placing in the seventeenth of thirty-three cantos, right in the center of the canticle, an apostrophe to the faculty of imagination (*Purg.* 17.13–18 "O imaginativa," etc.).

Dante's decision to make *Purgatorio* the canticle of the imagination is not motivated by some vague artistic whim. Rather, it suggests a certain understanding of religion: that various religions teach lessons on right practice to various differing historical communities by means of differing imaginative particulars appropriate to each community. Although the particulars of these moral lessons differ, the fundamental ethical principles are the same. At the center of the *Commedia* Dante shows the harmony between the moral laws revealed by the prophetic imagination and the practical intelligibles conceived by the philosopher.

Purgatorio begins to establish, and indeed emphasize, this link between scripture and imagination, from the moment when Vergil and Dante set foot on the first terrace of Purgatory proper. There Dante is amazed by the sculpted walls of the cliff at his side, the artistry of which (attributed to God) is so great that it almost literally brings to life the scenes depicted. The walls of this terrace, where the sin of Pride is purged, are covered with sculpted scenes representing three exemplary figures of Pride's opposite, the virtue of humility. The first of these scenes—the Virgin Mary's humble reply to the Angel Gabriel following the Annunciation of the Incarnation—is twice expressly referred to as an image:

> Dinanzi a noi pareva sì verace
>   quivi intagliato in un atto soave,
>   che non sembiava *imagine* che tace.
> Giurato si saria ch'el dicesse "Ave!";
>   perché iv' era *imaginata* quella
>   ch'ad aprir l'alto amor volse la chiave.

> Before us he appeared so vividly
> graven in gentle mien
> that it seemed not a silent image.
> One would have sworn that he was saying, *"Ave"*;
> for there was made an image of the woman
> who turned the key to open the supreme love.
>
> (*Purg.* 10.37–42)

Dante then sees (and hears, since one of the remarkable qualities of these images is that they are audible as well as visible: *Purg.* 10.60, 10.95), carved in the same marble cliff, a scene from the life of David, who was not ashamed to dance and mingle with his people (to the dismay of his embarrassed wife) following his success in returning the Ark of the Covenant to Jerusalem. The third carving depicts an episode from the life of the Roman emperor Trajan, who, in the urgency and hubbub of departing with his army for an important battle, allowed himself to be persuaded by a poor widow first to render justice in the matter of her son's murder. Taken together, these three sculpted narratives, collectively called "l'*imagini* di tante umilitadi" (*Purg.* 10.98 "the images of such humility"), amount to an ecumenical display of the virtue of humility—a virtue taught by stories from the Old Testament, the Gospels, and the legends of Roman history and exemplified by the actions of a Jew (David), a Christian (Mary), and a pagan (Trajan). Christians and non-Christians share a common faculty for one and the same virtue, although that virtue is "imaged" differently in different traditions.[40]

This notion that *scrittura* presents universal ethical principles mediated through and particularized by the faculty of imagination, is emphasized in an especially intense manner in *Purgatorio* 17, in a passage that follows immediately after the apostrophe to "imaginativa" (*Purg.* 17.13). Here Dante, through a vision that comes to his *imaginativa* (i.e., the faculty of imagination), sees within his mind three exemplary figures of Wrath (Procne, Haman, Amata), and their status as images is clearly marked: Procne appears in Dante's imagination (*Purg.* 17.21 "ne l'*imagine* mia"; "in my imagination"); the image (*Purg.* 17.31 "questa imagine"; "this imagination") of Haman appears in Dante's "alta fantasia" ("lofty fantasy," a synonym for the faculty of imagination); and, following his vision of Amata, Dante remarks that his imagining (*Purg.* 17.43 "l'*imaginar* mio"; "my imagining") has come to an end.

Recall that the very first of the dozens of exempla of virtues and vices that structure Dante's ascent up Mount Purgatory, a Gospel story involving the Virgin Mary, is twice referred to as an image. It will turn out, as we will see, that all of the exempla of right and wrong actions that Dante experiences on the seven terraces of Purgatory, insofar as he perceives them in the manner of a prophet, are linked to the faculty of imagination. Dante is guiding us to think of Gospel narrative as "imaginary." Scripture is presented as a mode of imagination—that is to say, a discourse that deals in concrete particulars rather than abstract universal essences.

To speak of religion as "imaginary" does not indicate that it is delusional or erroneous. It means that one of religion's primary functions is to present, for the masses of ordinary folk, "images" of truth—symbolic representations of things that philosophers can know as they really are. Al-Fārābi firmly established the view that the Law given by a prophet provides representation in particular, sensible imagery of universal intelligibles—things that philosophers understand without imagery.

In *Principles of the Views of the Citizens of the Perfect State*, al-Fārābi aims to direct humankind toward happiness, which for him means, above all, political happiness. It is the philosopher who knows what makes for the city's true felicity, and thus the perfect city is ruled by the philosopher; but not everyone is a philosopher. To the contrary, very few have the requisite acumen, inclination, and training. So the philosopher, in his role as prophet or religious lawgiver, presents knowledge leading to political happiness in symbolic or imaginative form—that is, as religion. The citizenry attains a kind of knowledge through images. But different sets and sorts of images are appropriate for the peoples of different communities, because human nature is "at one time different from [what it is] at another time" and the "accidents and states it has when existing in one country are different from the ones it has in another."[41]

Because the set of images appropriate for a particular community in a particular time and place may differ from the set of images appropriate for another community, it follows, in al-Fārābi's view, that there is a multiplicity of virtuous religions. As al-Fārābi says: "Therefore it is possible that excellent nations and excellent cities exist whose religions differ, although they all have as their goal one and the same felicity and the very same aims."[42] Moreover, says al-Fārābi:

> It is possible to imitate these things for each group and each nation, using matters that are different in each case. Consequently, there may be a number of virtuous nations and virtuous cities whose religions are different, even though they all pursue the very same kind of happiness. For religion is but the impression of these things or the impressions of their *images*, imprinted in the soul.[43]

What the reader learns by following Vergil and Dante up the terraces of Mount Purgatory, with its various images drawn from pagan, Hebrew, and Christian writings, is precisely that "it is possible to imitate these things for each group and each nation, using matters that are different in each case."

For al-Fārābi, the philosopher has cognition of the universals, whereas the ordinary believer is persuaded by imagery and rhetoric:

> Most men accept such principles as are accepted and followed, and are magnified and considered majestic, in the form of *images*, not cognitions. Now the ones who follow after happiness as they cognize it and accept the principles as they cognize them, are the wise men. And the ones in whose souls these things are found in the form of *images*, and who accept them and follow after them as such, are the believers.[44]

> Now, these things are philosophy when they are in the soul of the legislator. They are religion when they are in the souls of the multitude. For when the legislator knows these things, they are evident to him by sure insight, whereas what is established in the souls of the multitude is through an *image* and a persuasive argument. . . . The *images* and persuasive arguments are intended for others, whereas, so

far as he is concerned, these things are certain. They are a religion for others, whereas, so far as he is concerned, they are philosophy.[45]

The "things" known and followed by the philosopher through reason and believed and followed by the multitude through images are the same "things." Philosophy and religion are different yet wedded together as two aspects of (two manners of perceiving or being moved by) the same thing.

In *Purgatorio*'s central canto, Vergil gives Dante a philosophical explanation of the intelligible ethical principles that are "imaged" as the Seven Deadly Sins. *Purgatorio* 17 begins with a lengthy insistence on imagination (the whole first half of the canto) and ends with an extended lesson in philosophy (the whole second half). The canto's opening verses are filled with images (mountains, fog, and moles), which are explicitly designated as such: Dante tells the reader to use his or her imagination (*Purg.* 17.7 "la tua *imagine*") to conjure up the scene. In the canto's closing verses, language is now the vehicle of abstract rationality: Vergil tells Dante to reason out for himself the principles underlying Purgatory's three upper terraces (*Purg.* 17.138–39 "ma come tripartito si *ragiona*, / tacciolo, acciò che tu per te ne cerchi"; "but how it is distinguished as threefold / I do not say, that you may search it out for yourself"). The central canto of *Purgatorio* dramatizes a trajectory from *imagine* to *ragione*, from relative blindness (figured by the fog at *Purg.* 17.2 and the moles at *Purg.* 17.3) to insight. This movement from imagination to philosophical understanding is a progressive enlightenment: Dante at first compares himself to one who sees the sun shining weakly through a lifting fog; by the end of the canto he clearly sees the rational structure of Purgatory. This transition from the poetic to the philosophical indicates that the imaginary is grounded in the rational. We see that imagery (e.g., the exempla illustrating the Seven Deadly Sins) functions as a kind of philosophy for those who are non-philosophers. As al-Fārābī remarks in his *Book of Religion*: "Virtuous religion is similar to philosophy. . . . The practical things in religion are those whose universals are in practical philosophy."[46] Vergil understands (and, in his lecture on the fundamentals of moral philosophy at *Purg.* 17.85–18.75, teaches Dante to understand) the practical universals that, in religion, appear as particular "practical things."

As we have seen, Dante frequently points out that the exempla of virtues and vices which structure his journey up through the terraces of Purgatory are images. But even in those many cases in which he does not explicitly call them "images," it is clear that he receives these *exempla* through an event of the prophetic imagination. We can recognize this by bearing in mind two things: first, the strange, extraordinary nature of his perceptions (sometimes visible, sometimes audible, sometimes an unusual combination of the visible and the audible, e.g., the "visibile parlare" mentioned at *Purg.* 10.95, sometimes visible only to the inner eye of the *imaginativa*), which are unlike the usual perceptions of everyday life; second, the fact that these perceptions always occur near the threshold between one terrace and the next and thus always when Dante is close to the angel stationed at that threshold. One can mention here, as instances of the unusual nature of Dante's perceptions, the following: the "speaking spirits" (*Purg.* 13.26 "spiriti parlando") that are "heard but not seen" (*Purg.* 13.25–26 "sentiti / non però visti") as soon as Dante enters the terrace of Envy; the "ecstatic vision" (*Purg.* 15.85–86 "una visïone / estatica") that he experiences upon reaching the terrace of Wrath; the voice that, upon reaching the terrace of Gluttony, Dante hears call out from within some leafy branches (*Purg.* 22.140–41 "una voce per entro le fronde / gridò"); again—this time as Dante is exiting the terrace of Gluttony, and thus close to the threshold where awaits an angel, whom Dante will soon encounter as a voice [*Purg.* 24.134 "voce"] and as a shining [*Purg.* 24.138 "lucenti"] presence—an unidentifiable voice (*Purg.* 24.118 "non so chi diceva") emanating from within the leaves of a tree. This last-mentioned instance, in which Dante's proximity to the angel is manifest, suggests that the angels are the sources of Dante's imaged perceptions of the virtues and vices. This is in fact what we learn in *Purgatorio* 17: the apostrophe to *imaginativa* tells us that the source of those inner visions that Dante repeatedly calls images (*Purg.* 17.21 "ne l'*imagine* mia"; *Purg.* 17.31 "questa *imagine*"; *Purg.* 17.43 "l'*imaginar* mio") is "a light formed in Heaven" (*Purg.* 17.17 "moveti lume che nel ciel s'informa"); then, immediately following the cessation of his imagining, Dante experiences the angel's presence as a "light . . . / far brighter than the light to which we are accustomed" (*Purg.* 17.44–45 "lume . . . / maggior assai che quel ch'è in nostro uso"). Clearly it is the angel [i.e., the Intelligence] that has illuminated Dante's imagination.

Now, the *falasifa*, for whom prophetic revelation was among the most important of topics, characterize it as involving precisely these two elements: strange perceptions—very frequently involving disembodied voices, speech of unidentifiable provenance that does not come, as speech normally does, from a human speaker present to the auditor; and angels as the movers of the imagination and the mediators of divine truth. As Avicenna says:

> The best of people is the one whose soul is perfected by becoming an intellect in act and who attains the morals that constitute practical virtues. The best of the latter is the one ready to attain the rank of prophethood. This is the one who, in his psychological powers, has three distinctive properties which we have mentioned—namely, that he hears the speech of God, exalted be He, and sees His *angels* that have been transformed for him into a form he sees. We have shown the manner of this. We have shown that the *angels* take visible shape for the person who receives revelation and that there occurs in his hearing a voice, coming from the direction of God and His *angels*. He thus *hears it without this being speech from people* and the terrestrial animal. This is the one to whom revelation is given.[47]

As Dante crosses the thresholds of the terraces of Purgatory, his faculty of imagination is the vehicle of prophetic revelation. More precisely, *Purgatorio* dramatizes (as Dante relives) those various events of prophetic imagination by which revelation concerning right practice has been given in the past, to Christians and non-Christians alike.

What happens in prophetic revelation is that the Intelligence, which is a universal and always the same as itself, when it illuminates the imagination of a particular prophet, is mixed with the materiality of the prophet's *imaginativa* and thus rendered particular.[48] Prophets render in particular images, for the communities in which they have been raised, those things that philosophers (such as Vergil) know as universal intelligibles. As Howard Kreisel says, summarizing Judah Halevi's understanding of the variations among the Hebrew prophets:

> The depictions of the entities are figurative ones, the products of the prophet's imagination. They are formed in accordance with the influence of the intellect. The prophet thus sees in the eye of his imagination figures "to which he is accustomed"—that is, the images by means of which the prophetic knowledge is attained is borrowed from the prophet's own experience. . . . The prophets often employ different images in line with their particular historical circumstances. What Halevi is in effect saying is that the prophets affirm that the visions of their fellow prophets are appropriate figurative representations of the divine world, and it is clear that all

these visions are pointing to the same truths. . . . Just as the Active
Intellect's emanation to the imagination results in true visions
without it determining the actual figurative forms that are beheld by
the prophets in the philosophers view, so is God's role in prophecy in
the view of Halevi.[49]

Dante's prophetic experiences as he ascends Mount Purgatory are meant
to represent the underlying process common to all such prophetic experience. Prophecy is the reception in the imagination (and thus in a material and historically determined form) of what the philosopher knows
through practical intellect.[50] *Purgatorio*'s central canto shows us that
behind the curtain of the language of religious revelation stands Vergil,
with his philosopher's cognition of practical wisdom.

Once one has seen that Vergil's philosophy and the religious imagination revealed through prophecy are wedded together as two aspects
of the same truth, one can no longer claim without qualification that
Vergil stands outside, or prior to, religious revelation. Rather, Vergil's
relation to revelation is like the relation between al-Fārābi's philosopher and the Law: the universal intelligibles known by Vergil are the
very foundation of religious ethics. As Vergil tells Dante, moral philosophers, through "reasoning, reached the foundation" (*Purg.* 18.67 "ra-
gionando andaro al fondo"), the Law's source and essential truth.

But if Vergil, far from being alien to revelation, is in fact its intelligible foundation, this applies *only* when what is at stake is a matter of
praxis. This fact is in itself another reason why *Purgatory* 17 insists so
strongly on the bond between imagination and Vergil's practical intellect. For, as Averroës maintains, the faculty of practical intellect and
the faculty of imagination are inextricably wedded together: *practical
intelligibles are always linked with images*.[51]

The distinction between *theoria* and *praxis* is essential to the structure of the *Commedia*. Theory concerns those things that *are what they
are* entirely independent of human activity, while practice concerns
those things that humans themselves make or do. Dante describes this
distinction as the difference between things that are "outside human
control" (theoretical) and those that are "within our control" (practical).[52]
Theoretical knowledge, as al-Fārābi says, concerns things "whose existence and constitution owe nothing at all to human artifice")—things
such as "the celestial substances" (i.e., the stars and planets) and "the im-
material existents" (i.e., intelligences or angels).[53] But the paradigmatic

and ultimate object of theory is God—the highest of those beings that is what it is in complete independence of human activity. While God is the ultimate object of theoretical knowledge, the ultimate object of practical knowledge—the highest of those things that are "within our control"—is the perfect political state. In the *Commedia*, Vergil guides when the issue at stake is *praxis*, and Beatrice guides when the issue at stake is *theoria*. Beatrice's surpassing of Vergil in the itinerary of the *Commedia* does not signify the fact that Christian truth surpasses philosophy, for she herself *is* a philosopher. Vergil and Beatrice embody, respectively, the philosophical concern for things "within our control" and the philosophical concern for things "outside human control."

To analyze the implications of the distinction between *praxis* (which is a matter of right and wrong and pertains to the human) and *theoria* (which is a matter of true and false and pertains especially to the divine) lies beyond the scope of the present essay.[54] Suffice it to say that, reading the *Commedia* philosophically, one sees that the division of labor between Vergil and Beatrice is not a division between philosophy and religion, between reason and faith. Rather, it is a division *within* philosophy between two kinds of intellect: the practical intellect and the theoretical intellect. Beatrice guides in the realm of theory, whether the objects of theory happen to be disclosed in philosophical or in religious language. Vergil guides in the realm of practice, whether the principles of practice happen to be known philosophically or imagined religiously. Vergil's teaching, as the foundation for the formation of the perfect political state (Dante's monarchy), is addressed to all humans, since the peaceful civil society is meant for everyone. Beatrice addresses an elite group (*Par.* 2.10 "voi altri pochi"; "you other few"), those born with and having developed the potential eventually to *trasumanar* (*Par.* 1.70 "go beyond what is human"). As Averroës says, "practical understanding is common to all but knowing [i.e., theoretical knowledge] is not."[55] And, if Averroës is right that every revelation has intellect mixed in (in other words, that every religion contains philosophy), then we can say that Vergil's revelation (*Purgatorio*) has practical intellect mixed with it and is meant for all humans, whereas Beatrice's revelation (*Paradiso*) has theoretical (i.e., speculative) intellect mixed with it and is meant for a happy few.

Falconry as a Transmutative Art: Dante, Frederick II, and Islam

DANIELA BOCCASSINI

Dante's Purgatorio *and the Phenomenology of Falconry*

When Dante the pilgrim is about to turn his gaze toward the first penitent souls he encounters in *Purgatorio,* Dante the author interrupts the
narrative and addresses the reader. You should not, he argues,
"smagar[ti]/di buon proponimento" (*Purg.* 10.106–7 "be turned from
good resolution") as you hear what the "*forma* del martire" (*Purg.* 10.109
"form of suffering") is; you should instead focus on "la succession" (*Purg.*
10.110 "what follows"): the utter certainty that these souls *are* saved—no
matter how frightening their present "martire" ("suffering").

The reader is thus left to contemplate the dilemma that Dante has
just put into focus.[1] If these souls really *are* saved, why do they need to be
tortured? What lies between their future status as blessed-souls-to-be
and their current condition of saved yet suffering souls is precisely a re-
lentless process of penance *and* ascent, by means of which they will eventually become the magnificent creatures Dante so deftly evokes shortly
thereafter, the "angelica farfalla/che vola a la giustizia sanza schermi"
(*Purg.* 10.125–26 "the angelic butterfly/that flies without defenses toward
justice"). What has to occur, in sum, is nothing short of a metamorphic
miracle—a miracle intended to transmute a living soul into what nature,
or rather divinity, had meant it to become in the first place.[2]

Purgatory is unquestionably Dante's "newest" invention in the *Commedia.*[3] Hell and Paradise, traditionally the two opposite and self-excluding
loci of the beyond, were places that all Western cultures—classical,
Hebrew, Christian, and Islamic[4]—had previously visualized in their
own ways.[5] Each tradition had borrowed from the others, or argued
against them, in order to offer their followers images of the beyond

designed to instill fear of punishment, or hope of reward. While building on previous mappings of these two realms, Dante unquestionably creates his own unique version of each.[6] In particular, debate on the subject of Dante's alleged borrowings from the Muslim *mi'rāj* has flourished, and even at times become heated, without producing much in the way of agreement.[7]

Leaving aside issues pertaining to the realms of the damned and the saved, I will focus on the *Commedia*'s middle canticle in the attempt to understand first what cultural and ethical motives led Dante to give this intermediate realm the peculiar, and wholly positive, figurative form of a mountain to ascend and, second, what overarching theme sustained him in his enterprise. As has often been noted, *Purgatorio* is the canticle that most ostensibly mirrors the condition of human beings on earth, caught as they are between the often unbearable burden of their past actions and the uncertainty of the outcome of their lives. And this is also the canticle that provides the blueprint for Dante's own journey of inner transmutation—hence, salvation—a journey he takes upon himself to narrate so that his readers might do the same.[8]

Until Dante's time, the notion of a purgatorial fire was the only possibility envisaged by the Church as a temporary alternative to the definitive opposites of damnation and salvation, a path Dante clearly did not choose to follow in his visualization of the middle realm.[9] Rather, walking through a wall of fire will be, for Dante the wayfarer, the *culmination* of a process of ascent implying *inner* transformation through (a witnessing of the souls') *outer* coercion.[10] This process completed, Dante finds himself able to "soar" to the earthly Paradise (as presumably do all souls, once their purgation is complete) rather than helplessly scramble toward it as he did at the beginning of his ascent of the mountain—thus fulfilling the announcement made by Vergil at the outset of their laborious, initially ineffectual climb.[11]

If learning how to soar is the purpose of Purgatory (in preparation, one could argue, for Paradise), the stress Dante puts on the issue of divine art versus human art in the encounters with the proud on the first terrace makes clear that, in order to become saved souls, humans need to learn not just any kind of soaring,[12] but rather that particular *art* of soaring which will allow them to ascend toward God, like a butterfly leaving its chrysalis behind—or, as I presently argue, like a tamed falcon "ch'esce dal cappello" (*Par.* 19.34 "set free from its hood") at the falconer's command.

Upon reaching Purgatory's second terrace, Dante sheds tears of compassion in witnessing the kind of blindness imposed by Divine Justice on the envious to discipline them. This is in fact no ordinary, no "natural" form of blindness, but one that belongs to the preliminary procedures of the most sophisticated of all arts of taming: the art of falconry. In this perspective, the "seeling" of the souls' eyelids ought to be understood—figuratively, but at some level also literally—not as a punishment in and of itself, but rather as a redemptive device, and hence as an act of love which the penitent souls should learn to recognize as such. As we shall see in more detail soon, this is in fact *the* technique chosen by Divine Providence to enable the souls of the envious to learn to hear God's call so that they may eventually respond to it, in the same way that wild falcons are taught, through their forced blindness, to respond to the presence of the falconer and heed his call.[13]

Dante's Falconry in Context

If, as I believe, Dante saw both the condition of the penitent souls *and*, even more cogently, his own "taming" at the hands of Vergil, as a transmutative process most aptly understood in terms of falconry, then we should ask ourselves three questions. First, where and how did he become acquainted with the technical/textual aspects of falconry? Second, what ideological reasons or intercultural motives led him to adopt such a peculiar image as the most appropriate for his intermediate canticle?[14] Third, knowing Dante's highly distinctive way of handling any preexisting "given," how did his reworking of the theme of falconry fit his own inner vision in relation to the larger scenery of the Mediterranean world? There, after all, falconry had long generated its own "interdiscursivity," not only as a technique, but also as a symbolic construct.

Because this investigation entails by its very nature the study of Dante's text in its connections with multiple aspects of the medieval art of falconry, it may be useful to call on the "methods of approach" ("modi dell'approccio") that Maria Corti outlined in her attempt to probe the thorny issue of Dante's engagement with Islamic culture.[15] As will soon become apparent, an understanding of falconry symbolism in the *Commedia* contributes to a renewed appreciation of Dante's interest in Islamic lore.

Corti groups her observations in three separate yet complementary "methodological possibilities" ("possibilità metodologiche"):

> Prima: esistono nella cultura dell'epoca di Dante dei processi di *interdiscorsività*, cioè di circolazione fra i mondi culturali, per cui un dato, una notizia, un vocabolo tecnico divengono patrimonio comune in seguito appunto alla compenetrazione interdiscorsiva. In tali casi è impossibile, oltre che pericoloso, individuare una fonte diretta. Seconda possibilità: vi sono fenomeni definiti *intertestuali*, per cui può accadere che un testo x offra un modello di struttura a un testo y, come dire un modello analogico, il che non significa che il testo x sia necessariamente fonte di y, cioè che l'autore di y abbia letto, avuto sotto gli occhi il primo testo; può averne letto un riassunto, che già disegni la struttura, o averne udito un riassunto orale. . . . Terza possibilità: il testo arabo che si propone è, a parere dello studioso, *fonte diretta* di un'opera di Dante. In tale felice caso la derivazione dal testo arabo va provata dapprima con ragioni di storia letteraria (traduzione in latino o francese antico dal testo arabo; sua conoscenza nel contesto letterario dantesco). Successivamente va provata una corrispondenza non solo tematica, ma formale: estesa, perché non sia casuale, e isomorfa.

First possibility: in the culture of Dante's period there are processes of *interdiscursivity*, that is to say a circulation between cultural worlds, by which information, or a technical term, becomes common heritage immediately after the interdiscursive penetration. In such cases it is impossible, if not dangerous, to locate a direct source. Second possibility: there are definite *intertextual* phenomena, so it can happen that a text x offers a structural model to a text y, as an analogical model, which does not mean that text x is necessarily a source of y, that the author of y has read the text and had the first text in front of him, but he may have read a summary outlining the structure, or heard an oral summary. . . . Third possibility: the proposed Arabic text is, in the opinion of the scholar, a *direct source* of a work by Dante. In such a felicitous circumstance, the derivation from the Arabic text should be tested first by means of literary history (in Latin or Old French translations from the Arabic text; its currency in the literary context of Dante). Then not only a thematic, but a formal correspondence will be proven: a full parallel, because it is not random, and because it is isomorphic.[16]

Clearly these three "possible connections" ("possibilità di rapporto") between texts are meant to trace a progression from oral to written, from borrowing to source, from general to specific, from coincidental to deliberate. The underlying assumption is the old "philological golden rule," with which Corti no doubt wrestles, but to which she ultimately succumbs: thou shalt deem worth discussing nothing but the evidence of a direct textual source.

While I find Corti's categories useful, I also believe that we need to employ them differently. I will therefore reverse their order, so as to proceed from the textual to the intertextual to the discursive. By means of this reversal I intend to question the primacy of the "philological golden rule" as a parameter for inquiries that are inter- and multicultural in nature and thus ultimately to mitigate the (ideological?) strictures traditionally attached to an exclusively philological approach. Thus, rather than get caught between the rock of Dante's canonized originality and the hard place of his possible dependence on an ideologically objectionable "source," I will sail toward the open waters of the Mediterranean—where Dante's unique achievements may stand a chance to appear in the larger dialogical scenery of the multifaceted cultures that helped to shape his work, his mind, and his world.

"FONTE DIRETTA": DANTE'S TECHNICAL/TEXTUAL KNOWLEDGE OF FALCONRY

Although it is unlikely that Dante *practiced* falconry himself, we can rest assured that he saw it practiced—and close up. Where and by whom is the next question.

Dante's first references to falconry appear in the *canzoni* "Tre donne intorno al cor" (Three Ladies in My Heart), and "Doglia mi reca" (Leave, My Sorrow). This seems to indicate that Dante may have "discovered" falconry, along with its figurative potential, soon after he was exiled—more specifically via one of the two lords who hosted him at the time and whose "courtly" conduct he contrasts with the "savage" behavior of the Florentines.[17] As a guest of Scarpetta Odelaffi in Forlì and of Bartolomeo della Scala in Verona, Dante found himself in a Ghibelline milieu—among heads of a political coalition who still lived in the wake of Frederick

II and his royal habits, the most peculiar of which was, as we shall see in more detail below, the practice of falconry.[18]

Considering that Frederick II's many falconers must have sought (and found) employment among the rulers of northern Italy after Frederick's and Manfred's deaths and the demise of the Hohenstaufen curia, there is reason to believe that in the second half of the Duecento (i.e., the thirteenth century) falconry remained a practice that distinguished if not Guelfs from Ghibellines, then certainly urban, communal *gente nova* from the rulers of north Italian courts, where "solea valore e cortesia trovarsi / prima che Federico avesse briga" (*Purg.* 16.116–117 "valor and courtesy were once to be found / before Frederick met with strife")—and presumably for some decades after as well.[19] Not by coincidence, perhaps, the months following his stays in Forlì and Verona were also the time when Dante, having developed an increased awareness of the larger Italian political scene, decided to distance himself from the Whites so as to become "parte per [se] stesso" (*Par.* 17.69 "a party unto [him]self").[20]

As I mentioned earlier, in Canto 13 of *Purgatorio* Dante refers to the "seeling" of the envious' eyelids, not merely by naming this falconry technique but also by explaining it in technical detail:

> E come a li orbi non approda il sole,
> così a l'ombre quivi ond'io parlo ora
> luce del ciel di sé largir non vole:
> ché a tutti un fil di ferro i cigli fora
> e cusce sì come a sparvier selvaggio
> si fa però che queto non dimora.

> And even as the sun appears not to the blind,
> so to the shades in the place I speak of,
> Heaven's light denies its bounty,
> for all their eyelids an iron wire pierces
> and sews up, as is done to an untamed
> hawk, because it stays not quiet.
>
> (*Purg.* 13.67–72)

How did Dante learn about *ciliatio* ("seeling") in the first place, and why would he go to such lengths in depicting it for his readers? The practice of seeling falcons is meticulously described by Frederick II in his *De arte venandi cum avibus*, although it is not to be found in any other Western treatise. One could argue that no other treatise was at the time as detailed as Frederick's, yet if such an exacting practice had been current among Western falconers, we should expect to find at least cursory references to it elsewhere. However, the only other known reference appears in *Moamin*, a short Arabic treatise translated by Frederick II's philosopher Theodore of Antioch during the late 1230s. Furthermore, *ciliatio* was (and still is) a current practice among Arabic falconers (as its occurrence in *Moamin* attests). We can thus infer that Frederick II derived the technique of seeling falcons from the Arabs, along with other procedures on whose provenance he is quite explicit. Once he became convinced of its usefulness by testing it with his own birds, he proceeded to include it in his treatise and standardized the practice among his falconers.[21]

Dante's precise description of the seeling of the souls in *Purgatorio* seems to indicate the poet's awareness of the fact that not very many people in the peninsula were acquainted with this Frederician taming technique of Islamic origin. Did Dante learn about Arabic techniques such as *ciliatio*, or Persian ones such as the *capellum* ("hooding"),[22] from reading Frederick's treatise on falconry? Although this possibility cannot be ruled out, it is unlikely, as there is no documentary evidence that the massive *De arte venandi* ever circulated among north Italian rulers.[23] We may, however, easily visualize Dante watching falconers seeling falcons in one of the courts where he sojourned as a guest—and imagine perhaps that one of the falconers told him how he learned such a technique from one of his teachers in the emperor's service.[24]

In other words, from a technical/textual point of view, Dante's knowledge of falconry is objectively grounded in Hohenstaufen practices, even if Dante does not make any explicit reference to Frederick's treatise on falconry. For at least two falconry images highly relevant within the *Commedia*'s inner structure (seeling and hooding, on which more below), it is possible to indicate a direct link to Frederick II's practices, which in turn originated from the emperor's contacts with, and avid study of, Islamic falconry techniques.[25] While we cannot demonstrate Dante's *awareness* that these Frederician practices were of Islamic origin, it seems beyond doubt that there exists a direct connection between Dante's interest in the imagery of falconry and the Ghibelline heritage of curial practices related to an ideal of imperial sovereignty advocated by Frederick II in his *De arte venandi*.

INTERTEXTUALITY: DANTE'S ANALOGICAL FRAMEWORK
AND FREDERICK II'S FALCONRY VISION

We have, at best, scanty documentary records with regard to falconry in northern Italy in the years of Dante's exile. Paradoxically, the *Commedia* itself, through the richness of its references, testifies to the spread and consequence of this art among Dante's patrons more accurately than any other written or visual evidence we presently know of or may ever hope to identify.

One would like to imagine in particular that some of the splendor of Frederick's falconry practices lived on in Verona, where the Della Scalas had assumed the role of Ghibelline leaders.[26] Such may have been the case. In his poem *Bisbidis*, written to honor Cangrande, Immanuel Romano (or Manoello Giudeo, referred to as Dante's "Jewish friend") includes falcons and falconers among the wonders epitomizing the distinctiveness of this ruler's court:[27]

> Li falconi cui cui,   li bracchetti gu gu,
> li levrieri guuu uu,   per volersi sfugare.
> Qui falconieri,   maestri et scudieri,
> ragazzi et corrieri,   ciascun per sè andare.
> Et quanto et quanto   et quanto et quanto
> et quanto et quanto   li vedi spaz[i]are!

> The falcons screech screech,   the beagles bark bark,
> the greyhounds growl growl,   yearning for release.
> Their falconers, masters and squires,
> boys and runners,   each walk among them.
> And how much and   much and much and much
> And much and much   you see them swoop!
>   (101–12)[28]

Taken out of context, such references are so generic as to be virtually meaningless. Read within the poem, though, they help to project the aura of a court Frederician in flavor—complete with a zoo of exotic animals, open to wayfarers of any provenance, exiles from Guelph cities, and religious, political, or ethnic refugees of all kind, who were encouraged to share their thoughts in an atmosphere of acceptance, if not tolerance:

> Baroni et Marchesi   de tutti i paesi,
> gentili et cortesi qui vedi arrivare.

Quivi astrologia con Philosophia
et di Teologia   udrai disputare.
Quivi Tedeschi Latini et Franceschi
Fiammenghi e Ingheleschi   insieme parlare;

Barons and Marquises   of all countries,
genteel and noble,   you see arrive here.
Here you will hear   astrology dispute
with Philosophy and Theology.
Here Germans, Latins and Frenchmen,
Flemings and English   converse together;

(65–76)

Qui babbuini,   Romei et pellegrini,
Giudei et Sarracini   vedrai capitare

Here baboons,   Romans and pilgrims,
Jews and Saracens   you will see come together.

(121–24)[29]

Nor can we discount Dante's own recognition of the Della Scala brothers, Bartolomeo and Cangrande, who hosted him in 1303–4 and 1313, respectively. Their generosity toward him and other refugees, as well as their feats as rulers, shine—in Cacciaguida's prophecy—from under the wings of the imperial "santo uccello" (*Par.* 17.72 "sacred bird"),[30] against the murky backdrop of Clement V's vile betrayal of Henry VII (see *Par.* 17.79–93). As for Cangrande in particular, in the opening of his renowned *Epistola* 13, Dante refers to his wisdom as a ruler and magnificence as a sovereign in Solomonic terms. In so doing, Dante employs an imagery that harks back to the imperial rhetoric of the Hohenstaufen and, beyond that, to the Islamic understanding of sovereignty—one steeped, unsurprisingly, in the practice and symbolism of falconry.[31]

The very image of the imperial eagle had reached the Romans from the East. In Mazdaic and Sasanian traditions, the bird of prey represented the lord's sovereignty, wisdom, and power as emanating from a transcendental source and reaching down from the heavens into the realm of immanence. Such mythical birds were unrelated to falconry per se. However, once this iconography became integrated in the culture of the Arabic Islamic world, where the practice of taming birds of prey had long been widespread, the fusion of the symbolic and the cultural contributed to falconry's becoming the sovereign art par excellence. In this new context, the bird on the fist was still the sign of a superior wisdom, but now it was not so much received from above as it was acquired through the act of taming—taming the wild bird, and through that process, taming also one's own innermost self.[32]

Frederick II inherited from his Norman ancestors, and vigorously embraced, the blending of the symbolic potential of falconry with the traditional imagery of the imperial eagle of ancient Eastern origin. To see how, let us focus for a moment on the Stupor Mundi's accomplishments in falconry matters.

I shall deal first with Frederick II's desire to collect the best treatises available. Although we do not know exactly how many he managed to obtain, we know that he entrusted his personal philosopher, Theodore of Antioch, with the translation of two of these texts from Arabic into Latin. These two treatises, known in the West by the names of their Islamic authors, *Moamin* and *Ghatrif*, respectively, were widely circulated throughout Europe until the Renaissance. Today they are ranked among the most authoritative Islamic treatises on the subject. In fact, they were composed in the ninth century at the 'Abbasid court of Baghdad, where, thanks to the presence at court of numerous Iranian falconers, a superior tradition of falconry thrived.[33] By no means coincidentally, Frederick II would pride himself on doing much the same thing *chez lui*: as he repeatedly declares in *De arte venandi*, he regularly invited Islamic falconers to his court to learn from them directly.[34]

Second, more than any other Western ruler before (or, indeed, after) him, Frederick II advocated a daily practice of the art: this included closely observing the habits of birds (both those hunted and those doing the hunt), as well as testing various methods for taming and recalling birds of prey. This, he believed, would allow him to comprehend the world and his own place in it—better than would any other practice, science, and perhaps even religious doctrine. What Frederick intended to master was nothing less than an understanding of the workings of nature both in the animal world and in the human realm, so as to excel in the art that, to him, was eminently the emperor's own: that of taming, through the power of reason, the mind of nature *and* the human mind.[35]

Clearly, Frederick II superposed and merged two distinct concepts: the *dignitas hominis* within the created universe, on the one hand; and the supremacy of the ruler within the political realm, on the other. But

what truly stood out as original in the Swabian emperor's political philosophy was the fact that he established an actual analogy between
those well-known philosophical abstractions and the tangible workings of the art of falconry. Such an epistemological shift triggered, in
turn, a new approach to the morphological and technical aspects of
falconry, which were now legitimately considered the foundations of
an art that was noble as well as ennobling.

The imperial eagle—notably, in the form handed down by the Romans to later generations of European rulers—is the hypostasis of an
absolute power conceived as "naturally" divine in origin. In contrast,
the tamed falcon, at rest on the emperor's fist or being offered to him
by his falconers, became for Frederick II the emblem of an *acquired*
form of wisdom—of a nobility, that is, which must be educated so that
its inborn aggressiveness may be restrained and redeployed under the
superior command of reason. The falconer thereby becomes the image
of the ideal sovereign, he who succeeds in controlling the instinctive
aggressiveness of humankind by way of his "taming power." He is at
one and the same time the self-aware and responsible repository of natural law and the guarantor of positive law, that is, of justice. The study
and practice of falconry were therefore for Frederick II the best and
noblest ways for the sovereign to deepen his understanding of the laws
of the natural and of the human realm; to him they were indispensable
tools in his honorably dispatching his mission as universal sovereign.

Frederick's book of laws, the *Liber augustalis* or Constitutions of
Melfi (1231), states that universal peace and justice can only be achieved
through reason. Reason is the instrument entrusted by Divine Providence to sovereigns for leading humanity back to the state of perfection it possessed before the Fall. In this view, reason and law play in the
secular world a role parallel to that which Christ's redemption performs
at the eschatological level: accomplishing the *opus restaurationis* ("work
of restoration") which allows humankind to reach back to its primeval,
unspoiled *opus conditionis* ("work of creation [or foundation]"). This
political philosophy finds its most poignant symbol in the image of the
falconer, who trains the noble bird of prey to subject itself willingly to
the rule of reason so as to reach a higher degree of accomplishment than
it would ever do in nature.

Regardless of what the emperor's detractors claimed and in spite of
the actions he undertook in the face of the challenges he met during
the last years of his reign, there is no question that by identifying with

the figure of the falconer, Frederick wished above all to stress the importance, for himself and humankind at large, of the principle of self-taming, that is, self-education, which, at least as he conceived it, was implicit in the very act of ruling as a universal monarch.

Although I can adduce no textual proof (no "direct source," in Corti's terms) in support of this observation, I do believe that Dante developed a keen awareness of Frederick's understanding of imperial power as an act of taming. As we have seen, more than likely it was this very understanding that elicited Dante's own interest in the symbolic potential of falconry shortly after his exile. That, however, is just the beginning, for—and this is what really matters—through such a process of in-depth assessment of the emperor's worldview, Dante in turn undertook a radical critique of *that* notion of falconry as the epitome of the process of self-taming.

Despite the exemplary role he conferred to Frederick II as an earthly monarch, from the eschatological viewpoint Dante eventually condemns him to the depths of Hell, as foremost among those "che l'anima col corpo morta fanno" (*Inf.* 10.15 "who make the soul die with the body"). Not even allowing him, as the last among the universal sovereigns, a chance to state his own view regarding the eternity he seemingly disdained in life, Dante simply has Farinata evoke the emperor's name, almost in passing, at the very end of his exchange with Dante (*Inf.* 10.118–20).[36]

In this respect, it may be no coincidence if the *Commedia* introduces two revealing references to the transmutative worldview in locations numerologically correlated to Frederick's infernal "nomination"; they obviously contrast with the emperor's philosophical position and implicitly correct it. The first of these is to be found at the end of *Purgatorio* 10 (121–29), where Dante addresses those proud Christians who refused to believe in God's transmutative powers and rebukes them by using the image of the butterfly I have already alluded to. The second occurs in the three *terzine* that Dante dedicates to "l'anima santa che 'l mondo fallace / fa manifesto a chi di lei ben ode" (*Par.* 10.125–26 "the sainted soul who makes the fallacious world / manifest to any who listen to him")—none other than Boethius of Dacia and the transmutative book he authored while languishing in the exile of his unjust imprisonment at the hands of a sovereign turned tyrant, just like Frederick II had been toward Pier della Vigna.

Dante's condemnation of Frederick II to Hell was determined by what the poet considered to have been the emperor's ultimate blindness to—and transgression of—the most sacred core of the art of falconry, namely, the transmutative taming of one's instinctive pride as the only appropriate means of celebrating not the power of an absolute earthly monarch but rather "la gloria di colui che tutto move" (*Par.* 1.1 "the glory of the One who moves all"). From this point of view, Dante's understanding of falconry was strikingly similar to that of some of the greatest mystic poets of the medieval Islamic world.

INTERDISCURSIVITY: MEDITERRANEAN AND ISLAMIC FALCONRY SYMBOLISM

To my knowledge, no text in Western medieval culture other than the *Commedia* turns the image of falconry into an overarching theme of symbolic import. The one exception is Frederick II's *De arte venandi*, which, being a technical treatise, simply does not compare with Dante's poetic and visionary endeavor. Nevertheless, it is only after becoming conversant with Frederick's treatise that one can fully comprehend the importance and the careful layout of falconry imagery in Dante's *Commedia*. This in turn makes one realize the logic behind the scarcity of philosophical elaboration about falconry in Western medieval literature: since the ideological postulates of this art have deep-seated Eastern (for our purposes, Islamic) roots, they were bound to seem foreign to Western culture—outside the Frederician area of influence, that is.

Dante's figurative use of falconry in the *Commedia* should therefore be understood as his own interpretation of the symbolic potential of this art—the result of an "interdiscursivity" where, as Corti rightly sees, there can be scant hope of identifying borrowings, direct or indirect, with any precision. And yet, would our appreciation of Dante's achievements not be enhanced if we could project them against the backdrop of a reality created out of a multitude of other voices, no matter how remote from Dante's own? Did our understanding of Frederick's descant to Dante's own song not produce a powerful form of hermeneutical counterpoint?

Here, I shall limit myself to discussing three Islamic authors of canonical rank, one or two generations older than Dante, whose achievements as first-rate poets are acknowledged in the West as well.

Farīd od-Dīn 'Aṭṭār, a Sufi Persian poet active in the late twelfth and early thirteenth centuries (d. 1210–1230), stresses the importance of cleansing one's mind of its worldly components so as to direct it onto the path leading to the realm of the Lord—the mysterious and distant Simurgh. In his celebrated poem *Manṭeq al-Ṭayr* (Conference of the Birds) this process of self-transformation applies in various ways to all species of birds; but when it comes to the falcon, it is the power of the transmutative arts of taming that 'Aṭṭār evokes as a means of conversion. Such arts should in fact be understood as the earthly manifestation of the Supreme Lord's transcendental love:

> Rare falcon, welcome! How long will you be
> So fiercely jealous of your liberty?
> Your lure is love, and when the jess is tied,
> Submit, and be forever satisfied.
> Give up the intellect for love, and see
> In one brief moment all eternity;
> Break nature's frame, be resolute and brave,
> Then rest at peace in Unity's black cave [i.e., the "seeling"].
> Rejoice in that close, undisturbed dark air—
> The Prophet will be your companion there.[37]

Muḥammad Ibn al-'Arabī (1165–1240), who lived in Moorish al-Andalus, is perhaps best known among Dantists for having been signaled as one of Dante's possible "sources"—although no direct connection has so far been traced back to any of his writings.[38] I will not allude here to Ibn al-'Arabī's various inner *mi'rāj* and the interest they hold, as refined versions of the rougher *Liber scale Machometi*, with regard to the issue of the *Commedia*'s Islamic sources.[39] Nor shall I dwell on the appeal that Ibn al-'Arabī's *Tarjumān al-ashwāq* (The Interpreter of Desires) presents in relation to Dante's *Vita nuova*.[40] I will focus only on a single passage in the last-mentioned book and on one specific falconry image that Ibn al-'Arabī discusses in his own commentary to his poem. Dante visualizes that very image when Bonagiunta, in *Purgatorio* 24.55–60, voices to Dante the pilgrim his belated understanding of the knot which, in life, prevented him from following freely in the tracks of the *dittator*'s own soaring flight.[41]

In the *Tarjumān* Ibn al-'Arabī presents himself as a young lover-adept of divine beauty and wisdom. At one point in his crossing of the desert, he wishes to follow some enlightened travelers he has just chanced upon during his journey. However, he is prevented from doing so by these same beings, aware as they are of the fact that the poet-lover has not yet accomplished his earthly training. In his commentary Ibn al-'Arabī evokes falconry images in order to elaborate on the predicament of the young poet-lover:

> Son cœur prend, dès lors, son essor en voyageant derrière eux, comme le faucon attaché par une patte sur son perchoir et qui prend son envol par désir de s'élancer dans l'immensité des couches atmosphériques; cette attache le retient près de son perchoir. Il en est de même du lien qui maintient l'aspect subtil de cet amant pour qu'il gère cet habitacle corporel, attache comparable au perchoir du faucon, et qui le retient tant que Dieu l'ordonne.

> His heart rises up as it travels behind them, like the falcon tied by one leg to his perch that takes off out of a desire to launch itself into the vastness of the atmospheric layers; and this clip holds it near its perch. It is the same link that maintains the subtle appearance of this lover, on account of which he carries this corporal dwelling, attached in a manner similar to the falcon, which holds him as God directs.[42]

The best known and best loved among Sufi poets is undoubtedly Jalāl ad-Dīn ar-Rūmī, a Persian by birth who lived his adult life in Konya (Asia Minor) under Seljuk rule (1207–73) and whose mission may be described as the opening of poetry to the universal dimension of divine salvation for humankind. At a time and in a geographical context that no doubt lent themselves to either conflict or concord with neighboring religious traditions, Rūmī fervently chose the latter. Although resting firmly within the grounds of his own faith, he grasped and manifested in his spiritual teachings that higher, universal unity of the divine, which each established religious tradition casts in its own mold.[43] He also stressed the necessity of a process of inward transformation for the disciples, as *the* way for them to attain their higher nature and, ultimately, merge into God's.

Falconry images loom large in Rūmī's poetry. One of his favorite topoi is the image of the falcon as already tamed, single-heartedly devoted to returning to his lord's hand:[44]

> I am thy falcon, I am thy falcon, when I hear thy drum, O my king and Shahensha, my feather and wing come back.[45]

In his *Fīhī mā fīh* (Discourses) Rūmī discloses the very reason why we should consider the art of taming a bird of prey as an act of absolutely selfless, purely divine love:

> When someone lays a trap and catches little birds to eat and sell, that is called cunning. But if a king lays a trap to capture an untutored and worthless hawk, having no knowledge of its own true nature, to train it to his own forearm so that it may become ennobled, that is not called cunning. Though to outward appearance it is cunning, yet it is known to be the very acme of caring and generosity, restoring the dead to life, converting the base stone into a ruby, and far more than that. If the hawk knew for what reason the king wanted to capture him, it would not require any bait. It would search for the trap with soul and heart, and would fly to the king's hand.[46]

Had Dante been able to read this passage by Rūmī, he would have smiled approvingly.

Dante's Purgatorio *and Falconry as a Transmutative Art*

As I hope this last quotation from Rūmī makes clear, flying away from the safe yet constrained pond of the "fonte diretta" toward the open and no doubt challenging sea of the "interdiscursive" realm is a risk well worth taking. Such an approach allows us to sight what would otherwise remain inaccessible—literally invisible to a short-sighted mind's eye. That long-range vision is, I submit, nothing less than the very grounding of Dante's poetic enterprise; it is the hallmark of the *Commedia*'s stance in the intermediate, visionary realm of the "imaginal"[47]—a realm Christian Moevs has explored in his study of the poem's "metaphysics": "the awakening of the ultimate ontological principle to itself in us, which is revelation, or, in Christian terms, to know or receive Christ."[48] If the objective of the *Commedia* is to save humankind from itself and principally from its self-imposed rapaciousness,[49] then we can usefully ask ourselves which figurative means Dante could call upon to evoke a process of taming and conversion that by its very nature aims at transmuting the individual's instinctive ego-grasping into an artfully acquired—but nevertheless also gracefully received—form of absolute surrender and self-sacrifice to the highest manifestation of selflessness and boundless love. How are we to visualize the very nature of a learning process that must be experiential if it is to become effective? Such is, after all, the goal of the *Commedia* as a whole—in direct opposition, that is, to the treacherous attempts at rational grappling with reality, which leave human pride misleadingly in charge of transcendent affairs. While in our postmodern world of concept-based existence there seems to be little or nothing to call upon in order to suggest such a salvific becoming, I hope to have shown persuasively that Dante saw in falconry the art most apt to express that process of surrender and taming of an individual's own nature, in the form of a *return* to that very "hand" on whose universal fist the whole world is unknowingly perched.

For Dante, no art better than falconry could convey the sense of that sacrificial inner transmutation necessary for human consciousness to awaken to the vision of itself as a pure reflection of the transcendental source of all-encompassing love. No other art could as powerfully express the potential for universal salvation inscribed within a process meant to make human consciousness cognizant of its own divine origin—of its own participation in, and belonging to the very substance offered by the falconer to the falcon as its only rightful meal, as that "bread of angels" already evoked in the *Convivio*: purely celestial food, on which life itself unsuspectingly keeps feeding.

My principal aim so far has been to substantiate my contention that the art of falconry, along with its powerful symbolic potential, was a practice shared among Mediterranean cultures at the time. In this perspective, Dante's choice of falconry stands out as a central metaphorical component of his pilgrim's journey of conversion. Falconry is called upon to enact visually the universal potential that Dante, as poet and prophet, intended to ascribe to his transmutative poem.

But there is more. If in Dante's *Purgatorio* falconry techniques as images of inner growth apply to Dante the pilgrim, they do so just as fittingly for the souls undergoing penance. I have already discussed in some detail the case of the envious to be trained, through the seeling of their eyelids, for the hand of God. And we should equally bear in mind that the souls of the blessed—whose taming process is obviously completed—respond to Dante's question about God's justice with an eagerness comparable only to the proud countenance of a falcon suddenly freed from its hood: "Quasi falcone ch'esce del cappello, / move la testa e con l'ali si plaude, / voglia mostrando e faccendosi bello" (*Par.* 19.34–36 "As the falcon which, issuing from the hood / moves his head and flaps his wings / showing his will and making himself fine"). These very souls, who appear to Dante in the form of a celestial eagle, declare themselves blind to the depths of God's vision and ignorant of the un-fathomable workings of predestination (*Par.* 20.134–38). No reader fails to see that the eagle's very eye is made of souls that lived on earth both before and after the advent of Christ; and yet very few seem ever to notice the dramatic irony contained in that eye's—those blessed souls'—ultimate blindness.

The warning is therefore unambiguous: humans must learn to sus-pend all judgment with regard to God's justice. It is unthinkable for those on earth to scrutinize the unfolding of events "dentro al consi-glio divino" (*Par.* 13.141 "within the divine plan") when even blessed souls in Heaven are in a state comparable to that of a hooded falcon—who rejoices in the service of the only falconer-sovereign the universe knows, and to whose transcendence it willingly surrenders its very power of sight. This is to say that a human being aware of his own fini-tude would in no circumstance dare usurp the role of falconer. This insight into the ultimate nature of finite existence thus becomes Dante's answer to Frederick II's ill-advised wish to mold the human being (and the sovereign in particular) into the figure of the falconer: of the tamer, that is, rather than the one to be tamed.

At this point, we are left with one major unanswered question. What does Dante mean when he states (or rather indicates figuratively) that the very essence of Purgatory is a disciplinary process whose *transfor-mative* outcome allows the souls to move from one terrace to the next, so that they may reach the top of the mountain and eventually Para-dise?[50] How does the cleansing process, as Dante envisions it, relate to the issue of past, present, and future salvation? The difficulty clearly lies in the fact that the penitents encountered by the pilgrim are *already* saved, while for him and his readers such a happy outcome is still in the balance.

Unlike the principles traditionally predicated upon the mutually exclusive realms of Hell and Heaven, the theological grounds on which the Catholic institution of Purgatory rests are, to this day, difficult to define. More than one commentator has noticed—however elusively—the extent to which Dante's deeply cathartic view of Purgatory is at variance with a merely punitive one. A first example that can be adduced is to be found in the introduction to Robert M. Durling's and Ronald R. Martinez's edition of *Purgatorio*, where the authors highlight the unexpected presence of the process of moral discipline as the basis for the penitents' catharsis. Such an approach, they argue, is clearly at odds

with Catholic orthodoxy. They argue that Dante's comparing the process of moral discipline to the training of falcons or of horses

> constitute[s] a transferring of the idea of moral discipline in this life
> to the next. . . . The traditional Catholic conception of Purgatory,
> however, is quite different. In it, although when one's sins are
> forgiven the eternal punishment for sin—damnation—has been
> forgiven [*i.e., revoked*], one is still subject to temporal punish-
> ment. . . . In the traditional Catholic view, then, Purgatory is the
> place where satisfaction, begun in this life, is completed. There is not
> a trace, in Aquinas' (or pseudo-Aquinas') elaborate discussion of
> Purgatory, of Dante's idea of Purgatory as a place of moral discipline;
> for the author of *ST Supplementum* it is exclusively a place of punish-
> ment, and the only punishment envisaged . . . is fire. Dante repeat-
> edly draws on the traditional punitive conception of Purgatory (for
> instance, in *Purg.* 11.53), but his emphasis is radically different from
> the traditional one, according to which the idea of moral discipline
> [and hence free will] is inapplicable to the afterlife.[51]

Although Durling and Martinez do not elaborate further on the implications of Dante's emphasis on moral discipline as a basis for penance, they do highlight the connection that Dante establishes between
it and such procedures as the "training of falcons."[52] And even though
they fail to place their reference to "training" in the highly sophisticated context of the medieval "arts of taming," they realize that Dante's
understanding of the process of penance as one of moral discipline
implies that free will is still at work in the souls dwelling in the intermediate realm. This is all the more so in relation to the parallelism
that Dante draws between the souls' "taming" and that process of conversion which is the focus of the pilgrim's inner experience during his
ascent of the mountain—a process supervised by Vergil with loving
care.[53]

Furthermore, Peter Armour's *The Door of Purgatory* radically questions the soundness of the established scholarly interpretation of *Purgatorio* 9, whose episode of the door of Purgatory is typically understood
as an allegory of the sacrament of penance. By removing that construct
and exposing the inconsistency of the sacramental reading of that episode, Armour was able to reveal Dante's wholly positive, and hence
radically innovative, view of Purgatory as a *redemptive* intermediate
realm. In so doing, Armour also inevitably came to confront the issue
of the souls' involvement in the process of their inner transformation:

Traditionally, Purgatory was a negative place of punishment or testing by fire, the fires of Hell and Purgatory being contiguous. Dante wished not only to separate Hell and Purgatory very clearly, to contrast them, to introduce a variety of penances, to add extra theological, moral, and liturgical elements, but also, ultimately, to present Purgatory as positive and redemptive. Thus, when the actual discourse on the theology of Dante's Purgatory occurs in canto xvii, he employs a different technique, and there the theology is Dante's major contribution to the whole *cantica*—the crucial, positive, and all-pervading definition of love as the principle of action in man. Through Purgatory, the soul's rational or elective love and natural love are made absolutely identical and co-extensive, *so that the soul regains complete liberty of choice which is also the innate natural love of the Supreme Good*, the cause of the soul's existence (*causa efficiens*) and the goal of its *return* (*causa finalis*) (cf. *Purg.* 16.85–90). This doctrine is conveyed clearly in disquisitions from Marco Lombardo and Vergil on the relationship between corruption and free will, between natural and elective love, and between the three types of wrong love and the true love of God.[54]

A third and last quotation is in order. Faced with the challenge of summarizing the essence of Purgatory in just a couple of sentences for the benefit of the widest possible audience, Robin Kirkpatrick completely bypasses the dualism cleansing versus coercion and brilliantly takes the reader into the structural "beyond" that buttresses the entire canticle:

> The theme of the *Purgatorio* is freedom. . . . But how is Dante to reconcile his sense of the *potentialities* of human nature—a sense which increases throughout the *Purgatorio*—with his understanding—which also increases here—of the demands of Divine Law? . . . Slowly, Dante recognizes that the disciplines of purgation are not restrictions but the means by which the individual places himself in relation to other beings—both divine and human. Law *becomes* Love: and freedom finally is seen to reside in that interdependence of all beings which is fully enjoyed in Paradise.[55]

If, as logic suggests, the transmutation of law into love amounts to sameness becoming perfected (or being now perceived from a perfected mind), what does this tell us about Dante the wayfarer and the souls that must ascend the purgatorial mountain in order to perfect their salvation? How does this process of becoming affect their nature, their mind, their will as saved but penitent souls; and how does it affect our nature, our mind, our will as human beings on the path to salvation?

It may be that we ought to pay closer attention to the existential and experiential implications of the transmutative way to salvation explored and opened by Dante in his poem. As Christian Moevs rightly argues, "In the *Comedy* salvation is a self-awakening of the Real to itself in us, the surrender or sacrifice of what we take ourselves and the world to be, a changed experience that is one with a moral transformation. . . . The *Comedy*'s aim is self-knowledge, the self-experience of what is."[56]

That shift in vision has to happen through a process of taming that entails "death to the world" through the willing acceptance of a forced blindness (a temporary seeling of one's inner eye) as the necessary, painful preliminary (the "martyrdom" of *Purg.* 10.109) to the awakening of a new insight into the ultimate nature of Reality. While the souls of Hell individually and collectively refuse to submit to that temporary blindness, thus falling into the definitive blindness of their own blinding worldview, Dante seems to indicate that once a soul accepts becoming temporarily blinded as part of the divine design, he or she can begin truly partaking in the eternal vision of self-awakening of the divine Real to itself.

To enter the dimension of salvation thus means to open the doors of one's mind to the imaginal. As, regardless of their religious affiliation, all medieval visionaries knew, this is the only path to self-awakening, that is to say, a process of transmutation (and therefore of transcendental becoming) as inner taming at the hands of the Divine.

While the souls of the damned have condemned themselves to a quest for the summum bonum in an earthly, immanent perspective, the saved souls long for the eternal source of happiness. What they all have in common, regardless of their temporary separation from the First Cause, is the recognition of their transcendent belonging and hence of their inherent becoming: in Thomistic terms, they are aware—however dimly—of their *participatory* nature to the Divine. Without a doubt, that awareness stemmed from a free response of their earthly will to the call of divine grace. But that awareness—that repentance which is a turning-around of the soul—merely marks the initial step in a process of conversion whose purpose is the actualization of the participatory nature of the soul in the form of a journey of return—of ascent—to the First Cause.

Strange though it may seem, the very essence of that journey to freedom-as-love consists, as Armour puts it, in a reunion of the "amor d'animo" ("love of the mind") with the "amor naturale" ("natural love"), or even more precisely perhaps, in a surrender of the former to the latter. This means that "amor d'animo" (our reasoning mind, the seat of our free will) has to bend to "amor naturale," that other mind, which knows nothing but its participatory nature to the Divine, and desires nothing but its return to that First Cause. In essence, then, this is the purpose of Purgatory as Dante understands it: a taming of the wild(ly) reasoning mind so that it may (un)knowingly find its way back to the loving freedom of "amor naturale."

Indeed, at the very moment when Dante ascends from the earthly Paradise to the sphere of the moon by simply gazing into Beatrice's eyes fixed in the sun, "pur come pelegrin che tornar vuole" (*Par.* 1.51 "much like a pilgrim who would return home"), she explains to him the obvious, wholly natural logic of that apparently unnatural return. This is the return of the human soul to the state of perfect(ed) freedom in love which binds together "tutte nature, per diverse sorti" (*Par.* 1.110 "all natures, by different lots"). Simply by virtue of being alive, all natures partake of the self-realizing nature of ultimate Reality. In this perspective, the "freedom" of falling out of cosmic harmony, of not responding to the call, of *not returning*, amounts to perversion; it is a rupture of the natural bond between God and the whole created universe that is but a fall of the will into the unresponsiveness[57] of matter.

The ultimate goal of this transmutation lies in what, according to Beatrice, is *the* founding paradox of free will: the moment it fulfills itself as such, human free will ceases to stray from divine will and becomes one with it. By this metamorphic process the fallible "amore . . . d'animo" (*Purg.* 17.92–93) can be subsumed into the ever infallible natural love, "sempre sanza errore" (*Purg.* 17.94 "always without error").

It is not by accident that the necessity of this convergence is revealed by Vergil in the canto at the center of Dante's poem about love being the transmutative force that binds together in amorous longing the universe as a whole. And it is certainly no coincidence if, soon after being taught the lesson of "amore d'animo" and "amor naturale," in facing the choice between answering his master's call or heeding the seductive phantoms engendered by his own mind, Dante the pilgrim responds as a tamed falcon would, eager to receive his food from the hand of the Lord:

Quale il falcon, che prima a' piè si mira,
indi si volge al grido e si protende
per lo disio del pasto che là il tira;
tal mi fec'io; e tal, quanto si fende
la roccia per dar via a chi va suso,
n'andai infin dove 'l cerchiar si prende.

Like the falcon that first looks down,
then turns at the falconer's call and lunges
out of desire for the food that attracts him;
so I became; and so I remained, until,
through the rock cleft to make a road for the wayfarer,
I went up to where the circling begins.

(*Purg.* 19.64–69)

Images of Muḥammad in Dante

Dante's Muḥammad: Parallels between Islam and Arianism

MARIA ESPOSITO FRANK

Many scholarly works tackle different issues connected with Dante's Muḥammad, such as the question—first raised by Miguel Asín Palacios—of Muslim sources (the *miʿrāj* material in the traditional literature known as hadith) as inspirations or models for the *Commedia* or the significance of the Islamic figures Dante encounters in his journey beyond. Formal or stylistic influences of Arab poetry on medieval European poetry, Dante's poetry included, have also received attention. Here, I explore Dante's own understanding of the Prophet of Islam as encountered in *Inferno* 28 as a historical figure and religious leader.[1] The placement of Muḥammad in the eighth circle of Hell and the *contrapasso* ("counter-penalty") assigned to him did not simply result from views of Islam and its Prophet that were widespread in Dante's time. Rather, they express Dante's particular understanding of Muḥammad and reflect Dante's own experiences and predilections.

Modern scholars who have examined Christian responses to Islam from its inception throughout the Middle Ages agree almost unanimously in defining such responses from both Western and Eastern Christian writers as generally negative. Indeed, anti-Muslim sentiments, which led to misrepresentations of Islam's teachings and parody or caricature of its believers, emerged with the rising of this new faith in the seventh century and persisted throughout the Middle Ages and afterward.[2]

Lack of accurate information about Islam—that is to say, ignorance of authentic Islamic sources and misunderstanding of these sources as well—gave rise to many distortions and outright attacks. In certain regions and times, for example, Christian views of and attitudes toward Muslims reflected fear of the new, and a sort of "anxiety," as

María Rosa Menocal[3] aptly put it, especially in the face of significant loss of territories and of the political and cultural expansion of Islamic civilization, not to mention the increasing number of conversions. For instance, the spread of Islam in modern Syria, Turkey, and Iraq after the success of the Abbasids in 750 was characterized by government policies which fostered conversions of Christian, Jews, and Magians in those regions not only by means of doctrinal objections, but also by the promise of full political participation to converts. Hence, Christian treatises (in Syriac and Arabic) produced in such circumstances of pressure and dominance ought to be read as a response and a doctrinal defense of a politically unequal interlocutor to customarily voiced Islamic objections, a subject eloquently discussed by Sidney H. Griffith.[4]

Writings about Islam in medieval Eastern and Latin Christendom have often been characterized as apologetic or polemical. These labels help us understand the actual sentiments, conceptualizations, expectations, evaluations, and hopes that drove Christian authors to write those texts in the language and tone they chose. Yet the two categories often appear not so neatly separable, while the interaction of both apologetical and polemical tones and modes in one and the same text or one and same writer's production, poses challenges to our interpretation and evaluation of Christian literature on Islam. More often than not, the polemical aspect of a particular Christian text on Islam was accompanied by an apologetical purpose, and, vice versa, an apology of Christianity was suffused with polemical points.

According to John Tolan's nuanced distinction, apologetics and polemics indicate two different kinds of approaches and arguments used in Christian literature on Islam and Muslims.[5] Apologetical arguments are defensive, aimed at "protecting" and strengthening Christendom. Christian apologetical literature reflects fear and hope, while stressing the sense of Christian identity that is perceived as being threatened from outside. The tenor of this literature depends on the context in which it was produced, whether under direct Muslim rule or not, geographically close or less close to the Muslim world, and so forth.

Polemical arguments are "offensive" arguments, in which Islam is subjected to doctrinal refutation, criticism, or attacks. Crass ignorance, misinformation, or mere confusion about the new faith and the life of its Prophet punctuate the history of Christian reactions to Islam, as one finds in both apologetics and polemics, which were copiously produced in the East as well as the West. In the most influential Christian writings concerning Islam from the seventh to early fourteenth centuries, perceptions changed, with Islam appearing first primarily as a military threat and only gradually as a spiritual menace as well. All the while, the prevailing idea in Christendom was that Islam would not last.

In surveying apologetical or polemical Christian texts on Islam, we should start with Patriarch Sophronios's sermon, which has been viewed as apologetical. The sermon was delivered during Christmas of 634 in Jerusalem, at the very height of the Muslim/Arab invasions, which he personally witnessed. Sophronios speaks of the invaders as "godless Saracens" and "barbarians" who had been sent for punishment.[6]

The tone is similar to that used by a contemporary of Sophronios, Maximus the Confessor. A theologian and a monk who wrote in the immediate aftermath of Arab invasions (between 634 and 640), Maximus decried the invaders as "a barbarous nation of the desert overrunning another land as if it were their own! To see our civilization laid waste by wild and untamed beasts which have merely the shape of a human form!"[7] Also in the East (Melkite), the late seventh-century Syriac text known as Pseudo-Methodius's *Apocalypse* (ca. 692 but purportedly written in 311) reiterates the same views. In this work the invasion of the pagan Ishmaelites is "foretold" as the scourge of God—and Christians must repent.

As Rollin Armour has argued, "In the eyes of Christian writers, Arabs were another in the series of invading peoples, barbarians, who had attacked the Empire for centuries, this time from the south rather than the north, advancing against the Eastern Empire, not Western Europe."[8] Indeed, views of Muslims as barbarians, idolaters, or pagans sent to remind Christians to repent and reform can be found in a large number of texts by Christian authors, particularly during the first two centuries of Islamic expansion but also in the following centuries. Of course this kind of Christian response—that is, more in the apologetic than polemical mode—was predominant but not exclusive in this early period, when several polemical works were also composed: for example, in his *Hodegos* (Guidebook; it is among our earliest Melkite examples), Anastasius (d. 700), from the monastery of Saint Catherine on Mount Sinai, interestingly enough refers to the Muslims as Monophysites ("this heresy is the root of the errors of the Arab") and to their rejection of the Trinity. Having stated that, though, Anastasius does not engage in doctrinal refutations. Furthermore, we observe discrepancies in the actual understanding or labeling on the part of Anastasius of Sinai, who in his *Diegemata Steriktika* (Narratives of Moral Support) calls the Saracens "unbelievers" and people "worse than demons."[9] Decades later, however, we find real theological tracts, such as those of the prominent theologian John of Damascus (d. 749). With him, the level and the type of response to Islam appears to change. His *Disputatio Christiani et Saraceni* (Disputation between a Christian and a Saracen), much read and widely known for centuries thereafter, offers an apologia that seems aimed at reinforcing Christian beliefs while showing the deceptive ways of Muslim questioning (it ends without the conversion of the interlocutor). On the other hand, in his *De haeresibus* (On Heresies), which constitutes the second part of his *Fons scientiae* (Fount of Knowledge), John stresses that Islam is yet another expression of "deviant Christianities." In fact, he identifies the religion of the Ishmaelites as the hundredth in his catalogue of heresies.[10]

John of Damascus's oeuvre, which was influential in the East and West alike, mixes apologetic and polemic. John certainly met Islam at first hand, but his encounters did not result in full understanding and accuracy in his representation of the faith. The declared purpose of his writings was to *instruct* Christians in avoiding the evil of heresy: by the time he wrote, Christians had been converting to Islam in considerable numbers. In texts such as John's we can trace in its early stages a response to Islam that rests on doctrinal arguments, although they are often coupled with apologetical ones. Among such texts are *On True Religion* by Theodore of Carra, known under his Arab name Abū Qurrah (d. ca. 820), and Theophanes's *Chronographia* (Chronicle), in which the author, writing in 815, when Muslim rule was very well established in the Middle East, characterized Islam as a heresy that mixed Jewish and Christian elements, thereby reiterating the views of John of Damascus. Another interesting aspect of this chronicle is the explanation that the fault for the loss of Roman territory to the Arabs lies ultimately with the heresy of the Syrians and the adherence to it of the Byzantine emperor Heraclius.[11] To these texts one might add the exchange of letters in Arabic known as *Risalat al-Kindī* (The Apology of al-Kindī; formerly attributed to al-Masīh al-Kindī [d. 870], but probably composed in the tenth century), which can be considered both apologetical and polemical: it attacks Muslim doctrine, but its final part offers "an apologetical presentation of key Christian doctrines."[12]

Important works produced in the East, such as those already mentioned, were translated into Latin relatively soon, and became more easily accessible to the readership in the West. In the West the mixing of polemical and apologetical traits was characteristic of most literature on Islam from the very beginning, starting with the Venerable Bede (ca. 672–735), whose portrayal of the Saracens changes throughout his writings. Initially he depicts them as "quasi-Christian" (when they have gotten only so far as Damascus), but by the time the Islamic conquest reached the western Mediterranean he identified them as "unbelievers" and "idolaters who worshiped Venus/Lucifer."[13]

In the ninth century, most writings in the West about Islam became even more inflammatory or apocalyptic in tone. For example, the writings of Spanish Christian martyrs, such as the *Memoriale sanctorum* (Saints' Memorial) and *Liber apologeticus martyrum* (Defense of the Martyrs) by Eulogius of Córdoba and the *Indiculus luminosus* (The Little Illuminating Guide) by Paul Alvarus, discuss Muḥammad as "precursor Antichristi" ("forerunner of the Antichrist").[14]

Literary texts such as chansons de geste perpetuated the image of Saracens as idolaters, as did most chroniclers of the First Crusade. In contrast, Guibert of Nogent (1064?–1125), himself a chronicler of the Crusade, acknowledges that the Saracens are monotheists and that Muḥammad is not their God. After looking in vain in the books of the doctors of the Church, Guibert noticed and even lamented the lack of authoritative opinion on the subject. Consequently he relied on popular, folkloric sources in depicting Islam as heretical in its teachings and Muḥammad as lewd in his behavior, as did the four hostile biographies of Muḥammad that began to circulate in Latin during the twelfth century.[15] That same century saw attempts in Western Europe to begin a serious study of Islam: Peter the Venerable commissioned the translation of several texts from Arabic into Latin, including the *Apology of al-Kindī*, the Qur'an itself, and various Islamic tracts. A team of experienced translators, headed by Peter of Toledo and including Robert of Ketton, completed the project, which has been called the Corpus Toletanum, or Toledan Collection. These translations included works containing both facts and legends about Islam that were popular among Muslims, especially the stories of miracles and other wonders surrounding the life of the Prophet. At the head of the collection, Peter the Venerable placed his own apology as an introduction, *Summa totius haeresis ac diabolicae sectae Saracenorum sive Hismelitarum* (A Summary of the Entire Heresy or Devilish Sect of the Saracens or Ishmaelites). The importance of this collection has been discussed elsewhere, but for the sake of the present argument it is useful to repeat observations previously made about both the merits and faults of this great enterprise, namely, that while correctly describing the basic objections of the Muslims (to the Trinity, to the divinity of Jesus) and establishing with more accuracy certain facts, this collection still resorts to derogation ("barbarians," "idolaters"), insinuations of diabolical intervention (in the beliefs of Muslims), and tendentious interpretations of Muḥammad's motives. In conclusion, the Corpus Toletanum became the vehicle for disseminating some pieces of reliable information about Muslim beliefs and Islamic lore, together with Mozarabic polemical views of Islam and Peter's apologetic message. But Peter of Cluny's contribution went beyond this, and in his *Liber contra sectam sive haeresim Saracenorum* (Book against the Sect or Heresy of the Saracens) we find exhortations not to use force or violence—to approach the Saracens not with hatred or weapons but with love and words. Nonetheless, in this instance too there is something contradictory and rather disorienting (pun intended) in Peter's advocacy of nonviolence when he supports the Crusades and—at the same time—criticizes the Christians for failing to evangelize.[16]

While support for the Crusades was still voiced by people like Jacques de Vitry (d. 1240), Vincent of Beauvais in his *Speculum historiale* (Mirror of History, ca. 1250), and Fidentius of Padua in his *Liber de recuperatione terrae sanctae* (Book on the Recovery of the Holy Land, written between 1266 and 1291), there were also advocates for peace. For example, consider the missions of Oliver of Paderborn and Francis of Assisi to the Egyptian sultan al-Kāmil, during the Fifth Crusade. In the same irenic category one could also place the writings of William of Tripoli (1220–1273) and the anonymous *De statu Saracenorum* (On the Condition of the Saracens), a truly unusual book in that it speaks harmoniously of Islam and Christianity, showing the commonalities and basic agreement between the two faiths, and never referring to Muḥammad in derogatory terms. A final addition to this group (but not all scholars would equally include him under this rubric) would be the missionary work and writings, particularly the *Confutatio Alcorani* (Refutation of the Qur'an[17]) of Riccoldo of Monte Croce. With his death in 1321 we arrive at the chronological limits of the present study.

In the changing Christian perceptions—from viewing Muslims as barbarians or idolaters to considering them as heretics who departed to a greater or lesser extent from the Christian faith—we can chart a progression. For the first two centuries Islam to the Christian meant above all a call to repentance; during those times Christians looked at Islam mostly, in Tolan's words, as "a powerful military threat but a negligible spiritual menace," and thought it would go away.[18] Tolan concludes that by refusing to acknowledge Islam as a new faith, Christian authors "imposed familiar forms of the old Christian Roman Commonwealth on the new world of Islam." Only six centuries after the time of the Prophet did Christian authors in the West (especially in the areas that were part of the new Muslim empire) begin to confront "the irreversible nature of the advent of Islam."[19] After this realization they began to address the new faith on a doctrinal basis, as a Christological heresy.[20]

In my synthesis of a selected number of representative Christian responses to Islam from its inception to the early fourteenth century, we can indeed detect the shift at which I previously hinted: a growing awareness that led from an Islam primarily viewed as barbarism and idolatry (which translated into an immediate dismissal of serious theological consideration) to the gradual disappearance of such views, with greater emphasis placed on doctrinal issues. In other words, polemics prevailed over apologetics, as a different—though still faulty—understanding of Islam developed in Christendom in the late Middle Ages. Yet, as mentioned above, in relation to the Islamic world, Christian responses were not entirely clear-cut as either apologetic or polemic. The oscillation of authors between the two modes shows that their views of Islam were not absolutely fixed.

As we have seen above, in contrast to Crusade chronicles, chansons de geste, and other literary texts where the image of the Saracens as idolaters was perpetuated in twelfth-century Europe, Guibert of Nogent wisely stated that the Saracens were monotheists and that Muḥammad (whom he called "Mathomus") was their prophet, not their God, though at the same time Guibert denigrated and mocked the Prophet. On the one hand, Guibert openly acknowledged the need for a better knowledge of Islam and a sound refutation of Islam on theological grounds; on the other, he did not advance that cause himself. The case of Peter the Venerable is even more telling in this regard:

despite his great devotion to the study of Islam, he once wrote that he truly did not know whether to refer to Muslims as "heretics" on account of their faith or as "pagans" on account of their practices.[21] Often represented as a set of beliefs that included a mixture of Jewish and Christian elements, the newer faith was not understood as being based on a new revelation. The categories through which Christian authors of the Middle Ages read the phenomenon inevitably led to confusion and misidentification.

Turning to the Italian scene of the late thirteenth and early fourteenth century, I should also stress the role that millenarianism must have played in closing other possible approaches of Christians to Islam. Millenarian views of a final age that would bring to completion apocalyptic prophesies were certainly influential in certain circles and obviously held in high regard by someone like Dante, as the presence of Joachim of Fiore in his *Paradiso* unequivocally attests.

Dante's portrayal of Muḥammad, whom we meet in *Inferno* 28.22–42 in the ninth bolgia of the eighth circle, deserves to be examined within such a context:

> Già veggia, per mezzul perdere o lulla,
>   com' io vidi un, così non si pertugia,
>   rotto dal mento infin dove si trulla.
> Tra le gambe pendevan le minugia;
>   la corata pareva e 'l tristo sacco
>   che merda fa di quel che si trangugia.
> Mentre che tutto in lui veder m'attacco,
>   guardommi e con le man s'aperse il petto,
>   dicendo: "Or vedi com' io mi dilacco!
> vedi come storpiato è Mäometto!
>   Dinanzi a me sen va piangendo Alì,
>   fesso nel volto dal mento al ciuffetto.
> E tutti li altri che tu vedi qui,
>   seminator di scandalo e di scisma
>   fuor vivi, e però son fessi così.
> Un diavolo è qua dietro che n'accisma
>   sì crudelmente, al taglio de la spada
>   rimettendo ciascun di questa risma,
> quand' avem volta la dolente strada;
>   però che le ferite son richiuse
>   prima ch'altri dinanzi li rivada.
> Ma tu chi se' . . .

No barrel, through loss of board or lid,
gapes so wide as one I saw, cleft from
the chin to the part that breaks wind.
His entrails were hanging between his legs;
and the vitals could be seen and the foul sack
that makes shit of what is swallowed.
While I was all absorbed in gazing on him,
he looked at me and with his hands pulled
open his breast saying, "Now see how I
rend myself, see how mangled is Muḥammad!
In front of me goes ʿAlī weeping,
cleft in the face from chin to forelock;
and all the others whom you see here
were in their lifetime sowers of scandal
and schism, and are therefore thus cleft.
A devil is here behind that fashions us
so cruelly, putting again to the edge
of his sword each of this throng
when we have circled the doleful road;
for the wounds are closed up before any of us pass
again before him. But who are you . . .

Muḥammad appears ripped from the chin to his anus; his *contrapasso* is to be eternally severed by the sword of a devil as he completes his circle and his body's split closes up again. Dante places him among the sowers of discord, the dividers. This assignment indicates that he saw Muḥammad as a schismatic, a Christian schismatic as opposed to a heretic.

To grasp this point better, one should consult the oldest commentaries of the *Commedia* to see how they elucidated pertinent passages in *Inferno* 28. Commentators from Jacopo Alighieri (1322) to Cristoforo Landino (1481) refer to Muḥammad as either an impostor or an apostate-heretic. They cite and accept the legend widely spread in the Middle Ages (which Dante might have learned from Brunetto Latini's *Tresor* or Jacopo da Varazze's *Golden Legend*) according to which Muḥammad was a cardinal who failed to obtain election to the papacy and avenged himself by establishing a rival religion.[22]

Most commentators also refer to the legend of the "imposture," which Theophanes the Confessor's *Chronographia* helped to spread. In this legend the monk Baḥīrā of the genuine Islamic tradition undergoes major distortions at the hands of Christian apologists. In Islamic sources, the monk is presented as a holy hermit whom young Muḥammad encounters during a journey in Syria accompanied by his uncle Abū-Ṭālib. The holy hermit recognizes in Muḥammad the signs of his role as a prophet and instructs him in the pure monotheistic religion. But the anchorite of the Christian texts—under various different names, depending on the text transmitting the story—has now become a Nestorian, Jacobite, or Arian who wants to take revenge on the community that had rejected him and finds in Muḥammad an "ally," so to speak, for his plan. Alternatively, the monk is presented as a man as ambitious as Muḥammad, who follows his plans in order to achieve, thanks to a false faith, great political and economic power. Many variations occur on these two themes, which often include yet another monk (Waraqa ibn Nawfal) and many imaginative details illustrating tricks and gimmicks that were thought to have marked the foundation of Islam and made it believable.[23] For the sake of brevity, we simply note that such stories, which informed interpretations of Dante's Muḥammad as well as general views of Islam in the Italian peninsula, conveyed a view of Muḥammad as an apostate (the legend of the cardinal), or a deceiver, or an impostor.[24]

The general portrayal of Islam and Muḥammad in the oldest commentaries on *Inferno* 28 does not deviate from that of the Christian apologetics and polemics discussed above, since those works (and the views they fostered) had by the fourteenth century become well known. Dante's commentators therefore echoed and sometimes conflated or interwove themes and stories of that repertoire when glossing *Inferno* 28.22–40, in the belief that what they found reflected in Dante's portrayal of Muḥammad was the poetic counterpart of the purportedly historical Muḥammad discussed by major ecclesiastic as well as intellectual authorities from the seventh century to their own day. Of course, Dante too must have been familiar with the histories and stories (many coming from the East) that for centuries had circulated in the Latin West. These texts were highly regarded, because they were penned by ecclesiastic authorities or established intellectuals. Moreover, we should take into account the circulation of popular legends, perhaps similar in content to their most learned counterparts, that flourished in oral tradition.

In my view, however, Dante did not fully subscribe to any of the traditional accounts and interpretations of Islamic history and of its

Prophet. He approached the Islamic question with regard to its origins, by looking at the figure of Muḥammad and his role as a new religious leader who promoted division within Christianity. While it is not possible to list all Christian apologetics and polemics with which Dante was acquainted, it can be demonstrated that an intellectual of his stature in medieval Italy would have had significant exposure (direct or indirect) to the most authoritative Christian texts that dealt with Islam from historical and religious points of view. Indeed, the documentation collected and analyzed by Brenda Deen Schildgen confirms and illustrates clearly this level of familiarity.[25] Recent scholarship has also shown that Dante's interest in the Islamic world extended beyond religion to other areas as well, such as falconry, while Karla Mallette has traced intriguing connections between the figure of Manfred in *Purgatorio* 3 and Dante's perception of Islam and Arabic culture.[26]

Dante's study of Islam and Arabic culture has turned out to be multifaceted. My intent here is not to reiterate or corroborate the specific and important points made by other scholars or to remind of the old issues of Dante's borrowings from Islamic eschatology in general and from Islamic literature of the *mi'rāj* in particular, which date back to Asín Palacios's work. Rather, I wish to show that, although Dante most likely knew the origin of Islam through anti-Islamic Christian literature, his own outlook on the phenomenon was singular and insightful.

To begin with Hell, Dante the poet has Muḥammad himself illustrate what sort of denizens inhabit the ninth bolgia of the eighth circle: "E tutti li altri che tu vedi qui, / seminator di scandalo e di scisma / fuor vivi, e però son fessi così" (*Inf.* 28.34–36 "And all the others whom you see here / were sowers of scandal and schism / when alive, and for this they are treated in this way"). Thus Dante did not place Muḥammad among the heretics. Often in the Middle Ages *heretic* was used loosely in vituperation.[27] However, this particular canticle pays detailed attention to the meticulous classification of sins and to the corresponding topography of the infernal realm.[28] In Dante's Hell heretics are placed in the sixth circle in flaming tombs, right behind the gates of the city of Dis.[29] They are also the protagonists of Canto 10, where people of his own time and city—Farinata, Cavalcanti, and Frederick II, representatives of the "Epicurean" heresy—take the stage. Yet Muḥammad is placed in a different circle, in the company of 'Alī and of other dividers. Indeed, textual allusions and biographical facts have led me to believe that Dante's perception of Muḥammad was tied to the figure of the heresiarch Arius.[30]

John of Damascus, Eulogius of Cordoba, Peter of Cluny,[31] and Riccoldo da Monte di Croce had discussed Islam as a form of Arianism. None, however, had gone into great depth about the relationship, since apparently the mere mention of it sufficed. In the centuries during which Arianism was actively battled, the doctrine had been seen as an attack on the central dogmas of the Trinity and Incarnation. The parallel between Arianism and Islam that these authors drew is easily understood if we consider that the early fourth-century Libyan theologian Arius was known in his time, and throughout the Middle Ages, as a *negator* of the dogmas of Trinity and Incarnation, in the same way as Muḥammad came to be viewed later. But although Arius was an extremely controversial figure during his lifetime, his theological positions were not universally condemned. On the contrary, he had on his side powerful ecclesiastic authorities—Eusebius of Caesarea and Eusebius of Nicomedia among the most prominent—and many Asian churches favored his ideas, which contrasted with the orthodox dogma of the eternal deity of Christ and his equality with the Father (*homoousia*).[32] In short, over his entire life Arius was not cast entirely outside the Church, even when condemned by the Synod of Alexandria (320), banished by the Emperor Constantine, and anathematized by the Council of Nicea (325). During such periods, Arius moved elsewhere, such as Asia Minor and Illyria, where he was well received and supported.

At the end of Arius's life, the emperor himself ordered the Athanasians (that is, the followers of Arius's theological archenemy, Athanasius)[33] in Alexandria to receive Arius back in the Orthodox Church and give him communion. Various documents record that Arius died[34] in Constantinople, after an audience with the emperor at the imperial palace, and before receiving communion. His death took place in a public latrine, where he fainted and "falling headlong he burst asunder in the middle" (Athanasius, Letter 54 to Serapion). In the words of Socrates Scholasticus: "Together with the evacuations, his bowels protruded, followed by copious hemorrhage, and the descent of the smaller intestines. Moreover, portions of his spleen and liver were carried off in the effusion of blood, so he almost immediately died" (*Historia ecclesiastica* 1.38). Sozomen's account (*Historia ecclesiastica* 2.30) is very similar, while Epiphanius of Salamis in his *Panarion* (Books 2 and 3) notices that Arius's death is like that of Judas (Acts 1.8).[35]

It is worth noticing that Arius did not die (in 336) as a heretic, since he had been officially reinstated in the Church before his sudden expiration (which his supporters believed had been caused by poisoning). Unless we subscribe to the persistence of the Athanasian current, it would be hard to label Arius a heretic, especially if we consider, together with the circumstances of his life and work, that his were times of transition in the early development of the still nascent Christian church, during which doctrines were being constantly debated, and shifting interpretations with consequent divisions of various sorts were not uncommon: Athanasius himself was repeatedly driven out of his church and office by official authorities, and spent seventeen of his forty-five years as bishop in exile. Arius was, more than anything else, a heterodox theologian, a most striking and certainly memorable figure because of how Arianism developed in its manifold expressions in the succeeding two and a half centuries.

That the intriguing figure of Arius attracted Dante's interest is testified by his appearance in *Paradiso* 13, the fourth sphere, the Heaven of the Sun, where Saint Thomas warns against hasty judgment and unwise decisions.

> E questo ti sia sempre piombo a' piedi
>   per farti mover lento com'uom lasso
>   e al sì e al no che tu non vedi:
> ché quelli è tra li stolti bene a basso,
>   che sanza distinzione afferma e nega
>   ne l'un così come nell'altro passo:
> perch' elli 'ncontra che più volte piega
>   l'oppinïon corrente in falsa parte,
>   e poi l'affetto l'intelletto lega.
> Vie più che 'ndarno da riva si parte,
>   perché non torna tal qual e' si move,
>   chi pesca per lo vero e non ha l'arte.
> E di ciò sono al mondo aperte prove
>   Parmenide, Melisso e Brisso e molti,
>   li quali andaro e non sapëan dove;
> sì é Sabellio e Arrio e quelli stolti
>   che furon come spade a le Scritture
>   in render torti li diritti volti.
> Non sien le genti, ancor troppo sicure
>   a giudicar, sì come quei che stima
>   le biade in campo pria che sien mature.

And let this ever be as lead to your feet,
to make you slow, like a weary man, in moving
either to the *yes* or *no* which you do not see:
for he is right low down among the fools,
alike in the one and in the other case, who
affirms or denies without distinguishing:
because it happens that oftentimes hasty
opinion inclines to the wrong side, and
then fondness for it binds the intellect.
Far worse than in vain does he leave the shore
(since he returns not as he puts forth)
who fishes for the truth and has not the art.
And of this Parmenides, Melissus, Bryson,
are open proofs to the world, as are the many
others who went their way but knew not whither.
Thus did Sabellius, and Arius, and those fools
who were to the scriptures like blades,
in rendering straight countenances distorted.
Moreover, let folk not be too secure in judgment,
like one who should count the ears
in the field before they are ripe.

(*Par.* 13.112–32)

Since Arius as a heretic is obviously not a denizen of Heaven, he is
mentioned only briefly in Thomas's speech, which spreads over three
cantos (*Par.* 10–13).[36] Thomas's disquisition on necessary distinctions
begins in this context of kingly wisdom, that is to say, a kind of practical wisdom or prudence, and through the negative examples of ancient
philosophers and theologians (such as Arius), the Doctor Angelicus
warns against poor judgment and rash conclusions.

Although Dante mentions Arius by name only once (*Par.* 13.127),
he is not downplayed, and while Arius was too notorious to need
further elaboration in order to be identified, Dante's mere hint has
the effect of kindling the reader's curiosity about Arius's specific des-
tination, which remains untold. The Libyan theologian was an elusive, ultimately indefinable figure who seems to have intrigued and
inspired Dante, apparently for his heterodoxy. The *spade* (blades) of
Paradiso 13.127–29 are a metaphor that equates Arius (as well as Sabellius) to concave blades that, while mirroring, crook the straight
face of the scriptures. The image certainly carries overtones of heretical violence,[37] but it is also a vivid link with *Inferno* 28, where

Muḥammad tells of the devil's *spada* that splits open the bodies of the schismatic after each healing that takes place at the end of each circling (*Inf.* 28.38).

To Thomas's image of Arius as a sword distorting the truth of the scriptures and to the image of the sword of the devil in the ninth pouch of the eighth circle of Hell the reader familiar with the widespread ac- counts of Arius's death would almost automatically link the ripped- open body of this heterodox theologian in the latrine of Constantinople during his final hour. The fact that Dante chose to portray Muḥammad in Hell as ripped in the middle in the same way the dying Arius is de- scribed will hardly seem a coincidence. No coincidence at all, consider- ing also that, if Dante was simply looking for detractive ways to depict Muḥammad in Hell, he had ample materials at his disposal.[38] Dante could have drawn, for instance, from one of the widespread (in Italy and the Latin West in general) legends that narrated Muḥammad's death as eaten by pigs or dogs, in a state of drunkenness or of delusion about his resurrection.[39]

Dante's peculiar, implicit association between the role and signifi- cance of Arius's life and that of Muḥammad relates to another elo- quent presence in Dante's work and life: Anicius Manlius Severinus Boethius (ca. 480–524). Boethius's influence on Dante's thought and work goes well beyond the many mentions of or quotations from his writings (the most memorable of which may be *Inf.* 5.121–23)[40] and fre- quent references to him, especially in the *Convivio* (particularly *Conv.* 1.2.13). The echoes of Boethius's *Consolation* are innumerable when Dante discusses fortune, Providence, and, of course, philosophy (espe- cially *Inf.* 7.68–96, when Vergil explains fortune as a minister of the will of Providence). In each of Dante's representations of Providence as incomprehensibly benevolent (*Inf.* 20.28–30 or *Par.* 19), critics have de- tected Dante's philosophical allegiance to Boethius. Likewise, Boethi- us's influence can be discerned in Dante's casting of Lady Philosophy, his allegories in the *Convivio* (personification of Philosophy) and *Pur- gatorio* 19 (Dante's dream), and in Beatrice's speech at the end of *Para- diso* 1. V. E. Watts concluded that "*The Divine Comedy* as a whole could be regarded as a great elaboration of Boethius' concept of the ascent of the soul to the contemplation of the mind of God and its return to its true home or *patria* in the scheme of the universe."[41]

It is particularly relevant in this context that Boethius was also the first of the scholastics, and it is exactly in the scholastic perspective that, during Dante's time, Islam appeared not to be a religion of truth on account of its total reliance on divine revelation to the exclusion of any human capacity for reasoning in the pursuit of true knowledge of God.

In sum, the centrality of Boethius in Dante's professional life cannot be overemphasized. But biographical parallels in the lives of Boethius and Dante explain the latter's strong empathy for the former, for both men suffered false accusations of political corruption and an ensuing condemnation to exile and death. Boethius died as an orthodox martyr, or at least so the Middle Ages considered his life sacrifice.[42] Theodoric, the Ostrogoth king under whom Boethius rose to high distinction in political life, was Arian. Boethius's close relations with the growing power of the Byzantine East as a political and religious power played a role in Theodoric's distrust (and execution) of Boethius.[43]

Whether the accusation that Boethius had entered into treasonous negotiations with the Eastern Empire was well founded or not, Boethius was tortured for days and then bludgeoned to death at Pavia in 524 or 525.

The cult of Saint Severinus Boethius, although at least as old as the ninth century, became particularly popular in the thirteenth century in Pavia. Dante knew of Boethius's resting place in the church of San Pietro in Cielo d'Oro in Pavia:

> Or se tu l'occhio de la mente trani
>   di luce in luce dietro a le mie lode,
>   già de l'ottava con sete rimani.
> Per veder ogne ben dentro vi gode
>   l'anima santa che 'l mondo fallace
>   fa manifesto a chi di lei ben ode.
> Lo corpo ond' ella fu cacciata giace
>   giuso in Cieldauro; ed essa da martiro
>   e da essilio venne a questa pace.

> If now your mind's eye, following my
> praises, was drawn from light to light,
> you are already thirsting for the eighth.
> Therewithin, through seeing the Good,
> rejoices the sainted soul who makes the world's
> deceit plain to any who listen well to him.
> The body from which his soul was driven

lies down below in Cieldauro, and he came
from martyrdom and exile to this peace.
(*Par.* 10.121–29)

Indeed, Dante gives Boethius a notable place in Heaven as the eighth of twelve spirits that welcome and crown the pilgrim and Beatrice in the sphere of the Sun, the Heaven of Wisdom—where Arius is mentioned by Thomas Aquinas as a sword blade twisting the straight face of the scriptures.

Boethius took issue with Arius and Arianism in two of his four *Opuscula sacra* (Sacred Works), namely, *On Catholic Faith* and *On Trinity*, where he discussed the Trinity as three hypostases/*personae* as well as the crucial mystery of the union of both the divine and human nature in the person of Christ, through his own, new application of the methods of philosophy (logical methods and the terminology of Aristotle) to theological problems.

As Dante would have known, the controversy that Arius started in the early fourth century stemmed from a theological distortion akin to the one Muḥammad made in the seventh century, and as Dante observed firsthand, both Arianism and Islam had long-lasting divisive effects. In the Italian peninsula Arianism had been at the center of the well-known fourth-century polemic of Homoians versus anti-Homoians. This furor had involved many ecclesiastics, including the most prominent Church authorities of the time, first and foremost the pro-Nicene bishop of Milan, Ambrose. As Daniel H. Williams has stressed, Arianism represents several distinctly different theological viewpoints. The very term Arianism, "rhetorically conceived in a polemical context," is thus a misnomer "whose continued use . . . served only to cloud historical description of those groups who were at most indirectly related to the theology espoused by the presbyter Arius."[44] In this light it becomes even more understandable how during the Middle Ages parallels were easily drawn between the theologies of Arianism and Islam. Indeed, both were understood as having their origin within the Christian community and believed to be responsible for breaking the unity of Christendom while refusing the triune God and the theology of Incarnation, both of which Dante most solemnly celebrates in the climactic vision at the end of his celestial journey.

Writing of Dante's relations with the Islamic culture, Karla Mallette has observed that the poet worked at a time when Muslims and

Christians lived together in close proximity in Sicily and on the Iberian Peninsula. Despite what scholars believed for a long time, the frontiers between the Christian and Muslim communities in these areas were not impermeable. In fact, cultural contacts and exchanges were frequent and meaningful. For this reason medievalists such as Mallette have objected to Edward Said's view, expressed in his *Orientalism*, that Muslims and the Orient were seen by Christians as radically "other."[45] On the contrary, in northern Mediterranean areas an interpenetration (a "compenetrazione interdiscorsiva," in Maria Corti's expression)[46] enabled Dante to recognize the scientific work of the Arabs and to conceive of Islam and Christianity not as separate civilizations but as one (even if not homogeneous and uniform). Within that world religious differences or controversies that tore apart Christendom appeared to Dante as battles between an orthodoxy and various heterodoxies rather than between Christians and infidels or pagans.[47]

Dante assimilates the figure of Arius and his theology (which is significantly labeled today an archetypal heresy) to the Prophet of Islam and Islamic theology. Perhaps out of an uneasiness at classifying a figure as complex as Arius in a simple category, Dante does not indicate a precise place in the realms of the afterlife for the heterodox Libyan theologian. Yet he puts Muḥammad among the Christian schismatics. Furthermore, he shows the Prophet in the company of his son-in-law, ʿAlī, whom Dante so perspicaciously portrays as the one responsible for yet another schism within the Islamic heterodoxy.[48] In such instances, as well as in that of Manfred, the "Saracen,"[49] excommunicated by various popes yet placed on the threshold of Purgatory, enwrapped in an aura of martyrdom,[50] Dante selects unsettling and uncanny historical figures to address absolutistic claims or monopolies on the part of the official Christian orthodoxy, or to respond to divisive forces that he saw as undermining the core of orthodox theology (Trinity, Incarnation)—or to bridge a gap between them.

With his appeal to reason, as a skilled practitioner of Aristotelian logic, the *dialektikotatos* (acute reasoner) Arius, and the Ishmaelite Muḥammad, "the second Arius" ("God neither begets nor is He begotten," Qur'an, sura 112), proved themselves responsible for violating the unity of the Christian community. By lacerating the body of that community they damaged the foundational mystery of Christ's relation to God. That mystery opens *Paradiso* 10:

Guardando nel suo Figlio con l'Amore
  che l'uno e l'altro etternamente spira,
  lo primo e ineffabile Valore
quanto per mente e per loco si gira
  con tant'ordine é, ch'esser non puote
  sanza gustar di lui chi ciò rimira.

Looking upon His Son with the Love
which the One and the Other eternally breathe,
the primal and ineffable Power
made everything that revolves through the mind
or through space with such order that he who
contemplates it cannot but taste of Him.

(*Par.* 10.1–6)

With these words Dante introduces here the Sphere of the Sun, the Heaven where Thomas tells us of both Boethius and Arius in contrasting terms: the former "saw the Good" and has the merit of making "the world's deceit plain to any who listen well to him"; the latter, as to metaphysical topography, belongs to the unidentified crowd of those "who went their way but knew not whither" and "were to the scriptures like blades / in rendering straight countenances distorted."

At the end of *Paradiso* 33 the mystery returns—the mystery of the dual nature of Christ and of a triune God is disclosed to Dante the pilgrim: he sees three concentric, differently colored circles, and an image of man depicted on the second circle. The pilgrim is absorbed by that fact and tries to understand how the circle and the image can be united, how God and man can form a unity. In a momentary flash of intuition he understood what remains ineffable. With this vision, the impenetrability of the mystery is reasserted, and the poem ends.

Muḥammad in Hell

KARLA MALLETTE

T he title of this article nods to George Bernard Shaw's play "Don Juan in Hell." In every way that matters, of course, Dante's Muḥammad and Shaw's Don Juan differ. Don Juan, in Shaw's Hell, derides Hell. He is contemplating a move to Heaven; this is possible in Shaw's Hell. Juan's companions—including Lucifer, who is there to pass the time with Juan, a renowned conversationalist—are shocked at Juan's attitude. After all, everybody knows that Hell is the place to be. But Juan, wordy and remarkably dispassionate, argues his case with sangfroid. He finds Hell tedious, intellectually numbing; and he dreams of escape from its drearily earnest denizens, although the viewer may find it difficult to picture his vision of Paradise. A libertine in life, Shaw's Don Juan in Hell seems little more than a mouthpiece for the author's critiques of intellectual and moral hypocrisy and of organized religion.

In Dante's Hell, of course, characters cannot change their eternal address at will; Lucifer does not participate in witty table talk, and Hell is nothing other than horrific. However, Shaw depicts Juan and Dante depicts Muḥammad as bons vivants who now pay a steep price for their lives of libertinage. In both cases, the sideshow curiosity of their appearance derives from seeing what transformations the physical and psychological discipline of Hell will wreak upon a creature who lived for physical pleasure. And both Shaw's Juan and Dante's Muḥammad function less as characters than as mouthpieces. Like Juan, Dante's Muḥammad is a psychological nullity, a character whose emotional response to his eventful life is of little interest to his creator. Rather more important is the stark contrast between his current state and the well-known drama of his earthly life.

Medieval Christians viewed the historical Muḥammad as a frankly theatrical character. One need only scan the fourteenth-century commentaries on *Inferno* 28 to get a sense of this. Muḥammad was a renegade Christian, enraged by the cardinals who promised him the death of the current pope so that he himself could be made pope.[1] Or he was a puppet, controlled by a shadowy figure named Sergius, who plotted the downfall of Christendom.[2] Or he put bird seed in his ear and trained a dove to eat it so that his followers would believe that he was in communication with the Holy Spirit.[3] We see traces of the medieval perception of the Prophet as consummate showman even in Gibbon's reflections on his life in *The Decline and Fall of the Roman Empire*. Concluding his biography of Muḥammad, Gibbon wonders "whether the title of enthusiast or impostor more properly belongs to that extraordinary man. . . . From enthusiasm to imposture the step is perilous and slippery; the daemon of Socrates affords a memorable instance how a wise man may deceive himself, how a good man may deceive others, how the conscience may slumber in a mixed and middle state between self-illusion and voluntary fraud."[4] Here is an image of Muḥammad as a confidence man who builds an empire out of words—not, after all, that far from Shaw's Don Juan.

The Muḥammad of the *Inferno* is an enigma, in no small part because of the exceptionally writerly way that Dante blocks out this scene.[5] Dante seems more concerned with literary special effects than with developing Muḥammad's emotional and psychological back story; he adorns his portrait of Muḥammad with diverse (and at times conflicting) rhetorical flourishes. The canto begins with Dante's only attempt at writing martial poetry: he invokes the war dead of Puglia in order to set the stage for the grotesque mutilations we will meet in the ninth bolgia. In modern poetry the bodies of anonymous war heroes at rest beneath the earth of the fatherland nurture the nation. ("Make these ashes," Walt Whitman sang in honor of the Civil War dead, "to nourish and blossom"—addressing himself expansively not to this side or that but to all slain Americans, "soldiers South or North," in his poem "Ashes of Soldiers.") This, of course, is not the case with the dead of *Inferno* 28, who teem futilely beneath the soil of Puglia. Robert Hollander likened *Inferno* 28 to a Sam Peckinpaugh movie, and the comparison seems apt.[6] Though the dead exhibit their ostentatious mutilations with outrage, the reader recognizes them as a kind of celestial frontier justice: the mark of God's just punishment.

The poetic exceptionalism of *Inferno* 28 continues when Vergil, rather than the pilgrim, addresses Muḥammad. There are, of course, other occasions in the *Inferno* when Vergil interviews the dead—most notably, in the encounters with Pier della Vigna and with Ulysses. In those episodes, however, Dante explains why Vergil speaks. In the first case Dante is shocked into silence. And in the second the motive is linguistic: Vergil addresses Ulysses because Ulysses, in his Greek haughtiness, might be put off by Dante's Italian. But Dante does not explain why Vergil speaks for him in *Inferno* 28. It may be because (as in the case of Pier) the pilgrim is too horrified to speak. It may be for linguistic reasons, as in the case of Ulysses. Or there may be some other motive—Dante simply doesn't explain.

If Dante puts Vergil between the pilgrim and the damned in order to distance himself from Muḥammad, Muḥammad, on the contrary, stresses the connection between himself and Dante. Muḥammad assumes that Dante is one of the damned stopping for a bit of sightseeing on his way to his eternal home. This too is a strategy that Dante had used earlier in the *Inferno*. Pope Nicholas II mistook Dante for his archenemy Boniface VIII, dead before his time (*Inf.* 19.52–53), and Guido da Montefeltro disbelieved that he was talking to a living man (*Inf.* 27.61–66). What makes the use of the device in *Inferno* 28 intriguing is the way that the rhetorical strategy by means of which the damned claim intimacy with the pilgrim collides with the rhetorical strategy that the poet uses to create distance between himself and the damned.

In this essay I propose new sources for Dante's (somewhat conflicted) portrait of the Prophet of Islam. My aim is to sketch the outlines of an invigorated reading of one of the cagiest and stagiest figures in the *Commedia*—a figure whose emotional significance, certainly not accidentally, has eluded readers since Dante's day. My proposals will not be backed in every instance by documentary sources. Like an art restorer who must use guesswork to undo the depredations of time, I will at times advance my argument by inductive leaps rather than deductive increments. Where an insufficient record remains, only informed speculation can advance the philological argument; but it is worth remembering that speculative arguments have in the past guided scholars toward the fruitful resolution of a crux.[7]

Previous readers have, of course, entertained the possibility that Dante worked from an Islamic source in framing the *Commedia* in

general and *Inferno* 28 in particular. Most of this scholarship has focused on the parallels between the *Commedia* and the tradition known
in the Islamic world as the *mi'rāj*—Muḥammad's miraculous midlife
journey to Heaven and Hell; and I will discuss the *mi'rāj* tradition
later in this essay.[8] However, the Islamic source that I am chiefly interested in is not the *Liber scale Machometi* (The Book of the Ladder of
Muḥammad, as the *mi'rāj* narrative was known in Latin translation)
but rather the Qur'an—more precisely, one of the episodes from the
Prophet's life mentioned in the Qur'an. Two translations of the Qur'an
into Latin were made in Spain in the century and a half before Dante's
birth. Robert of Ketton translated it in 1142–43 for Peter the Venerable,
and Mark of Toledo made his version in 1210–11.[9] Although no decisive
evidence has been found to prove that Dante knew the Qur'an, it was
certainly known in Dante's Italy—and apparently better known than
the *mi'rāj* tradition. Riccoldo da Monte di Croce, to whom I will
return later, brought an intimate knowledge of the Qur'an back to
Florence when he returned from his long sojourn in Palestine, Syria,
and Iraq in 1300.[10] And three of the fourteenth-century commentaries
mention the Qur'an when discussing the career of the Prophet in their
comments on *Inferno* 28—Guido da Pisa (on *Inf.* 28.25–27); the Codice
Cassinese (on *Inf.* 28.23); and Benvenuto da Imola (on *Inf.* 28.22–24).[11]
No commentators, of course, mention the *Liber scale* or the *mi'rāj* tradition in general.

The Qur'an could not serve as a source on the *mi'rāj* episode in
Muḥammad's life. The *mi'rāj* merits only the briefest of mentions in
the Qur'an.[12] However another event in the Prophet's life may have
contributed to Dante's personification of Muḥammad in *Inferno* 28.
There is an ancient tradition in Islam known as *al-sharh*—the opening, or expansion—that describes an episode in which God opens
Muḥammad's chest and removes and purifies his heart.[13] In some versions of the tale God sends angels to split Muḥammad's body open; in
others it is birds that, as divine agents, open his chest.[14] Again, some
tales report that the angels or the birds removed something dark and
impure from Muḥammad's chest,[15] or that they purified Muḥammad's
heart by packing it full of snow or by washing it with cool water drawn
from the Zamzam well at Mecca.[16] In others the cleansing is figurative
rather than literal, and the accounts give no specifics regarding the
means by which it is achieved.[17] In some versions the purification functions as preparation for prophecy: God prepares Muḥammad's heart to

receive the Qur'an.[18] And in others it serves as a prelude specifically to the *mi'rāj*—Muhammad's journey to the next world.[19] Popular tradition elaborated the *sharh* material significantly; in some versions God's agents open Muhammad's chest and stir his innards about, stitching his chest closed when they have finished their business.[20] The mainstream and intellectual traditions, however, toned down the tale considerably, seeing it as an allegory for Muhammad's vocation, his calling to prophecy.[21] At present, we have no evidence that any of these *sharh* narratives were transferred to the Christian world. But the episode is mentioned—in an allusive and poetic way—in the Qur'an; and the Qur'an was, of course, accessible to Christians in Latin translation.

The Qur'an refers to the *sharh* twice. In particular, it is the subject of a brief sura, *al-Inshirāh* (solace, consolation, relief).[22] *Al-Inshirāh* (sura 94) is a prayer for release from troubles, a meditation on the difficulty of the believer's life—whether he be the Prophet of Islam or a humble Muslim—and the Arabic original uses allusive and powerful poetic language to evoke the episode so vividly elaborated in the popular tradition. I mentioned above that two Latin translations of the Qur'an were made before Dante's life: Robert of Ketton's and Mark of Toledo's. I have found comparison of Dante's portrait of Muhammad to Mark of Toledo's translation to be particularly intriguing, and so I will concentrate on that text in this discussion, despite the apparent *unpopularity* of Mark's version among medieval readers. At least twenty-five manuscripts of Robert's translation survive; by contrast only six manuscripts of Mark's translation are known.[23] However, as I argue below, Mark's translation may have better suited Dante's purposes both geographically (its presence in northern Italy, while not attested by extant manuscripts, is plausible) and temperamentally (the urgency and mystic density of Mark's language grant his version a suggestive quality lacking in Robert's translation).

Following is Mark's version of sura 94, *al-Inshirāh*, in its entirety:

> 1. Did I not throw open your heart / 2. and remove from you your sin / 3. which burst asunder [*or* shattered] your back? / 4. And I have exalted your memory / 5. since with incapacity there is capacity, / 6. and with incapacity, capacity. / 7. And when you have fulfilled [your obligation], / 8. contemplate and pray to your Creator.[24]

The reference to the physical trauma of the opening of Muhammad's chest scarcely registers in the Arabic text. Mark's translation, however, heightens the physical drama of the episode. In the Arabic, God *expands* (*sharaḥa*) Muḥammad's chest. Mark uses the verb *adaperio* to translate the Arabic: God "lays bare" or "opens fully" Muḥammad's chest. (In contrast, Robert of Ketton uses the phrase "fecit amplum" to translate this verb; in his version God "made wide" the heart of the believer.)[25] Again, in the original God relieves the believer's back of a burden that weighs heavily upon it (*anqaḍa*).[26] Mark uses *disrupit*—to burst asunder, or shatter—to render this verb. (Robert of Ketton's translation says, "tergusque graue fecimus," "and we made your back heavy.") Thomas Burman has demonstrated that the medieval Christian translators of the Qur'an often introduced extraneous material—sometimes from theological works and Qur'anic commentaries—into their translations.[27] Here, Mark's translation seems to be informed by the popular versions of the *sharḥ* legend that emphasized the physical trauma of the event, depicting it as a corporeal ordeal.[28]

The potential relevance of this material to the portrait of Muḥammad in the *Inferno* will be immediately apparent to those who remember *Inferno* 28 (despite the absence of lexical echoes of Mark's translation in the passage). In that canto Dante meets the "sowers of schism and scandal." As punishment for his rupture of the Church Muḥammad's chest is ruptured, *opened* from the front to the back, as in the *sharḥ* episode.[29] Dante does not repeat the terminology of Mark's translation in his portrait of Muḥammad in *Inferno* 28. In the *Inferno*, Dante uses common, even crude vocabulary; the abstract verbs and nouns of Mark's translation have no place in Dante's description of Muḥammad, his torso gaping like a staved-in barrel, his organs visible in the breach. If there is a response to Mark's translation in *Inferno* 28, it is found in the dissonance between the significance of Muḥammad's ruptured body in the two texts. Like Mark's Muḥammad, Dante's Muḥammad is riven by God's touch, his body opened from chest to back. In Mark's translation, God shatters Muḥammad in order to exalt him; the opening of Muḥammad's chest serves as a preparation for prophecy in general or for Muḥammad's mystical journey to the next world in particular. God recalls this episode in the sura *al-Inshirāḥ* in order to comfort Muḥammad, as if to say, "where you find my awesome power, you will also find my mercy." In the *Inferno*, in contrast, when Muḥammad displays his wounds, he seems at once shamed, scandalized, and self-pitying. God has split his torso not to exalt him but rather to humiliate him. The opening of Muḥammad's chest in the *Inferno* reverses the significance of the expansion of Muḥammad's chest in the Qur'an. Recall the words that Muḥammad speaks to Dante, in childish horror at his own mutilation: "Or vedi com' io mi dilacco! Vedi come storpiato è Maometto!" (*Inf.* 28.30–31 "See how I open myself! See how Muḥammad is burst!"). The scene is a grotesquerie, a carnivalesque inversion of an episode recounted with awe in the Islamic popular tradition.

The proposition that Christian Europe knew the details of an episode in the life of the Prophet of Islam used within the Islamic tradition to confirm his prophetic mission may strain credulity. Yet Christian witnesses, even overtly hostile Christian witnesses, might at times produce neutral reportage on events in the Prophet's life that functioned in the Islamic tradition as evidence of God's preferential treatment of him. A striking example of this phenomenon can be found in Christian accounts of one element from the Islamic legend of the *miʿrāj*, the Prophet's miraculous journey to Heaven and Hell. I turn now to Christian discussions of the physical affect of God's touch on Muḥammad as evidence of a startlingly nonpolemical treatment of an Islamic tradition on the part of Christians and thus as a useful corrective to the aggressively hostile depiction of Muḥammad in the commentary tradition. As we will see, this episode exhibits an intriguing thematic parallel with the *sharḥ* tradition. Furthermore, the dissemination of the legend in the Christian world illustrates both the spread of knowledge about Islam in Christian communities (indeed, we can situate one discussion of the legend in Dante's own backyard) and the tenuous survival of manuscript witnesses to Christian knowledge about Islamic belief.

The work regularly cited as Dante's most probable source of information on the Islamic afterworld, the *Liber scale Machometi*, reports that when Muḥammad ascended to Heaven and stood finally in the presence of the Almighty, God "suddenly placed his hand upon my head, so that I felt the chill of his hand penetrate to my heart." God then invested Muḥammad with the knowledge of everything "which had happened until that moment and which would happen in the future."[30] The episode serves to demonstrate God's election of his last prophet and to confirm his epistemological exceptionalism, his privileged access to divine understanding. It occurs in some popular Islamic accounts of the *miʿrāj*,[31] and it became a standard element in Christian versions of the Prophet's ascension. It is also included in summaries of the *mi'rāj* that appeared in two anti-Islamic polemics: the *Liber denu-dationis* (The Book of Denuding), to which I return below, and the *Contra legem Saracenorum* (Against the Law of the Saracens) by Ric-coldo da Monte di Croce.

Riccoldo was one of the most significant and remarkable figures in the history of communications between medieval Muslims and Chris-tians during the late Middle Ages.[32] Born in Florence, he was invested as a Dominican at Santa Maria Novella in 1267. In 1288 Riccoldo trav-eled to the Holy Land in order to undertake a pilgrimage and to preach the Gospel to Muslims. He would journey through Syria and as far inland as Baghdad before his return to Italy. During his travels Ric-coldo learned Arabic thoroughly[33] and studied the Qur'an and Islamic theological traditions—an *impresa* (feat) that is remembered in Fazio degli Uberti's epic recollection of Riccoldo in the *Dittamondo* (written mid-fourteenth century):

> L'arabico linguaggio quivi appresi;
> la legge *Alcoran* di Macometto
> di punto in punto per latin distesi.
>
> The Arabic language he learned there;
> The law of the Qur'an of Muḥammad
> He refuted in Latin, point for point.
> (*Dittamondo* 5.9.109–11)

Riccoldo's presence in Florence is next attested in about 1300. He died in Florence in 1320.

Riccoldo wrote two texts that were very widely disseminated in late medieval Italy: the *Liber peregrinationis* (Book of Pilgrimage), de-scribing his travels, and *Contra legem Sarracenorum*, a point-by-point refutation of the Qur'an. In *Contra legem Sarracenorum*, which sur-vives in twenty-nine manuscripts, Riccoldo recounts the tale of the *mi'rāj*. At the climax of his brief summary of Muḥammad's journey to Heaven and Hell, Riccoldo reports the same episode recorded in the *Liber scale Machometi*. Muḥammad stands "in the presence of God and his tribunal. God touched me," Riccoldo writes, speaking in the voice of Muḥammad, "with his hand between the shoulders in such a way that the frigidity of his hand penetrated all the way through to the marrow of my spine."[34] Dante scholars—accustomed to the crude anti-Islamic sentiments of the commentary tradition—may be forgiven if we respond with astonishment to the rhetorical complexity of this moment, in which a scholar engaged in writing an anti-Islamic polemic speaks in the voice of the Prophet of Islam in order to record Muḥammad's own astonishment when he is touched by the hand of God.

Yet *Contra legem Sarracenorum*, although it is clearly the product of Riccoldo's sustained scrutiny of Islamic traditions, here cites an earlier polemical work. And so, while the work corroborates Riccoldo's intimacy with Islamic belief, at the same time it attests to the complexities of the transmission of information concerning Islamic beliefs and practices—at second and third hand and beyond—in medieval Christian Europe. Riccoldo lifted the phrase under discussion from an anti-Muslim polemic, written by a Muslim convert to Christianity, known as the *Liber denudationis*, also known as *Contrarietas alpholica* (with much debate over the precise meaning and origin of the second element).[35] The *Liber denudationis* survives in a single late twelfth- or early thirteenth-century manuscript, bound with Mark's translation of the Qur'an, currently in the Bibliothèque nationale de France (MS lat. 3394, fols. 238r–63v). Thus while no smoking gun survives to demonstrate lines of affiliation in early fourteenth-century Italy, a web of possibilities emerges. Did the *Liber denudationis* regularly circulate along with Mark's translation of the Qur'an? If Riccoldo had access to the *Liber denudationis* (and possibly to a composite volume of the *Liber denudationis* and Mark's Qur'an) while living in Florence, does that mean that the text circulated in northern Italy during the early fourteenth century? Could Dante have been aware of any of these texts: Riccoldo's *Contra legem Sarracenorum*, the *Liber denudationis*, or Mark's Qur'an itself? Mark's Qur'an survives in a fifteenth-century manuscript in Turin; does the presence of this later copy of the work suggest that other versions circulated earlier in Italy, perhaps providing the source from which this version was made? Such speculations, like any philological argument that proceeds by means of inductive leaps rather than deductive analysis, must be validated or annulled by subsequent scholarship. What can be argued from the surviving evidence is precisely the paucity of the surviving evidence: those who sought knowledge about Islamic belief in early fourteenth-century Italy turned to resources that do not survive to the present day (or have not yet been discovered and discussed by modern scholars).

Of the three texts under discussion—*Contra legem Sarracenorum*, the *Liber denudationis*, and the *Liber scale Machometi*—not one refers explicitly to popular versions of the legend of the opening of

Muḥammad's chest. Yet the tale (both in the Islamic versions and the Christian cognates) uses elements found also in the *sharḥ* tradition to signal Muḥammad's vocation. God (or God's agent) touches Muḥammad. The contact is marked by a physical trauma—it penetrates Muḥammad's chest—and by a supernatural chill (the sundering of Muḥammad's breast in the Qur'an and the *sharḥ* tradition; the snow or the cool water of the Zamzam used to cleanse Muḥammad's heart in the *sharḥ* tradition; the penetrating chill of God's touch in the *Contra legem, Liber denudationis*, and *Liber scale Machometi*). The episode illustrates God's intimacy with his last prophet. And the Christian redactions of the two tales—the *sharḥ* sura from the Qur'an on the one hand, the *mi'rāj* on the other—do not attempt to delegitimize Muḥammad; they do not posit a shadowy Sergius orchestrating an assault on Christian orthodoxy or doves trained to eat birdseed from the Prophet's ear. God himself, in this instance, designs his Prophet's corporeal ordeal: the chill of God's touch penetrates Muḥammad's marrow; God's angel splits Muḥammad's breast.

Approaching the *Inferno* from a reading of Christian recapitulations of Islamic belief, it is tempting—though not, on the basis of the evidence presented, philologically defensible—to read the physical abjection of the Muḥammad of *Inferno* 28, in which God splits Muḥammad's breast not to exalt but rather to debase him, as an inversion of (Islamic) orthodoxy. Speculation aside, this exploration of the portrait of Muḥammad in *Inferno* 28 illuminates the subtlety both of medieval Christian knowledge of Islam and of Dante's Muḥammad. Medieval Christian representations of Islamic belief nearly always served an explicit tactical purpose: they refuted while they reported. But at the same time, medieval writings on Islam varied in their efforts to polemicize with precision. Some scholars spoke out of a profound knowledge of Islamic practice, acquired through study of intellectual traditions and observation of customs, and aimed to produce a comprehensive account of those traditions for a Christian audience. Despite Riccoldo's explicit and oft-voiced hostility toward Islamic belief, no polemical coloring is evident in the detailed description he (or the *Liber denudationis*) gives of God's interview of Muḥammad in the presence of the angels: God's hand between Muḥammad's shoulders and the life-altering chill of God's touch. Whether Riccoldo found God or the devil in the details seems for the moment a matter of indifference; he intended to reproduce them in their multitude for the edification of his reader.

We have no evidence that Dante interested himself in Christian discussions of Islamic practice. We know that he availed himself of Islamic philosophical traditions.[36] And our increasingly sophisticated understanding of contemporary Italians' involvement with Islamic philosophy allows us to begin to measure with greater accuracy Christian responses to those traditions in Dante's Italy.[37] Furthermore, Dante lived in an Italy linked by mercantile connections with the port cities of the Arab Mediterranean, as *Inferno* 28 itself demonstrates. Dante puts the word *risma*—which means ream (of paper)—in Muḥammad's mouth, and it is the first attested usage of the word in the Italian language.[38]

> Un diavolo è qua dietro che n'accisma
> sì crudelmente, al taglio de la spada
> rimettendo ciascun di questa risma,
> quand' avem volta la dolente strada . . .
>
> A devil is here behind that fashions us
> so cruelly, putting again to the edge
> of his sword each of this throng
> when we have circled the doleful road . . .
> (*Inf.* 28.37–40)

The Italian *risma* comes from the Arabic *rizma*, which referred to the bundles of rags used in the production of paper. The Italian word came to signify (as the English cognate does today) the bundles made of paper in order to transport it to market. But Dante's use of the word suggests a meaning closer to the semantic range of the Arabic *rizma*. Dante rhymes *risma* with the verb *accismare*, an Italian borrowing from the Occitan that meant to bedeck, to adorn, or to dress in fine clothes. In this tercet Dante reduces the damned with brutal swiftness from the finery they wore in life to the abjection they will know eternally in the afterlife. The meaning of the Arabic *rizma*—a bundle of rags, slashed with blades or nails to reduce them to the fibers which would form the paper—suits Dante's poetic purpose much better than the meaning that the Italian *risma* would acquire: a bundled stack of paper.[39] Dante's Italy was closer to the Arab world than we imagine, thanks in large part to the mercantile activities that built the prosperous Italian communes of Dante's age.

However, Dante did not engage Islam as a competing religion outside of *Inferno* 28, where he represents it not as a religion, per se, but rather as an aberrant form of Christianity: a schism.[40] New evidence may change this perception, of course (as has happened so often in the past). The strongest textual evidence I can offer, as of this writing, to support the contention that Dante knew and responded to Islamic sources in his depiction of Muḥammad is the argument from literary efficacy. A series of strong characters provide the psychological and literary scaffolding upon which Dante structures the *Inferno*, from Paolo and Francesca through Brunetto Latini and Pier della Vigna all the way to Muḥammad's own neighborhood—Ulysses and Ugolino. In this company, Muḥammad seems a cipher, too emotionally sketchy to carry the weight of an Ugolino or to pack the punch that Francesca does. He appears to crumble under the barrage of rhetorical munitions that Dante deploys around him: the martial verses that open *Inferno* 28; the fact that Vergil, not Dante, addresses him; and his overweening identification of Dante as a fellow traveler.

In certain cases modern scholarship has transformed our understanding of key concepts in the *Commedia* by making us aware of the contours of the medieval landscape within which Dante worked (think, for instance, of Amilcare Iannucci's authoritative work on Limbo).[41] Sustained scholarship on the nuances of Dante's Muḥammad might enable us to see the character in a different light, as a commanding reading of a figure that in Dante's age possessed a dark charisma. "Official" Christian reportage depicted Muḥammad as a confidence man, a sideshow barker, and an impostor. Word of mouth, however, might paint him in a different light: as a powerful general, for instance, who set the armies of Islam in motion toward the Mediterranean.[42] Translations of Islamic texts and accounts of Islamic belief—like Mark's Qur'an and Riccoldo's anti-Muslim polemic—mobilized information from a variety of sources to challenge the validity of Islam. And translations of philosophical treatises made Islamic readings of Greek philosophy accessible to medieval Christians. How much of this material did Dante use in his portrait of Muḥammad? Did he give thought, as Riccoldo so publicly did, to Muḥammad's claims of prophetic exceptionalism?[43] Certainly *Inferno* 28 becomes a much more powerful portrayal of a prophet manqué if we read it as an inversion of a traditional pious representation of Muḥammad. Rather than a curiously flat caricature of one of the most provocative figures to find his way into the *Commedia*, the Muḥammad of *Inferno* 28 emerges as a vivid abnegation of the Prophet's claims and of the claims of his followers. This

Muhammad, in his abjection, is worthy both of Dante's convictions and his literary powers; and, as a canny reading of an Islamic tradition, he witnesses the complexity of Muslim-Christian cultural communications in the medieval Mediterranean.

I hedge my conclusion by couching it in speculative terms out of both respect for philological method—which works best when it balances inductive and deductive approaches in proper measure—and awareness of the damage done to scholarship on Dante and Islam in the past by incautious argument. Miguel Asín Palacios inaugurated the twentieth-century debate on the question of Islamic influence on Dante's afterlife with his 1919 monograph, *La escatología musulmana en la Divina Comedia* (Muslim Eschatology in the *Divine Comedy*). In 1924 Asín Palacios would publish a pamphlet summarizing the controversy sparked by his book between 1919 and 1923 ("Historia y crítica de una polémica" ["History and Criticism of a Polemic"]); this bibliography would be reprinted, along with supplemental notes on the continuation of the polemic, in the 1943 edition of *La escatología musulmana*. Asín Palacios's thesis provoked a firestorm of response, much of it voiced with a bellicose intensity that the author himself found dismaying. He seems to find a certain comfort in a comment made by an English Dantist named MacDonald at the beginning of the controversy: Dante scholars are "no peaceful folk."[44] In truth, in *La escatología musulmana* Asín Palacios ignored a component crucial to framing a successful philological argument: he did not present a plausible means of transmission of Islamic notions of the afterlife to Dante. And so, in his eagerness to demonstrate the unity of medieval Mediterranean civilization, Asín Palacios sent the noses of Dante scholars around the world out of joint, despite the sensitivity, the probity, and the beauty of his readings of Dante and of Islamic depictions of the afterlife. I argued earlier in this essay that where an insufficient record remains, only informed speculation—scholarship that balances the demonstrable and the probable—can advance our understanding of the past. And in such cases speculative conclusions are, by an ironic twist, the most conclusive: the most optimistic, and the most likely to spur further research.

Islam in Dante's Italy

Mendicants and Muslims in Dante's Florence

JOHN TOLAN

E poi che, per la sete del martiro,
  ne la presenza del Soldan superba
  predicò Cristo e li altri che 'l seguiro,
e per trovare a conversione acerba
  troppo la gente e per son stare indarno,
  redissi al frutto de l'italica erba,
nel crudo sasso intra Tevero e Arno
  da Cristo prese l'ultimo sigillo,
  che le sue membra due anni portarno.

And when, in his thirst for martyrdom,
in the proud presence of the sultan
he preached Christ and those who followed Him,
but found the people too unripe for conversion,
so as not to stay in vain he returned
to the harvest of Italian fields,
where on the harsh rock between Tiber and Arno
he received from Christ the last seal,
which his limbs bore for two years.

—(*Par.* 11.100–108)

I n the eleventh canto of the *Paradiso*, Dante paints a vivid portrait of Francis of Assisi, a new rising sun in the Orient, an *alter Christus* ("second Christ") who married Lady Poverty and who toward the end of his life was marked with the *ultimo sigillo* ("final seal"), the wounds that Christ had borne. A key episode in the spiritual itinerary of the saint is his preaching Christ in the "proud presence" of the sultan, into whose presence he was driven by his "thirst for martyrdom."

Francis of Assisi was thirteenth-century Europe's best-known and most venerated saint, and Dante gives him a prominent place among the blessed in the celestial rose (*Par.* 32): just beneath the Virgin Mary and John the Baptist, before Saints Benedict and Augustine. Francis himself never speaks in the *Commedia*, but Thomas Aquinas narrates his life at length in *Paradiso* 11: indeed, it is the longest biographical narration in the *Commedia*. Dante probably studied in the Franciscan convent of Santa Croce in Florence and read in its library—and probably as well in the library of the Dominican convent of Santa Maria Novella. He no doubt attended the sermons and lectures of mendicant friars in both convents. As has often been noted, Franciscan ideas and ideals are central to Dante's vision of the world: he was a fervent admirer of Francis, a strong advocate of the ideals of religious renewal and evangelical poverty embodied in the Franciscan (and Dominican) way of life, and a fierce critic of what he and others saw as deviation from that way of life among some contemporary friars.[1]

Much of the scholarship on Dante and the Muslim world has focused on the poet's knowledge and use of Arab texts: philosophical and scientific works as well as the traditions of the *mi'rāj* ("ascension").[2] Various Franciscan and Dominican friars wrote about Islam and advocated (and in some cases practiced) mission to Muslim lands. Francis of Assisi himself traveled to Egypt in 1219, in the midst of the Fifth Crusade, and met with Sultan al-Malik al-Kāmil;[3] for Dante, this is one of the central, defining events in the saint's life. To what extent is Dante's vision of this central event in Francis's life shaped by what he read, heard, and saw in Florence, particularly in the Franciscan convent of Santa Croce? How did this shape both his understanding of Francis and of Francis's mission to the Egyptian sultan? We will see that in this, as in many things, Dante borrowed extensively from earlier models but shows considerable originality and innovation.

In order to comprehend the key place given by Dante to Francis's preaching to the sultan, I will first briefly study the presence of the two mendicant orders in thirteenth-century Florence and of representations of Francis—and particularly of his encounter with the sultan—in the texts and pictorial representations with which Dante was familiar. I will then consider what Dante does with these sources in his portrayal of the saint.

Franciscans and Dominicans in Dante's Florence

The friars were a major force in the religious, intellectual, and civic life of Dante's Florence.[4] Indeed, the Franciscans had been present in Florence since the life of their founding saint; Francis sent two friars, Bernard and Giles, to the city in 1208 or 1209. Francis himself passed through Florence perhaps in 1211; he was at any rate there in 1217, when he met Cardinal Ugolino (the future Pope Gregory IX), who became cardinal protector of the order. At the time, the Friars Minor already had a small convent in the city, near the Porta San Gallo. A few years later, they transferred it to a more central site, on an island in the Arno, where they built a church dedicated to the Holy Cross (Santa Croce).[5] The primitive church and convent were no doubt quite modest: in the beginning, the church essentially served the needs of the friars. They slept in the convent, but their mission was in the city, with the Florentines. On September 14, 1228, the feast of the Holy Cross, Gregory IX promulgated a bull in favor of the Florentine convent in which the pope took "the Florentine church of Santa Croce under Saint Peter's protection and our own." In other words, Gregory affirmed the independence of the friars and their church from the bishop of Florence. He also proposed a solution to a thorny judicial problem: the Rule prohibited the Friars Minor from possessing anything: how could they then have convents and churches and accept donations from laymen? In this bull, the pope affirmed his power over the Friars Minor and their Florentine church; at the same time, the friars did not disobey the Rule, which prohibited them from owning property, since the church belonged to the pope. This became the doctrine of *usus pauper* (referring to "poor" or "restricted" ownership of goods), confirmed by Gregory in the bull *Quo elongati* on October 4, 1230.

The early convent of Santa Croce was soon too small for the Florentine brothers, all the more so since more and more prominent citizens wished to be buried there—a practice that Pope Innocent IV formally authorized in 1245. In 1252 the same pope accorded indulgences to anyone who would make donations for the construction of a new Franciscan church at Santa Croce.[6] And new Franciscan churches were springing up all over Italy for similar reasons.[7] Before the end of the thirteenth century the Florentine friars began plans for a third church, even bigger and more sumptuous, to replace the second. This project provoked the ire of certain friars, notably Ubertino da Casale, one of the heads of the nascent spiritual movement, whom the young Dante may have heard preach at Santa Croce.[8] According to a contemporary legend, the construction project was the brainchild of Giovanni degli Agli, a friar from a prominent Florentine family: he wanted a church more luxurious than Santa Maria Novella, Florence's Dominican church. After his death, Giovanni appeared to a spiritual friar and announced that he was condemned to the eternal flames for having transgressed Francis's Rule.[9] But the spirituals could not stop the project: in 1295 the Florence commune granted 1,200 pounds for the new church and the construction began; in 1297 the Franciscan pontifical legate Matteo d'Aquasparta obtained an indulgence promising the remission of sins for those laymen who contributed alms for the construction. The new church was consecrated in 1320.

With a nave 115 meters long and 38.23 meters wide (and a transept 73.73 meters wide), Santa Croce is much larger than its Dominican rival, Santa Maria Novella. As Rona Goffen has remarked, the wooden roof is in accord with the rules proclaimed at the chapter of Narbonne in 1260 concerning the construction of churches, which were supposed to be simple. But nothing else in this church respected the spirit of these rules: neither the dimensions, nor the elaborate program of decorative sculptures, frescoes, and stained glass. Santa Croce was one of the largest Franciscan convents in Europe: in 1300 there were 123 friars.[10]

While Dante was in exile when the new church was consecrated in 1320, he frequented Santa Croce during its construction. We do not know what Dante thought of the controversy surrounding the new grandiose church. In his portrait of Francis in the *Paradiso*, he presents the saint above all as the spouse of Lady Poverty; he may have seen the grandiose church as yet another proof that the order had abandoned the heritage of the "poverel di Dio" (*Par.* 13.33 "pauper of God"). In *Paradiso* 12 he has Bonaventure deliver a ringing condemnation of the strife within the order: while one can still find a few friars who respect Francis's rule, Bonaventure says, they will not be found among the followers of either conventual leader Matteo di Aquasparta or of spiritual leader Ubertino da Casale: one strives to "flee it"; the other, to "constrict it further."[11] As Nick Havely and others have noted, Dante frequently evokes the ideal of poverty, in the *Commedia* and in other writings, often echoing Franciscan ideals (and in particular spiritualist ideals) of renunciation. This is particularly seen in *Purgatorio*, where Dante appropriates the discourse of Franciscan poverty in order to imagine Purgatory as a restored church. Dante's apocalyptic vision in *Purgatorio* 32 is influenced by the spirituals, but it is distinct from their vision, since Dante foresees a revitalized Empire and a reformed Church faithful to the ideal of poverty.[12]

The Dominican convent of Santa Maria Novella also enjoyed considerable success in the thirteenth century and similar patronage from the commune and from prominent Florentine families. Daniel Lesnick has shown that the two orders did not cater to exactly the same clientele: the Franciscans recruited among the Florentine *popolo* ("commoners") and among recent arrivals in the city; the Dominicans, on the contrary, received a large number of members of the Florentine patriciate.[13] The popularity of Francis and his order are manifest in the whole of Tuscany: by 1330 Francesco becomes the most popular male name given to Tuscan boys; there are more than twice as many Francescos as Domenicos. In some villages 6–11 percent of the males are named Francesco. We have seen that Dante gives Francis a far more prominent place than Dominic among the saints in the Empyrean.

In Florence, as elsewhere in northern Italy, the new major Dominican and Franciscan churches reshaped the spiritual geography of the city, making the new mendicant convents (in the *borghi*, or "boroughs") into centers alongside the traditional center of the cathedral.[14] By the time of Dante's birth, Santa Croce and Santa Maria Novella both boasted *studia generalia* ("schools of higher learning"). Dante himself says in the *Convivio* (2.12.7) that he "frequented the schools of the religious." He may have studied with, or at least listened to lectures and sermons of, the principal teachers of both convents: the Dominican Remigio de' Girolami, who taught both Thomist theology and Roman history, and the Franciscans Peter of Trabibus, John Peter Olivi, and Ubertino da Casale. Dante probably read Aristotle and Thomas Aquinas in the library of Santa Maria Novella and Bonaventure in Santa Croce.[15] Sylvain Piron has found a quodlibetical question by Peter of Trabibus "on whether the knowledge of human letters or the goodness of intellect confers sanctity to the soul" and argues convincingly that Dante himself may have posed this question to Peter.[16] It is also possible that in Santa Maria Novella Dante met Riccoldo da Monte di Croce, a friar who set off in 1288 on a mission to Muslim lands that took him to Baghdad; he returned to Florence around 1300 and composed a polemical work against the Qur'an, the *Contra legem Saracenorum* (Against the Law of the Saracens). If he indeed returned to Florence before Dante's exile in 1301, he may have proved an important source of information on Islam.[17]

Mendicants also played a central role in the inquisition; in Florence the Franciscans took over as inquisitors from the Dominicans in 1254; this proved to be a source of considerable wealth and power for the order.[18] The friars are key players in civic affairs as well: in 1282 the

Florentine Guelfs recommended Franciscan inquisitor Salamone da
Lucca as supervisor of communal elections; Franciscan minister general Matteo di Aquasparta in 1300–1302 attempted (and failed) to ne-
gotiate peace between the black and white factions of Florentine
Guelfs.[19] Throughout northern Italy, friars increasingly direct and control lay piety, at times creating clashes as mendicant inquisitors condemn cults of saints deemed heretical and destroy their shrines.[20]

The growing presence of the friars and their accumulation of land
in the Italian cities at times provoked resentment and hostility. In the
mid-thirteenth century the Bologna city council forbade the dumping
of trash or dead animals onto Dominican property and tried to put an
end to throwing rocks at the Franciscan convent.[21] In 1325, four years
after Dante's death, the commune of Florence took measures to ban
friars from civic office.[22] Dante himself, while expressing admiration
for the two founding saints of the orders and the lives they preached,
harshly criticized abuses within the two orders. Thomas Aquinas follows his narration of Francis's life with a severe condemnation of the
abuses in his own Dominican order:

> Ma 'l suo peculio di nova vivanda
>   è fatto ghiotto, sì ch'esser non puote
>   che per diversi salti non si spanda;
> e quanto le sue pecore remote
>   e vagabunde più da esso vanno,
>   più tornano a l'ovil di latte vòte

> But his flock has grown so greedy
> for new fare that it cannot help but
> be scattered through varied pastures;
> and the farther his sheep, remote
> and vagabond, stray from him, the more
> empty of milk they return to the fold.
>
> (*Par.* 11.124–29)

In a parallel passage, Bonaventure, after relating the life and deeds
of Dominic, denounces the conflicts within the Franciscan order. This
theme of clerical corruption recurs throughout the *Commedia:* Saint
Benedict, for example, bemoans the degeneracy of Benedictine monks
(*Par.* 22.73–93); Peter Damian complains of the venality of modern
clerics (*Par.* 21.127–35). The Franciscans and Dominicans were an essential part of urban Italian life for Dante, but many of them were

cruelly lacking in the qualities so brilliantly displayed by their saintly founders.

Dante's Francis in the Context of His Sources

At the same time that the two principal mendicant orders were establishing convents in Florence and other Italian (and more generally European) cities, playing an increasing role in their religious and civic life, each order pursued missionary activities to non-Christians: Jews, Muslims, Mongols, and in some cases Oriental Christians. In the case of the Franciscans, it was Francis himself who initiated mission to "Saracens," preaching to the Egyptian sultan al-Kāmil in 1219 and, in 1221, including a chapter on missions to Saracens in the *Regula non bullata* (Rule without a Papal Bull), the first extant written rule of the Friars Minor. In 1220 five friars were put to death in Marrakech for having insulted Muhammad and the Qur'an; others emulated their active search for martyrdom throughout the thirteenth and fourteenth centuries.[23] For these Franciscans, preaching to infidels was part of the apostolic life, indeed the culmination of that life, for it led to an apostolic death: martyrdom at the hands of the infidels.

Dante's knowledge of Franciscan mission, and particularly of Francis's preaching to al-Kāmil, would have come from his discussion with Santa Croce's friars as well as his reading of Bonaventure's life of Francis, the *Legenda maior* (Longer Life of Saint Francis). It would also have been nourished by his contemplation of the painted images of the saint, such as those of the Bardi dossal at Santa Croce and perhaps the frescoes of the upper basilica at Assisi.

In 1228 Friar Thomas of Celano, at the bidding of Gregory IX, wrote a life of Francis, known as the *Vita prima* (First Life of St. Francis), for the saint's canonization process.[24] Thomas describes Francis's conversion from a life of carefree pleasure to a life of pursuing the apostolic ideal. He then tells how Francis and a band of companions joyfully lived in poverty, simplicity, and communal prayer, and how the saint sent off his companions two by two, like the apostles, to preach. Francis himself, driven by a "great desire for martyrdom," set off for "Syria" and, braving the dangers of fierce wars between Christians and "pagans," crossed over to the enemy camp to meet with and preach to the sultan. Francis and his companion were beaten by the infidel soldiers, but then well received by the sultan himself, who listened to him with interest. Francis, however, succeeded neither in converting the sultan nor in obtaining the martyrdom he so desired, for God had reserved for him "the prerogative of a unique grace": the stigmata. For Thomas, Francis's voyage testifies first and foremost to his great desire for martyrdom: the saint wanted to live the apostolic life to its logical end, to die the glorious death of the apostles, achieving martyrdom at the hands of the infidels. In Thomas's *Vita*, Francis's passage to the East marks a turning point in his life. Before his departure Thomas describes the saint's conversion and the foundation of a brotherhood living in poverty and in joyous devotion, recreating the simple life of the apostles. Francis is above all a model, an inspiration, a companion in the pursuit of this ideal life. After his return from the East, he is a singular, inimitable man: one who speaks to animals and makes them obey him, who performs miracles, and who receives the divine mark of the stigmata.

While Dante probably did not read Thomas's *Vita prima*, he may well have been acquainted with the Bardi dossal, a large altarpiece probably painted in the 1240s, which is now in the Bardi Chapel of Santa Croce and which may well have been in Santa Croce when Dante frequented the church.[25] It is an important early example of a dossal, or altarpiece, probably meant to be placed above and behind an altar in Santa Croce (Figures 1–3). In the center stands Francis, haloed, in Franciscan habit (brown with pointed hood, with a knotted rope in place of a belt). He is tonsured. The stigmata, in black, are clearly visible on his hands and feet. His right hand is raised in a Christ-like gesture of blessing, while his left hand holds a book with a golden cover marked with a large cross. Is this book the Gospels, as some commentators have affirmed, or rather the Franciscan Rule, as others have argued? Are the two not the same for Francis and his followers? To live according to the Rule is to live according to the Gospels; Francis himself had presented the *Regula non bullata* as the "life of the Gospel of Jesus Christ."[26] The artist seems to affirm the same here. This sentiment is confirmed by the scene above the saint's head: the hand of God emerges from the blue vault of the firmament and unfurls a parchment, toward which two angels point. On the parchment, we read: "Hunc exaudite perhibentem dogmata vitae" ("Obey this man, bearer of the precepts of life"). God orders the viewer to obey Francis, who bears in his hand the "precepts of life," that is, the rule of the Gospel.

Figure 1. Saint Francis, surrounded by scenes from his life (Master of Saint Francis, Bardi dossal, Santa Croce, Florence). (Scala / Art Resource, NY)

How is one to follow this divine order, to live according to the precepts of the Rule/Gospel? That is what the artist shows in the twenty scenes placed around the central standing figure of the saint, who is both a model to follow and a saint to venerate. The twenty scenes present a narration, more or less chronological, of the life, death, and several post mortem miracles of Francis. The narrative begins on the top left. Francis, on the right of the scene, haloed (in this scene and in all the others), is freed by his mother: according to Thomas of Celano, he had been imprisoned by his father, who was furious that his son gave away his money in order to pay for repairing a church (1C 12–13). In an act of maternal love and charity, the mother liberates her son; on the left is the father, who has returned and who seems to oppose in vain his wife's act. Directly underneath, the second scene shows Francis breaking the ties with his parents. Before the cathedral and the episcopal palace of Assisi, Francis tosses his clothes at his father's feet; the bishop of Assisi, a tall man with a gray beard, holding a book in his hand, puts his arm and his cloak around Francis, in a gesture of welcome and protection. In the center are the blue and white clothes that Francis has spurned, symbols of the worldly life that he now renounces. In the third scene, Francis traces, using a stick as the bishop looks on, the habit in the form of a cross that he will wear in the seventeen other scenes. In the following scene, Francis listens to mass at the church of Portiuncula: when he hears Christ's injunction to the Apostles: "Provide neither gold, nor silver, nor brass in your purses, nor scrip for your journey, neither two coats, neither shoes, nor yet staves," he removes his shoes and henceforth goes barefoot.[27]

These initial scenes emphasize Francis's rupture with a world ruled by monetary and material values. Francis has chosen to renounce his parental heritage. The dress and appearance of Francis and his friars clearly show this rupture: the habit in the shape of the cross, the bare feet, the simple cord instead of a belt, the refusal to handle money. In the fifth scene, the pope gives his approval to Francis, who kneels at the center of the composition; the pope hands Francis a book with his left hand and blesses him with his right hand. Behind the pope, several cardinals look on; behind Francis are a friar and a priest. It has often been said that the pope here is Innocent III, but nothing indicates whether the scene is meant to represent the first approbation of the order by Innocent in 1209/1210 or the approval of the *Regula bullata* by Honorius III in 1223, or a mix of the two. In any case, the mes-

Figure 2. Francis preaches to the birds and to the Saracens (Master of Saint Francis, Bardi dossal, Santa Croce, Florence). (Scala / Art Resource, NY)

sage is clear: both Francis and his Rule have received the blessing of the pope and hence of the Church. The book, like that held by the saint at the center of the dossal, is both Rule and Gospel since, according to Thomas of Celano, Francis, in composing the first rule "used primarily words of the Holy Gospel, longing only for its perfection" (1C 32).

The artist presents preaching as a central concern for Francis and his friars, as we see in two images of Francis preaching: to the birds and to the Saracens. In both cases, a group of friars is on the left: at least three behind Francis above, two below (even though all the texts give Francis only one companion). In the preaching to the birds, Francis holds a closed book in his left hand; his right hand is pointed toward his audience, his index finger raised. Before the Muslims, the book is open; the pages are blank; his right hand is raised toward Heaven. In both cases, he preaches to an attentive and well-ordered audience. The birds, all shown in profile, are aligned in five rows, on the ground and on four perfectly horizontal branches of a tree; they face Francis and seem to listen to him. They all have the same size and coloring; some hold their wings open. Other artists will take pleasure in depicting a great variety of birds before the saint, with a multiplicity of species, sizes, and colors—no doubt for aesthetic reasons, but also to symbolize the great diversity of the men and women to whom Francis and his friars are called to preach. Here, on the contrary, the accent is on the fundamental uniformity of God's creatures, all of whom should sing praises of their Creator. Below, the Saracens are also neatly aligned in five rows. Here, however, the artist has depicted them in all their diversity, with clothes of different colors (red, pink, blue, white) and both women and men (though it is not always possible to distinguish a woman from a young beardless man). Some of the men have black or white beards, most of which (including the sultan's) are long and pointed, marking them as Oriental: the other men depicted in the dossal have closely trimmed beards. Many of them have turbans. The seated position of the men in the first row is also visibly Oriental: they are on the ground, with legs crossed or, in one case, arms around knees—positions that we find nowhere else on the panel. As for the sultan, apart from his long beard, nothing distinguishes him from a Christian king: he holds all the essential symbols of royal power: crown, scepter, throne, royal robes, and, behind him, his *spatharius*, or arms-bearer, holding his spear and shield. The sultan and his subjects have their eyes riveted on the saint; they seem to be listening to him closely.

In the scene of Francis's preaching to the sultan in the Bardi dossal, the artist has first of all had to make a choice: he devotes only one image to Francis's mission to the East. He could have chosen, taking inspiration from Thomas of Celano's text, to paint the context of the crusade, placing the encounter in the midst of the tents of the sultan's army; on the contrary, he chose an urban setting that—alongside the bucolic venue of the preaching to the birds—underlines the universal character of the Franciscans' preaching mission. He could have shown the saint being "insulted and beaten" (as Thomas affirms) by the sultan's soldiers. Yet here nothing suggests the slightest threat of violence: the only weapon, the spear held by the *spatharius*, presents no danger because it is pointed upward. The artist could have shown the rich gifts that the sultan offered Francis, "trying to turn his mind towards worldly riches." Yet he chose to portray Francis preaching to the sultan who "was moved by his words and listened to him very willingly."[28]

Several scenes later, Francis receives the stigmata: kneeling before the door of a sanctuary in a mountainous landscape, the saint raises his hands in prayer and contemplates the image of the crucified Christ superimposed on a seraph. Golden rays emanate from the seraph to the saint's halo. I have described the scenes that find echoes clearly in Dante's text. The one aspect of Dante's text that has no clear visual representation in the Bardi dossal is his marriage with Lady Poverty. Yet the spirit of poverty is clear: a number of the scenes emphasize the extreme ascesis of Francis and his brothers—their simple habit, their bare feet, Francis's penance, his care for lepers. Francis is clearly presented as a model to be followed by the Franciscans of Santa Croce. Other thirteenth-century representations, by contrast, present Francis as a saint and miracle worker to be venerated.

But the central source on Francis for Dante, as for anyone in the early fourteenth century, was Bonaventure's *Legenda maior*. In 1260 the general chapter of Narbonne asked Bonaventure (minister general of the order) to compose a new life of Francis. Bonaventure completed the text before May 1263, when the general chapter meeting at Pisa approved the *Legenda maior*.[29] In 1266 the general chapter of Paris ordered that any other biography of Francis be destroyed: Bonaventure's *Legenda* became henceforth the only authoritative text on the founder of the order. Thus Dante is unlikely to have encountered, in Santa Croce or elsewhere, earlier texts on Francis, such as Thomas of Celano's *Vita prima*. Every Franciscan convent had at least one copy of Bonaventure's text. While Bonaventure based his narrative on earlier hagiographical works, notably Thomas's, he transformed those works to present a saint whose spiritual itinerary led him inexorably upward toward Christ.

The culminating point and central miracle of this itinerary is the stig-matization, for Bonaventure as for Dante. In the prologue to the *Legenda maior*, Bonaventure applies to Francis the words of Apocalypse 7:2: "Vidi alterum angelum ascendentem ab ortu solis" ("I saw another angel ascending from the rising of the sun"). Dante, as we will see, goes further and makes Francis into a sun rising in the East.

For Bonaventure, the ardent longing for martyrdom played a key role in Franciscan spirituality. It was the highest form of love—at once a longing for union with God and a desire to bring the souls of infidels to him. Bonaventure's *Legenda* insists on the burning desire for martyrdom that drove Francis East. Bonaventure takes up and expands on Thomas of Celano's version of Francis's series of failed attempts to obtain the crown of martyrdom from the Saracens. He embellishes the interview with the sultan, having Francis propose an ordeal: he and the sultan's "priests" would enter into a fire; he who came out unscathed would have proven that he followed God's true law. When the Saracen priests refused, Francis urged the sultan to light a fire anyway so that he could enter the flames alone. The sultan refused, fearing a revolt among his people. Francis then spurned the gifts that the sultan offered him; the sultan, "was overflowing with admiration, and developed an even greater respect for him." Since the sultan did not wish or did not dare to convert, Bonaventure concludes, Francis left him. This apparent failure is but a step on the way to the stigmata, the ultimate expression of his burning love for Christ.

Fire, heat, and light are the dominant metaphors in Bonaventure's portrayal of Francis: in the description of quest for martyrdom, we repeatedly find the terms *fervens* ("boiling"), *flamma* ("flame"), *successus* ("kindled"), *flagrans* ("blazing"), *ardor* ("heat"), *ignis* ("fire"), *comburere* ("combust"), and *aestuare* ("seethe").[30] Bonaventure's fiery metaphor finds graphic expression on the walls of the upper basilica at Assisi, where in the final years of the thirteenth century a series of twenty-eight large frescoes was executed that presents Francis as a prodigious miracle worker.[31] Among these frescoes, traditionally attributed to Giotto, is an image of a confrontation between Francis and Saracen "priests" (Figure 3). Drawing inspiration from the trial by fire that (according to Bonaventure) Francis proposed to the sultan, the artist places the saint in the middle of the composition, before a fire that separates him from the Saracen "priests" and causes them to flee. Francis glances back at the sultan, who, seated on his throne and surrounded by armed men, with

Figure 3. Trial by fire of Saint Francis (Fresco, School of Giotto, Upper Basilica, Assisi). (Scala / Art Resource, NY)

a sweep of his arm exhorts Francis to enter into the fire. Francis's mission to Egypt has become a dramatic confrontation, an ordeal whose final outcome is uncertain but that has succeeded in chasing away the clerics of the rival religion, shown the superiority of Christianity, and displayed Francis's courage.

Bonaventure is Dante's principal written source for the life of Francis. Dante also no doubt had in his mind the images from the

Bardi dossal and perhaps those of the frescoes at Assisi. He was also acquainted with the *Sacrum commercium Sancti Francisci cum domina Paupertate* (Sacred Exchange of Saint Francis with Lady Poverty), a text probably composed in the thirteenth century; it is not clear whether it was composed before or after Bonaventure's *Legenda maior*.[32] Dante may have at some point read the text, may merely have heard of it, or may have read a text that had reworked elements of it, such as Ubertino's *Arbor vitae crucifixae Jesu* (Tree of the Crucified Life of Jesus).[33]

Dante's Francis

Let us now consider what Dante does with these sources to paint a portrait of Francis in *Paradiso* 11.[34] In Canto 10, Dante and Beatrice ascend into the Sphere of the Sun, where they meet the wise—in particular, theologians—and speak with Thomas Aquinas, who explains how "The Providence that rules the world" ordained two princes:

> L'un fu tutto serafico in ardore;
> l'altro per sapïenza in terra fue
> di cherubica luce uno splendore

> The one was all seraphic in his ardor;
> the other, for wisdom on earth was
> a splendor of cherubic light.
> (*Par.* 11.37–39)

In Canto 12, the Franciscan Bonaventure narrates the life of Dominic; here it is the Dominican Thomas who tells Francis's story. This crossed narration is meant no doubt to show that fraternal admiration between two rival orders reigns in Heaven and that the two saints and their orders are fundamentally compatible. Taking his cue from Bonaventure, Dante presents Francis as the expression of "seraphic ardor."[35] Thomas begins, in two stanzas, by evoking the Umbrian landscape where the saint was born and continues:

> Di questa costa, là dov' ella frange
>   più sua rattezza, nacque al mondo un sole,
>   come fa questo tal volta di Gange.
> Però chi d'esso loco fa parole
>   non dica Ascesi, ché direbbe corto
>   ma Orïente, se proprio dir vuole.

From this slope, where its steepness
is most broken, a sun was born to the world,
much like this one arising from the Ganges.
Therefore let him who talks of this place
not say *Ascesi*, which rises not to the occasion,
but *Orient*, if he would alight on the proper name.

(Par. 11.49–54)

Assisi is the East, source of the rising sun that is Francis: it is compared
with the Ganges and equated with the Orient. Dante plays on the
word *Ascesi*: a contemporary spelling for "Assisi" but also a verb meaning "I have risen," here applied to the new rising sun, Francis. This description is appropriately set in the Sphere of the Sun. This can only
highlight the comparison between Francis and Christ, whom Luke
(1:78–79) presents as a new rising sun. In Canto 11, Bonaventure presents Dominic's home, Spain, as the land of the setting sun, emphasizing both the universality and complementarity of the two friars'
missions. Thomas goes on to describe Francis's love for Lady Poverty
and how that love brought him into conflict with his father, leading to
a dramatic confrontation:

ché per tal donna, giovinetto, in guerra
    del padre corse, a cui, come a la morte,
    la porta del piacer nessun diserra;
e dinanzi a la sua spiritat corte
    et *coram patre* le si fece unito;
    poscia di dì in dì l'amò più forte

for a certain Lady in his youth he rushed
into conflict with his father, a Lady for whom,
like death, no one willingly unlocks the gate;
and before his spiritual court
et coram patre he was joined unto her;
and day by day, he loved her more and more.

(Par. 11.58–63)

Bonaventure describes the dramatic scene of Francis's renunciation of
his worldly wealth, how the saint stripped naked "coram episcopo"
(before the bishop; he later adds "coram omnibus," before everyone)
and gave his clothes to his father, "ad quod faciendum se promptum
exhibuit verus paupertatis amator" ("in so doing showed himself ready
to be a true lover of poverty"). This dramatic confrontation is a key

episode in Franciscan iconography, seen in both the Bardi dossal and in the Assisi frescoes. Dante dramatizes this image of Francis as "lover of poverty": "coram patre," before his father, he joins himself, against his father's wishes, to the lady he loves, a woman feared and despised as death. This lady, he continues, is "privata del primo marito, millecent' anni e più dispetta e scura" (*Par.* 11.64 "bereft of her first husband, for eleven hundred years and more, despised and obscure"). Her husband of course is Christ: Francis, the new sun, *alter Christus*, is her new mate, to the great consternation of Francis's father. While Bonaventure presented Francis as *paupertatis amator*, this idea was given fuller allegorical expression in the *Sacrum commercium*. Yet, as Erich Auerbach has noted, Dante's portrayal of the love between Francis and Poverty is quite different from that of the *Sacrum commercium*, whose Poverty chastely addresses Francis and his friars as her "brothers and sons." Dante portrays their love in clearly sexual terms: Francis, enamored of a spurned and despised woman, joins himself to her in love *"coram patre"*; in this striking metaphor, the poet dramatizes the rupture with his father and with the values of the Italian merchant community that the father represented. What had been a rather bland and chaste metaphor for spiritual love becomes an image of "fole amors," a mad love that drives Francis to spurn his father and his own reputation in the pursuit of his love.[36] Thomas goes on to tell how this same love inspired others to follow Francis's example:

> . . .'l venerabile Bernardo
> si scalzò prima, e dietro a tanta pace
> corse e, correndo, li parve esser tardo.
> Oh ignota ricchezza! oh ben ferace!
> Scalzasi Egidio, scalzasi Silvestro
> dietro a lo sposo, sì la sposa piace.

> . . . the venerable Bernard
> first went barefoot to rush toward such peace,
> and as he ran, his pace seemed to him too slow.
> Oh unknown riches! Oh fruitful good!
> Egidius goes barefoot, and Silvester too, both
> following the groom, the bride delights them so.
>   (*Par.* 11.79–84)

These three first recruits run after the groom out of desire for the bride. Their act of conversion is expressed in one dramatic action: the verb *scalzarsi* (to take off one's shoes) used three times. We have seen that the Bardi dossal portrays Francis removing his shoes to respect the Gospels' injunction to live simply; Bonaventure too presents Francis's shedding his shoes as the first key act marking his conversion.[37]

Dante then presents how Francis obtains "three seals." The first two are the approval of his life and order by two popes: Innocent III (who, according to Franciscan tradition, gave his approval to the order in 1209 or 1210) and Honorius III (who confirmed the Franciscan *Regula bullata* in 1223). Next comes his preaching to the sultan, which for Dante is inextricably related to the saint's obtaining the third and final seal, the stigmata:

> E poi che, per la sete del martiro,
>   Ne la presenza del Soldan superba
>   predicò Cristo e li altri che 'l seguiro,
> e per trovare a conversione acerba
>   troppo la gente per non stare indarno,
>   redissi al frutto dell'italica erba,
> nel crudo sasso intra Tevero e Arno
>   da Cristo prese l'ultimo sigillo,
>   che le sue membra due anni portarno.

> And when, in his thirst for martyrdom,
> in the proud presence of the sultan
> he preached Christ and those who followed Him,
> but found the people too unripe for conversion,
> so as not to stay in vain he returned
> to the harvest of Italian fields,
> where on the harsh rock bewteen Tiber and Arno
> he received from Christ the last seal,
> which his limbs bore for two years.
>   (*Par.* 11.100–108)

It is Francis's "thirst for martyrdom" that drives him to preach to the sultan: Francis preached in the *presenza superba* of the sultan—a description that could call to mind the image of the sultan sitting straight and regally on his throne, as seen in both the Bardi dossal and the Assisi fresco. Yet Dante emphasizes preaching, as in the Bardi dossal, not the proposed trial by fire seen in Assisi. Dante gives a prominent place to the preaching to the sultan, one of the few events of the saint's life that he narrates. In Canto 12 (*Par.* 12.130), Bonaventure follows his diatribe against contemporary Franciscans by presenting exemplary ascetics in Heaven: the first name he mentions is that of Illuminatus, Francis's companion to the sultan's court.

Francis realizes the futility of his quest. Bonaventure says that he learned through divine revelation that he would succeed neither in converting the Saracens nor in obtaining martyrdom. Dante uses an agricultural metaphor: Francis found the sultan's people "unripe for conversion," so he "returned to the harvest of Italian fields." Bonaventure explains that while Francis had not been martyred in a traditional manner at the hands of the infidel, he was later received the palm of martyrdom through his stigmatization (which Bonaventure recounts just before relating the saint's death).

Dante places the stigmatization immediately following the saint's return to Italy. This is the third and final seal: the first two seals, the approval by popes Innocent III and Honorius III, had marked the acknowledgment of Francis and his order by the institutional Church. The third is imprinted by Christ himself and shows his recognition of Francis as one who had followed in his footsteps and had wed his bereaved bride Poverty.

Thomas then relates how the saint bequeathed Lady Poverty to his brothers and ordered them to love her faithfully, how he then chose to set forth from the bosom of Lady Poverty, "e al suo corpo non volle altra bara" (*Par.* 11.117 "and wished no other casket for his corpse"). Bonaventure had described how Francis wished to depart naked from the world, "nudus voluit de mundo exire" (*Legenda maior* 14.4): he removed his clothes, lay naked on the bare earth, and there died.

Dante follows this evocation of Francis's seraphic ardor with a condemnation of the lack of zeal of current friars; his Thomas is too polite to criticize the Franciscans, so he lambastes the shortcomings of his own, the Dominicans; similarly, in Canto 12, Bonaventure follows his portrayal of Dominic with a ringing condemnation of current Franciscans.

Dante's sultan is little more than a foil for Francis's sanctity. His "proud presence" provides a stage where Francis can shine forth, showing his exemplary imitation of Christ and the Apostles. Francis's mission, and Franciscan mission in general, seems less about converting Muslims than about leading lives of exemplary sanctity. Francis preaches to the sultan in the East, while Dominic (in *Par.* 12) evangelizes heretics in the West. The sultan is another fleeting Muslim presence in the *Commedia:* a proud and dignified presence, perhaps, reminiscent of the regal figure in the Bardi dossal or the Assisi fresco, but a mute figure. Indeed, the only Muslim who speaks in the *Commedia* is Muhammad himself, and it is to utter a fierce condemnation of the "schism" he founded and of that subsequently perpetrated by his nephew Ali. Saladin, the historical uncle of al-Kāmil, is a stately and dignified—but silent—figure in the City of Light in the first circle of Hell. Unlike Saladin, al-Kāmil does not directly appear in the *Commedia*: he is merely a silent, nameless figure, proud and regal, in Thomas Aquinas's narration of Francis's exemplary life.

Here as elsewhere, Dante uses and transforms his sources, creating a portrait of Francis that bears the clear traces of Bonaventure, the *Sacrum commercium*, and the visual images of Florence and Assisi, but transcends them all, forming a unique and original image. Dante sketches Francis's life in bold and clear strokes: his marriage to poverty, approbation by two popes (his first two seals), his preaching to the sultan, the *ultimo sigillo* of the stigmata, and his exemplary death. His Francis is both immediately recognizable and striking, an exemplar of evangelical poverty who shows how far his followers have fallen from the ideal he represents. It is perhaps in part this kind of alchemical transformation of his source material that led his biographer and admirer, Giovanni Boccaccio, to present the *Commedia* as inimitable, in terms that strangely echo the Muslim doctrine of the inimitability of the Qur'an:

> De' quali tre libri egli ciascuno distinse per canti e i canti per rittimi, sì come chiaro si vede; e quello in rima volgare compose con tanta arte, con sì mirabile ordine e con sì bello, che niuno fu ancora che giustamente quello potesse in alcuno atto riprendere.

> He distinguished each of its three books with songs, and the songs with rhythms, as is clearly perceptible; and he composed it in common rhymes with such skill, with such amazing order and with such beauty, that there has been no one who could justly find fault with it in any aspect.[38]

Dante and the Three Religions

GIORGIO BATTISTONI

I nklings of Dante's interest in non-Christian religions and cultures began to make their way into the sphere of Dante studies around 1919–21. I refer specifically to *La escatología musulmana en la Divina Comedia* (Muslim Eschatology in the Divine Comedy) by the Spanish Jesuit Miguel Asín Palacios, himself a student of Arab culture.[1] This work, which arrived in Italy during the celebrations commemorating the six-hundredth anniversary of Dante's death, aimed to show that the basic conception of the *Commedia* and many of the ideas contained in it were found by Dante in Arab texts that narrated the voyage of Muḥammad through Hell and into the Islamic Paradise.[2]

Having thoroughly analyzed various versions of the legend of Muḥammad's voyage into the world of eternal punishments and rewards, Asín Palacios concluded that the many points of contact with the *Commedia* could not have resulted from pure chance. Rather, in his view they demonstrated that Dante had access to various eschatological and metaphysical Muslim texts and that he used this knowledge in creating his own Christian realm of the afterlife. Unfortunately Asín Palacios did not provide any proof that Dante had available to him any sources other than those which had been translated into Latin and circulated in the Latin-speaking world.

Before continuing with the history of Muslim eschatology within the *Commedia*, I would like to recall an incident that took place at Verona during that commemoration of the six-hundredth anniversary of Dante's death. In the wake of the national celebrations, the city of Verona decided to open the tomb of Cangrande (on July 27, 1921) in order to see if that great patron of Dante had taken with him, on his final journey, the third canticle, or even the entire *Commedia*, or at least *Epistola* 13 in which the *Paradiso* had been dedicated to him. Although no manuscript of or by Dante was found in the tomb, the embalmed cadaver was found with a shroud entirely of Islamic fabrics wrapped around it.[3] One of the pieces was in the style associated with the Mongol Ilkanide dynasty that held sway in Iran and Iraq from 1251 to 1335. It symbolizes, with its astronomical animals (Raven, Fish, Lion/Dog, and Rabbit/Hare), the route of the soul through the astral sphere. Another of the swatches has an Arabic eulogy woven into it with the name of Allah.[4]

On the basis of these fabrics, I set out to delve into the perilous nexus between Dante, Cangrande, and the Islamic world. In fact, the first question that arose was why a Christian prince would have been interred with a funeral shroud of Muslim origin. I attempted to respond to this question by linking the strange burial of Cangrande with the presence in the *Commedia* of the Islamic traces pointed out by Asín Palacios: although the reason may have been yet incomprehensible, the common eschatology that connected the afterlives of Dante, Cangrande, and Muḥammad warranted note. It was just this search for a reasonable answer (causal, rather than casual) as to the perilous nexus that gave way to my study, "Dante, l'Islam, ed altre considerazioni" (Dante, Islam, and Other Considerations, 1985). Since this study, I have examined the religious paradigm of the "three rings" (as popularized in Boccaccio's *Decameron*) and the idea of empire in hopes of finding the explanation.

Thirty years after Asín Palacios's study appeared, an Italian scholar discovered the documentary proof that had eluded the Spaniard. Following a clue from Ugo Monneret de Villard,[5] Enrico Cerulli fixed his attention on manuscripts in Oxford and Paris, and found within the *Corpus Toletanum* (Toledan Collection) French and Latin translations of the famous *Kitab al-mi'rāj* (Ascension of Muḥammad). Furthermore, another manuscript of the Latin translation, the *Liber scale Machometi* (Book of the Ladder of Muḥammad), occurs in Rome, Biblioteca Vaticana, MS Vat. lat. 4072, also within the *Corpus Toletanum* that was translated into Latin under the direction of Peter the Venerable, Abbot of Cluny. Cerulli comments on the significance of the surviving manuscript witnesses:

Questa provenienza, dunque, prova un'altra linea di diffusione del
"Liber Scalae" negli scriptoria del primo Trecento. . . . Questo fatto
ne assicurava la diffusione e insieme ne garantiva, agli occhi degli
occidentali, il carattere di libro considerato sacro dai musulmani.

This provenance, therefore, demonstrates a different route of dissemination of the "Book of the Ladder" in the scriptoria of the early
fourteenth century . . . . This fact ensured the dissemination and
simultaneously guaranteed, in the eyes of Westerners, the character
of a book considered sacred by Muslims.[6]

The importance of the discovery of this text in terms of the West
and Italy lay not so much in its contents, which do little to distinguish
themselves from the collage of Arabic texts used by Asín Palacios in
elaborating his argument, as in the fact that a single book could contain the evidence to support the hypothesis that Dante would have
had access to Muslim eschatology detailing the voyage of Muḥammad
to the afterlife. That this text circulated in Latin during Dante's age
served to demonstrate the proper grounding of Asín Palacios's thesis.

The *Liber scale Machometi*—a medieval Andalusian version of the
nocturnal journey (*isrā'*) and ascension or stairway (*mi'rāj*) of the
prophet Muḥammad—had been translated into Castilian from Arabic
by the Toledan Jewish physician Abraham Alfaquím between 1260 and
1264, as part of the translation project supported by Alfonso X the
Wise.[7] Shortly thereafter the text would be translated from Castilian
into French and Latin by the notary Bonaventure of Siena, and it becomes disseminated throughout the Christian West. The connection
with Bonaventure may tie the book to Dante's Tuscany. In fact, a citation from the *Liber scale Machometi* appeared in the work of an Italian
poet. In a volume entitled *Il Dittamondo* (The Sayings of the World),
composed around 1350, Fazio degli Uberti wrote, in speaking of the
Muslim religion, "Ancor nel Libro suo che Scala ha nome" ("Yet in that
book that has as its name *Scala*").[8]

Let us turn again to Cerulli:

Fazio degli Uberti, che scriveva il suo *Dittamondo* tra il 1350 e il 1360,
conosceva il *Libro della Scala*. . . . Fazio degli Uberti, immediato
epigono di Dante, attesta insieme la conoscenza nella Toscana del
medio Trecento del *Libro della Scala*.

Fazio degli Uberti, who wrote his *Sayings of the World* between 1350
and 1360, knew the *Book of the Ladder*. . . . Fazio degli Uberti,

immediate follower of Dante, also attested familiarity with the *Book of the Ladder* in mid-fourteenth-century Tuscany.[9]

Cerulli, however, was a bit too hasty in stating as a fact that this book was known in Tuscany at that time. In fact, the family of Farinata degli Uberti, constrained in 1266 to abandon Florence, chose for their new home that Verona of the della Scala family, at the time ruled by Mastino I (d. 1277). They were just one of many Ghibelline families forced by historical events to remake themselves as Lombards.[10]

It was at the court of Mastino II della Scala (1308–1351), the nephew and immediate successor to Cangrande, that Fazio degli Uberti belonged to a coterie of artists, poets, and musicians. Thus if one wishes to trace the physical and political roots of Fazio degli Uberti (and therefore of his reference to the *Liber scale Machometi*), one would have to look not to Florence and Tuscany but rather to Verona and Lombardy. In this artistic circle, three musicians stand out as composers of madrigals. Their names signal a program of transfiguration. In the Synoptic Gospels (Matthew 17:1–9, Mark 9:2–8, Luke 9:28–36) Jesus ascends an unnamed mountain (identified since the third century with Mount Tabor) with the apostles Peter, James (son of Zebedee), and John the Apostle, and is transfigured before them. The three madrigalists are named Maestro Piero, Jacopo da Bologna, and Giovanni da Cascia, their personal names corresponding directly to the names of the three apostles.

We find ourselves between the years 1336 and 1350, while these three musicians imagined themselves to be in an earthly Paradise, obviously "in scale" (according to the analogy of proportion between the model and its copy, commonly used in the Middle Ages), that in their madrigals was referred to as "il bel giardino" ("the beautiful garden") and "il verziere" ("the orchard"). In this Paradise there ran a "fiume chiaro" ("clear river") of "perla" ("pearls") "corrente" ("flowing"); there also grew an "albero di perla" ("tree of pearls") "bei fiori adorno" ("adorned with beautiful flowers") giving "grande ombra" ("plentiful shade").[11] The interesting thing is that these musicians truly found themselves in a Paradise: that is, the gardens of the della Scala family along the banks of the Adige, where the shade that covered them was provided by a real tree of pearls, that is, a tree known in Italian as *perlaro*. These songs, these compositions are in fact known today as the "Ciclo del perlaro" (Cycle of the *Perlaro*).[12]

The *perlaro* referred to by these musicians is also known as a *bago-laro* ("hackberry, nettle-tree") or *loto* ("lotus, lote tree").[13] Mattioli, in his *Volgarizzamento di Dioscoride* (Translation of Dioscorides), writes:

> Se pure a tempi nostri si ritrovano loti in Italia, non penso che fallerebbe chi dicesse che fusse il vero loto, e massimamente quello cui intesero Dioscoride e Plinio, quello che in su 'l Trentino si chiama bagolaro et in alcuni altri luoghi (così come ancora a Verona) si chiama perlaro.

> If the lotus is indeed found in contemporary Italy, I do not think one would err in calling it the true lotus, especially if one means the plant known to Dioscorides and Pliny, which in Trentino is called hackberry and in some other places (so even now in Verona) is called "pearl tree."[14]

In this place, both real and symbolic, these musicians sang of the woman named Anna, the flame that kindled their poetic-erudite passions.

Scholars generally, besides looking at who could have been the flesh-and-blood *donna angelicata* ("angelic lady, the woman as angel") veiled under the pseudonym of Anna, have investigated the botanic name of the tree referred to as the *perlaro*. However, had they given more attention to the poems themselves, they would have understood that the *perlaro* (Melia azedarach) was above all else a tree that gave the water running by the feet of the musicians a pearl-like color. As Jacopo said, it was "il bel perlaro fiume" ("the beautiful pearl river"). Also, they would have seen that Anna, rather than containing a surname, hid within her name's etymology the meaning of "grace," just as Giovanna, for Dante, signified the "Grace of God" (*Par.* 12.79–81).

Here I will not concentrate on this "donna di grazia" (or alternatively, of "merzé" or "mercede"), this woman of Grace. Rather, I will focus on the description of the Muslim Paradise, the place in which Muḥammad obtained the divine gift of Grace that would transform a common man into a prophet, the representative of God. Having visited the place where curtains soared in covering and housing the "beautiful women," the *donne angelicate* that were given by God to those worthy souls in Paradise, Muḥammad continues his narration thus:

> When I, Muḥammad . . . had seen these great marvels, of which I just spoke to you . . . Gabriel and Ridhoan, who were with me, brought me to the place which was called the Lotus of Forgetful-

ness . . . and they showed me a certain tree, so great and so extremely beautiful that I can hardly describe it even a little bit. For the tree was *completely of one pearl, marvelously white.* It was so beautiful that its beauty surpassed all others, except the beauty of God and his angels. And similarly all of its leaves, its flowers, and its fruits were like Him. And all its fruits had all the good flavors that a man's heart could imagine.

At the foot of this tree arose *a spring of water, brighter and clearer than anything,* sweeter than honey. I asked Gabriel what kind of spring. He replied that the spring was called "Halkaufkar," which means *the source of complete grace* [my emphasis].[15]

It is properly the infusion of Grace (Anna for our three musicians!) that transforms (and transfigures) those who arrive at the "loto del termine" or the "tree of pearls" into a poet and into a prophet, a representative, a scribe of God: "In every truly inspired man there is the nature of a prophet, and the prophet is in his way a poet," as Boccaccio would have written.[16]

Dante would also speak of this "grace" by comparing it with the beauty and nature of the *perla.*

Ogni attimo dato e ogni dono perfetto di suso viene, discendendo dal Padre de' lumi. Dice adunque che Dio solo porge questa *grazia* a l'anima di quelli cui vede stare perfettamente ne la sua persona, acconcio e disposto a questo divino atto ricevere. . . . onde se l'anima è imperfettamente posta, non è disposta a ricevere questa benedetta infusione: si' come una *pietra margarita* [a pearl] è male disposta, o vero imperfetta, la virtù celestiale ricever non può.

Every given moment and every perfect gift comes from above, descending from the Father of lights. It then says that God alone bestows this *grace* on the soul of him whom he sees abiding perfectly in his own person, ready and disposed to receive this divine act. . . . hence, if the soul is imperfectly situated, it is not disposed to receive this blessed infusion: just as if a *precious stone* [a pearl] is situated badly, or indeed imperfectly, it cannot receive the celestial virtue. (*Conv.* 4.20.7, emphasis added)

At this point, it will be useful yet again to slow our course to underline several facts and advance a hypothesis. The first fact concerns the Islamic features that are present in the *Commedia* and in the tomb of Cangrande. The second regards the explicit citation of the *Liber scale Machometi* made by Fazio degli Uberti in his *Dittamondo*. Thirty years after the death of Dante and twenty years after that of Cangrande, Fazio degli Uberti attests to the knowledge of *Liber scale Machometi* in the Lombard / della Scala and not the Roman/Florentine circle among the elite of Verona. The third fact concerns the concordances between the *Liber scale Machometi* and the "Ciclo del perlaro," which demonstrate that within the court of Mastino II della Scala, there must have been access to the *Liber scale Machometi* and its divine symbolism.

One other piece of information, not proof in itself but lending itself to a useful supposition, leads me to believe that there could have been no Italian family other than the della Scala family that would have had a greater interest in possessing this *Liber* (that was held to be sacred): the book had their family name in its Italian title, *Libro della Scala* (The Book of the Ladder).

After this brief aside, it will be useful to return to Asín Palacios's hypothesis and to those who, according to him, could have been the means by which Dante acquired his knowledge of Muslim culture. Asín Palacios was preoccupied with recording dozens of probable names, texts, and sources that could have brought Muslim eschatology to Dante's attention. His preoccupation reflected the reality that at that time no single book was known from which Dante could have derived ideas and suggestions for his own poetic journey. However, once such a book and its historical, geographical, and political circumstances had been found to link the Islamic text and the use that Dante could have made of it, many of the names and texts (Brunetto Latini above all others)[17] that had been indispensable to Asín Palacios in establishing a broad context turn out to be of minor relevance.

Thus having identified the source from which Dante could have drawn in creating his otherworldly voyage—a voyage that he certainly would have wanted to be incomparable with the one taken by Muḥammad, with Hebrew eschatology, and on a poetic level with any other text written before the *Commedia*—I would like to mention two Jewish personages cited in passing by Asín Palacios.[18] These two could have brought to Verona pertinent Islamic knowledge in addition to privileged Hebrew knowledge that sheds light on Dante's work.[19] The names of these two men linked to Dante's Verona are Hillel ben Samuel of Verona and Manoello Giudeo (also known as Immanuel ben Solomon).

Hillel of Verona

Hillel's great-grandfather was Samuel, his grandfather was Eleazar ben Samuel, and his father was Samuel. He was born in 1220 and died well into his seventies, not before 1295. His heritage can be traced in Verona from the first years of the twelfth century.

From 1144 to 1146 Abraham ibn Ezra, a Jew who was a translator of Arabic in the translation "school" of Raimundo (Raymund, archbishop of Toledo from 1125 to 1141), was a guest in Verona. Ibn Ezra, grammarian, poet, philosopher, and greatest astrologer of all the medieval Jews, was also the author of a Hebrew work entitled *Hai ben Mekits* (literally, "Living Son of the Vigilant"), which narrates the ascension (*mi'rāj*) of the philosopher toward the intelligible, across the various states of being under the auspices of intellect. Ibn Ezra's text clearly recalls a preceding text, that of the mystic Avicenna, *The Story of Hayy Ibn Yaqzān* (1100, "Alive" Son of "Awake"), in which

> Hayy means the Living, Yaqzān the Vigilant. Hayy is the name of the Angel that, across the tale, is the Messenger, the Guide, and the Interpreter. He has the same role as that of the archangel Gabriel in the vision of Daniel; the role of Raphael or Michael in the visions of Enoch; that of the archangel Uriel in the Fourth Book of Esdras. In the account of Avicenna, the Guide is Gabriel, the archangel of the Revelations given successively to all of the prophets up to Muhammad; he whom the Koran identifies with the Holy Spirit and the philosophers identify with the Agent of Intellect. The Messenger, the Guide of the mystic tales of Avicenna just as of Sohrawardi, is both the Angel of Knowledge and the Angel of Revelation.[20]

Another ascension story is told by Ibn Tufayl (d. 1185) of Guadix, known to the Scholastics as Abubacer, a "rationalist mystic" contemporary of Ibn Ezra. He was the author, roughly forty years after Avicenna, of the *Epistle of Hayy ibn Yaqzān*,[21] which was translated from Arabic into Hebrew by Moses of Narbonne (d. after 1362) and which would later become famous in Europe in the seventeenth century under the title *Philosofus autodidacticus* (The Autodidact Philosopher). Abubacer's *mi'rāj* was translated from Arabic, in Rome, by Kalonymos ben Kalonymos (a friend of Manoello Giudeo) who then presented the translation of the *Epistle* and described its author, philosopher and emir, as "iudex excellens Avobacher Aventafel" ("Abubacer Ibn Tufayl, exceptional judge").[22]

Returning to our Hebrew family of Verona, we know that Eleazar, the grandfather of Hillel, was the head and promoter of a Talmudic school in Verona, which seems to be the first of its kind in northern Italy. Eleazar was a student of Yishaq ben Shemuel di Dampierre (d. 1195), a teacher who during his lifetime was credited as a seer of visions of heavenly pilgrimage and who gained fame as a prophet.[23] The title was not merely honorary, but indicated those who had dedicated themselves to the mysticism of the *Merkavà* (Chariot). This mysticism entailed an education and an authority, as exemplified by Magister Liazarius in Verona (as Eleazar came to be known), that was renowned in centers as distant as Vienna, Cologne, and the Rhenish communities of Speyer, Worms, and Mainz.

We do not know much about Hillel's father, Shemuel, but we can say of Hillel himself that he was a student of the Talmud at Barcelona and of medicine at Montpellier. In 1250 he was in the Naples of Frederick II. In 1265 he was in Capua, where he met and became friends with Abraham Abulafia: with Abraham he studied *The Guide for the Perplexed* of Maimonides.[24] Abulafia was the greatest Hebrew Kabbalist of all times, the prophet who challenged Pope Nicholas III in 1280, as Moses did Pharaoh: he desired that the new pharaoh of Rome liberate the Jews from the yoke of Christianity.[25] This demand would have earned him a spot on the pyre already prepared in a Roman piazza if not for the fact that (providentially) the pope died the day before the execution and Abulafia somehow escaped from prison.

With the end of Frederick II's reign around 1267, Hillel moved to Rome, where he studied at an academy of biblical exegetes and translators from Arabic.[26] In Rome Hillel encountered and befriended (even if there was no scarcity of doctrinal disputes between the two) that same Manoello Giudeo who would be a guest at the court of Cangrande and a friend to Dante. From the Guelphan Rome of Robert of Anjou, Hillel moved (this time definitively) to Forlì, the Ghibelline city where Guido Bonatti still served as the astrologer and Arabic translator for Ezzelino III da Romano, lord of Verona until Ezzolino died in 1259. (After Ezzelino, Mastino I della Scala initiated the rule of the della Scala family.) In addition to Guido Bonatti, Salione da Padova was also present at Ezzelino III's court. Salione, together with Michael Scot (astrologer and translator for Frederick II), was a translator of Arabic in Toledo during the first half of the thirteenth century.[27]

Hillel's most notable work, *Tagmule ha-Nefesh* (Book of the Rewards of the Soul),[28] was intended to clarify for his coreligionists the issue of the immortality of the soul. The text aims to definitively resolve the problems regarding the issue of eternal recompense, as reward or punishment, which the soul will receive as a result of the actions of an individual in this earthly life. It is an eschatological text written by a Jew for Jews; however, the author does not hesitate to draw upon the three worlds of Islam, Christianity, and Judaism. Together with texts from the Hebrew tradition (Maimonides and Nachmanides) are joined two Arab texts (Avicenna and Averroës) and a Christian text (Thomas Aquinas). Hillel therefore found himself together with other Hebrew scholars before him (Baḥya Ibn Paquda and Maimonides, to cite the most notable) and others who would come after him (Dante, first and foremost) in sharing a truth of reason that transcends the walls imposed by the truth of faith and the respective dogmas of the three religions.

Manoello Giudeo

Some think that it was Manoello's friendship with Hillel of Verona (natural by their participation in the Roman academy as translators from Arabic and biblical exegetes) that brought Manoello to the city of the della Scala family. Whether for this reason or possibly because the liberality and hospitality of Cangrande guaranteed protection to those ostracized by the Church, Manoello, himself an author, poet, and biblical exegete, was at Verona at the same time as Dante. Manoello, who wrote in both Hebrew and the vernacular, is the author of the most interesting poem from the court of Cangrande, a poem entitled (untranslatably) *Bisbidis*.

Manoello begins his poem, as Dante does *Epistula* 13, by singing the praises of the city of Verona. According to Manoello, Verona surpasses in magnificence any other place he had visited as well as any other place of which he had heard great things, such as the seat of the "Gran Cane" (Great Khan) of the Tartars. He almost cannot believe what his eyes reveal to him, and like Dante he finds in Cangrande's Verona a locale worthy of its name "del dire e del fare "in word and in deed." Here, Manoello sees the representatives of different nations: Germans, Latins (meaning Italians), French, and English. He watches barons and marquises arriving from different lands; he hears debates on questions of astrology, philosophy, and theology; and he is an eyewitness to the presence of the three religions. Romans and pilgrims from Compostella are present as well as "Giudei e Sarracini ("Jews and Saracens"). This was all intended to bring glory to that Lord whose valor and honor spread over the earth and sea.

At this court, the "donna cara" ("dear lady," dear to both the Hebrew poet[29] and the della Scala court) ensures the reign of Virtue: this is *Sapienza* (Wisdom). Manoello continues that Love is also present " 'n la sala / del Sir della Scala" ("In the court / of the Lord della Scala"). These presences, Virtue, Wisdom, and Love, remind us of the sustenance of the "Veltro," the celestial dog that would chase the she-wolf in the *Inferno*:

> Questi non ciberà terra né peltro,
>   ma sapïenza, amore e virtute,
>   e sua nazion sarà tra feltro e feltro.

> He will not feed on earth or pelf,
> but on wisdom, love, and virtue,
> and his birth shall be between felt and felt.
>   (*Inf.* 1.103–5)

With regard to Cangrande, Manoello Giudeo (albeit in a cryptic way) likens him to a new Cyrus the Great, the one chosen by God, the Persian king and non-Jew, who liberated the Jews (exiles par excellence) from their Babylonian captivity.[30] Dante, however, as we shall see, likened Cangrande to Darius the Great, giving to himself the function of converter that the prophet Daniel fulfilled in the court of the king of the Medes.

Manoello Giudeo's *Inferno and Paradiso* (*Ha-Tofet ve-ha-Eden*), written in Hebrew as a celebration of the recently deceased Dante Alighieri, deserves to be quoted:

> When sixty of my own years had passed by, and the quickening signs of death made their advance, a vital, generous man, progeny of the saints, who was younger than I, saw his days come to an end. Seeing this, I was seized with terror and said, "Alas, Reason seems to vanish!" . . . And while I contemplated this, and my heart ached in my chest, and my tears were released as a torrent, and my sobbing ran like water, I was filled with a heavy sense of mourning . . . and I said: "Where then, O Daniel, are you, you enviable man, and where is your Wisdom? If only I could find you, come upon your greatness,

ask you and have you enlighten me, to have you satiate me with the stream of your blessedness, and you could let me know the length of my days, my end; you could show me the place of my repose and final rest."[31]

Manoello may have referred to Dante as Daniel for several reasons. Perhaps during the Middle Ages it was not proper to publicize a friendship between a Hebrew and a Christian. It was also customary for a poet to conceal the true identity of a subject through the use of an alias in order to protect the subject from prying eyes. Etymology could also make an alias attractive. The syllable *Dan* is common to both names, while the letter *i* and the phoneme *el* of Dani*el* recall principal attributes of the Creator. The *I* of IEVE (which was the Italian transliteration in the Middle Ages that would correspond to the modern English YHWH) indicates mercy and divine love; the *el* of Elhoim, justice and divine power.[32] These attributes also echo Dante, who according to Manoello himself, "ha perdonato il peccato di molti ma colpisce i peccatori" ("has pardoned the sin of many but punishes the sinners").[33] Finally, Manoello could have chosen the name of Daniel because the prophet was, for Dante, the biblical model that he had appropriated for himself, considering his activity at the court of Cangrande as analogous to that which Daniel performed at the court of Darius.[34] For this last reason Manoello, having just invoked his recently departed friend Dante/Daniel, has the biblical prophet show up at his side. This Daniel, the biblical alter ego of Dante, accompanies Manoello Giudeo through the circles of Hell and along the steps of the Judaic Paradise.

Another surprise awaits us, as we learn that in this Judaic Paradise a throne is set up to welcome the Christian poet-prophet as soon as he arrives. In addition, Dante's throne is the same that would welcome Judah "il leoncello" (the young cousin of Manoello) and also Manoello himself.

> And it occurred that when I heard these words [used by Daniel to indicate that this throne would welcome both Manoello and his cousin] I remembered the excellence of my brother Daniel, who had guided me along the path of truth, who had corrected my course and who was close to me when I was in exile: a sacred crown upon my head, the life of my own flesh, my soul, and my spirit. And the ends of the Earth were filled with praise for him, his greatness, his generosity, his intellect and his judgment, his humility and his justness. . . . And the Man said to me: "Come with me and I will

show you the grandeur and honor of his place of rest" . . . There we saw the great throne, covered in gold, that would give life to he who would occupy it, would give health to his flesh. It was adorned with precious gems and fabrics of blue, purple, and scarlet were spread upon it. And there were plumes of copper, beautifully shining for all of the nations of earth [that is for all pious, sage, or just people, of any religion or nation]. At the top of the throne there was a crown composed of a talent of gold and a precious gem whose value was greater than gold or silver. And a voice said: "Behold! For that crown is the reward to those who sit beside the Lord." And the man who was speaking to me said: "Have you seen the crown and the throne on which your friend Daniel will resurrect himself like a cub and from which he shall raise himself like a lion? This will be his eternal rest, and here he will sit because he listened to the Word of the Lord, and no one on Earth was wiser or a greater philosopher than he."[35]

Several points regarding this passage must be clarified. First, Judah ben Moses of Rome (also known as Giuda Romano and Leone Romano, d. after 1330), Manoello Giudeo's cousin, who with Hillel of Verona was among the first to introduce the philosophy and theology of the Scholastics (led by Thomas Aquinas) into Hebrew literature. He also transcribed into Hebrew characters and translated into Judaeo-Roman dialect the verses of the *Commedia* that speak of free will, the divine light, and the necessity of being faithful to vows.[36] Thus for Dante's throne to be the same as that of Giuda Romano, his admirer and translator, as well as that of Manoello Giudeo, "brother" to Dante, is less incomprehensible than it might appear at first glance. And here the question arises as to who the mediator was who put into Giuda Romano's hands part of the (or perhaps the entire?) *Commedia* after its drafting in Lombardy.

I would also like to return to what the biblical prophet says to Manoello about the deceased Daniel: "Egli ha perdonato il peccato di molti ma colpisce i peccatori" ("has pardoned the sin of many but punishes the sinners"). This is precisely what Dante had done with the *Commedia* and what Manoello sought to do with his *Inferno and Paradiso*.

The third point that I would like to highlight is Manoello Giudeo's emphasis on the link that arises through the conditions of a shared exile ("who was close to me when I was in exile?"[37]) and that becomes a bond when the Great Mind, through the mouth of the prophet Daniel, declares its desire to have the two joined together in eternal life: "As the Great Mind knew that without you he would not have found peace and tranquility, he will raise his tent by your own."[38]

Thus a Manoello who defined Dante as a brother would have done this with difficulty, had Dante judged him according to the standards by which medieval Christians judged the Jews: as deicides, as the living damned, as spiritually and civically dead wandering the earth. The bond between Dante and Manoello is very strong, notwithstanding the inferiority that Manoello feels when confronting himself with Daniel:

> And with regard to your own valor being lesser than his, the Creator knowing that he would find delight in being at your side, he will be for you like Moses, and you for him like Joshua. In this way, all will see that your two souls are together and are not separated, and they say, "Can two people go about together if they did not arrange that meeting among themselves?"[39]

A "meeting" in a Paradise that is "open to the just of all the nations," as forged between the Hebrew poet and the Christian poet, could have proved costly for both. Along these lines, Cino da Pistoia writes of this "meeting" in the afterlife in a sonnet that he sends to Bosone da Gubbio upon the death of Manoello; Cino, having gone *in fine dierum* ("at the end of [his] days") from the Empire to the Church,[40] sends the sonnet to the man who together with Manoello Giudeo had given birth to the exchange of poems that lamented the death of Dante, his having been taken up by the Supreme Judge "in glorioso scanno" ("on the glorious throne"):[41]

> Messer Boson, lo vostro Manoello,
> seguitando l'error de la sua Legge,
> passato è ne lo Inferno e prova quello
> martir ch'è dato a chi non si corregge.
>
> Non è con tutta la comune gregge,
> ma con Dante si sta sotto al cappello
> del qual, come nel Libro suo si legge,
> vide coperto Alessi Interminello.
>
> Tra lor non è sollazzo, ma corruccio,
> del qual fu pieno Alessi com' un orso
> e raggia là dove vede Castruccio.

E Dante dice: "Quel satiro morso
ci mostrò Manoello in breve sdruccio
de l'uom che innesta 'l persico nel torso."

Lord Bosone, your Manoello,
following the error of his religion,
has passed into Hell and undergoes
the punishment given to the unrepentant.

He is not with the common crowd,
but stands with Dante under the same cap
with which, as is read in his Book [the *Commedia*],
Alessio Interminei was seen to be covered.

Among them there is no cheer but only anger,
with which Alessio was filled, just like a bear,
and he rages there, where he sees Castruccio.

And Dante says: "This biting satire
Manoello showed us in a brief composition
of the man who grafts the peach on the trunk."

The first four lines say essentially: "Dear Bosone, your Manoello, having continued to err in his religion [Judaism], has ended up in Hell and now undergoes the penalty that is meted out to those who do not repent." The second stanza clarifies the area of Hell as well as the pains that Manoello suffers alongside Dante: "Manoello is not with the common people; rather, he finds himself, with Dante, under the same *cappello* as covers Alessio Interminei [alternatively, Interminelli] in the *Commedia*."[42] And, going back to the *Commedia*, we see that the penalty that awaits the panderers (or, more vulgar yet accurate, the asskissers, *leccaculi*) is to have their roofs or heavens (metaphorically, their hats), with their heads covered with human excrement (*Inf.* 18.112–14).

In the third stanza, the author continues: "There is no joy or felicity between those two covered in excrement, but rather deaf grief, mixed with rage, the same as Alessio has already been filled with, just like a bear." In the final stanza Cino has Dante speak in the first person, admitting that this particularly biting satire (that is, the terrible and vulgar punishment that is worthy of one of Juvenal's *Satires*) was not properly his own idea; rather, it was suggested to him by Manoello in one of his brief poetic compositions, in the passage in which we see that this happens to those who wish to join together things that are irreconcilable.

The Three Rings

I would like to end by clarifying the moral of the story that informed my scholastic itinerary. To do so I will return to the parable of the three rings that became famous through the writings of Boccaccio.[43]

Saladin poses to the wise Jew Melchizedek the disconcerting question of which of the three religions, Judaism, Islam, or Christianity, is the true religion. Melchizedek responds with the parable of the father who, possessing a beautiful and precious ring, so as not to disappoint or irritate any of his three wonderful sons and heirs, has two other rings made by a great craftsman. These two rings were so similar to the first that it was impossible to distinguish the original from the copies. At his death, the father secretly left one ring to each of his sons, each believing that he had the original. Each of the sons thus believed himself to be the legitimate heir of the ring and the paternal inheritance.

> E così vi dico, signor mio, delle tre leggi alli tre popoli date da Dio padre, delle quali la questione proponeste: ciascun la sua eredità, la sua vera legge e i suoi comandamenti direttamente si crede avere e fare, ma chi se l'abbia, come degli anelli, ancora ne pende la quistione.

> And therefore I speak to you, my lord, of the three Laws given to the three peoples by God the Father, about which you have asked me: each people believes that they possess and execute their own inheritance, their own true Law, and their own commandments directly from God, but as with the rings, who actually has them is still an open question.[44]

The parable of the three rings has a long history, which we cannot retrace here. Suffice it to note that in 1270 it was used by Abraham Abulafia, friend of Hillel of Verona; that it is present in the prose collection *Il Novellino* (a collection of one hundred Tuscan *novelle*, "short fictions"),[45] which was famous during Dante's time; and that another author (close to Dante and Manoello) who used it was Bosone da Gubbio, in his *L'avventuroso siciliano* (The Adventurous Sicilian).[46] A German scholar has traced the parable back to eighth-century Baghdad, representing in his opinion another version of the parable of the "three impostors": Moses, Jesus, and Muḥammad. Also, having been expanded upon by the Hebrew philosopher Maimonides as well as those wise medieval philosophers intent on liberating themselves from the yoke of religious censorship, it would crop back up at the end of the eighteenth century to give impetus to the Enlightenment.[47] The above serves to demonstrate the general apologia of tolerance that was ascribed to this fable.[48]

As to the symbolism of the three rings and its underlying allegory, we can say that the parable was used by the Hebrew Kabbalists who visualized the tetragrammaton as three concentric and dynamic circles, one of which was red as fire.[49] It was also used by Gioacchino da Fiore, whom I discuss below. The "moral of the story," other than a generic religious tolerance, in fact drives a metaphysical unity that transcends the three religions;[50] it guides a point of view subsuming the religions under the three in one that recalls YHWH, God, and Allah (three names of a single God, not three divinities) as the Sole Creator.[51]

That said, and strengthened by this parable that invites religious tolerance through the symbolism of three interlocking rings that give way to a (monotheistic) truth superior to its individual parts, it seems to me quite natural to recall here Dante's own verses written about his Trinity, composed of three rotating *giri* (circles) by which Dante is literally captured, absorbing it within himself and having it incarnated through his very person.[52]

> Ne la profonda e chiara sussistenza
>   de l'Alto Lume parvemi tre giri
>   di tre colori e d'una contenenza;
> e l'un da l'altro come iri da iri
>   parea riflesso, e 'l terzo parea foco
>   che quinci e quindi igualmente si spiri.

> Within the profound and shining essence
> of the Exalted Light appeared to me three circles
> of three colors and one magnitude,
> and one seemed reflected by the other,
> as rainbow by rainbow, and the third seemed fire
> breathed forth equally from the one and the other.
>   (*Par.* 33.115–20)

As is well known, Dante was waiting for the age of the world that would come after the age of the Father and of the Son, that is, the age of the Holy Spirit. Joachim of Fiore, the abbot "di spirito profetico dotato" (*Par.* 12.141 "endowed with prophetic spirit"), was a proponent of the millennialist expectations that were awaiting a world filled with peace prior to the end of the world and the Last Judgment. Between 1180 and 1190 Joachim gave form to the Holy Trinity by depicting it as three interlocking rings. The first ring represented the biblical age of the Father; the second, the evangelical age of the Son; and the third, the spirituality of a new age, which was imminent and would be of brief duration, driven by the third member of the Trinity, the Holy Spirit.

Dante certainly knew the image of the Trinity in Joachim's *Liber figurarum* (Book of Figures), but he did not use it as did Joachim, for whom the future of humanity depended on Providence and on the victory of Christianity over the other religions. Joachim's was a God who, despite mankind, would have soon put an end to the world and celebrated the affirmation of Christianity against the Hebrew and/or Muslim Antichrist.

Dante refutes the linear time of Joachim, as he would rather overlap the determinism of Joachim with the circularity of the three invisible circles tracked by the stars. This is a path that anyone gifted with intellect can deduce from the heavens: from the circle of the *sphera mundi*, the celestial horizon, and from the oblique circle of the zodiac.[53] Dante hinges this notion not on a providence that is too similar to the fate of the pagans—a providence that bends with the desires or fears of mankind—but rather on the potentialities of the human race (*Mon.* 1.3, the possible intellect). This man, Dante's man of intellect, is able to learn from nature in order to understand the highest and most profound mysteries of the Father of nature[54] and in order to advance himself ever more, both in time and in the sublunary world, toward the perfect man that as a new Adam would have to recreate the new earthly Paradise.

Around these three circles, Dante envisions a materialized Trinity both in nature and in the nature of man, in the macro- and in the microcosm, which is thus comprehensible to the reader of the *Commedia* through both psychological and experimental means.[55] The circles themselves are invisible to the human eye but are recognizable through the circular motion (*giri*) of the polar stars around the Earth's axis, through the constellations around the heavenly equator and through the planets around the ecliptic plane, all functioning to demonstrate to those watching on Earth the influences and lessons of the Creator

(*Par.* 8.127–28 "La circular natura, ch'è suggello / a la cera mortal" "Circular nature, which is a seal / on the mortal wax"). This is a Trinity of faith to which one could approach by means of reason and science; a Trinity that, indeed, beginning from the Argonauts, could be glimpsed by those looking to the stars and seeing there the three-dimensionality of the Creator and the created; a trinity that would then be revealed to humanity, toward whom the *Commedia* was aimed. It is not a Trinity that is solely a question of a single faith or dogma; it can become the sole truth for all by overcoming the restricted margins offered by orthodox Christianity. It is a Trinity of faith, reason, and science that is given as a reading to any who would wish to know it by the very act of Creation by the single Creator, the single Universal God. We could define it as a propaedeutic rationale that has the goal of demonstrating the *preambula fidei* ("preambles to faith") from which Dante never moves.[56]

> At the beginning of the *Summa contra gentiles* [Treatise against the Pagans], Saint Thomas clarifies the method that he will follow in order to display according to his analysis the truth professed by the Catholic faith and to reject the errors that are contrary to this truth: "Thus it is necessary to find recourse in the natural reason to which all must adhere . . . how the truth that is established through the path of demonstration is in accordance with the faith of the Christian religion."[57]

Dante took the figure of the three rings from Joachim of Fiore, but how did Joachim himself come by this figure? Joachim, along with the papal curia, was in Verona with Pope Lucius III on July 22, 1184, when the pope was to meet with the emperor Frederick Barbarossa. A subsequent visit by Joachim to Verona is known to have occurred in 1186, this time following with Pope Urban III.

At Verona Joachim delved into the mysteries of the tetragrammaton, thanks to his discussions with a "highly knowledgeable Jew." This acquaintance earns him the accusation, or defamation, that referred to him as a "Jew son of Jews" ("ebreo figlio di ebrei"). Hence Geoffrey of Auxerre:

> He is a Jew, born of the Jews and educated for many years in Judaism, an education that it seems has not yet been expelled out of him. His Hebrew origin, which he and his family keep well-hidden, is already shown in his foreign name.

Gian Luca Podestà writes:

> But the wise figure alluded to in Joachim turns to look . . . at that same Hebrew community in Verona, the city where that papal curia resided between 1184 and 1187 and where Joachim found himself in 1186. This was precisely the time in which he brought into focus his new version of history, connected to a profound rethinking of the mystery of and the relations of the Trinity. Numerous testimonies reveal the lofty cultural levels achieved by several members of the Jewish community in Verona, among whom the Spanish grammarian and exegete Abraham ibn Ezra had sojourned in 1146. . . .
> Thanks to the Jewish community's continuous presence in Verona, [Joachim] was able to receive information on the tradition of thought based on speculations as to the significance of the tetragrammaton (which during the twelfth century generally came from Spain and Provence) that was understood as a code related to the mystery of the divine creative force.[58]

And in fact, during these years the most famous Jew in Verona was the Magister Liazarius mentioned in conjunction with Hillel.

To conclude, I would like to recall the voyages into the afterlife that circulated around the city of Verona where Dante found his "rifugio" ("refuge") and "ostello" ("lodging") and perhaps wrote the entire *Commedia*.

First, Abraham ibn Ezra, a guest in Verona for two years, authored *Ḥai ben Meḳits* (The Living Son of the Watchful), a work that narrates the ascension (*miʻrāj*) of the philosopher toward the Intelligible, across the various states of being under the auspices of the Agent of Intellect.[59] Second, Eleazar ben Samuel of Verona (grandfather of Hillel), who frequented the circle of Isaac ben Samuel the Elder of Dampierre and who earned fame during his lifetime as a prophet and credit for "having visions of celestial pilgrimages," had access to the ecstatic and kabbalistic experiences tied to the mysticism of the *Merkavà* and to the mysteries of the "trinitarian relations." Joachim of Fiore, in his two-year sojourn in Verona, could have come in contact with these traditions. Third, Giacomino da Verona's *De Babilonia civitate infernali* (On the Infernal State of Babylon) of the middle of the thirteenth century narrates the horrors of Hell, as does his *De Ierusalem coelesti* (On the Heavenly Jerusalem). Fourth, between 1288 and 1291 Hillel of Verona at Forlì focused on the treatise *Tagmule ha-Nefesh* (The Rewards of the Soul), in which he speaks of Paradise and of Hell, of the future world, of the age of the Messiah, and of the resurrection of the dead.

Beyond these four other possible connections, Dante could have had access to the Islamic *Liber scale Machometi* in the library of the della Scala family. This same della Scala circle would see Cangrande accompanied into the afterlife with a funeral shroud made of Islamic cloth, and would host Fazio degli Uberti (the first to have cited this work) after having hosted Dante and the composers of madrigals responsible for the "Ciclo del perlaro."

Finally, there is Manoello Giudeo, who praised the court of Cangrande with his *Bisbidis* and who also, to commemorate Dante among his coreligionists, wrote in Hebrew section 28 of the *Maḥbarot*. Eschatalogically, this is the final section of the entire book, and it became known, for that very reason, as *The Inferno and the Paradiso* (*Ha-Tofet ve-ha-Eden*).

No other European city can boast similar precedents or demonstrate a more closely woven web among the three sons of the one Father.

Translated by Kyle M. Hall

The Last Muslims in Italy

DAVID ABULAFIA

D uring Dante's lifetime, the only Muslim city on the Italian peninsula ceased to exist.[1] Dante does not mention Lucera Saracenorum (a Latin placename meaning "Lucera of the Saracens") in his writings, despite his references to the struggle between the Angevins and first the Hohenstaufen, then the Aragonese (for instance, in *Purgatorio* 6 and 7), or indeed his references to Muḥammad and to crusaders. And yet during its brief history of less than eighty years, up to its conquest by Charles II in 1300, Lucera was a source of controversy and of fascination, the seat of Christian rulers who employed the inhabitants of the town as soldiers and craftsmen, taking particular advantage of their skill in the production of military equipment, including armaments and tents.[2] Its existence serves as a reminder that contact with Islam in Dante's Italy did not consist solely in translation projects; in any case, the Angevin court mainly employed Jews, not Muslims, on these projects, as had Frederick II. Nor did it consist solely of commercial links through Genoa, Venice, and other ports. As soldiers in the armies of Frederick II (1194–1250), Manfred (ca. 1232–1266), and Charles I (1226–1285), the Muslims of Lucera aroused awe in lands where they served, which included northern Italy, Albania, and possibly the crusader states. They were a source of worry to the popes, partly because their establishment in Lucera had resulted in the displacement of the local Christians and partly because it was unsettling to see arms-bearing Muslims living no great distance from the papal state in the flat lands of Capitanata (the region around Foggia); indeed, they resisted the papal champion Charles I when he conquered the kingdom of Sicily in 1266, and they rebelled against him following the tragic attempt by Frederick's grandson Conradin (1252–1268) to recover the throne of Sicily for the house of Hohenstaufen. Yet they were permitted to continue to live in Lucera and were only arrested and deported in 1300, in circumstances that still arouse controversy among historians, for at that stage there is no evidence that they were actively opposing the Crown, nor did they possess any known links to the outside world that would have enabled their opponents to argue that they were the allies of hostile Muslim powers in North Africa or elsewhere (unlike the Muslims of Minorca and Valencia in the same period). There was unease at the idea that they were a permanent element in the population of southern Italy. After founding the colony, Frederick II encouraged the Luceran Muslims to cultivate the soil around Lucera as part of a wider plan to bring back prosperity to the Capitanata. And some evidence suggests that, at least initially, attempts were made to convert the Lucerans to Christianity.

Frederick II established the Muslim colony at Lucera to solve the problem of continuing rebellion among the Muslims of Sicily. The rebellion had begun in the last years of the twelfth century: longstanding disaffection among the Sicilian Muslims turned into open revolt as rival claimants to the Sicilian throne—Norman, Sicilian, and German—competed for control of the kingdom of Sicily. One writer, the anonymous author of the letter to Peter, treasurer of the church of Palermo, lamented that the "Sicilians" were unable to work together against the common enemy from outside and looked to the Muslims of Sicily for cooperation, for, he said, if Christians and Saracens worked together under a king whom they all respected, the island could be saved from the insane fury of the Germans, rude foreigners from the north, with their grunting speech and bestial ways, who would rape the Sicilian women and cut down with the sword those who resisted them: "The madness of the Germans is not accustomed to being controlled by reason."[3] Yet he was aware that the Muslims felt they had been persecuted long enough, and there was a danger that they would act independently, perhaps seizing strongholds in the mountains (as in fact happened) or along the coast.

It is already clear from the travel diary of the Granadan pilgrim Muḥammad ibn Jubayr, who visited Sicily in 1184–85, that the Muslim communities of Sicily were under increasing pressure from the Crown, while the hostility of Christian settlers from northern Italy had resulted in pogroms twenty years earlier. By granting extensive estates in western and southeastern Sicily to the abbey (later cathedral) of Monreale, King William II placed the greater part of the Muslim peasantry under ecclesiastical lordship, bringing to an end an era of relative autonomy in the Muslim villages of western Sicily. Rebellious Muslims sought to recover this autonomy, whose roots can be traced back to the surrender treaties made at the time of the Norman conquest in the late eleventh century. Exploiting the disorder of Frederick II's childhood, the Muslims created a statelet of their own at Entella and Jato, which even minted its own coins. Disorder spread to Girgenti (Agrigento), threatening the overseas grain trade that had long been a prime source of income for the Crown. Pope Innocent III inveighed against the Muslim rebels, seeing them as allies of the German warlord Markward of Anweiler, who for a time had the young Frederick of Hohenstaufen in his power. Innocent even threatened Markward with a crusade, on the grounds that he made use of Saracen military allies; his threats marked an important moment in the evolution of the "political crusades" launched against enemies of the Church within Western Europe.[4]

Frederick II's intentions in founding the colony at Lucera can be compared with those of the Iberian monarchs who, in the same period, were engaged in wars of conquest against the "Moors." The crucial difference was that Frederick's Muslims were seen as rebels, whereas those in Spain were treated in various ways according to whether they submitted peacefully or resisted. Majorca fell to James of Aragon in 1229, Minorca in 1231, and Valencia City in 1238; Córdoba and Seville were taken in 1236 and 1248, respectively, falling within the Castilian-Leonese sphere; and the Portuguese made significant advances in the Algarve as well. What was original about Lucera was that it did not simply involve the expulsion of the Muslims from the conquered lands, as happened in parts of Andalusia; the entire Muslim population of Sicily of between 15,000 and 30,000 people was uprooted and taken to a distant location, isolated from the Islamic world. Thus this case falls halfway between the mass expulsions often carried out by the Castilians and the policy of retention of the Mudejar population characteristic of Aragon.[5] It is impossible to reconstruct the history of their transportation. That this was a complex exercise is obvious; much misery must have been involved. But the scale of the deportations should not be exaggerated. They were spread over many years, from 1223 onward, and as late as 1246 Frederick was still facing resistance in the Sicilian highlands. In 1241, 681 Muslim families apparently still lived on

Malta, constituting the vast majority of the population, though they were in the minority on Gozo. Ibn Khaldūn reports that the Muslims of Malta were expelled in 1249—some historians argue for a later date—and they were mostly gone by 1271.[6] Deportations were thus scattered and slow. The aim, certainly, was to reduce Sicily's Muslim population as much as possible, though Sicily continued to host Muslim slaves as well as merchants and craftsmen who arrived from North Africa. Malta too served as a bridge to North Africa—it was through Malta that animals such as Barbary leopards were obtained for the royal menagerie.[7]

Nor did the expulsion of the Muslims completely end the Arabized culture of Sicily. Sicilian Jews, whose fate was closely intertwined with that of the Muslims, continued to speak Arabic for at least another century and to write Arabic (in Hebrew characters) in Jewish documents up to the time of their own expulsion from Sicily in 1492–93. Frederick II and Charles I of Anjou turned to Jewish scholars for translations of works available in Arabic, whether they were texts by Averroës or medical tracts such as that presented by the Jewish Faraj of Girgenti to King Charles. Frederick also relied on the Jews as a source of technical know-how, inviting Jews from Garbum (either the Maghreb in general or the island of Jerba) to settle in Palermo in 1239–40 and to cultivate indigo, henna, and other plants that had largely disappeared following the loss of the Muslim population.[8] The presence of the Jews must be stressed for another reason: it was they who provided a model for the classification of first the Sicilian and then the Luceran Muslims as *servi* of the royal chamber—an important aspect of the Luceran community that merits further discussion.

Regardless of what it reveals about Frederick's Muslim policy, the deportation fits into an ancient tradition of population transfers in the region. Southern Italy was dotted with small communities of Greeks, Bulgars, and others whose origins lay in earlier deportations by the Byzantine rulers of Langobardia.[9] Indeed, Frederick deported Christians as well as Muslims: the siege of Celano in 1223 was reportedly followed by the deportation of the inhabitants to Malta, which, as has been seen, was a center of Muslim settlement; Frederick clearly wished to dilute the Muslim presence there.[10]

After the settlement of Muslims at Lucera, a small Christian community continued to exist, most probably in the suburbs. Bishops of Lucera continued to be invested, though it is unclear whether they were able to reside within the city; by 1300 the cathedral was evidently in a bad state of repair, and the bells of the Luceran churches were deposited in the castle—evidently there was no longer any point in ringing them.[11]

Yet Frederick's intention was not to create a fossilized community of Sicilian Muslims at Lucera. He saw the isolation of the Saracens at Lucera as a means of assimilating them into the Christian world. Alone *in media Christianorum planitie* ("in the middle of Christian country"), the Luceran Muslims were expected to assimilate into Latin society. Keeping them together was not, perhaps, the obvious way to achieve assimilation. Yet many already understood Italian, and there is good evidence from the end of the thirteenth century that names of Christian or Romance origin such as Riccardus were used alongside Arabic names.

In 1233 Gregory IX solicited Frederick's help in ensuring that the Dominicans be allowed to preach Christianity to the Lucerans.[12] Frederick insisted that he too was keen to convert all the Saracens in Lucera; he assured the pope that many had already converted.[13] At a time when Gregory IX, Ramon de Penyafort (Raymond of Peñafort, d. 1275), and others were beginning to plan ambitious preaching campaigns against Jews and Muslims, based on the close study of Arabic and Hebrew in special language academies set up for training missionaries, this self-contained group of Muslims was an obvious first candidate for conversion. Ramón Llull, that great enthusiast for these methods, was in the kingdom of Sicily during 1294, planning a trip to Lucera; but there is no hard evidence that he actually reached the town or that he converted a single soul in Lucera (or anywhere else he traveled).[14]

Frederick was still interested in converting the Luceran Muslims in 1236. He asserted (though this must have been an exaggeration) that one third of the population had already decided to become Christians, thereby rebutting accusations that he had shown little interest in converting them. Frederick claimed credit not merely for the deportations to Lucera; he also claimed credit for Christianizing western Sicily by strengthening Christian settlement there and by removing the Muslim menace from the island. Lucera has to be seen as part of a two-pronged policy intended to benefit the Christians.[15] The great majority of Lucerans certainly remained Muslims until 1300, though the strength of their commitment is unknown. Some evidence suggests that pigs were reared by Luceran Muslims, implying that they were eaten as well by some of the *Saraceni*.[16] Yet it has been reasonably suggested that they had their own madrasa for the teaching and study of Islam. No Arabic books survive from Lucera, however, and there is no evidence that it was a significant cultural center. Undoubtedly, as in Spain, these Muslims who fell under Christian rule became increasingly isolated from the religious and intellectual life of the Islamic world. The Spanish evidence shows that the leading families tended to migrate to North Africa, and the Mudejar communities even of regions such as Valencia, with a high concentration of Muslims, were shorn of their upper class, leaving communities without the leadership traditionally supplied by the imams and the Muslim nobility. As will be seen, a local Luceran elite did emerge, but there are no indications that it was particularly distinguished in descent; rather, its power stemmed from success in fighting, gaining lands, and building ties to the Crown. Yet Islamic learning must have persisted at least in the practice of law: the Luceran Saracens were guaranteed the right to operate their own law courts, in accordance with the general principle borrowed by the Norman conquerors from their Muslim predecessors that religious minorities should govern themselves according to their own code of laws.[17] This *dhimmī* principle, to use the Arabic term, was borrowed and modified in Iberia as well in the same period.

The secret of Lucera's success lay in its fertility.[18] Frederick II was keen to promote agricultural production throughout the realm, partly in the hope of effecting a recovery from the fiscal chaos of his childhood; revenues from grain sales, especially from the sale of grain grown on royal estates, were a source of financial security for the Crown. The thirteenth century saw a general extension of large estates in Apulia, marked by the creation of the granges, or *masserie*—pockets of productive land that were increasingly consolidated into contiguous holdings. Wheat and barley dominated agricultural production in the region, while sheep, goats, and pigs were also reared; the great age of sheep farming in Apulia began in the fifteenth century, under Alfonso V (the Magnanimous), but Frederick's legislation, itself based on that of William II in the late twelfth century, makes plain the importance of cycles of transhumance well before the Aragonese period. Most of the Muslims lived within the city, but some of the lands they cultivated were several miles outside of Lucera; the presence of resident Muslims, officially or otherwise, in the surrounding countryside is fairly well documented: there were Muslims at Stornara, twenty-seven miles (forty-four kilometers) southeast of Lucera, at Castelluccio, sixteen miles (twenty-six kilometers) southeast of Lucera, and at San Giacomo, less than four miles (six kilometers) from Lucera.[19] Some Muslims commuted from the town, walking or riding to their lands several miles from Lucera to cultivate the soil.

Skilled craftsmen in the town were given commissions by the Sicilian kings, and some at least of the male Lucerans became soldiers, serving as far away as northern Italy, Albania, and Tunis during the thirteenth century.[20] As mentioned, the city was not a major cultural center, although the royal palace in Lucera was a favorite residence of Frederick II and his successors. Many of the Saracen dancers and trumpeters in the emperor's service were probably Muslim slaves brought from overseas, not local Lucerans, even if they eventually settled in Lucera.

The continuing presence of the Muslims in southern Italy irritated rulers after Frederick. In 1258, when the English king Henry III (1207–1272) decided to accept a papal offer of the throne of Sicily on behalf of his second son Edmund, the presence of the Luceran Muslims was cited as good grounds for a crusade against King Manfred.[21] After conquering the kingdom of Sicily, Charles I was uneasy about the Luceran Muslims. Yet neither their resistance to the conquering Angevin armies in 1266 nor their rebellion in favor of Conradin in 1268 led Charles to suppress the colony. His intention to do so at some stage in the future need not be doubted. Yet he was well aware of their usefulness as farmers, soldiers, and makers of military equipment, and he would have been aware too of how Iberian rulers preserved and benefited from the subject Muslim communities over whom they were acquiring dominion during Charles's lifetime, a period when Christian power was greatly extended into southern Spain and Portugal. The clearest evidence that the Angevin kings sought to replace the Muslim farmers of Lucera with a Christian population can be found in Charles I's attempts to encourage Provençal settlement in and around Lucera. Julie Taylor maintains that his original intention was to settle Lucera itself with these Provençaux, and that this policy motivated the construction of a fortress in the town.[22] Charles's first intention, then, seems to have been the creation of a Christian population in a walled-off area of Lucera as a counterbalance to the massive Muslim majority; his second aim was the replacement of the Saracens by Provençal Christians, but their numbers were insufficient, and they became diffused across the surrounding region of Capitanata. Franco-Provençal dialects have persisted in nearby villages, suggesting that the newcomers found rural locations less constricting and more amenable.[23]

One of the most important and difficult questions to answer pertains to the legal status of the Luceran Muslims. The latest account of the community, by Taylor, offers plenty of detailed information about the Lucerans as craftsmen, farmers, and soldiers, but, unfortunately, adds nothing to our understanding of this fundamental question.[24] The deeper one looks at this issue, the clearer it becomes that Frederick II's model was not that of subject Muslims in Spain but of his Jewish subjects in Germany. In 1236 he had issued a privilege in favor of the German Jews that brought them under his direct protection; in part he sought to ensure that it was the emperor, and not the Church, who would exercise financial and legal authority over the Jews, who, he was aware, needed protection at a time of blood libels and other attacks. Frederick described the German Jews as *servi camere nostre*, a term indicating direct dependence on the emperor; the word *servus* did not, in this context, indicate a state of abjection but merely that the Jews were the king's dependents and, in some measure, his agents or ministers.[25] Similar terminology was also applied to the Jews in Spain, starting in the statutes of the Aragonese city of Teruel (1176) and the Castilian city of Cuenca (1190).[26] It is clear that the concept of Jewish servitude was closely linked to the observation of St. Augustine that the Jews were destined to serve the Christians, preserving the books of the Old Law just as a *servus* would carry the books of his master. Additionally, the Theodosian and Justinianic law codes insisted in a similar spirit that Jews must not exercise dominion over Christians but must always be subordinate to them. These theological and legal verdicts on Jewish status helped determine the status of Muslims under Christian rule as well.

The first evidence that this terminology was being applied to non-Christians in Sicily occurs in a privilege issued by Frederick II at Brescia, in northern Italy, in November 1237, in which Frederick exempts a Jewish doctor called *magister* ("Master") Busach, described as *iudeus medicus, servus camere nostre*, from taxes customarily paid by the Jews of Palermo then and in the future.[27] General tax exemption would no doubt have been quite valuable to a physician, who would have needed to import high quality ingredients from abroad, such as the sugar Frederick is known to have enjoyed.[28] A reference in this document to the *servicia* rendered to Frederick by Busach is a reminder that Busach ministered to his king; *servicia* is a neutral term that could apply to anyone who wins the ruler's favor by helping him: this man is no slave or serf. Later, the term *servicia* is used in the same document to mean taxes, imposts, and other obligations to the Crown, just as it might be used to describe the dues owed by a land tenant or by Christian citizens of any town.

This was a privilege in favor of a single person. We cannot show that Frederick II employed the term *servi camere nostre* for all his Jewish subjects in southern Italy and Sicily, in the way that he certainly did in Germany. However, it is clear that he did think of the Jews of the kingdom in similar terms to those of Germany since there was a long tradition in southern Italy of treating the Jews as financial assets of their Norman rulers, granted collectively to cooperative bishops or other beneficiaries.[29] The papacy complained in August 1236 that Frederick had stamped on the rights of the Church in Sicily, and one issue concerned "the Jewries seized from certain churches" ("de Iudecis ablatis quibusdam ecclesiis").[30] To this complaint Frederick replied significantly that

> We did not take the Jews, who are immediately subject to us both in the empire and the kingdom according to a similar law, from any church that might assume a special right over them.[31]

It is thus abundantly clear that Frederick wished to treat all Jews, whether in Germany or Sicily, as existing in a state of "immediacy," directly linked to the Crown without intermediaries, unless he himself chose to make an exception.

The first evidence for a Sicilian Muslim being classified in the same way as a Jew comes from the register of Frederick II of 1239–40, where a figure called 'Abd Allah or Abdolla appears as the *servus* of the *camera*:

> By the mandate of Lord John the Moor, John of Otranto wrote to Alexander son of Henry, to the effect that at the request of Master Joachim he should provide expenses for Abdolla, *servus* of the Chamber, who is being sent to learn how to read and write Arabic letters, since he will be traveling to him, and will stay with him.[32]

Thus Abdolla was sent to study under an otherwise unknown Master Joachim, apparently a Greek or a Latin.[33] Here, as in the case of Master Busach, it appears that the term *servus* is applied to a specific individual. The idea of needing to train someone to read and write Arabic should come as no great surprise: the Muslims of Sicily had nearly all been deported to Lucera by this point. Although Sicilian Jews continued to speak Arabic, Jews normally wrote Arabic in Hebrew characters; it must have made sense to train individuals in the use of Arabic script. It is even possible that Frederick wanted to train someone to read advanced scientific or philosophical texts in Arabic. Frederick's instructions concerning Abdolla were sent to John the Moor, described by the chronicler Nicholas de Jamsilla as "quidam servus niger de domo Imperatoris" ("a certain black *servus* of the Emperor's household") who had been born into servitude ("ancilla natum"). Here we seem to encounter a slave, the son of a slave—the classic figure present at many another Mediterranean and oriental courts—who later became *qaʾid* of the Muslims of Lucera.

It is possible that Abdolla was also a Muslim court slave; and Jeremy Johns has actually rendered *servo camere* as "a slave of the Chamber" without explaining the intended meaning.[34] Yet the term *servus camere* seems to be used by Frederick in a Sicilian (but not a German) context to indicate Jews and Muslims personally close to him, members of his intimate entourage, who might be slave or free. We can contrast this status with the position of the Muslims possessed by the royal court (*curia*) who still lived in Malta, where they were liable for a series of taxes and corvées; the *villani curie* paid the Crown 3,100 *tarí* (over 33 ounces of gold) each year in the 1240s. They lived alongside Maltese Jews, who were also evidently regarded as dependents of the Crown and who paid a *gisia*, or poll-tax, based on Islamic models. Most of the Maltese Muslims were apparently deported to Lucera, although many may have converted and remained as *villani curie* (helping to explain the survival of Siculo-Arabic as the Maltese vernacular). Slaves were a separate phenomenon on Malta. The slave population included captives from the islands of Jerba, raided by Frederick II a few years earlier: sixty *servi* and *ancille* working in the three royal castles (Mdina, Birgu, Gozo) appear to have been slaves.[35] To take a specific but unusual example, a Maltese slave was sold by a Florentine merchant in Genoa in 1248; her name was Maimona and, exceptionally, she indicated her consent to the sale—an odd and inexplicable set of circumstances.[36] However, the *servientes* who formed the island garrison should not be confused with slaves or servants; these were soldiers—"sergeants"—who were presumably free men from Sicily and southern Italy.[37]

Servitude thus took many forms, and what we need to discover is the meaning of the term *servus* when applied to the Luceran Saracens in particular. The starting point is the entourage of Frederick II. In what senses were the apparent slave Abdolla and the physician Busach of similar status? Both Busach the Jew and Abdolla the Saracen were *servi* of the ruler's chamber; Abdolla may also have been a slave in the sense of having been bought as a slave or of being the son of a slave, but the term *servus camere* itself did not convey that meaning. A *servus camere*, Jewish or Muslim, who was present at court had a special bond to the ruler, a status not as grand as that of the *familiares regis* of the Norman period but nevertheless one that allowed these people to enjoy exceptional closeness to the ruler. The concept was applied to communities too: the Jews and Muslims were available to provide the king with services (including direct taxes); they had a direct, immediate, almost personal bond to the ruler.

The difficulty in accommodating Muslims in Christian society was met in Sicily and Iberia by approximating their status to that of Jews, even if Muslims did not carry the theological baggage that was heaped on the shoulders of Jews.[38] It was a neat and simple solution that came to define the status of the Muslims in southern Italy until their mass arrest in 1300 and even beyond. Under Charles I and Charles II, even the leaders of the Luceran community, such as 'Abd al-'Azīz (Adelasisius), were *servi camere nostri*; this did not prevent them from being knighted or from attending the king's parliaments.[39] The term was applied both to all Luceran Muslims ("universis hominibus Lucerie Sarracenis Camere Sue servis") and to many individuals, such as Adelasisius, "sarracenus, milex, camere nostre fidelis et servus." In an earlier article, I argued that their fragile status as the king's *servi* could, by 1300, be exploited with the help of the civil lawyers to justify the sale of virtually the entire population of Lucera as slaves and the dispersal of the Muslim colony at Lucera.[40] The term *servus* was itself ambiguous, applied to people as diverse as the pope and real slaves; but, armed with their knowledge of the Roman law of slavery, Charles's advisers, such as his minister Bartolomeo da Capua, decided to read *servi camere nostre* as a statement that the Lucera Saracens were fully possessed by the king—they were slaves of the royal chamber. After 1300 a specific Latin term for slaves was also applied to former Lucera Muslims, who appeared in the marketplaces of the Mediterranean or occasionally lingered on estates in Apulia: by 1309 we read of "duos sclavos de servis olim Lucerie" ("two slaves from among the *servi* formerly of Lucera").[41] The term *sclavi* had occasionally been applied in the past to Lucerans who were full slaves.[42] From a group possessed, in a certain sense, by the Crown, the Lucerans became individuals possessed by those who could pay the state for them. In effect, King Charles II had decided that the Muslims of Lucera, as his property, would be sold to private buyers to raise cash and to extirpate the extraordinary, and to him highly offensive, Islamic city in his domains.

Some comparisons can be made. Thirteen years before the Lucerans were sold as slaves, the king of Aragon, Alfonso III, sold into slavery virtually the entire population of Minorca (perhaps 40,000 people), which had submitted to the king of Aragon under the highly advantageous terms of a surrender treaty in 1231. Between 1231 and 1287 the Minorcans led what was to all intents and purposes an autonomous existence as free Muslims within the Catalan-Aragonese kingdom of Majorca; they could even ban Christians and Jews from settling in their midst. But in 1287 they were classed as rebels because they were said to have collaborated with North African emirs to frustrate Aragonese enterprises in the Maghreb. Thus the complete depopulation of a Muslim territory had precedents; and there were also clearances in Andalusia following the fall of Córdoba and Seville in 1236 and 1248. However, the Minorcans were enslaved as punishment, whereas the Lucerans were already identified as *servi*, and the term was given its most stringent meaning; therefore, they were not sold into slavery but sold as existing slaves to new masters.[43] Still, it is very probable that Minorca provided an example of how to treat, or rather mistreat, a subject Muslim population by selling them en masse.

The extinction of Muslim Lucera should also be understood alongside Charles II's vigorously anti-Jewish policy, beginning with the expulsion of the Jews from Anjou and Maine in 1289 (amid lurid accounts of Jewish usury and the seduction of Christian maidens), followed by an intense persecution of the south Italian Jews in about 1290.[44] The aim in the latter case was the conversion of the Jews, who were accused of putting a Christian boy to death in mockery of Christ's Passion.[45] Eight thousand Jews are said to have converted; the rest are said to have fled from southern Italy. One of those involved in this policy was the eminent Crown lawyer and minister Bartolomeo da Capua, who was also heavily involved in the suppression of the Muslim colony at Lucera.[46] That there was a strong religious component to the decision to end the Muslim community at Lucera is clear from the pronouncements of Charles II. Among the documents collected by Pietro Egidi in his *Codice diplomatico dei saraceni di Lucera* (Documentary Collection Concerning the Muslims of Lucera) are letters from Charles II in which he insists that his intention in suppressing the colony has been to increase the Christian faith. Indeed, he states that he has decided to dedicate the new, Christian city to the Virgin Mary (renaming it Città Santa Maria), considering it for "the common good, the safety of the province, and the advantage of his subjects" that the seed of Belial should be uprooted and wiped out in Capitanata, for the Saracens had committed "many horrendous and detestable things inimical to the Christian name."[47] While the accusation of (unspecified) horrendous acts bears comparison with the abuse directed against the Jews and Judaism, the exclusion of the Saracens from the wider community of *regnicoli* is made clear in the king's insistence that they are being suppressed for the general good of his subjects.

The sale of the Lucerans into slavery also brought Charles II much-needed funds at a critical time in his struggle against the Aragonese for control of Sicily, and much of the grain of Lucera was sent in 1300 to feed the Angevin armies.[48] The immediate result of the depopulation of Lucera was a collapse in revenues from the region as agricultural productivity collapsed. Indeed, in 1302 special permission was granted for small groups of Muslims (some interestingly described as *liberi*, others as *servi*) to remain in Capitanata, without explicitly insisting that they convert to Christianity, though they were denied the right to a mosque or to form a religious congregation.[49] In 1301, five and a half months after the arrest of all the Luceran Muslims, deported males were sold for two ounces of gold (craftsmen for three), women and children for one ounce; there was apparently no further attempt to distinguish among slaves by physique, health, or age, though (for reasons it would be more delicate not to explore) attractive young females would attract better prices on the international markets than older women.[50] Merchants could recoup the cost of a young woman by putting her to work as a sex slave: it is unlikely that much pity was shown for the misery of the Lucerans. Maybe prices had been higher immediately after the sale of the Lucerans began, but it needs to be stressed that these prices were far below those being paid in the same period at Palermo, where a black "Saracen" slave named Miriam was sold in 1287 for five ounces and twenty-two and one half tarí, and a white Saracen slave was sold for five ounces; the Maltese slave Maimona, sold in Genoa in 1248, fetched five and a half *librae* of silver, which (depending on exchange rates) was only about an ounce and a half, according to Peter Spufford's tables of exchange rates.[51] However, around 1287 four or five ounces seems to have been the standard price at least in Palermo, though later in the year, as Minorcan slaves flooded the market, the price plummeted.[52] Many a merchant must have bought Luceran slaves with a view to selling them on to purchasers overseas, at a handsome profit.

Assuming that 10,000 Luceran slaves were sold and that one third were male, one third female, and one third children, we can assume a total value of about 15,000 ounces of gold (taking into account the extra fee for artisans). Then there was the property of the Lucerans: considerable attention was paid to the disposal of cattle owned by the Muslims, while the wealthy Luceran 'Abd al-'Azīz (Adelasisius) suffered the loss of precious items such as robes and articles made of silver—these were returned to him after he converted to Christianity, but only after some effort.[53] With allowance for overheads—the Muslims had to be fed as they were sent to points of sale in Naples and Apulia—and after commission from merchants who presumably helped the royal agents dispose of these living goods, not to mention endemic corruption, the king would have been lucky to receive 10,000 ounces. Still, that was a massive injection of funds, 333 pounds of gold, and yet it served little purpose, since within two years even Charles's supporter Pope Boniface (who had praised the suppression of Lucera) had to admit that the time had come for peace with the Aragonese, which was secured with the Treaty of Caltabellotta.[54]

Ultimately, both Jews and Muslims were victims not so much of Angevin failure in the War of the Sicilian Vespers as of Angevin failure to come to the aid of the beleaguered Latin Kingdom of Jerusalem, which had fallen to the Mamluks in 1291 while Charles II was preoccupied with Sicilian affairs. After his father bought the Crown of Jerusalem from Maria of Antioch in 1277, the Angevin kings of Naples called themselves *Rex Jerusalem et Sicilie* ("King of Jerusalem and Sicily"), even though they lost the latter in 1282 (and the former nine years later). The escutcheon of the kings of Naples proudly bore the gold cross on a white field of Jerusalem. Charles II fondly produced plans for a great crusade that would recover Latin power in the Holy Land, and all the evidence suggests that he saw himself as an *athleta Christi* ("athlete of Christ") charged with the moral and military defense of Christendom against Muslims and Jews. It is perhaps no surprise that, in search of an easy victory against Islam, he turned against the Muslim farmers and craftsmen of his own kingdom, impotent as he was in the face of Mamluk power.

Notes

INTRODUCTION
Jan M. Ziolkowski

1. For publications with the Spanish title, see Miguel Asín Palacios, *Dante y el Islam*, Colección de manuales Hispania, serie B:1 (Madrid: Editorial Voluntad, 1927); and Ricardo Horacio Shamsuddín Elía, *Dante y el islam: El pensamiento musulmán en la Europa del siglo XIV* (Buenos Aires, Argentina: Ediciones Mezquita At-Tauhid, 1998). With the Italian title, see Giuseppe Gabrieli, *Dante e l'Islam: Contro la memoria di Mig. Asin interno alla Escatalogia musulmana nella Divina Commedia* (Varallo Sesia: Unione tipografica valsesiana, 1921); Enrico Cerulli, "Dante e l'Islam," published in similar forms in *Convegno di scienze morali, storiche e filologiche, 27 maggio–10 giugno 1956. Tema: Oriente ed Occidente nel Medio Evo* (Rome: Accademia nazionale dei Lincei, 1957), 275–94, and *Al-Andalus* 21 (1956): 229–53; Peter Russell, *Dante e l'Islam* (Terranuova Bracciolini: Biblioteca comunale, Assessorato alla cultura, 1991); Peter Russell, "Dante e l'Islam: Una introduzione generale," "Dante e l'Islam oggi," and "Assunzione celeste: Quarta conferenza su Dante e l'Islam," in *Poetic Asides*, 2 vols., Salzburg Studies in English Literature: Poetic Drama & Poetic Theory 77:3, Outsiders 5–6 (Salzburg: Institut für Anglistik und Amerikanistik, Universität Salzburg, 1992–1993), 2:5–23, 24–33, and 34–51, respectively. Miguel Asín Palacios, *Dante e l'Islam*, trans. Roberto Rossi Testa e Younis Tawfik, introduction by Carlo Ossola, 2 vols., Nuovi saggi 94 (Parma: Pratiche 1994; repr., Milan: NET, 2005); and Karla Mallette, "Dante e l'Islam: sul canto III del *Purgatorio*," *Rivista di storia e letteratura religiosa* 41 (2005): 39–62. With the French title, see Werner Söderhjelm, "Dante et l'Islam," *Neuphilologische Mitteilungen* (1921); and Giorgio Levi della Vida, "Dante et l'Islam: d'aprés de nouveaux documents," *Revue de la Méditerranée* no. 60 (1954). With the English title, see Thomas Walker

Arnold, "Dante and Islam" (review of Asín Palacios), *Contemporary Review* (August 1921); and Fuat Sezgin, ed. *Dante and Islam: Texts and Studies*, Publications of the Institute for the History of Arabic-Islamic Science at the Johann Wolfgang Goethe University: Islamic philosophy 119 (Frankfurt am Main: Institute for the History of Arabic-Islamic Science, 2000).

2. If there is need to demonstrate that the *Commedia* passes muster as a summa, consider the title of *Dante, Summa medievalis: Proceedings of the Symposium of the Center for Italian Studies, SUNY Stony Brook*, ed. Charles Franco and Leslie Morgan, Filibrary 9 (Stony Brook, N.Y.: Forum Italicum, 1995). On Dante as a Catholic author, see J.F. Makepeace, "The Dante Sexcentenary," *New Blackfriars* 2, no. 14 (1921): 92: "For Dante was, first and foremost, a Catholic and regarded everything from a Catholic standpoint."

3. Paul A. Cantor, "The Uncanonical Dante: The Divine Comedy and Islamic Philosophy," *Philosophy and Literature* 20, no. 1 (1996): 138–53.

4. Teodolinda Barolini, *The Undivine Comedy: Detheologizing Dante* (Princeton, N.J.: Princeton University Press, 1992), 6 (on the Dominicans, especially Guido Vernani) and 267–68 n. 9 (cited by Cantor). For a fuller exploration of the topic, see James Miller, editor, *Dante and the Unorthodox: The Aesthetics of Transgression* (Waterloo, Ont.: Wilfrid Laurier University Press, 2005).

5. The incident has been discussed by Jeffrey Einboden, "Voicing an Islamic Dante: The Problem of Translating the *Commedia* into Arabic," *Neophilologus* 92 (2008): 77. For original reporting, see for example Philip Willan, "Al-Qaida Plot to Blow Up Bologna Church Fresco," in *The Guardian* (London), June 24, 2002, Guardian Foreign Pages, 13.

6. Richard Owen, "Muslims Say Fresco Must Be Destroyed," *The Times* (London), June 9, 2001, Overseas News.

7. The term "clash of civilization" owes its vogue to an article that appeared first in 1993, the title of which had lost its concluding interrogative and had been transformed into a slogan for future political conduct by the time the book by the same author was published in 1996: Samuel P. Huntington, "The Clash of Civilizations?" *Foreign Affairs* 72, no. 3 (Summer 1993): 22–49; and Huntington, *The Clash of Civilizations and the Remaking of World Order* (New York: Simon & Schuster, 1996). The "pushback" both from within Near Eastern studies and from those allied with the theory of Orientalism was strong. For two instances, see Roy P. Mottahedeh, "The Clash of Civilizations: An Islamicist's Critique," *Harvard Middle Eastern and Islamic Review* 2, no. 2 (1996): 1–26; and

Edward W. Said, "The Clash of Ignorance," *The Nation* 273, no. 12 (October 22, 2001): 11–13.

8. A classic tallying of debts to Islam is *The Legacy of Islam*, ed. Joseph Schacht, 2nd ed. (Oxford: Clarendon Press, 1974). Specifically focused upon the Middle Ages are Norman Daniel, *The Arabs and Mediaeval Europe* (London: Longman, 1975); Norman Daniel, *Islam and the West: The Making of an Image* (Edinburgh: University Press, 1960); and W. Montgomery Watt, *The Influence of Islam on Medieval Europe* (Edinburgh: University Press, 1972).

9. Gregory B. Stone, *Dante's Pluralism and the Islamic Philosophy of Religion* (New York: Palgrave Macmillan, 2006), 54. Stone has contributed to this issue an essay entitled "Dante and the *Falasifa*: Religion as Imagination."

10. By referring to pluralism, I draw attention once again to Stone, *Dante's Pluralism*, but I hasten to point out that he does not use the term *convivencia* in his book. Nor does María Rosa Menocal, the most prominent exponent in the Anglophone world of the idea that Dante was heavily influenced by Arabic culture, in her earliest major treatment of Dante, although she does emphasize medieval connections between al-Andalus and Italy. See *The Arabic Role in Medieval Literary History: A Forgotten Heritage* (Philadelphia: University of Pennsylvania Press, 1987), esp. 115–35.

11. Jonathan Ray, "Beyond Tolerance and Persecution: Reassessing our Approach to Medieval *Convivencia*," *Jewish Social Studies* 11, no. 2 (Winter 2005): 1–18.

12. For examples, see David L. Lewis, *God's Crucible: Islam and the Making of Europe, 570 to 1215* (New York: W.W. Norton, 2008); Chris Lowney, *A Vanished World: Medieval Spain's Golden Age of Enlightenment* (New York: Free Press, 2005); Vivian B. Mann, Thomas F. Glick, and Jerrilynn D. Dodds, eds., *Convivencia: Jews, Muslims, and Christians in Medieval Spain* (New York: G. Braziller in association with the Jewish Museum, 1992); María Rosa Menocal, *The Ornament of the World: How Muslims, Jews, and Christians Created a Culture of Tolerance in Medieval Spain* (Boston: Little, Brown, 2002); and Lucy K. Pick, *Conflict and Coexistence: Archbishop Rodrigo and the Muslims and Jews in Medieval Spain* (Ann Arbor: University of Michigan, 2004).

13. For a broad consideration of the Arab contribution to Italian culture in the Middle Ages, see Francesco Gabrieli and Umberto Scerrato, *Li Arabi in Italia: Cultura, contatti e tradizioni* (Milan: Garzanti/Scheiwiller, 1979). With particular attention to literary history, see Karla Mallette, *The Kingdom of Sicily, 1100–1250: A Literary History* (Philadelphia: University of Pennsylvania Press, 2005).

14. (New York: Pantheon Books, 1978), 70. Said's views on Dante have been critiqued in two essays (the interrelationship of which resists easy disentanglement) by Kathleen Biddick, "Coming Out of Exile: Dante on the Orient(alism) Express," *The American Historical Review*, 105 (2000): 1234–49, and "Coming Out of Exile: Dante on the Orient Express," in *The Postcolonial Middle Ages*, ed. Jeffrey Jerome Cohen (New York: St. Martin's Press, 2000), 35–52; as well as by Elizabeth A. Coggeshall, "Dante, Islam, and Edward Said," *Telos* 139 (Summer 2007): 133–51. They are also discussed in the present volume by Maria Esposito Frank, "Dante's Muḥammad."

15. See (though without any particular reference to medieval studies) *Occidentalism: Images of the West*, ed. James G. Carrier (Oxford: Clarendon Press, 1995).

16. For *convivencia*, see Américo Castro, *España en su historia: Cristianos, moros y judíos* (Buenos Aires: Editorial Losada, 1948), 198–202. On recent turns in the application of the term, see Jonathan Ray, "Beyond Tolerance and Persecution: Reassessing our Approach to Medieval *Convivencia*," *Jewish Social Studies* 11, no. 2 (Winter 2005): 1–18. For Orientalism, the earliest citation in any sense in the *Oxford English Dictionary* is dated to 1769.

17. On the place of the Orient in Dante's geography, see Brenda Deen Schildgen, *Dante and the Orient* (Urbana: University of Illinois Press, 2002), 19–44.

18. María Rosa Menocal, *The Arabic Role*, 127, 130.

19. See Alessandro Niccoli, "Saracino," *Enciclopedia dantesca*, 5:30–31.

20. On the chansons de geste, see C. Meredith Jones, "The Conventional Saracen of the Songs of Geste," *Speculum* 17 (1942): 204–6. In Dante, see *Convivio* 2.8.9, *Inferno* 27.87, and *Epistole* 11.4.

21. On Dante's outlook on the reality and concept of the Holy Land Crusade, see Schildgen, *Dante and the Orient*, 66–91.

22. Marshall Hodgson, *The Venture of Islam: Conscience and History in a World Civilization*, 3 vols. (Chicago: University of Chicago Press, 1974), 1 ("The classical age of Islam"): 59, coined the adjective "Islamicate" (on the model of Italianate) as referring "not directly to the religion, Islam, itself, but to the social and cultural complex historically associated with Islam and the Muslims, both among Muslims themselves and even when found among non-Muslims."

23. A sense of the researches that had been done can be gleaned from Edgar Blochet, *Les sources orientales de la Divine Comédie*, Les Littératures populaires de toutes les nations 41 (Paris: J. Maisonneuve, 1901).

24. Asín Palacios himself summarized the reaction to his book in an addendum that accompanied it when it was reprinted in 1943 ("Historia y crítica de una controversia"). On the occasion of a much later reprinting of Asín Palacios's collected works, María Rosa Menocal discussed the problems and peculiarities in the reception of his work: see "An Andalusianist's Last Sigh," *La corónica* 24 (1996): 179–89.

25. Colección de manuales Hispania, Serie B:1 (Madrid: Editorial Voluntad, 1927).

26. *Dante e l'Islam*, trans. Roberto Rossi and Younis Tawfik, 2 vols., Nuovi Saggi 94 (Parma: Pratiche Editrice, 1994).

27. *Islam and the Divine Comedy*, ed. and trans. Harold Sunderland (London: J. Murray, 1926).

28. Dieter Kremers, "Islamische Einflüsse auf Dantes 'Göttliche Komödie,'" in *Orientalisches Mittelalter*, ed. Wolfhart Heinrichs, Neues Handbuch der Literaturwissenschaft 5 (Wiesbaden: AULA-Verlag, 1990), 202. In the early years of the reception, the only extended study by an Italian Dantist that shows signs of having responded positively to Asín Palacios's book is Luigi Valli, *Il linguaggio segreto di Dante e dei "Fedeli d'amore,"* Biblioteca di filosofia e scienza 10 (Rome: Optima [L'universale], 1928).

29. María Rosa Menocal, review of *Il Libro della scala di Maometto*, trans. Roberto Rossi Testa (Milan: SE, 1991), in *Lectura Dantis* 13 (1993): 106.

30. Francesco Gabrieli, "Dante e l'Islam," *Cultura e scuola* 13–14 (1965): 195.

31. Philip F. Kennedy, "The Muslim Sources of Dante?" in *The Arab Influence in Medieval Europe: Folia Scholastica Mediterranea*, ed. Dionisius A. Agius and Richard Hitchcock (Reading: Ithaca Press, 1994), 63.

32. Leonardo Olschki, "Mohammedan Eschatology and Dante's Other World," *Comparative Literature* 3 (1951): 2.

33. Alexander Knysh, "Ibn ʿArabī," in *The Literature of Al-Andalus*, ed. María Rosa Menocal, Raymond P. Scheindlin, and Michael Sells (Cambridge: Cambridge University Press, 2000), 331–44; James Winston Morris, "The Spiritual Ascension: Ibn ʿArabī and the Miʿrāǧ," *Journal of the American Oriental Society* 107 (1987): 629–52 and 108 (1988): 63–78.

34. For the latest studies of such material by a scholar who has long been active in this domain, see Peter Dinzelbacher, *Von der Welt durch die Hölle zum Paradies—das mittelalterliche Jenseits* (Paderborn: Ferdinand Schöningh, 2007). English translations of many key works can be found in Eileen Gardiner, *Medieval Visions of Heaven and Hell: A Sourcebook*, Garland Medieval Bibliographies 11, Garland Reference

Library of the Humanities 1256 (New York: Garland Publishing, 1993).
German translations, with the texts in the original languages en face,
are available in *Mittelalterliche Visionsliteratur—eine Anthologie*, ed. and
trans. Peter Dinzelbacher (Darmstadt: Wissenschaftliche Buchgesellschaft, 1989). For an overview of such visions of the otherworld up to
Dante, see Cesare Segre, "Viaggi e visioni d'oltremondo sino alla *Commedia* di Dante," in his *Fuori del mondo: i modelli nella follia e nelle
immagini dell'aldilà*, Einaudi Paperbacks 204 (Turin: G. Einaudi, 1990),
25–48. For a consideration of Asín Palacios's investigations as a test case
for determining the laws of literary imitation, see Louis Massignon,
Opera minora: Textes recueillis, classés et présentés avec une bibliographie,
ed. Youakim Moubarac, 3 vols. (Beirut: Dar al-Maaref, 1963), 59–81.

    35. Richard W. Southern, "Dante and Islam," in *Relations Between
East and West in the Middle Ages: Papers Delivered at the Second Colloquium
in Medieval History to be held at the University of Edinburgh, March 1969*,
ed. Derek Baker (Edinburgh: Edinburgh University Press, 1973), 140.

    36. For details about Bonaventure, see Enrico Cerulli, "Bonaventura
da Siena," in *Dizionario biografico degli Italiani* (Rome: Istituto della
Enciclopedia Italiana, 1960–), 11: 640–42.

    37. The foundational edition, with the Latin and Old French en
face, was by Enrico Cerulli, *Il "Libro della scala" e la questione delle
fonti arabo-spagnole della Divina Commedia*, Studi e testi 150 (Vatican
City: Biblioteca Apostolica Vaticana, 1949). Presently the standard
editions of the Latin are *Liber scale Machometi: Die lateinische Fassung
des Kitāb al miʻrādj*, ed. Edeltraud Werner, Studia humaniora 4
(Düsseldorf: Droste, 1986); and (with French translation) *Le livre de
l'échelle de Mahomet = Liber scale Machometi*, trans. Gisèle Besson and
Michèle Brossard-Dandré, Lettres gothiques 4529 (Paris: Librairie
générale française/Le Livre de poche, 1991). These have been translated
into French, German, and Italian, but not yet into English. For the
German and Italian, see *Die Jenseitsreise Mohammeds = Liber scale Machometi = Kitab al-miʻraj*, trans. Edeltraud Werner, Religionswissenschaftli-
che Texte und Studien 14 (Hildesheim: Olms, 2007), and *Il libro della
scala di Maometto*, trans. Roberto Rossi Testa, Oscar classici 464 (Milan:
A. Mondadori, 1999). For the Old French, see *Le livre de l'Eschiele
Mahomet: Die französische Fassung einer alfonsinischen Übersetzung*, ed.
Peter Wunderli, Romanica Helvetica 77 (Bern: Francke, 1968). For an
English translation of the Old French, see *The Prophet of Islam in Old
French: The Romance of Muḥammad (1258) and the Book of Muḥammad's
Ladder (1264)*, trans. Reginald Hyatte, Brill's Studies in Intellectual
History 75 (Leiden: E. J. Brill, 1997), 97–198.

38. Muñoz, followed by Kennedy, "The Muslim Sources," 76–77.

39. The most readily available edition is *Peter the Venerable and Islam*, ed. James Kritzeck, Princeton Oriental Studies 23 (Princeton, NJ: Princeton University Press, 1964), but the new standard is now *Petrus Venerabilis: Schriften zum Islam*, ed. and trans. Reinhold Glei, Corpus Islamo-Christianum, Series Latina 1 (Altenberge: CIS-Verlag, 1985).

40. Cerulli, followed by Kennedy, "The Muslim Sources," 78.

41. The work was familiar already around 1350 to the Tuscan Fazio degli Uberti (ca. 1305–after 1367), grandson of the Farinata evoked in *Inferno* 10. In a poem entitled *Il Dittamondo* Fazio mentions the Muslim paradise as described in *Liber scale* (and he also invokes Riccoldo da Montecroce). The *Liber scale* was also familiar later to the Franciscan Roberto Caracciolo (1425–1495) of Apulia who in his *Specchio della Fede* (Mirror of Faith) refers to it. See Francesco Gabrieli, "Dante und der Islam," trans. Werner Eicke, *Diogenes: Internationale Zeitschrift für die Wissenschaften vom Menschen* 9–10 (1978): 25; and Francesco Gabrieli, "New Light on Dante and Islam," *Diogenes* 6 (1954): 65. The Castilian translation, although no longer available, was probably a source for the close résumé given by San Pedro Pascual (1227–1300) in his *Sobre la seta mahometana* (On the Muḥammadan Sect). For the latest estimation of these and other testimonia, see *Die Jenseitsreise*, trans. Werner, 39–48.

42. *La Escala de Mahoma: Traducción del arabe al castellano, latín y francés, ordenada por Alfonso X el Sabio* (Madrid: Ministerio de Asuntos Exteriores, 1949).

43. Cerulli offered a concise form of his conclusions in "Dante e l'Islam." A very careful, albeit now somewhat dated, sifting of evidence is performed by Theodore Silverstein, "Dante and the Legend of the Mi'rāj: The Problem of Islamic Influence on the Christian Literature of the Otherworld," *Journal of Near Eastern Studies* 11 (1952): 89–110 and 187–97.

44. This observation is made in Southern, "Dante and Islam," 141.

45. I am inspired here by Olschki, "Mohammedan Eschatology," 14.

46. Vicente Cantarino, "Dante and Islam: History and Analysis of a Controversy," in *A Dante Symposium in Commemoration of the 700th Anniversary of the Poet's Birth (1265–1965)*, ed. William De Sua and Gino Rizzo, sponsored by the 1965 Dante Centenary Committee: Dante Society of America, South Atlantic Region, University of North Carolina Studies in the Romance Languages and Literatures 58 (Chapel Hill: University of North Carolina Press, 1965), 175–98.

47. An exhaustive annotated bibliography that appeared at nearly the same time is Peter Wunderli, "Zur Auseinandersetzung über die

muselmanischen Quellen der *Divina Commedia*: Versuch einer kritischen Bibliographie," *Romanistisches Jahrbuch* 15 (1964): 19–50. Slightly later appeared Edoardo Crema, *La leyenda de un Dante islamizado*, INCIBA centenario 1 (Caracas: INCIBA, 1966).

48. Maria Corti, "Dante e la cultura islamica," in *"Per correr miglior acque . . .": Bilanci e prospettive degli studi danteschi alle soglie del nuovo millennio, Atti del convegno internazionale di Verona-Ravenna, 25–29 ottobre 1999*, 2 vols., Pubblicazioni del "Centro Pio Rajna" Sezione prima, Studi e saggi 9 (Rome: Salerno, 2001), 1:183–202. An interview of Maria Corti on the topic "Dante e l'Islam," recorded on April 20, 2000, is available in transcription at Enciclopedia multimediale delle scienze filosofiche, http://www.emsf.rai.it/interviste/interviste.asp?d=490.

49. Al-Qaeda, also known as al-Qaida, is more properly transcribed as al-Qāʿida and means "base" or "foundation" in Arabic.

50. For a few examples, see David G. Dalin and John F. Rothmann, *Icon of Evil: Hitler's Mufti and the Rise of Radical Islam* (New York: Random House, 2008); Philip Jenkins, *God's Continent: Christianity, Islam, and Europe's Religious Crisis* (Oxford: Oxford University Press, 2007); and David Selbourne, *The Losing Battle with Islam* (Amherst, N.Y.: Prometheus Books, 2005).

51. For a subtle exploration of such elision by both sides, see Bruce Holsinger, "Empire, Apocalypse, and the 9/11 Premodern," *Critical Inquiry* 34 (2008): 468–90. For a darkly humorous investigation of unfavorable assumptions about the Middle Ages, see Fred C. Robinson, "Medieval, the Middle Ages," *Speculum* 59 (1984): 745–56.

52. For a quick overview of these developments, see Archibald R. Lewis, "The Islamic World and the Latin West, 1350–1500," *Speculum* 65 (1990): 833–44.

53. See also John Tolan, "Du sage arabe au Sarrasin irrationnel: vers une idéologie de la supériorité occidentale," in *Culture arabe et culture européenne: L'inconnu au turban dans l'album de famille: colloque de Nantes, 14 et 15 décembre 2000*, ed. Malika Pondevie Roumane, François Clément, and John Tolan (Paris: Harmattan, 2006), 189–201; and John V. Tolan, *Saracens: Islam in the Medieval European Imagination* (New York: Columbia University Press, 2002), 245–54.

54. The earliest use of "European" to refer to "a native of Europe" is early seventeenth-century. See the *Oxford English Dictionary*, s.v.

55. To appreciate how monstrous Jews and Muslims were often made to appear in the art of Latin Christendom, see Debra Higgs Strickland, *Saracens, Demons, and Jews: Making Monsters in Medieval Art* (Princeton, NJ: Princeton University Press, 2003).

56. A recent study devoted to Immanuel is Fabian Alfie, "Immanuel of Rome, alias Manoello Giudeo: The Poetics of Jewish Identity in Fourteenth-Century Italy," *Italica* 75 (1998): 307–29. For earlier studies, see Umberto Cassuto, "Dante und Manoello," *Jahrbuch für jüdische Geschichte und Literatur* 24 (1921–1922): 90–121; Umberto Cassuto, *Dante e Manoello* (Florence: Israel, 1921); and Theodor Paur, "Immanuel and Dante," *Jahrbuch der Deutschen Dantegesellschaft* 3 (1871): 451–62. The interrelatedness of Dante's views on Jews and Muslims is examined most broadly by Jesper Hede, "Jews and Muslims in Dante's Vision," *European Review* 16 (2008): 101–14.

57. Paola Manni, *Storia della lingua italiana* 2, ed. Francesco Bruni, "Il Trecento toscano: la lingua di Dante, Petrarca e Boccaccio" (Bologna: Il Mulino, 2003), 156.

58. J. S. P. Tatlock, "Mohammed and His Followers in Dante," *The Modern Language Review* 27 (1932): 195.

59. Einboden, "Voicing an Islamic Dante," 84, and Richard Lemay, "Le Nemrod de l' 'Enfer' de Dante et le 'Liber Nemroth,'" *Quaderni degli "Studi danteschi"* 40 (1963): 57–128.

60. Tatlock, "Mohammed and His Followers," 186.

61. These images have been examined repeatedly, in greatest detail by Richard Schröder, *Glaube und Aberglaube in den altfranzösischen Dichtungen: ein Beitrag zur Kulturgeschichte des Mittelalters* (Erlangen: A. Deichert, 1886), and Norman Daniel, *Heroes and Saracens: An Interpretation of the Chansons de Geste* (Edinburgh: Edinburgh University Press, 1984). For a distillation of the images, see Tolan, *Saracens*, 105–34.

62. The threesome can be seen most clearly in *Chanson de Roland*, *laisse* 187, verses 2580–2591, in *The Song of Roland: An Analytical Edition*, ed. and trans. Gerard J. Brault, 2 vols. (University Park: Pennsylvania State University Press, 1978), 2:156–59.

63. For concise commentary, see Robert Hollander and Jean Hollander, translators, *Dante Alighieri: Paradiso* (New York: Doubleday, 2006), 16–20.

64. For instance, consider Charlemagne and Roland (Orlando: *Inf.* 31.16–18, *Par.* 18.43; Ganellone: *Inf.* 32.122), and William of Orange and Renouard (Rinoardo: *Par.* 18.46–48).

65. This perception of Islam took shape many centuries before Dante. Consider for example John of Damascus, as analyzed in Daniel J. Sahas, *John of Damascus on Islam: The "Heresy of the Ishmaelites"* (Leiden: Brill, 1972). For examination of the twelfth-century roots of this tradition, see Tolan, *Saracens*, 135–69.

66. Here I am indebted to Tolan, "Du sage arabe au Sarrasin irrationnel," at 190.

67. See Edmond Doutté, *Mahomet cardinal* (Châlons-sur-Marne: Martin frères, 1899).

68. Rasha Hamood Al-Sabah, "*Inferno* XXVIII: The Figure of Muḥammad," *Yale Italian Studies* 1 (1977): 158.

69. See Robert Hollander and Jean Hollander, translators, *Dante Alighieri: Purgatorio* (New York: Doubleday, 2003), 680.

70. The basic monograph on Muḥammad as represented in Western legends is Alessandro d'Ancona, *La leggenda di Maometto in Occidente*, ed. Andrea Borruso, Omikron 51 (Rome: Salerno Editrice, 1994), which was printed first in *Giornale Storico della Letteratura Italiana* 13 (1889): 199–281 and later (in revised form) in Alessandro d'Ancona, *Studi di critica e storia letteraria* (Bologna: Zanichelli, 1912), 2:167–306. For more recent coverage, see Stephan Hotz, *Mohammed und seine Lehre in der Darstellung abendländischer Autoren vom späten 11. bis zur Mitte des 12. Jahrhunderts: Aspekte, Quellen und Tendenzen in Kontinuität und Wandel*, Studien zur klassischen Philologie 137 (Frankfurt am Main: Lang, 2002). For a rapid overview, see Albrecht Noth, "Muḥammad 3. The Prophet's Image in Europe and the West," in *The Encyclopedia of Islam*, 11 vols., Web-CD editions (Leiden: Brill, 2003), 7:377–81. The lengthiest examination of Muḥammad in relation specifically to Dante has been Giuseppe Macaluso, *Dante e Maometto* (Rome: Edizioni Ruiz, 1951).

71. On the interplay between Muḥammad's status as a schismatic and his bodily mutilation, see Al-Sabah, "*Inferno* XXVIII: The Figure of Muḥammad," and Southern, "Dante and Islam," 137–38.

72. Tatlock, "Mohammed and His Followers," 192.

73. Einboden, "Voicing an Islamic Dante," 79–82.

74. For a simple diagram of the opposition inherent in Dante's views as emblematic of Western attitudes in general, see Fernando Cisneros, "Dante y el Islam. Enfoques a partir del texto de la *Commedia*," *Estudios de Asia y África* 36, no. 1 (2001): 79.

75. On the roles of the three in Dante, see Giuseppe Macaluso, "Tre Mussulmani illustri nella *Divina Commedia*," in his *Conferenze e scritti sull'islâm antico e moderno (seconda dispensazione)* (Rome: Pensiero e azione, 1974), 287–360. Despite the paucity of space allocated to Avicenna when he is named, his influence in the *Commedia* may be more extensive. See Rudolf Palgen, "Dante und Avicenna," *Anzeiger der philosophischen-historischen Klasse der Österreichischen Akademie der Wissenschaften* 1951, no. 12, 160–172, and Gotthard Strohmaier, "Ibn

Sīnā's Psychology and Dante's *Divine Comedy*," *Journal for the History of Arabic Science* 9 (1991): 107–11.

76. See Marcia Colish, "The Virtuous Pagan: Dante and the Christian Tradition," in *The Unbounded Community: Papers in Christian Ecumenism in Honor of Jaroslav Pelikan*, ed. William Caferro and Duncan G. Fisher, Garland Reference Library of the Humanities 1822 (New York: Garland, 1996), 43–92; Gino Rizzo, "Dante and the Virtuous Pagans," in *A Dante Symposium*, ed. De Sua and Rizzo, 115–31; and Cindy L. Vitto, *The Virtuous Pagan in Middle English Literature*, Transactions of the American Philosophical Society 79, pt. 5 (Philadelphia: American Philosophical Society, 1989), 36–49.

77. Jo Ann Hoeppner Moran Cruz, "Popular Attitudes Towards Islam in Medieval Europe," in *Western Views of Islam in Medieval and Early Modern Europe: Perception of Other*, ed. David R. Blanks and Michael Frassetto (New York: St. Martin's Press, 1999), 61.

78. An illuminating parallel was drawn at the very end of the twentieth century to the reasonable reflex to differentiating between dictators and reputable military leaders or scientists under their regimes. See Alauddin Samarrai, "Arabs and Latins in the Middle Ages: Enemies, Partners, and Scholars," in *Western Views of Islam in Medieval and Early Modern Europe*, ed. Blanks and Frassetto, 141: "Contrast, for example, the Western attitudes toward Adolf Hitler on the one hand, and Marshal Erwin Rommel and the German physicist Werner Heisenberg on the other; or Joseph Stalin vs. Marshall Georgi Zhukov and the Soviet physicist Peter Kapitza."

79. On Saladin, see Gaston Paris, "La Légende de Saladin," *Journal des savants* (May–August 1893): 284–299, 354–364, 428–438, 486–498; Américo Castro, "The Presence of the Sultan Saladin in the Romance Literatures," in *An Idea of History: Selected Essays of Américo Castro*, ed. and trans. Stephen Gilman and Edmund L. King (Columbus: Ohio State University Press, 1977), 241–69; Hannes Möhring, *Saladin, the Sultan and His Times, 1138–1193*, trans. David S. Bachrach (Baltimore: Johns Hopkins University Press, 2008); and John V. Tolan, *Sons of Ishmael: Muslims through European Eyes in the Middle Ages* (Gainesville: University Press of Florida, 2008), 79–105 (with reference to Tolan's earlier studies on the topic).

80. For the influence of Averroës and Averroism on Dante, see Maria Corti, *Percorsi dell'invenzione: Il linguaggio poetico e Dante* (Turin: Einaudi, 1993).

81. On the history of the term "Latin Avicennism," see Kenelm Foster, "Avicenna and Western Thought in the Thirteenth Century,"

New Blackfriars 32, no. 381 (1951): 591–602. On Latin Averroism, see S.-T. Bonino, "Averroès chez les latins: Vues cavalières sur la réception d'Averroès dans la scolastique latine médiévale," *Bulletin de littérature* 100 (1999): 133–52.

82. Vincent Cantarino, "Dante and Islam: Theory of Light in the *Paradiso*," *Kentucky Romance Quarterly* 15 (1968): 3–35.

83. Rocco Murari, "Il *De causis* e la sua fortuna nel Medio Evo," *Giornale storico della letteratura italiana* 34 (1899): 93–117.

84. For a sampling of articles on the furor, see Éric Aeschiman, "Aristote, un détour arabe contesté," *Libération*, April 30, 2008, Culture, 29; Aeschiman, "Du rififi chez les intellos: Littérature," *Libération*, July 19, 2008, Cahiers Été, 8; Jean Birnbaum, "Averroès," *Le Monde*, July, 25, 2008, Le Monde des livres, 4; Birnbaum, "Polémique sur les 'racines' de l'Europe," *Le Monde*, April 25, 2008, Le Monde des livres, 2; Roger-Pol Droit, "Et si l'Europe ne devait pas ses savoirs à l'islam? L'historien Sylvain Gouguenheim récuse l'idée que la science des Grecs ait été transmise à l'Occident par le monde musulman," *Le Monde*, April 4, 2008, Le Monde des livres, 6; Droit, "Jacques de Venise, passeur oublié," *Le Monde*, April 4, 2008, Le Monde des livres, 6; Historiens du *moyen âge*, "Oui, l'Occident chrétien est redevable au monde islamique," *Libération*, April 30, 2008, Rebonds, 32; *Le Monde*, "Gouguenheim," *Le Monde*, July 11, 2008, Le Monde des livres, 9; *Le Monde*, " 'Le Monde des livres' à Blois," October 10, 2008, Le Monde des livres, 8; Gabriel Martinez-Gros and Julien Loiseau, "Une démonstration suspecte," *Le Monde*, April 25, 2008, Le Monde des livres, 2; Nicholas Weill, "Kurt Flasch: Un regard 'démembré' sur le *moyen âge*," *Le Monde*, July 4, 2008, Le Monde des livres, 10; Thomas Wieder, "Penser l' 'affaire Gouguenheim,' " *Le Monde*, October 17, 2008, Le Monde des livres, 2.

85. John Vinocur, "Europe's Debt to Islam Given a Skeptical Look; Politicus," *The International Herald Tribune*, April 29, 2008, News, 2.

86. Shawkat M. Toorawa, "Muḥammad, Muslims, and Islamophiles in Dante's *Commedia*," *The Muslim World* 82 (1992): 133–44.

87. The epithet is known best from Matthew Paris (*Chronica majora*, no. 141a, 5.190): see Andrea Sommerlechner, *Stupor mundi?: Kaiser Friedrich II. und die mittelalterliche Geschichtsschreibung*, Publikationen des Historischen Instituts beim Österreichischen Kulturinstitut in Rom: I. Abteilung, Abhandlungen 11 (Vienna: Verlag der Österreichischen Akademie der Wissenschaften, 1999), 9, 226, 470, and 479.

88. Thomas E. Burman, "Michael Scot and the Translators," in *The Literature of Al-Andalus*, 404–11.

DANTE AND ISLAM: HISTORY AND ANALYSIS
OF A CONTROVERSY
Vicente Cantarino

The article was originally printed in *A Dante Symposium in Commemoration of the 700th Anniversary of the Poet's Birth (1265–1965)*, ed. William De Sua and Gino Rizzo, sponsored by the 1965 Dante Centenary Committee: Dante Society of America, South Atlantic Region, University of North Carolina Studies in the Romance Languages and Literatures 58 (Chapel Hill: University of North Carolina Press, 1965), 175–98. It is reprinted with the permission of the author and of the Dante Society of America.

The text has been edited to bring its style into conformity with other essays in this book. Additionally, a descriptive bibliography that had been separate has been integrated into the notes of the article proper. Finally, typographical errors and miscitations or incomplete citations have been corrected or expanded. It is hoped that these changes, for which the author has accorded his approval, will make the article easier to read.

   1. [Cantarino includes in his bibliography an exceedingly rare item that presents a résumé of the scholarship up to 1961 by an Italian scholar who taught in Cairo: Doménico Càntele, *L'Islam e Dante: La controversa influenza delle fonti musulmane su la "Divina Commedia"* (Cairo: Casa editrice Mondiale, 1961). This short study was reviewed favorably though inconclusively by Giuliano Bonfante in *La rassegna della letteratura italiana* 67, no. 1 (1963): 71–72.]

   2. Juan Andrés, *Dell'origine, progressi e stato attuale d'ogni letteratura* (Parma, 1782–98), published in Spanish as *Del origen, progresos y estado actual de toda la literatura* (Madrid: A. de Sancha, 1784–1806).

   3. Francesco Cancellieri, *Osservazioni intorno alla questione promossa dal Vannozzi, dal Mazzocchi, dal Bottari, especialmente dal p. abate D. Giuseppe Giustino di Costanzo, sopra l'originalità della Divina Commedia di Dante: Appoggiata alla storia della Visione del monaco casinese Alberico* (Rome: Bourlie, 1814)—a work ridiculed by Ugo Foscolo in "Dante," *Edinburgh Review* 30 (September 1818): 317–51; Charles Labitte, "La Divine Comédie avant Dante," [in *Revue des deux mondes*, quatrième série, 31 (1842), 704–742, and] in Dante Aligheri, *Oeuvres: La Divine Comédie*, trans. Auguste Brizeux (Paris: Charpentier, 1843); Pasquale Villari, *Antiche leggende e tradizioni che illustrano la Divina Commedia* (Pisa: Nistri, 1865).

   4. Alessandro d'Ancona, *I precursori di Dante* (Florence: Sansoni, 1874). D'Ancona pursued his work later in "La Leggenda di Maometto in Occidente," *Giornale storico della letteratura italiana* 13 (1889): 199–281. In

the same year Tomasso Vitti, in "Le origini della *Divina Commedia*," *Alighieri* 1 (1889): 33–45, admitted, albeit vaguely, that the *Commedia* is connected with previous Oriental literatures; but he was wrong in quoting the Mahabharata, which certainly has nothing to do with the work of Dante.

Some additions to D'Ancona's findings were supplied by Lucien Bouvat, "Le Prophète Mohammed en Europe: Légende et literature," *Revue du monde musulman* 9 (1909): 264–72. The possibility of Iranian influences was pursued further by Jivanji Jamshedji Modi, *Dante Papers: Virâf, Adamnan, and Dante, and Other Papers* (Bombay: J. J. Modi, 1914), 1–71, and Reynold A. Nicholson, "A Persian Forerunner of Dante," *Transactions of the Royal Asiatic Society* 19 (1943): 1–5.

5. Another work of the fin de siècle was Ernest J. Becker, *A Contribution to the Comparative Study of the Medieval Visions of Heaven and Hell* (Baltimore, Md.: Murphy, 1899), on the possible relationship between the Bridge and as-Sirat in Iranian visions and those in the medieval Western visions. A few years earlier, Angelo De Gubernatis maintained that prior to Dante, Christian art had never represented Purgatory as a mountain, the summit of which was the Earthly Paradise, and further, that this representation is only a copy of the Muslim system. According to De Gubernatis, Dante's Inferno is only a copy of the Buddhist Hell. See "Le Type indien de Lucifer chez le Dante," *Giornale Dantesco* 3 (1896): 49–58.

6. Edgar Blochet, *Les sources orientales de la Divine Comédie* (Paris: J. Maisonneuve, 1901), xv: "s'il n'y a pas dans la Divine Comédie et dans les légendes antérieures qui appartiennent au même cycle qu'elle des traces de cette Oriental influence."

7. Ibid., 155. The pre-Islamic Iranian sources of the *Commedia* were also source for the legend of Muḥammad.

8. Ibid., 11: "Dante a pu entendre de la bouche d'un des chevaliers qui entrèrent a Jerusalem avec l'empereur de l'Allemagne" and "ne connaissait les lettres arabes."

9. Ibid., 19: "Il faut chercher ses [Dante's] véritables sources dans les formes occidentales de cette légende qui ont été répandues dans le monde chrétien durant tout le Moyen-Age."

10. Ibid., 32 ff. Blochet also recognized the fact that Muslim eschatology had Hellenistic elements (54 ff.).

11. Edgar Blochet, "Études sur l'histoire religieuse d'Iran: II. L'Ascension au ciel du Prophète Mohammed," *Revue de l'histoire des religions* 40 (1899): 1–25, 203–36. Blochet tried to prove that the Iranian legend of the Ascension had entered Greece at an early period and that it

is found in two writers who were read throughout the centuries—Plato and Plutarch.

12. Blochet, *Les Sources orientales*, 195: "la gloire de Dante consiste moins à avoir inventé le cadre de la légende, qu'à y avoir fait entrer des épisodes qui n'ont de correspondants dans aucune autre littérature et surtout dans les formes orientales de la Légende de l'Ascension."

13. Rudolf Leszynsky, *Mohammedanische Traditionen über das jüngste Gericht: Eine vergleichende Studie zur jüdisch-christlichen und mohammedanischen Eschatologie* (Kirchhain N.-L.: Druck von M. Schmersow, 1909).

14. Marcus Dods, *Forerunners of Dante: An Account of Some of the More Important Visions of the Unseen World, from the Earliest Times* (Edinburgh: Clark, 1903), 3. Also worth noting is the speculation that Dante was influenced by biblical lore and Jewish tradition through "the Vision of the Other-world composed by [his] friend, the learned Jew Immanuel ben Salamone." See Charles Stuart Boswell, *An Irish Precursor of Dante: A Study on the Vision of Heaven and Hell, Ascribed to the Eighth-Century Irish Saint, Adamnán, with Translation of the Irish Text* (London: Nutt, 1908), 241.

15. Cited by Miguel Asín Palacios, *Islam and the Divine Comedy*, trans. Harold Sunderland (London: Murray, 1926), xiv "Egli [Blochet] ragiona così: Dante conobbe le narrazioni occidentali di altri viaggi al mondo di là; ma queste narrazioni derivano dalla leggenda orientale; dunque è la fonte prima della Divina Commedia." French, German, Italian, and Arabic translations of this work were announced but never published.

16. Francesco Torraca, *I precursori della Divina Commedia* (Florence: Sansoni, 1905), 30: "Dante non ha precursori perciò non al tenebroso Medio Evo europeo appartiene la Divina Commedia, ma alla nuova complessa varia luminosa civiltà italiana."

17. Angelo de Fabrizio, "Il 'Mirag' di Maometto esposto da un frate salentino del XV secolo," *Giornale storico della letteratura italiana* 49 (1907): 309: "molto sommariamente, come se si trattasse di cose già note al lettore."

18. Ibid., 313: "Che i Visionarì medioevali conoscessero il Mirag è probabile; che lo conoscesse Dante pur essendo amissibile, non si può allo stato odierno degli studi affermare . . . esclusa l'ipotesi d'una imitazione diretta, consapevole . . . rimarrebbe la possibilità d'una impercettibile efficacia che nell'orditura della Commedia la leggenda avrebbe avuta, confusa con altre più importanti narrazioni affini, se non assorbita da esse."

19. Raffaele Ottolenghi, *Un lontano precursore di Dante* (Lugano: Coenobium, 1910), originally printed in *Coenobium* 2–5 (1909); reviewed in *Giornale Dantesco* 19 (1911): 121; and in *Giornale storico della letteratura italiana* 56 (1910): 250.

20. Paolo Amaducci, *La fonte della Divina Commedia*, 2 vols. (Rovigo: Tipografia Sociale Editrice, 1911).

21. Bruno Nardi, "Pretese fonti della *Divina Commedia*," *Nuova antologia* 90 (July 1955): 383–89, reprinted in *Dal "Convivio" alla "Commedia": Sei saggi danteschi*, Studi storici 35–39 (Rome: Istituto storico italiano per il Medio Evo, 1960): "Ad agitare le acque della letteratura dantesca, che da alcuni decenni insigni maestri s'adopravano a purgare da elementi torbidi e a ricondurre entro gli argini d'una sana critica, furono improvvisamente gettati, alla fine dell'inverno 1911, due volumi— dove Paolo Amaducci dava il sensazionale e alquanto chiassoso annunzio di avere scoperta la 'fonte della Divina Commedia.'" See also Friedrich Schneider, "Bruno Nardis angebliche Quellen der Göttlichen Komödie," *Deutsches Dante-Jahrbuch*, n.F. 34–35 (1957): 25–26, 177–82.

22. *La escatología musulmana en la Divina Comedia* (Madrid: Real Academia Española 1919). The author's arguments are summarized in *Dante y el Islam*, with an introduction by Emilio García Gómez (Madrid: Voluntad, 1927).

23. Miguel Asín Palacios, *Abenmasarra y su escuela: Orígenes de la filosofía hispano-musulmana* (Madrid: Maestre, 1914), 160, reprinted in *Obras escogidas*, vol. 1, *Ibn Masarra y su escuela, El Místico Abū-l-'Abbas ibn al-'Arif de Almería y su "Mahasin al-Maŷālis," Un Precursor hispano-musulmán de San Juan de la Cruz* (Madrid: Escuelas de Estudios Arabes de Madrid y Granada, 1946–48), 158.

24. See Miguel Asín Palacios, *Islam and the Divine Comedy*, xiv; and *Escatología*, 2nd ed. (Madrid: Consejo Superior de Investigaciones Científicas, 1943), 3.

25. Asín Palacios claimed, in a note added after the publication of the Spanish original of *Islam and the Divine Comedy* (xiv) not to have known of Blochet's work.

26. Asín Palacios, *Escatología*, 2nd ed., 371n; Asín Palacios, *Islam and the Divine Comedy*, 253: "los conductos más próximos, constantes y estables de comunicación entre la cultura oriental y occidental."

27. Ibid., 254.

28. Ibid., 255; see also Asín Palacios, *Escatología*, 2nd ed., 586n (note added after publication of the Spanish original). On the same topic, see Levi della Vida, "Nuova luce sulle fonti islamiche della Divina Commedia," *Al-Andalus* 14 (1949): 404n: "Dopo gli studi di U. Cassuto (p. es.

L'elemento italiano nelle Mehabberoth in *Rivista Israelitica* 1–2 [1905–6];
Dante e Manoello [Florence: Israele, 1921]), è fuor di luogo continuare a
parlare di relazioni culturali tra Dante e gli Ebrei suoi contemporanei."
Levi della Vida's article also appeared as "Dante e l'Islam secondo nuovi
documenti," in *Aneddoti e svaghi arabi e non arabi* (Milan: Ricciardi,
1959), 149–61, and in French as "Dante et l'Islam d'après de nouveaux
documents," *Revue de la Méditerranée* 14, no. 60 (1954): 131–46. The
argument concerning Dante's Jewish friends, however, was used again by
Georges Cattaui, "Les Sources orientales de la 'Divine Comédie,'"
Annales du Centre Universitaire Méditerranéen 10 (1956–57): 163, and 11
(1957–58): 159–67, identical with *Bulletin de la Société d'études dantesques
du Centre Universitaire Méditerranéen* 7 (1958): 7–15.

29. Asín Palacios, *Islam and the Divine Comedy*, 259.

30. Miguel Asín Palacios, "La Escatología musulmana en la *Divina
Comedia*: Historia y crítica de una polémica," *Il Giornale Dantesco* 26
(1923): 289–307 and 27 (1924): 15. This article was also published in
Boletín de la Real Academia Española (1924): 5–53; and in French translation as "L'influence musulmane dans la Divine Comédie: Histoire et
critique d'une polémique," in *Revue de littérature comparée* 4 (April–June
1924): 369–407.

31. "en la Divina Comedia existen ideas e imágenes escatológicas que
son específicamente islámicas y cuyo conocimiento exige el de la lengua
árabe en Dante o en quien se las hubiera traducido." However, about the
importance of this documentary evidence Asín Palacios said, "El testimonio histórico, el documento escrito, caso de existir, comprobaría las
inferencias basadas en los hechos, pero no añadiría ni un adarme de
fuerza a la convicción científica engendrada por las inferencias antes que
el testimonio fuese descubierto" ("The historical witness, the written
document, if it existed, would corroborate the inferences based on the
facts, but it would not add even an ounce of strength to the scientific
conviction engendered by the earlier inferences that the witness was
discovered"). *Escatología*, 2nd ed., 387 (Sunderland's translation, *Islam
and the Divine Comedy*, 255, is somewhat milder).

32. Among the most important reviews of Asín Palacios's book and
other important articles to appear soon after publication were André
Bellessort, "Pour le sixième centenaire de Dante: Dante et Mahomet,"
Revue des deux mondes, April 1, 1920, 556–79; Mohammed Bencheneb,
"Sources musulmanes dans la 'Divine Comédie,'" *Revue africaine* 60
(1919): 483–93; Antoine Cabaton, "'La Divine Comedie' et l'Islam,"
Revue de l'histoire des religions 81 (1920): 333–60; Giuseppe Gabrieli, "Dante
e l'Islam (Contro la memoria di Msg. Asin intorno alla 'Escatologia

musulmana nella Divina Commedia')," in "Scritti vari pubblicati in occasione del sesto centenario della morte di Dante Alighieri," *Rivista di filosofia neo-scolastica* 13 (1921): 97–139; Giuseppe Gabrieli, *Intorno alle fonti orientali della "Divina Commedia"* (Rome: Tipografia Poliglotta Vaticana, 1919), identical to article, *Arcadia* 3 (1920): 237–318; Angel Licitra, *De la originalidad de "La Divina Comedia" y de la leyenda islámica del Isrá y del Mirach* (La Plata: Olivieri, 1921); Pierre Félix Mandonnet, "Dante et le voyage de Mahomet au Paradis," *Comité français catholique pour la célébration du sixième centenaire de la mort de Dante Alighieri: Bulletin du jubilé* 5 (1921–22): 544–53 (Mandonnet advances the hypothesis that the otherworldly journey of Muḥammad could have come to Dante's knowledge through Riccoldo of Monte Croce); Louis Massignon, "Les Études islamiques à l'étranger, en Espagne: Les recherches d'Asín Palacios sur Dante," *Revue du monde musulman* 36 (1919): 23–58; Carlo Alfonso Nallino, review of *La escatología musulmana, Rivista degli Studi Orientali* 8 (1919–21): 800–19, reprinted in *Raccolta di Scritti editi ed inediti* 2 (1940): 436–53; Ernesto Giacomo Parodi, review of *La escatología musulmana, Bulletino della Società dantesca italiana* 26 (1919): 163–81; Werner Söderhjelm, "Dante et l'Islam," *Neuphilologische Mitteilungen* 22, no. 5 (1921): 89–99; and Vladimiro Zabughin, "Dante e l'Oriente," *Roma e l'Oriente* 21 (1921): 6–19.

33. The article appeared concurrently in *Il Giornale Dantesco, Litteris* (1924), *Boletín de la Real Academia Española* (1924), and, as "L'Influence musulmane dans la Divine Comédie: Histoire et critique d'une polémique," in *Revue de littérature comparée* 4 (April–June 1924): 392.

34. Appended to the second edition of Asín Palacios's *Escatología* (1943) was the survey of the polemic he had previously published, which was cursorily brought up to date: *La Escatología musulmana en la Divina Comedia: Seguida de la Historia y crítica de una polémica* (Madrid: Consejo Superior de Investigaciones Científicas, 1943). Since this edition was a reprint of the first, it failed to contribute to the polemic or to stir up new interest.

35. Louis Massignon, "Les études islamiques à l'étranger, en Espagne: Les Recherches d'Asín Palacios sur Dante," *Revue du monde Musulman* 36 (1919): 23–58, reprinted in Massignon, *Opera minora: Textes recueillis, classés et présentés avec une bibliographie*, ed. Youakim Moubarac (Paris: Presses Universitaires de France, 1969), 1: 57–81.

36. See, for example, Werner Mulertt, "Östliche Züge in der 'Navigatio Brendani,'" *Zeitschrift für romanische Philologie* 45 (1926): 306–27. Arguing against the Islamic origin of the *Commedia* and of Western

Christian legends, Mulertt places their origin in remote prototypes from other eschatologies that could easily have come to the West without Islamic intermediaries. Charles Hall Grandgent, "Islam and Dante," *Studi Medievali*, ser[o]. 2., 3 (1930): 1–5, repeats Mullertt's arguments. Asín Palacios answered in *Al-Andalus* 1 (1933): 451–53.

37. Asín Palacios, *Escatología*, 2nd ed., 65. Owing no doubt to the Second World War, the controversy saw little progress in the late 1930s and early 1940s. See Giovanni Galbiati, "Dante e gli arabi," in *Studi su Dante*, ed. Francesco Orestano, vol. 1, 181–211 (Milan: Hoepli, 1939); Louis Gillet, *Dante* (Paris: Flammarion, 1941), 67–96 (chapter 3 "Dante et l'Islam"), which presents an unconditional and uncritical defense of the theses of Asín Palacios; Francisco Siniscalco La Sala, *Dante y Abena-rabi* (Montevideo: Talleres gráficos "Centenario," 1940), which offers an uncritical approval of Asín Palacios's theory, especially as it refers to the allegorical interpretation of Muslim eschatology by Ibn al-'Arabī; and Armando Troni, *Dante et Mahomet*, trans. Roger Cimarosti, Quaderni di Cultura 3 (Palermo: Centro Studi e Scambi Internazionali, 1948).

38. [Cantarino pointed out that this statement held true equally well in the Arabic world, where interest was directed chiefly toward Dante's eschatology, as presented by Asín Palacios, but without any further extension of his theories: see Hassan Osman, "Dante in Arabic," *73rd Annual Report of the Dante Society* (Cambridge, MA, 1955), 47–52.]

39. Leonardo Olschki, "Dante e l'Oriente," *Giornale Dantesco* 39 (1936): 65–90: "il contributo musulmano alla scienza ed alla filosofia cristiana di quei secoli."

40. Ibid., 65: "per reazione tendono ad annullarla, ritenendo Dante del tutto ignaro delle cose d'oriente e poco curioso di esse."

41. Ibid., 69: "nella universale sinossi di dottrina e di storia che fu presente alla mente di Dante come fonte di meditazione e d'ispirazione, l'oriente ebbe la sua parte" and 72: "quegli immensi territori già inaccessibili agli occidentali."

42. Ibid., 89: "Le dottrini dei filosofi arabi furono accolte in Occidente in virtù del loro puro contenuto speculative . . . come eredi di quella tradizione antica cui si riconnettevano per le loro stesse origini e per la loro stessa dialettica i padri e i dottori della Chiesa. . . . Questi autori arabi erano, dunque, studiati e seguiti in occidente in virtù della continuità spirituale che essi rappresentavano."

43. Ibid., 89: "Mahometto non ha parte alcuna; e se Algazali, Averroè e altri autori d'oriente tentarono l'accordo sostanziale, dialettico, allegorico, teologico e mistico col Corano, nulla di tutto questo potè entrare e penetrò nel pensiero occidentale, così come rimase del tutto

escluso da esso ciò che faceva parte della 'legge' di Mahometto e della morale pratica e religiosa dell'Islam."

44. Ugo Monneret de Villart, *Lo studio dell'Islam in Europa nel XII e nel XIII secolo*, Studi e testi 110 (Vatican City: Biblioteca Apostolica Vaticana, 1944), 54. Monneret de Villart is due credit for having called attention to the manuscripts of the French translation and the Latin translation of this work existing, respectively, in the Bodleian and the Bibliothèque Nationale de Paris, p. 53.

45. August Rüegg, *Die Jenseitsvorstellungen vor Dante und die übrigen literarischen Voraussetzungen der "Divina Commedia,"* 2 vols. (Einsiedeln: Benzinger, 1945).

46. For something like a comprehensive survey of the whole field, with a valuable bibliography, see Howard R. Patch, *The Other World* (Cambridge, MA: Smith College Studies in Modern Languages, 1950).

47. Rüegg, *Die Jenseitsvorstellungen* 436: "selbstverständlich, dass das Mittelalter in der Arabischen wie in der germanischen Welt kulturell, weil auf demselben Traditionsboden erwachsen, in der Hauptsache ähnliche Grundzüge aufweist, wenn es auch im Norden des Mittelmeers mehr römisch-germanisch-keltische und im Süden mehr orientalisch-griechische Färbung hat."

48. Ibid., 440: "wären wir gezwungen anzunehmen, Dante hätte eine ganze Bibliothek aus verschiedenen Jahrhunderten stammender Schriften arabischer Mystiker, Philosophen und Dichter zur freien Benutzung gehabt."

49. Ibid., 440: "Wenn Dante alle diese Muslim Vorbildsmotive so massiert und geordnet, wie sie bei Asín figurieren, bequem in einer Schrift vorgefunden hätte, dann musste man fast an eine Mohammeda-nische Quelle denken."

50. Key works by Enrico Cerulli are "Dante e l'Islam" *Al-Andalus* 21 (1956): 229–55, and "Dante e l'Islam e Oriente ed Occidente nel Medio Evo," in *Oriente ed Occidente nel Medio Evo[o]: Convegno di scienze morali storiche e filologiche, 27 maggio–10 giugno 1956* (Rome: Accademia Nazionale dei Lincei, 1957), 275–94, 445–58. His edition is *Il "Libro della scala" e la question delle fonti arabo-spagnole della Divina Commedia*, ed. Enrico Cerulli, Studi e testi 150 (Vatican City: Biblio-teca Apostolica Vaticana, 1949). [Later Cerulli published *Nuove ricerche sul Libro della scala e la conoscenza dell'Islam in Occidente*, Studi e testi 271 (Vatican City: Biblioteca Apostolica Vaticana, 1972).] The Spanish edition is by José Muñoz Sendino, *La Escala de Mahoma: Traducción del árabe al castellano, latín y francés ordenada por Alfonso X el Sabio* (Ma-drid: Ministerio de Asuntos Exteriores, Dirección General de Relaciones

Culturales, 1949). The two scholars offer different approaches to their work. Muñoz reproduced the French and Latin texts. Cerulli attempted, not always with great fortune, to correct the text found in the manuscript. As for the authors' commentaries on the *Liber scale Machometi*, Levi della Vida says in "Nuova luce sulle fonti islamiche," 406: "Il lavoro di Muñoz, benchè condotto con grande zelo e con evidente fatica di ricerca, è troppo ingombro di digressioni non pertinenti all'argomento, troppo debole nell'analisi storica e letteraria e troppo viziato da errori e distrazioni [here we could add also "too prejudiced in favor of Asín Palacios's theories"] per poter essere collocate sullo stesso livello di quello di Cerulli, il quale sarà certamente completato da ricerche ulteriori . . . ma è, e rimarrà, un poderoso e mirabile contributo allo studio della penetrazione della cultura ispanoislamica nell'Europa cristiana e all'intelligenza del complicato processo della formazione ed elaborazione della *Divina Commedia*" ("The work of Muñoz, although it is conducted with great zeal and evident effort in its research, is too cluttered with digressions inconsequential to the argument, too weak in its historical and literary analysis, flawed by errors and distractions [here we could add also "too prejudiced in favor of Asín Palacios's theories"], to be placed on the same level as that of Cerulli, which will certainly be supplemented by later research . . . but it is, and will remain, a powerful and wonderful contribution to the study of the penetration of Hispano-Islamic in Christian Europe, and to the understanding of the complicated process of the composition and elaboration of the *Divine Comedy*.")

51. Pierre Groult, "La 'Divine Comédie' et 'L'Eschiele Mahomet,'" *Louvain, Les Lettres Romanes* 4 (1950): 137–49. While Groult claims that the *Liber scale Machometi* proves the essentials of Asín Palacios's theory, he severely criticizes Cerulli's edition of the French text: "Ce manuscrit vraiment méritait mieux qu'une édition negligée ("This manuscript certainly merited more than a negligent edition") (149).

52. Levi della Vida, "Nuova luce sulle fonti islamiche," 392: "Oggi non è più possibile dubitarne, che il *Libro della Scala* reso accessibile all'Occidente latino in duplice se non triplice versione, fosse rimasto ignoto a Dante sarebbe fuori di ogni verosimiglianza. La tesi di Asín intorno alla possibilità non solo, ma alla realtà di relazioni tra Dante e l'escatologia islamica rimane dunque definitivamente confermata."

53. Francesco Gabrieli, "New Light on Dante and Islam," *Diogenes: An International Review of Philosophy and Humanistic Studies* 6 (Spring 1954): 66, translated into German as "Dante und der Islam," *Diogenes: Internationale Zeitschrift fur Wissenschaft von Menschen* 3, nos. 9–10

(1956): 19–33, and in Italian as "Nuova luce su Dante e l'Islam," in Francesco Gabrieli, *Dal mondo dell'Islam. Nuovi saggi di storia e civiltà musulmana* (Milan: R. Ricciardi, 1954), 156–72. [Francesco Gabrieli had touched earlier upon the question of Dante and Islam in his *Storia e civiltà musulmana* (Naples: R. Ricciardi, 1947), 236–50 ("Una *Divina Commedia* musulmana").]

54. Nardi, "Pretese fonti della *Divina Comedia*," 356: "Poichè sembra che da parte di taluno si sia dimenticata la vecchia regoletta del loicare: *a posse ad esse non datur illatio.* . . . Una simile affermazione non può esser fatta se non dopo un attento e accurato esame comparativo, per il quale sono stati apportati molti materiali, ma che a me sembra non sia ancora stato fatto come doveva esser fatto."

55. Levi della Vida, "Nuova luce sulle fonti islamiche," 401: "Il *Libro della Scala* . . . ha fornito alla *Divina Commedia* alcuni elementi importanti, sia nel disegno generale o sia nei particolari."

56. Manfredi Porena, "La *Divina Commedia*: Il Viaggio di Maometto nell'oltretomba narrato nel *Libro della Scala*," *Atti della Accademia nazionale dei Lincei*, ser. 8, vol. 5 (1950): 58: "Circa la relazione fra il libro della Scala e la *Divina Commedia* l'unica cosa che a me par quasi certa si è che in Dante non si abbiano non dico imitazioni ma neanche riecheggiamenti o reminiscenze sicure del libro musulmano."

57. Beyond the articles already cited, the controversy came to the fore in Carlo Grabher, "Possibili conclusioni su Dante e l'escatologia musulmana," *Siculorum Gymnasium* 8 (1955): 164–82 (a denial that Dante knew the *Liber scale Machometi:* reviewed favorably by Bruno Maier in *Rassegna della letteratura italiana* 61 [1957]: 277); Giuseppe Macaluso, *Dante e Maometto* (Rome: Edizioni Ruiz, 1953); and Jacques Monfrin, "Les Sources arabes de la 'Divine Comédie' et la traduction française du livre de l'Ascension de Mahomet," *Bibliothèque de l'école des chartes* 109, no. 2 (1951): 277–90; Enrico Morpurgo, "Dante tra l'Islam e il medioevo: A proposito di una nuova pubblicazione," *Neo-Philologus* 37 (1953): 116–18; Silvio Pelosi, "Il Paradiso e il *Libro della Scala*," *Veltro* 3 (1959): 5–18; and Maxime Rodinson, "Dante et l'Islam d'après des travaux récents," *Revue de l'histoire des religions* 140, no. 2 (October–December 1951): 203–36. [An additional source from the same period is Alessandro Bausani, "Fonti orientali della *Divina Commedia*," *Palatino* 1 (1957).]

58. Umberto Bosco, "Contati della cultura occidentale di Dante con la letteratura non dotta Arabo-spagnuola," *Studi danteschi* 29 (1950): 85–102, at 101 [reprinted in Umberto Bosco, *Dante vicino: Contributi e letture*, Aretusa 23 (Caltanissetta-Roma: Salvatore Sciascia, 1966),

197–212]: "Qui dobbiamo ammettere che per ciascuna di quelle analogie si può legittimamente restare in dubbio; ciascuna, forse, può essere spiegata con una fonte comune o con la comune fondamentale esperienza umana. Ma resta il loro complesso, che è imponente."

59. Gustave Soulier, *Les influences orientales dans la peinture toscane* (Paris: Laurens, 1924), illustrates the relationships between Tuscany and the Levant and shows the knowledge and interest by Italians in Muslim art from the eleventh century.

60. Marie-Thérèse d'Alverny, "Les Pérégrinations de l'âme dans l'autre monde d'après un anonyme de la fin du XIIe siècle," *Archives d'histoire doctrinale et littéraire du moyen âge* 13, years 15–17 (1940–42): 239–79. See also Enrico Cerulli, *Il "Libro della scala,"* 519.

61. Dante might not have been aware that the *Liber de causis* contained Arabic philosophy; see Cerulli, *Il "Libro della scala,"* 513. On the *Liber de causis*, see Rocco Murari, "Il *De Causis* e la sua fortuna nel Medio Evo," *Giornale storico della letteratura italiana* 34 (1899): 93–117; and Manuel Alonso, "El *Liber de Causis*," *Al-Andalus* 9 (1944): 43, and 10 (1945): 429.

62. On this very important aspect of Eastern-Western relations, see Norman Daniel, *Islam and the West: The Making of an Image* (Edinburgh: University Press, 1960).

63. Leonardo Olschki, "Mohammedan Eschatology and Dante's Other World," *Comparative Literature* 3 (1951): 15.

64. Ibid., 17.

65. Theodore Silverstein, "Dante and the Legend of the Mi'rāj: The Problem of Islamic Influence on the Christian Literature of the Other-World," *Journal of Near Eastern Studies* 11 (1952): 89.

66. Ibid., 98.

67. Ibid., 109.

68. Ibid., 196.

69. Richard Lemay, "Le Nemrod de l' 'Enfer' de Dante et le 'Liber Nemroth,'" *Studi danteschi* 40 (1963): 109: "Si donc Dante connaissait l'arabe, le problème de ses emprunts à des sources littéraires arabes deviendrait fort simplifié, n'est-il pas vrai? Dante avait les moyens de lire ce qu'il voulait ou qui l'intéressait: qu'il s'agisse de la *Risalat al-Ghoufran* d'abou 'l-'ala al-Ma'arri [not Ma'āri!] ou des divers ouvrages du grand mystique de Murcia Ibn el-'Arabi, ouvrages célèbres parmi les Arabes et très répandues tout au long de l'aire culturelle de 1'Islam, les inspirations connues et surtout les nombreux passages parallèles relevé par Asín Palacios entre ces ouvrages et la *Divine Comédie* n'auraient rien pour nous surprendre!"

DANTE AND ISLAMIC CULTURE
Maria Corti

This article was originally printed as "Dante e la cultura islamica," in *Per correr miglior acque . . . : Bilanci e prospettive degli studi danteschi alle soglie del nuovo millennio*, Atti del convegno internazionale di Verona-Ravenna, 25–29 ottobre 1999, 2 vols., Pubblicazioni del Centro Pio Rajna, Sezione prima, Studi e saggi 9 (Rome: Salerno, 2001), 1: 183–202. This English translation is published with the permission of Salerno Editrice S. R. L., thanks to the gracious assistance of Enrico Malato. Beyond being translated, both the text and the notes of this article have been edited to bring them into conformity with the conventions of *Dante Studies*. Additionally, typographical errors and miscitations or incomplete citations have been corrected or expanded. It is hoped that these changes will make the article easier to read and that the author would have approved.

1. Ernst Robert Curtius, *European Literature and the Latin Middle Ages*, trans. Willard R. Trask, Bollingen Series 36 (Princeton, N.J.: Princeton University Press, 1990), 379.

2. Miguel Asín Palacios, *Dante y el Islam* (Madrid: Voluntad, 1927), trans. Harold Sunderland as *Islam and the Divine Comedy* (London: J. Murray, 1926). [For analysis of the impact that Asín Palacios's book had on subsequent scholarship, see Vicente Cantarino, "Dante and Islam: History and Analysis of a Controversy," in this volume.]

3. [This interpretive strategy is turned on its head in Daniela Boccassini, "Falconry as a Transmutative Art: Dante, Frederick II, and Islam," in this volume.]

4. Maria Corti, *Percorsi dell'invenzione: Il Linguaggio poetico e Dante* (Turin: Einaudi, 1993), 122–26.

5. On the continual contact between the Arabs and the Spanish, see Juan Vernet, *La Cultura hispanoárabe en Oriente y Occidente* (Barcelona: Ariel, 1978).

6. Book 2 (folio 4v), ed. Nathaniel Edward Griffin (Cambridge, Mass.: Mediaeval Academy of America, 1936), 10.

7. 228–32, in *Il gatto lupesco e Il mare amoroso*, ed. Annamaria Carrega, Orsatti 7 (Alessandria: Edizioni dell'Orso, 2000), 74.

8. On the structure of the monument, see Reinhart Pieter Anne Dozy, *Recherches sur l'histoire et la littérature de l'Espagne pendant le moyen âge*, 3rd ed. (Leiden: Brill, 1881), 2:300–314; and René Basset, "L'aqueduc et la statue de Cadix," *La Tradition* 6 (1892): 97. Upon a stone square was placed a second square, connected to the first by copper pilasters between 60 and 100 cubits in height. The sides of the second,

upper square were one-third the size of the first one. Above this was a triangular construction that tapered upward. On this rested a block of white marble, upon which stood the brass statue, 6 cubits in height, of Muḥammad, with a long beard and a gilded mantle over his shoulders. His left arm was stretched out in the direction of the strait, signifying for the Arab geographers, "No one shall proceed further," or "return to the place from which you have come."

9. Mario Fubini, "Il peccato di Ulisse," *Belfagor* 2 (1947): 461–75; reprinted in Mario Fubini, *Il peccaato di Ulisse e altri scritti danteschi* (Milan: R. Ricciardi, 1966), 1–36.

10. Maria Corti, "Le metafore della navigazione, del volo e della lingua di fuoco nell'episodio di Ulisse ('Inferno' XXVI)," in *Miscellanea di studi in onore di A. Roncaglia* (Modena: Mucchi, 1989), 2:479–91.

11. Maria Corti, *Percorsi dell'invenzione*. [Ed.: Corti may have had in mind the treatment of shipwreck in Aeschylus, *Agamemnon*, and Sophocles, *Oedipus Rex*.]

12. Ramón Menéndez Pidal, *Historia de España* (Madrid: Espasa-Calpe, 1956–).

13. [Ed.: At this point Corti's Italian text expands with the following remark about Myrleia:]more noted today for the trial of Ocalan [Abdullah "Apo" Öcalan (1948–), founding leader of the Kurdish party Kurdistan Workers Party (PKK), has been held since his capture in 1999 under solitary confinement as the only prisoner on İmralı Island in Turkey] than for the armistice reached between the Greeks and the Turks in 1922[o].

14. For similar wording of the same passage, see *Libro de la destructione de Troya: Volgarizzamento napoletano trecentesco da Guido delle Colonne,* ed. Nicola De Blasi, I Volgari d'Italia 3 (Rome: Bonacci, 1986).

15. [Ed.: The source of information for the last two statements appears to be Snorri Sturluson, *Ólófs saga Helga,* chapter 18, in Snorri, *Heimskringla,* ed. Bjarni Aðalbjarnarson, Íslenzk fornrit 26–28, 3 vols. (Reykjavík: Hið Íslenzka fornritafélag, 1941–1951), 2: 25. With his ship in a place named Karlsá, Olaf is on the verge of sailing through the Straits of Gibraltar, when he has a dream in which he is visited by "merkiligr [variant: göfugligr] maðr ok þekkiligr ok þó ógurligr" ("a remarkable [glorious] and handsome man and yet awful"). This figure tells him to go back to Norway, where he and his descendants will be the kings of Norway.]

16. In addition, see *Inferno* 1.26 ("lo passo / che non lasciò già mai persona viva" "the pass / that never left anyone alive"), *Inferno* 26.132

("poi che 'ntrati eravam ne l'alto passo" "since we had entered on the passage of the deep"). One also observes the rhymes within the text at *Inferno* 1, lines 26, 28, and 30 (*passo, lasso, basso*) and *Inferno* 26, lines 128, 130, and 132 (*basso, passo, casso*)[o].

17. Jurij Lotman, *Testo e contesto* (Rome: Laterza, 1980), 96.

18. Madrid, Biblioteca Nacional, MS 7563, folios 106r–107v.

19. For the transcription of the unedited text, I am very thankful to Prof. Giuseppe Mazzocchi, who chose the best manuscript from the fifteenth century (as the original is lost) and photographed it for me in Madrid, and Prof. Paolo Pintacuda, who rendered the Castilian text legible for me. Both are members of the Iberian section of the Dipartimento di Lingue e Letterature Straniere Moderne at the Università di Pavia.

20. Arno Borst, *Der Turmbau von Babel: Geschichte der Meinungen über Ursprung und Vielfalt der Sprachen und Völker*, 4 vols. in 6 books (Stuttgart: A. Hiersemann, 1957–1963).

21. Hans-Josef Niederehe, *Die Sprachauffassung Alfons des Weisen: Studien zur Sprach- und Wissenschaftsgeschichte* (Tübingen: M. Niemeyer, 1975), 64–68.

22. Maria Corti, "Dante e la Torre di Babele," in Maria Corti, *Il viaggio testuale: Le ideologie e le strutture semiotiche* (Turin: Einaudi, 1978), 243–57.

23. Maria Corti, "La 'Commedia' di Dante e l'oltretomba islamico," *Belfagor* 50, no. 3 (1995): 301–14, also printed as *L'Alighieri* 36, n.s., 5 (1995), 7–19.

24. See Georges-Henri Luquet, "Hermann l'Allemand," *Revue de l'histoire des religions* 44 (1901): 407–22; and Jaime Ferreiro Alemparte, "Hermann el Alemán traductor del siglo XIII en Toledo," *Hispania sacra* 35 (1983): 9–56. Alemparte provides the unusual statement that Brunetto would have begun his *Tresor* in Toledo on September 15, 1260. He comments as well that "no sólo conoció la obra de Hermann, sino que pudo conocer también personalmente al autor" "not only knew the work of Hermann, but also could have gotten to know the author personally."

25. Maria Corti, *La felicità mentale: Nuove prospettive per Cavalcanti e Dante* (Turin: Einaudi, 1983), 96–109.

26. [For this text, see *Alfonso el Sabio: Setenario*, ed. Kenneth H. Vanderford (Buenos Aires: Instituto de filología, 1945; repr., Barcelona: Editorial Crítica, 1984).]

27. [On Avicenna's views on the dead, see Brenda Deen Schildgen, "Philosophers, Theologians, and the Islamic Legacy in Dante," in this volume.]

28. The materials connected with this polemic (which began in 1919) are gathered most conveniently in Miguel Asín Palacios, *La Escatología musulmana en la Divina Comedia: Seguida de la Historia y crítica de una polémica*, 4th ed., Libros Hiperión 79 (Madrid: Hiperión, 1984).

29. Ugo Monneret de Villard, *Lo studio dell'Islam in Europa nel XII e nel XIII secolo*, Studi e testi 110 (Vatican: Biblioteca Apostolica Vaticana, 1944). Five years after Monneret de Villard's article appeared, Cerulli published his *Il "Libro della scala" e la questione delle fonti arabo-spagnole della Divina Commedia*, Studi e testi 150 (Vatican: Biblioteca Apostolica Vaticana, 1949).

30. Gonzalo Menéndez Pidal, "Como trabajaron las escuelas Alfonsíes," *Nueva revista de filología hispánica* 5 (1951): 363–80.

31. Antoine Cabaton, "La 'Divine Comédie' et l'Islam," *Revue de l'histoire des religions* 81 (1920): 351. "Il est absolument impossible qu'à cette cour mi-chrétienne mi-arabe . . . Brunetto Latini n'ait pas vu, connu les traducteurs Tolédans: qu'allant de Tolède à Seville, où résidait tour à tour le roi, il ne les ait pas interrogés."

32. I refer here to the research of Anna Longoni, a scholar from Pavia who is preparing a Latin edition of the *Liber scale Machometi* for the "Bembo" collection from Guanda. [Ed.: The edition has not appeared.]

33. Of the Collectio, containing the Qur'an, three Arabic texts (*De doctrina*, *De generatione*, one *Cronica*) as well as texts of rebuttal (the *Apologia* of the pseudo-Kindi, letters exchanged between an Arab Christian and a Muslim, two Summas in favor of Christianity), there are roughly thirty specimens, of which only nine are complete. Within two of these can be found the two manuscripts of the *Liber scale Machometi*.

34. [Cerulli, Il *"Libro della scala"* (1949) 355–57, 504–6.]

35. Maria Corti, *Percorsi dell'invenzione*, 147–63.

36. [On the impact of Averroës (among others) on Latin Christendom at this time, see Schildgen, "Philosophers, Theologians, and the Islamic Legacy in Dante," in this volume.]

37. *Liber scale Machometi*, chap. 32, in Cerulli, ed., Il *"Libro della scala,"* 107 (par. 78).

38. Ibid. chap. 17, 75 (par. 42).

39. Medieval Islamic mysticism and the entire Sufi movement developed a metaphysics of light and of the Light of Lights that causes one to lose all memory as one approaches it. This is discussed in further detail by al-Ghazali. Regarding Sufism, see Mario Satz, *Umbría lumbre: San Juan de la Cruz y la sabiduría secreta en la Kábala y el Sufismo*

(Madrid: Hiparion, 1991), 153–88, where the *Book of the Brightness* (*Bahir*), a very important text on Islamic mysticism, is also cited. Luce López Baralt, *San Juan de la Cruz y el Islam: Estudio sobre las filiaciones semíticas de su literatura mística* (México: Universidad de Puerto Rico-Recinto de Río Piedras, 1985) gives a panoramic view of Arab mystical literature of the twelfth and thirteenth centuries and also discusses the mystical language of Ibn al-ʿArabī and Ibn al-Fārid al-Dīn and the symbolic and esoteric characteristics of light, suggesting a far-flung influence of Oriental Christian monasticism. There would then also be a double-sided process: from Christianity to Islam and then from Islamic mysticism to Christian mysticism (Meister Eckehart). I am very thankful to Giovanni Caravaggi for various bibliographical suggestions.

40. Manuela Colombo, *Dai mistici a Dante: Il linguaggio dell'ineffabilità* (Florence: La Nuova Italia, 1987), 61–71.

41. Maria Corti, "La 'Commedia' di Dante e l'oltretomba islamico."

42. [Corti may have in mind the four rivers of Paradise (Gen. 2:10–14) or, if she is thinking of two in particular, the Tigris and Euphrates.]

TRANSLATIONS OF THE QUR'AN AND OTHER ISLAMIC TEXTS
BEFORE DANTE (TWELFTH AND THIRTEENTH CENTURIES)
José Martínez Gázquez

This article was completed with the assistance of the Research Projects "Percepción del Islam en la Europa cristiana" HUM2004-03957-C02-02 of the DGI of the MEC and 2005SGR00538 of the AGAUR of the Generalitat de Catalunya.

1. Peter the Venerable, *Summa totius haeresis Saracenorum*, in *Peter the Venerable and Islam*, ed. James Kritzeck, Princeton Oriental Studies 23 (Princeton, NJ: Princeton University Press, 1964), 208, and in *Petrus Venerabilis. Schriften zum Islam*, ed. and trans. Reinhold Glei, Corpus Islamo-Christianum Series Latina 1 (Altenberge: CIS-Verlag, 1985), 14 (no. 13): "Quae quidem olim diaboli machinatione concepta, primo per Arrium seminata, deinde per istum Sathanan scilicet Mahumet, prouecta, per Antichristum uero, ex toto secundum diabolicam intentionem complebitur." In the prologues to the Latin translations of these Islamic texts we find such ideas to be commonplaces that motivate these translations.

2. Miguel Barceló, "'Per sarraïns a preïcar' o l'art de predicar a audiències cautives," *El debat intercultural als segles XIII i XIV: Actes de les I jornadas de filosofia catalana: Girona, 25–27 d'abril de 1988*, ed. Marcel Salleras (Barcelona: Universitat Autònoma de Barcelona, 1989), 120.

3. On the description of Muḥammad's alleged sin and punishment, see Jan M. Ziolkowski, "Introduction," in this volume.

4. *L'ottimo commento della Divina Commedia: Testo inedito d'un contemporaneo di Dante*, ed. Alessandro Torri, 3 vols. (Pisa, 1827–1829; repr., Bologna: Arnaldo Forni Editore, 1995), 1:481–82, comment on Canto 28.22–38: "Dicono alcuni, ma non è vero, ch'egli fu cardinale, e savio scienziato; e che in servigio de la fede cristiana andò a predicare in Affrica; . . . e che quando elli andò di là, li fue promesso per li cardinali il papato, se 'l Papa morisse anzi ch'egli ritornasse, la qual cosa non fecero: per lo quale sdegno predicò alla gente convertita il contrario e diè loro nuov[a] legge; per la qual cosa fu pronu[n]ziato scismatico." "Some say, though this is not true, that he was a cardinal, a knowledgeable scientist; and that he went to preach in Africa in the service of Christianity; . . . and that when he went there, he was promised the papacy by the cardinals if the Pope should die before his return, which they did not do: enraged at this, he preached the opposite message to the converted people and spoke to them about a new law; on this account, he was pronounced a schismatic."[o]

5. For further discussion of Mark of Toledo, see Karla Mallette, "Muhammad in Hell," in this volume. For an overview, see Marie-Thérèse d'Alverny, "Deux traductions latines du Coran au moyen âge," *Archives d'histoire doctrinale et littéraire du moyen âge* 16 (1947–48): 69–131, reprinted in d'Alverny, *La connaissance de l'Islam dans l'Occident médiéval*, ed. Charles Burnett (Aldershot: Variorum, 1994). An updated account can be found in José Martínez Gázquez, "Trois traductions médiévales latines du Coran: Pierre le Vénérable—Robert de Ketton, Marc de Tolède et Jean de Segobia," *Revue des études latines* 80 (2003): 223–36, and in the articles compiled in Miguel Barceló and José Martínez Gázquez, eds., *Musulmanes y cristianos en Hispania durante las conquistas de los siglos XII y XIII* (Barcelona: Bellaterra, 2005). Most recently, see Thomas E. Burman, "Tafsir and Translation: Traditional Arabic Quran Exegesis and the Latin Qurans of Robert of Ketton and Mark of Toledo," *Speculum* 73 (1998): 703–32; and Thomas E. Burman, *Reading the Qur'ân in Latin Christendom, 1140–1560* (Philadelphia: University of Pennsylvania Press, 2007). For the overall attitude of the Cluniacs, see Dominique Iogna-Prat, *Ordonner et exclure: Cluny et la société chrétienne face à l'hérésie, au judaïsme et à l'islam 1000–1150* (Paris: Aubier, 1998).

6. Charles Julian Bishko, "Peter the Venerable's Journey," in *Petrus Venerabilis, 1156–1956: Studies and Texts Commemorating the Eighth Centenary of his Death*, ed. Giles Constable and James Kritzeck (Rome: Herder, 1956), 163–75.

7. As stated in the various allusions in the texts of Peter the Venerable and the incipits of the manuscripts that transmit them, the translations that constitute the Corpus Islamolatinum were done in cities in the north of Castile and Aragon, outside of the city of Toledo.

8. Peter the Venerable, *Liber contra sectam siue haeresim Saracenorum*, in *Peter the Venerable and Islam*, 228–29: "Vnde concaluit cor meum intra me, et in meditatione mea exarsit ignis. Indignatus sum causam tantae perditionis Latinos ignorare, et ipsa ignorantia nullum ad resistendum posse animari, nam non erat qui responderet, quia non erat qui agnosceret."

9. Marie-Thérèse d'Alverny, "Deux traductions latines du Coran," 77–109; d'Alverny, "Quelques manuscrits de la 'Colectio Toletana,'" in Constable and Kritzeck, *Petrus Venerabilis, 1156–1956*, 215. See also *Catalogue des manuscrits de la Bibliothèque de l'Arsenal*, vol. 2 (664–2387) (Paris, 1886), 315 (on MS 1162).

10. Fernando González Muñoz, *Exposición y refutación del Islam: La versión latina de las epístolas de al-Hāšimī y al-Kindī* (Coruña: Universidade de Coruña, 2005).

11. *Peter the Venerable and Islam*, 14: "As important as the financial results of Peter's journey undoubtedly were for Cluny, it produced an infinitely more important result, totally incidental to the others and probably also unpremeditated, which marks that journey as a momentous event in the intellectual history of Europe. For in its course Peter conceived, planned, and sponsored his project to study, comprehensively and from original sources, the religion of Islam."

12. Peter the Venerable, *Liber contra sectam*, 230–31: "Non errabo plane, si simplici oculo fecero quod meum est, et Deo, ut dixi, seruauero quod suum est. Non poterit, certe non poterit omnino, labor causa Dei assumptus euadere absque fructu, si autem conuersis profuerit, aut hostibus obstiterit aut domesticos munierit aut saltem horum scriptori 'pax bone uoluntatis hominibus' repromissa non defuerit."

13. José Martínez Gázquez, Óscar de la Cruz, Cándida Ferrero, and Nàdia Petrus, "Die lateinischen Koran-Übersetzungen in Spanien," in *Juden, Christen und Muslime: Religionsdialoge im Mittelalter*, ed. Matthias Lutz-Bachmann and Alexander Fidora (Darmstadt: Wissenschaftliche Buchgesellschaft, 2004), 232.

14. Peter the Venerable, *Liber contra sectam*, 220–91.

15. Ibid., 220–21: "Causa plane scribendi haec michi fuit, quae multis et magnis patribus extitit. Non potuerunt illi pati quamlibet uel paruam iacturam fidei Christianae, nec aduersus sanam doctrinam insanientem multiformium hereticorum uesaniam tolerarunt. Cauerunt

esse muti ubi loquendum erat, aduertentes immo plenissime scientes—
non minus se addicendos in suptili apud Deum statera iudicii de infruc-
tuoso uel, quod maius est, dampnoso silentio, quam de uerbo otioso uel
noxio. Ideo aepistolis, ideo libris, ideo diuersis ac robustis tractatibus
obstruxerunt 'os loquentium iniqua,' et 'omnem' iuxta apostolorum,
'Sathanae altitudinem extollentem se aduersus scientiam Dei' loquente
per eos Spiritu Dei, prostrauerunt, calcauerunt, destruxerunt."

16. José Martínez Gázquez, "Observaciones a la traducción latina del
Corán (Qur'an) de Robert de Ketton," in *Les traducteurs au travail: Leurs
manuscrits et leurs méthodes. Actes du colloque international organisé par
le "Ettore Majorana Centre for Scientific Culture," (Erice, September
30–October 6 1999)*, ed. Jacqueline Hamesse (Turnhout: Brepols, 2001),
115–27; Martínez Gázquez, "El lenguaje de la violencia en el prólogo de la
traducción latina del Corán impulsada por Pedro el Venerable," *Cahiers
d'études hispaniques médiévales* 28 (2005): 243–52, the prologue on
244–45: "Latinitas tamen omnis hucusque—non dicam perniciosis
incommodis ignorancie, negligencieue—pressa, suorum hostium causam
et ignorare et non depellere passa est."

17. Robert of Ketton, *Praefatio*, in Martínez Gázquez, "Observaciones," 117: "Lapides igitur et ligna, ut tuum deinde pulcherimum et
commodissimum edificium cementatum et indisolubile surgat, nil excer-
pens, nil sensibiliter nisi propter inteligenciam tantum alterans attuli."

18. Ibid.: "Ius igitur exigit ut hostium castrum, immo caueam,
delendo, puteum exsiccando, cum tu sis dextre mundi pars optima, cos
religionis acutissima, caritatis manus largiflua, tuorum munimen
corrobores, tela diligenter acuas, fontemque suum forcius emanare.
Sueque caritatis uallum protensius atque capacius efficias."

19. Hartmut Bobzin, *Der Koran im Zeitalter der Reformation:
Studien zur Frühgeschichte der Arabistik und Islamkunde in Europa*
(Stuttgart: Beiruter Texte und Studien 42, 1995), 222–36. Upon analyzing
Bibliander's edition Bobzin studies the internal structure of Robert of
Ketton's Latin text and its differences with respect to the Arabic text.
See also Burman, *Reading the Qur'ān*, 78–87.

20. Marie-Thérèse d'Alverny, "Deux traductions latines du Coran,"
100–102.

21. Robert of Ketton, *Azoara 17*, in Martínez Gázquez, "Observaciones," 120: "Azoara [XVII] [[Septima]]. Hic intexit fabulas infinitas de
Adan et Eua et Beelzebub et prophetis quibusdam inauditis et de Moyse
solita deliramenta et insanias et uerba stultissima reiterare non cessans,
agitante se spiritu maligno." The cardinal number seventeen in the
Roman numeral indicates the number of the sura in Robert's translation,

while the ordinal seventh refers to the number of the sura according to the count in the Qur'an.

22. Georges Vajda and Marie-Thérèse d'Alverny, "Marc de Tolède, traducteur d'Ibn Tūmart," *Al-Andalus* 16 (1951): 1–56, reprinted in d'Alverny, *La connaissance de l'Islam dans l'Occident médiéval*, cited at 2:266: "Cumque per fantasticas delusiones ut magicus populos rudes seduceret et interdum legatum Dei, interdum autem prophetam Dei se uocaret, et lecciones quas confingebat eis exponeret." We give the text of the *Prologus* provided in the edition of Nàdia Petrus i Pons, whose critical edition of Mark of Toledo's *Alcoranus Latinus* is forthcoming as a doctoral thesis.

23. John Tolan, "Las traducciones y la ideología de reconquista: Marcos de Toledo," in Barceló and Martínez Gázquez, *Musulmanes y cristianos en Hispania durante las conquistas de los siglos XII y XIII*, 80: "Contingit peccatis exigentibus quod tum per predicacionem eius fallacem, tum per bellicam cladem, tam ipse quam successores eius ab Acquilone usque ad mare Mediterraneum et ab Indiis usque ad occiduas partes omnes fere ad suam heresim coegit, proth dolor, non solum regiones has subiugauit, quarum quedam iam fidem susceperant Ihesu Christi, uerum etiam quasdam partes Yspanie per prodicionem sequaces eius occuparunt et in quibus olim multi sacerdotes diuinum Deo prestabant obsequium, nunc scelerati uiri exsecrabilis Mafometo supplicaciones impendunt, et ecclesie que condam per manus episcoporum fuerant consecrate, nunc in templa sunt redacte profana."

24. Ibid.

25. Vajda and d'Alverny, "Marc de Tolède, traducteur d'Ibn Tūmart," 2:268 (*Prologus Alcorani*): "Ego autem, Marchus, humilis eiusdem canonicus, iustis utriusque uotis et desideris obedire sattagens in fauorabili opere, quantocius operam dedi et ut uotum et desiderium eorum effectui manciparem librum Mafometi ad peticionem eorum et comodum ortodoxie fidei de arabica lingua in latinum transtuli sermonem."

26. Ibid., 2:269 (*Prologus Habentometi*): "Ille uero Mahometus in preceptis inhonestus, in uerbis confusus, in dictis inuerecundus, in factis ipsius Nouae Legis Christi contrarius, ut in pluribus Veteri autem Testamento, in paucis consors, extitisse probatur."

27. Ibid.: "Ego autem Marcus, diaconus, Toletanus canonicus, qui librum Mafometi transtuli, rogatus postmodum a Magistro Mauricio, Toletano archidiacono et Ecclesie Burgensis electo, libellum Habentometi de Arabica lingua in Latinum transtuli sermonem; in catolicis uiris utrumque librum inspicientibus Maurorum secreta uia patet impugnandi."

28. "How an Italian Friar Read His Arabic Qur'an," in this volume.

29. Julia Bolton Holloway, "Alfonso el Sabio, Brunetto Latini and Dante Alighieri," *Thought* 60 (1985): 468–83.

30. Although there had previously been hints as to the importance of the Arabic tradition in Dante, particularly with respect to Muhammad's voyage to Paradise, it was Miguel Asín Palacios's *La escatología musulmana en la Divina Comedia* (Madrid: E. Maestre, 1919) that definitively set forth the question of Muslim influence in the work of Dante. Giuseppe Gabriel, *Dante e l'Oriente* (Bologna: N. Zanichelli, 1921) insisted on this orientation, and later José Muñoz Sendino, ed., *La escala de Mahoma: Traducción del árabe al castellano, latín y francés, ordenada por Alfonso X el Sabio* (Madrid: Ministerio de Asuntos Exteriores, Dirección General de Relaciones Culturales, 1949), and Enrico Cerulli, *Il "Libro della scala" e la questione delle fonti arabo-spagnole della Divina Commedia*, Studi e testi 150 (Vatican City: Biblioteca Apostolica Vaticana, 1949) published, respectively, transcriptions of the *Liber scale Machometi* in Latin and French versions, both of which made evident the parallel in content in Dante's poem and Muhammad's voyage to paradise.

31. Thus this essay enriches and complicates the status quaestionis when Vicente Cantarino wrote, who concludes his article by assuming that Dante had to have known Arabic in order to have had access to Islamic culture and Arabic texts: see Cantarino, "Dante and Islam: History and Analysis of a Controversy," in this volume. At the same time, it amplifies considerably the context constructed by Maria Corti, "Dante and Islamic Culture," also in this volume.

HOW AN ITALIAN FRIAR READ HIS ARABIC QUR'AN
Thomas E. Burman

1. William McGuckin DeSlane, *Catalogue des manuscripts arabes*, 2 vols. (Paris: Imprimier nationale, 1883–95). See also *Catalogus codicum manuscriptorum Bibliothecae Regiae*, vol. 1, *Pars prima complectans codices manuscriptos orientales* (Paris, 1739).

2. François Déroche, *Catalogue des manuscrits arabes*, Deuxième partie, *Manuscrits musulmans*, vol. 1, 2, *Les manuscrits du coran du Maghreb à l'Insulinde* (Paris: Bibliothèque nationale, 1985), 53.

3. To my knowledge, I am the only scholar to mention it, and mostly not in connection with its Latin notes. See Thomas E. Burman,

"Polemic, Philology, and Ambivalence: Reading the Qur'an in Latin Christendom," *Journal of Islamic Studies* 15, no. 2 (2004): 191; and Burman, *Reading the Qur'an in Latin Christendom, 1140–1560* (Philadelphia: University of Pennsylvania Press, 2007), 81, 212, 286.

4. There is reason to think that this earlier set of notes might be the work of Riccoldo's older confrere, Ramón Martí, who also knew Arabic extremely well. In his anti-Jewish work, *Pugio fidei*, he quotes from the Qur'an several times, and his quotations of verses from sura 3 in particular may be connected to MS Arabe 384. Not only are there verbal similarities to the relevant verses as translated by the larger hand on fol. 24r, but his citation system—indicating sura number and decade (*denarius*) number—conforms to this Qur'an manuscript, which, like many Qur'an manuscripts, has '*ashr* (decade) markings after each ten verses. At other points, however, he does not cite the Qur'an in this way, and there are no parallel translations in MS Arabe 384. See Ramón Martí, *Pugio fidei adversus Mauros et Judaeos* (Leipzig, 1687; repr., Farnborough, Hants., UK: Gregg Press, 1967), 3.3.7 (p. 749), and 2.8 (p. 365). See also Angel Cortabarria, "La connaissance des textes arabes chez Raymond Martin O. P. et sa position en face de l'Islam," in *Islam et chrétiens du Midi (XIIe–XIVe s.)*, Cahiers de Fanjeaux 18 (Toulouse: E. Privat, 1983), 279–300, esp. 285–91.

5. See the lists of Qur'anic errors in Paris, Bib. nat. MSS Lat. 3668 and 3669, on which see my *Reading the Qur'an*, 93, 243 nn. 34, 35.

6. See especially MS Arabe 384, fols. 2r, and 237r, where the note in the smaller hand seems certainly to have been written after the note in the larger hand immediately above it.

7. For an overview with bibliography on these figures, see John V. Tolan, *Saracens: Islam in the Medieval Imagination* (New York: Columbia University Press, 2002), 233–74.

8. See J.-M. Mérigoux's edition of Riccoldo's *Contra legem Sarracenorum* in his "L'Ouvrage d'un frère prêcheur florentin en Orient à la fin du XIIIe siècle: Le 'Contra legem Sarracenorum' de Riccoldo da Monte di Croce," in *Fede e controversia nel '300 e '500*, Memorie domenicane, n.s., 17 (Pistoia, Italy: Centro riviste della Provincia romana, 1986), 35–58, where he discusses the many manuscripts, translations, and printed editions of this text. Hereafter this edition will be referred to as "*CLS*" and cited by chapter and page number.

9. On Riccoldo and especially on the composition of his *Contra legem Sacracenorum*, see Karla Mallette, "Muḥammad in Hell," in this volume.

10. See, for example, Jalāl al-Dīn al-Suyūti's list of alternative names in *al-Iqtān fī 'ulūm al-Qur'ān* (Beirut, n.d.), 1.116–22.

11. MS Arabe 384, fol. 249r; *CLS* 3.76.

12. MS Arabe 384, fol. 36r; *CLS* 15.134. This translation is quite different from the only known literal Latin version of the Qur'an available in Riccoldo's day, Mark of Toledo's *Liber Alchorani* (Turin, Biblioteca Nazionale Universitaria, MS F. v. 35, fol. 11va): "Deus enim non parcit eis qui cum eo statuunt participem" ("For God does not spare those who have agreed upon a partner with Him"). Robert of Ketton's mid-twelfth-century Latin Qur'an is an energetic paraphrase and therefore not relevant. For another example see the note at 4:82 (fol. 38r) and the quotation of it in *CLS* 6.82. Compare Mark of Toledo, *Liber Alchorani* (fol. 12rb): "Si non venisset a deo plures quidem diversitates invenientur" ("If it did not come from God many contradictions will indeed be found").

13. "¶ Iste liber est ¶ contra sanctos apostolos quia dicit quod ipsi fuerunt saraceni et imitatores macometti ¶ contra euangelistas . . . ¶ contra sanctos prophetas . . . ¶ contra patriarchas . . . ¶ contra sanctos angelos . . . ¶ contra beatam virginem . . . ¶ contra filium dei . . . ¶ contra spiritum sanctum . . . ¶ contra deum patrem . . . ¶ contra deum simpliciter . . . ¶ est autem acceptus demonibus quia ipse [Muḥammad] dicit . . . millia ex eis facti sunt saracenos" ("That book is against the holy apostles because it says that they were Saracens and imitators of Muḥammad—against the evangelists, the holy prophets, the patriarchs, the holy angels, the Blessed Virgin, the Son of God, the Holy Spirit, God the Father—simply, against God . . . The demons, however, hold it to be true that he [Muḥammad] says that thousands of Saracens arose from him"). MS Arabe 384, fol. 2r. The Italianate form of Muḥammad here, *Maccometus*, is quite unusual in Latin texts of this period, but it appears from time to time in *CLS* (see, for example, 8.94)—another sign of Riccoldo's authorship of these notes.

14. "Reducuntur autem principales falsitates eius ad decem genera. Dicit enim falsa de seipso, de Christianis, de Iudeis, de Apostolis, de Patriarchis, de Demonibus, de Angelis, de Virgine Maria, de Christo et de Deo" (*CLS* 9.100).

15. "De patriarchis autem idem asserit Mahometus. Dicit enim in pluribus locis in Alchorano quod Abraham, Ysaac et Iacob et filii eorum fuerunt Saraceni" (*CLS* 9.102). Compare MS Arabe 384, fol. 2r: "Iste liber est . . . contra patriarchas. Dicit enim quod Habraam fuit Saracenus et etiam Iacob et filii eius" ("That book is . . . against the

Patriarchs. For he says that Abraham was a Saracen, as well as Jacob and his sons").

16. "Item etiam quod deus et angeli eius salutant Maccometum et orant pro eo . . . capitulo 330" (MS Arabe 384, fol. 2r "Likewise about the statement that God and His angels greet Muhammed and pray for him . . . in chapter 330"); "Preterea, Mahometus dicit in capitulo *Elehzab* quod Deus et angeli eius orant pro Mahometo (*CLS* 9.106 "Muḥammad, moreover, says in a chapter of *Elehzab* that God and His angels pray for Muḥammad").

17. Mérigoux, "L'ouvrage d'un frère prêcheur," 9–11 and plates 2–7 (Florence, Bibl. Nazionale, Conv. Sopp. C 8.1173).

18. See note 1, above.

19. MS Arabe 384, fol. 226r; Riccoldo, *CLS* 9.107. Compare Mark of Toledo, *Liber Alchorani*: "Et si Alchoranum hunc super montem mitteremus desursum" (fol. 75va "And if we would send this Qur'an down upon a mountain . . ."").

20. For another example, see his marginal translation of part of 33:53 (fol. 172r "et quando provocati fueritis exite et nolite dicere ystorias quia hoc est molestum prophete et verecundatur propter vos et deus non verecundatur dicere veritatem"; "and when you will be provoked, leave and do tell stories, for this is odious to the prophet, and he is ashamed of you, and God is not ashamed to speak the truth") and the quotation of the same passage in *CLS* 12.117. Compare Mark of Toledo, *Liber Alchorani* (fol. 57ra): "verum quando vocati fueritis ingredimini et cum procurati [sic] fueritis dispergimini et historias non referatis quia hoc est prophete molestum" ("But when you will be called, enter, and when you have been looked after, leave and do not tell stories, for this is odious to the prophet").

21. On such polemic and apologetic, see José Martínez Gázquez, "Translations of the Qur'an and Other Islamic Texts before Dante (Twelfth and Thirteenth Centuries)," in this volume.

22. See, for example, the marginal translations of all of sura 95, and sura 96:1–10 (MS Arabe 384, fol. 248r).

23. "Comedatis et bibatis usque dum discernitur a vobis filum album a nigro" "eat and drink until a white thread is discerned from a black one by you," a close translation of part of 2:187, which Riccoldo—also in the margin—then interprets to mean the following: "de nocte licet commedere et luxuriari cum mulieribus" (MS Arabe 384, fol. 13v "by night it is allowed to eat and to be wanton with women"). See also Daniel, *Islam and the West*, 246–48. Compare Mark of Toledo, *Liber Alchorani*: "comedite et bibite donec distingatur filum album a filo nigro aurore"

(fol. 4rb "eat and drink until a black thread is distinguished from a white one by dawn").

24. MS Arabe 384, fol. 138v. Compare Mark of Toledo, *Liber Alchorani* (fol. 45va): "[Abraham] vos appellavit Sarracenos" ("[Abraham] has called you Saracens").

25. "Non est equum ut accedatis ad domos a dorso earum id [est] equum est ut timeatis et accedatis ad domos earum ab hostiis *glossa id est non cognoscatis uxores vestras in membro non concesso* (MS Arabe 384, fol. 13v, emphasis in original "it is not righteous that you enter the houses from their backs, that is, it is righteous that you fear and enter the houses by their gates. The gloss: that is, do not have sex with your women in the disallowed rump"). As we will see below, the Latin translation here is actually taken directly from Mark of Toledo's *Liber Alchorani* (fol. 4va). Adding the gloss based on Qur'anic commentaries is entirely Riccoldo's work.

26. "Al-āyah mathal fī jimāʿ al-nisāʾ, amr bi-ityānihinna fī al-qubul lā min al-dubur. . . . qāla Ibn ʿAṭīyah wa-hādhā baʿīd mughayyir namaṭ al-kalām" ("The verse is a metaphor for intercourse with women, a command to approach them in the front, not from behind . . . . Ibn ʿAṭīyah says this is far-fetched, altering the mode of speaking [in this passage]"). See Abū Abd Allāh Muḥammad ibn Aḥmad al-Anṣārī al-Qurṭubī, *Al-Jāmiʿ li-aḥkām al-Qurʾān*, 21 in 11 vols. (Beirut, n.d.) on 2:189; 2, p. 231. Compare Abū Muḥammad ʿAbd al-Haqq Ibn ʿAṭīyah, *Al-Muḥarrar al-wajīz fī tafsīr al-kitāb al-ʿazīz*, ed. al-Raḥḥālī al-Fārūq et al., 15 vols. (Doha, 1977–91) on 2:189; 2, p. 138.

27. Burman, *Reading the Qurʾan*, 28.

28. *CLS* 15.128; MS Arabe 384, fol. 134r. Compare Mark of Toledo, *Liber Alchorani*: "aperuimus in ea de spiritu nostro (fol. 44ra "we have opened up our spirit into her"). For another example see Riccoldo's quotation of 3:42, *CLS* 15.128; MS Arabe 384, fol. 24r.

29. MS Arabe 384, fol. 51v; *CLS* 15.135.

30. See my *Reading the Qurʾan*, 122, 131–32.

31. MS Arabe 384, fol. 118v: "dic. Si convenirent homines et demones ut simile huic alcorano componerent. Non facerent tale" ("Say: if humans and demons agreed to compose something similar to this Qurʾan, they would not create anything similar"). Mark of Toledo, *Liber Alchorani*, 38rb: "Si convenirent homines et demones ut simile huic alchorano componerent non facerent tale" ("If humans and demons agreed to compose something similar to this Qurʾan, they would not create anything similar"). *CLS* 9.100–101: "Quod si congregarentur omnes homines et omnes spiritus vel angeli non possent facere talem

Alchoranum qualis est iste" ("But if all men and all spirits or angels would gather, they could not make such a Qur'an such as this one"). Here is Riccoldo's comment on his unfinished Qur'an translation (*CLS* prol.62): "Et cum inceperim eam in Latinum transferre, tot inveni fabulas et falsitates et blasphemies, et eadem per omnia in locis creberrimis repetita, quod tunc attediatus dimisi" ("And when I had begun to translate it into Latin, I found so many fables and falsities and blasphemies, and these same repeated throughout in multitudinous places, that, disgusted, I quit").

32. See note 23, above.

33. See Mérigoux, "L'ouvrage d'un frère prêcheur," 31–32, and the notes to his edition, passim. He refers to it, as most modern scholars have, as the *Contrarietas alfolica*, a title written in a much later hand on the first folio of work as it appears in the single surviving manuscript, Paris, Bib. nat., MS lat. 3394, even though the work clearly names itself *Liber denudationis sive ostensionis aut patefaciens* within the text. For these and the other details in this paragraph concerning this work and the manuscript that contains it, see Thomas E. Burman in *Religious Polemic and the Intellectual History of the Mozarabs, c. 1050 to 1200* (Leiden: E. J. Brill, 1994), 37–70, 215–39.

34. *CLS* 6.86: "Unde in capitulo *Prophetarum* dicit quod Deus dixit ei: 'Non misimus te nisi ad universitatem gentium.' Sed quomodo ibit ad omnes gentes in septuaginta linguis qui nescit suum recitare sermonem nisi in lingua Arabica" ("Therefore in a chapter of the *Prophets* he says that God said to him: 'I did not send you if not to all of the people.' But how will he go to all the people of seventy different languages, he who does not know how to deliver his own speech except in the Arabic language?"). *Liber denudationis* 8.4, in Burman, *Religious Polemic*, 298: "Et iterum in Capitulo Prophetarum, fingit Deum dicentem sibi, *Non destinavimus te nisi misericordiam sapientibus* [21, 107]. Et iterum in capitulo Seba: *Non misimus te nisi ad universtitatem gentium* [34, 28]. Respice et attende presumptionis tue mendatium quod te fingis nuntium Dei. Vadis ad universitatem gentium in septuaginta linguis. Nescis tuum nuntium recitare nisi in Arabica lingua" ("Again, in a chapter of the *Prophets*, he imagines God speaking to him, *I did not destine you for anything except mercy for the wise* [21, 107]. Again, in a chapter of the *Seba*: *I did not send you if not to all of the people* [34, 28]. See and consider the presumptuous lie that you imagine yourself to be the messenger of God. You go to all of the people in their seventy languages. You do not know how to deliver your message except in the Arabic language"). Compare Mark of Toledo, *Liber*

Alchorani (fol. 58r): "Non misimus te nisi in universis hominibus" ("I did not send you if not to all men").

35. MS Arabe 384, fol. 174v.

36. Burman, *Religious Polemic*, 149–50.

37. *Liber denudationis* 9.11, in Burman, *Religious Polemic*, 318; *CLS* 4.78.

38. MS Arabe 384, fol. 217v (my italics throughout). Compare Mark of Toledo, *Liber Alchorani* (fol. 72rb): "Approqinquavit hora et scissa est luna" ("The hour approached and the moon was rent").

39. *CLS* 8.91: "Tunc dixit sententiam in Alchorano in capitulo *Elmeteharrem*, quod interpretatur vetatio, vel anathema, que sic dicit: 'O propheta, quid vetas quod Deus concessit tibi? Placare uxores tuas expostulas, iam legem vobis posuit Deus ut soluatis iuramenta vestra" ("Then he spoke a passage in the Qur'an in the chapter of *Elmeteharrem*, which translates as 'Prohibition,' or 'Anathema,' which reads thus: 'O prophet, why do you prohibit what God has conceded to you? You seek to do the will of your wives, but already God has laid down a law before you so that you may break your oaths'"). See also ibid., 12.116, where he refers to sura 66 by this title as well. *Liber denudationis* 7.1, Burman, *Religious Polemic*, 280: "Item in Capitulo *Eltahrim*, quod interpretatur 'vetatio' sive 'anathema:' *O propheta, quare anathematizes seu vetas quae Deus concessit ad quid quaeris facere voluntatem uxorum tuarum? Et Deus est propitius et misericors. Iam posuit legem vobis Deus ut soluatis iuramenta vestra*" ("Likewise in the chapter *Eltahrim*, which means 'the Prohibition' or 'the Anathema': *O prophet, why do you anathematize or prohibit those things which God has conceded regarding that which you seek, namely, to do the will of your wives? God is well-disposed and merciful. God has already laid down a law for you so that you may break your oaths*"). Compare MS Arabe 384, fol. 231v who here, as elsewhere, is following Mark of Toledo, *Liber Alchorani* (fol. 77rb): "O propheta quare interdicis quod absolvit tibi Deus quaeris gratiam uxorum tuarum et Deus parcit et miseretur" ("O prophet, why do you forbid what God absolves you of, [that] you seek the favor of your wives, and God is restrained and merciful").

40. MS Arabe 384, fol. 16r.

41. *Liber denudationis* 10.3 in Burman, *Religious Polemic*, 342.

42. "Item in capitulo de *Vacca*, concedit sodomiam tam cum masculo quam cum femina. Dicit enim Saracenis quod 'non polluant se cum infidelibus nisi credant'" (*CLS* 6.84 "Likewise in the chapter *On the Cow*, he allows sodomy, both with a man and with a woman. For he says to the Saracens that 'they do not defile themselves with the unbelievers

except if they believe"). See Mérigoux, "L'ouvrage d'un frère prêcheur," nn. 17 and 18 on this passage. Notice that immediately afterward Riccoldo quotes a following verse (2:223) that Christians frequently took as allowing licentious behavior ("Your women are your tilth; plow them however you wish"). His translation in *CLS* is identical to that found in a note next to this verse in his Arabic Qur'an (*CLS* 6.84; MS Arabe 384, fol. 16r): "Mulieres uestre aratura uestra, arate eas ut uultis" ("Your women are your tilth, plow them however you wish").

43. See my *Religious Polemic*, 46–48, and note 4 above. That Riccoldo cites both *Liber denudationis* and Mark's translation so extensively serves as corroboration, by the way, for Mérigoux's implicit suggestion that these two works, which appear together in a sixteenth-century manuscript, Paris, Bib. nat., MS lat. 3394, may well have appeared together in a much earlier manuscript to which Riccoldo had access. See his "L'Ouvrage d'un frère prêcheur," 30–31.

PHILOSOPHERS, THEOLOGIANS, AND THE ISLAMIC LEGACY IN DANTE: *INFERNO* 4 VERSUS *PARADISO* 4
Brenda Deen Schildgen

I wish to thank Christian Moevs for his careful reading of this essay. He helped me straighten out theological or philosophical errors, imprecise expression, and other egregious missteps. Any errors that remain are mine alone.

1. Dante Alighieri, *The Divine Comedy*, trans. Charles S. Singleton (Princeton, N.J.: Princeton University Press, 1970–75).

2. Although not within the scope of this essay, examples of Dante's allegorical approaches can be found elaborated in, for example, Augustine, *De doctrina Christiana*, ed. Joseph Martin, CCSL 32 (Turnhout: Brepols, 1962), 1–167; Hugh of Saint-Victor, *De Arca Noe morali*, PL 176:617–80; and Hugh of Saint-Victor, *Commentariorum in hierarchiam coelestem S. Dionysii Areopagitae*, PL 175:923–1154.

3. For passing observations on citations of Averroës in Bartolomeo da Bologna's *Tractatus de luce*, see Maria Corti, "Dante and Islamic Culture," in this volume.

4. See Pierre Mandonnet, *Siger de Brabant et l'averroïsme latin au XIIIme siècle* (Genève: Slatkine Reprints, 1976); and Fernand van Steenberghen, *Maître Siger de Brabant*, Philosophes médiévaux 21 (Louvain: Publications universitaires, 1977).

5. For Dante and the Arabs, the reception of Miguel Asín Palacios through 1965 is covered by Vicente Cantarino, "Dante and Islam," in this

volume. More recently, María Rosa Menocal, *The Arabic Role in Medieval Literary History: A Forgotten Heritage* (Philadelphia: University of Pennsylvania Press, 1987), continues these debates, taking up Western censorship of Islamic influence by "Eurocentric" cultural historians; see chapter 5, 115–35. Maria Corti, *Percorsi dell'invenzione: Il linguaggio poetico e Dante* (Turin: Einaudi, 1993) considers the influence of Averroës and Averroism on Dante.

6. For other information on Avicenna and al-Ghazali in Dante, see Corti, "Dante and Islamic Culture," in this volume.

7. *Convivio*, ed. Cesare Vasoli and Domenico De Robertis, in *Opere minori*, vol. 1, pt. 2 (Milan and Naples: Ricciardi Editore, 1979).

8. As R. W. Southern wrote in *Western Views of Islam in the Middle Ages* (Cambridge, Mass.: Harvard University Press, 1962), for the learned in the Middle Ages, Arabic philosophy was considered "classical learning."

9. Larry Peterman, "Reading the *Convivio*," *Dante Studies* 103 (1985): 135.

10. For a thorough discussion of Statius's discourse on the origins of the human soul in *Purgatorio* 25, see Howard Needler, "The Birth and Death of the Soul," *Dante Studies* 122 (2004): 71–93.

11. For a nuanced view of the complex issues at stake in the *Convivio*, see Richard Lansing, "Dante's Intended Audience in the *Convivio*," *Dante Studies* 110 (1992): 17–24.

12. Averroës was known in the Middle Ages as "the commentator" because he wrote commentaries or summaries of all of Aristotle's major works. See Harry Austryn Wolfson et al., eds., *Corpus commentariorum Averrois in Aristotelem*, Publications of the Medieval Academy of America 54 (Cambridge, Mass.: Medieval Academy of America, 1953–56).

13. For Avicenna, for example, and the influence of the stars on human actions, see below, Peter Heath, *Allegory and Philosophy in Avicenna (Ibn Sina) with a Translation of the Book of the Prophet Muhammad's Ascent to Heaven* (Philadelphia: University of Pennsylvania Press, 1992), 131–32.

14. Teodolinda Barolini, *The Undivine Comedy: Detheologizing Dante* (Princeton, N.J.: Princeton University Press, 1992), 187.

15. John Freccero, "The Dance of the Stars: *Paradiso* X," *Dante: The Poetics of Conversion*, ed. Rachel Jacoff (Cambridge, Mass.: Harvard University Press, 1986), 221–23.

16. See Anthony Esolen's notes to *Purgatorio* 4 in *Dante: Purgatory* (New York: Random House, 2003). This issue of the status of the soul is critical for Aquinas because "he wishes to avoid having to see the human

being as a soul imprisoned in the body, as Plato sometimes suggests it is—for that would contradict the doctrines of the Incarnation of Christ and the resurrection of the body. At the same time, he must avoid seeing, as the Arab philosopher Averroës did, the human soul as so determined by the body that it cannot, as an individual entity, survive death" (421).

17. For a thorough discussion of this issue in Dante, see Giuseppe Mazzotta, "Logic and Power," chapter 5 in his *Dante's Vision and the Circle of Knowledge* (Princeton, NJ: Princeton University Press, 1993), 96–115.

18. For these points I am indebted to Christian Moevs's cogent discussion in "Miraculous Syllogism: Clocks, Faith and Reason in *Paradiso* 10 and 24," *Dante Studies* 117 (1999): 70–72.

19. "Allegory, Time, and Space in the *Mi'raj* and Its Commentary Tradition," *Allegorica* 22 (2001): 31–46. The discussion of Avicenna's and al-Ghazali's commentaries on the *mi'rāj* come from this essay. For other perspectives on Islamic commentaries on the *mi'rāj*, see, in this volume, Vicente Cantarino, "Dante and Islam: History and Analysis of a Controversy," and Corti, "Dante and Islamic Culture."

20. For Dante's response to this controversy and his expansive synthesizing project, see Mazzotta, *Dante's Vision and the Circle of Knowledge*. For further information on the *falasifa* (though without specific reference to the Sufis), see Gregory B. Stone, "Dante and the *Falasifa*: Religion as Imagination," in this volume.

21. *The Encyclopaedia of Islam*, new ed., s.v. "*Mi'rādj*." For an overview of *mi'rāj* and its influence on Islamic culture, see Annemarie Schimmel, *And Muhammad Is His Messenger: The Veneration of the Prophet in Islamic Piety* (Chapel Hill: University of North Carolina Press, 1985), especially "The Prophet's Night Journey and Ascension," 159–75; Étienne Renaud, "Le Récit du *Mi'râj*: Une version arabe de l'ascension du prophète, dans le *Tafsîr* de Tabarî," in *Apocalypses et voyages dans l'au-delà*, ed. Claude Kappler (Paris: Les Éditions du Cerf, 1987), 267–90; and Angelo M. Piemontese, "Le voyage de Mahomet au Paradis et en Enfer: Une version persane du *Mi'râj*," in *Apocalypses et voyages*, 293–320.

22. *The Encyclopaedia of Islam*, new ed., s.v. "Al burak." In the *mi'rāj*, Burāq is described as an animal larger than an ass but smaller than a mule, and with a man's face; its hair is pearls, the mane emeralds, and the tail rubies; its feet and hooves were like a camel's, and its color pure light.

23. For the history of the translations in the Latin Middle Ages, see Corti, "Dante and Islamic Culture," in this volume. Also, see Reginald White, *The Prophet of Islam in Old French: The Romance of Muhammad*

(*1258*) *and the Book of Muhammad's Ladder* (*1264*) (Leiden: E. J. Brill, 1997), 19–25, 78–80. The Latin and French versions of the *miʿrāj* are printed in Cerulli, *Il "Libro della scala" e la questione delle fonti arabo-spagnole della Divina Commedia*, Studi e testi 150 (Vatican City: Biblioteca Apostolica Vaticana, 1949), 24–247. See also *Le Livre de l'Échelle de Mahomet*, which provides the Latin text with a modern French translation, trans. and ed. Gisèle Besson and Michèle Brossard-Dandré (Paris: Librairie Générale Française, 1991). E. Blochet, *Les sources orientales de la Divine Comédie*, deals with parallels between the *miʿrāj*, which he traces to Persian origins, and the *Commedia*.

24. For Riccoldo's history, see Riccoldo da Montecroce, *I saraceni: Contra legem Sarracenorum*, ed. Giuseppe Rizzardi, Biblioteca medievale 13 (Florence: Nardini, 1992), 7–24. For Riccoldo, see also Ugo Monneret de Villard, *Il libro della peregrinazione nelle parti d'Oriente di frate Ricoldo da Montecroce* (Rome: ad S. Sabinae, 1948), 84, 104–18. For Dante and Riccoldo, see F. Gabrieli, "Dante e l'Islam," *Cultura e scuola* 13–14 (1965): 194–97, and Thomas Burman, "How an Italian Friar Read His Arabic Qur'an," in this volume. For Santa Maria Novella and Dante, see Charles T. Davis, "The Florentine Studia and Dante's 'Library,'" in *The Divine Comedy and the Encyclopedia of Arts and Sciences*, ed. Giuseppe Di Scipio and Aldo Scaglione (Amsterdam: John Benjamins, 1988), 339–66.

25. See Riccoldo da Monte Croce, *Pérégrination en Terre Sainte et au Proche Orient*, Latin text and French translation (Paris: H. Champion, 1997); and da Monte Croce, *Viaggio in Terra Santa di fra Ricoldo da Monte di Croce, volgarizzamento del secolo XIV* (Siena: A. Mucci, 1864).

26. Riccoldo, *I saraceni: Contra legem Sarracenorum*, 7–24. On Riccoldo's activities and writings, see Burman, "How an Italian Friar Read His Arabic Qur'an," in this volume.

27. Ibid., the section on the vision, see 149–53; Cerulli, *"Libro della scala,"* 346–57.

28. For a recent discussion of this, see my "Middle Eastern Apocalyptic Traditions in Dante's *La Divina Commedia* and Muhammad's *Miʿraj* or Night Journey," *Studies in Medieval and Renaissance History* 4, ed. Roger Dahood and Peter E. Medine (New York: AMS Press, 2007), 171–93. For classic earlier studies, see Asín Palacios, *Dante y el Islam*; Asín Palacios, *La escatología musulmana en la Divina Comedia*; Cerulli, *"Libro della scala"*; and Enrico Cerulli, *Nuove ricerche sul Libro della scala e la conoscenza dell'Islam in Occidente* (Vatican City: Biblioteca Apostolica Vaticana, 1972). On the history of scholarly responses to the relationship between Dante's poem and the Islamic work, see in this volume Cantarino, "Dante and Islam," and Corti, "Dante and Islamic Culture."

29. On Avicenna's life and intellectual contribution, see Heath, *Allegory and Philosophy in Avicenna*, 24–27.

30. Ibid., 111.

31. Heath, "The *Mi'raj* Nâma," in *Allegory and Philosophy in Avicenna*, 123. For further insights into intelligibles as well as Avicenna, see Gregory B. Stone, "Dante and the *Falasifa*: Religion as Imagination," in this volume.

32. Ibid., 64.

33. Ismail M. Dahiyat, *Avicenna's Commentary on the Poetics of Aristotle* (Leiden: E. J. Brill, 1974), 34, 61–62.

34. Ibid., 42.

35. Ibid. (*Poetics* 26.6), 119.

36. *Early Islamic Mysticism: Sufi, Qur'an, Mi'raj, Poetic and Theological Writings*, ed. Michael A. Sells (New York: Paulist Press, 1996), 47.

37. Qassim al-Samarrai, *The Theme of the Ascension in Mystical Writings* (Baghdad: National Printing and Publishing, 1968), 187–88.

38. Al-Ghazali, *Freedom and Fulfillment: An Annotated Translation of Al-Ghazali's al-Munqidh min al-Dalal and Other Relevant Works of al-Ghazali*, trans. Richard Joseph McCarthy (Boston: Twayne, 1980), 89–90.

39. Al-Ghazali, *The Remembrance of Death and the Afterlife: Book XL of the Revival of the Religious Sciences*, trans., intro, and notes T. J. Winter (Cambridge: Islamic Texts Society, 1989), xvi–xvii.

40. Al-Ghazali, *The Incoherence of the Philosophers*, trans. Michael E. Marmura (Provo, Utah: Brigham Young University Press, 1997), 218–19.

41. Qassim Al-Samarrai, *The Theme of the Ascension in Mystical Writings* (Baghdad: National Printing and Publishing, 1968), 183–244.

42. *Itinerarium mentis in Deum*, in *Opera omnia* 12, ed. A. C. Peltier (Paris: Vives, 1866–71), 1–24. See also Bonaventure, "The Soul's Journey to God," in *Bonaventure*, trans. Ewert Cousins (New York: Paulist Press, 1978), 53–116.

43. Albertus Magnus, "In Apocalypsim B. Joannis Apostoli," in *Opera omnia* 38, ed. Auguste Borgnet and Émile Borgnet (Paris: Vives, 1899), 465–796.

44. For a brief discussion of his commentary style, see my *Power and Prejudice: The Reception of the Gospel of Mark* (Detroit: Wayne State University Press, 1999), 79–82.

45. See Bernard F. Huppé and D. W. Robertson, Jr., *Fruyt and Chaf: Studies in Chaucer's Allegories* (Princeton, N.J.: Princeton University Press, 1963); and D. W. Robertson Jr., *Preface to Chaucer: Studies in Medieval Perspectives* (Princeton, N.J.: Princeton University Press, 1962).

46. Erich Auerbach, "Figura," *Scenes from the Drama of European Literature* (Minneapolis: University of Minnesota Press, 1984), 70–71.

47. Lee Patterson, *Chaucer and the Subject of History* (Madison: University of Wisconsin, 1991), 10, 280–321.

48. The genres Jauss identifies include those breaking loose from biblical exegesis, whose purposes tend to be strictly religious didacticism directed at individual reform; transformations of *Physiologus* and the bestiaries, which can be political, moral, and satirical; apocalyptic and other world visions; allegorical epics with a wide range of veiled purposes. See Hans Robert Jauss, "La transformation de la forme allégorique entre 1180 et 1240: D'Alain de Lille à Guillaume de Lorris," in *L'humanisme médiévale dans les littératures romanes du XII au XIV siècle*, ed. Anthime Fourrier (Paris: Klincksieck, 1964), 107–46; Jauss, "Entstehung und Strukturwandel der allegorischen Dichtung," in *La littérature didactique, allégorique, et satirique* 1, ed. Hans Robert Jauss (Heidelberg: Carl Winter, 1968), 146–244; and Jauss, "Genèse et structure des genres allégoriques," in *La littérature didactique, allégorique et satirique* 2, ed. Hans Robert Jauss (Heidelberg: Carl Winter, 1970), 203–280.

49. Barolini, *The Undivine Comedy*, 226–27.

50. For an expansive discussion of Dante's achievement in this regard, see Mazzotta, *Dante's Vision and the Circle of Knowledge*.

51. On Muḥammad and Ali as schismatics, see Jan M. Ziolkowski, "Introduction," in this volume.

52. On Thomas Aquinas and Muḥammad, see *Summa contra Gentiles* in *Opera omnia*, ed. Roberto Busa (Stuttgart: Günther Holzboog, 1980), 2, 1.6.7. See also my *Dante and the Orient* (Urbana: University of Illinois Press, 2002), 55–57.

DANTE AND THE *FALASIFA*: RELIGION AS IMAGINATION
Gregory B. Stone

1. All emphasis of Dante's text (indicated by italics) is mine.

2. A variation of the same verb (*sternere*, from the Latin meaning "to spread out," "to unfold") is used for the teaching provided by Aristotle (*Par.* 26.37 *sterne*), Moses (*Par.* 26.40 *sternel*), and John (*Par.* 26.43 *sternilmi*). The effect of this repetition is to emphasize the equivalence, the interchangeability, of the truth content of philosophy and various revealed religions.

3. For the suggestion that "Peter" (the examiner) in *Paradiso* 24 is an impostor and a figure for Dante's archenemy, Boniface VIII, see Ernest L. Fortin, *Dissidence et philosophie au moyen âge: Dante et ses antécédents*

(Montreal: Bellarmin, 1980), 148–53. In Fortin's view, Dante does not reveal to "Peter" his true views on faith but rather conceals them, in the manner of one facing a papal inquisition. I develop Fortin's interpretation further in *Dante's Pluralism and the Islamic Philosophy of Religion* (New York: Palgrave Macmillan, 2006), 272–81, where I treat in greater detail some of the points made in the present essay.

4. The *Book of Kuzari*, written by the great twelfth-century Andalusian Hebrew poet Judah Halevi (Yehudah ha-Levi), argues passionately in favor of the notion that Judaism is the sole true religious law. Although an opponent of the philosophers, Halevi is well-versed in their teachings, and he offers, through the words of a character in his dialogue named simply "the Philosopher," a succinct distillation of what one can call "the religion of the philosophers": "Once you have integrated this philosophy within yourself, you need not concern yourself with which specific dogma, set of rituals and other actions, choice of words or language that you will practice. If you like, you could even fabricate your own religion, which promotes humility, exalts the Prime Cause, helps you correct your traits, and does the same for your family members and your fellow countrymen (if you can get them to listen to you). Or, you might adopt the intellectually stimulating rituals of the philosophers. But your ultimate objective should be purification of the soul [so you can perceive things more accurately]. In summation, seek purification of the heart with whatever method works for you, as long as you understand the principles of wisdom clearly." *The Kuzari: In Defense of the Despised Faith*, trans. N. Daniel Korobkin (Northvale, NJ: Jason Aronson, 1998), 6–7. My point here is not to imply a direct link between Halevi's text and Dante; rather, it is to suggest that Dante's dialogue with John the Evangelist in *Paradiso* 26 is one place where we can glimpse the possibility that Dante was cognizant of this "religion of the philosophers." For an excellent treatment of the "religion of the philosophers," including extensive discussion of medieval Islamic and Jewish thinkers, see Carlos Fraenkel, *Philosophical Religions from Plato to Spinoza: Reason, Religion, and Autonomy* (Cambridge: Cambridge University Press, 2012).

5. The notion that a scripture—and the *Commedia*, the "poema sacro / al quale ha posto mano e cielo e terra" (*Par.* 25.1–2 "the sacred poem / to which Heaven and earth have so set hand"), *is* a kind of scripture—has multiple discursive levels, each aimed at a certain audience, is the basis of Averroës's analysis, in *The Decisive Treatise, Determining What the Connection is Between Religion and Philosophy*, of the manner in which the Law (for him, the Qur'an) operates to gain the assent of every audience. For Averroës, revelation is simultaneously

aimed at three kinds of people: the masses of ordinary folk, the theologians, and the philosophers ("For people are of three sorts with respect to the Law. One sort is in no way adept at interpretation. These are the rhetorical people, who are the overwhelming multitude. . . . Another sort is those adept in dialectical interpretation [i.e., the theologians]. . . . Another sort is those adept in certain interpretation [i.e., the philosophers]. . . . This [i.e., the philosophical] interpretation ought not to be declared to those adept in dialectic [i.e., to the theologians], not to mention [to] the multitude." Averroës, *Decisive Treatise and Epistle Dedicatory*, trans. Charles E. Butterworth (Provo, UT: Brigham Young University Press, 2001), 26.

6. After discouraging those whom one might call (to borrow a phrase from Averroës) "the overwhelming multitude" from reading *Paradiso*, Dante tells who *are* the intended audience of the poem's final canticle: "Voi altri pochi che drizzaste il collo / per tempo al pan de li angeli" (*Par.* 2.10–11 "You other few who lifted up your necks / betimes for the bread of angels"). This is an obvious allusion to the *Convivio* 1.1.7 ("O beati quelli pochi che seggiono a quella mensa dove lo pane delli angeli si manuca!;" "O, blessed are the few who sit at the table where the bread of angels is eaten!"). In the *Convivio*, the phrase "bread of angels" clearly refers to philosophy, that study that will feed our desire for "scienza" (*Conv.* 1.1.1 "knowledge"). Robert Hollander, commenting on Dante's use of "bread of angels" in *Paradiso* 2.11, insists that, whereas in the *Convivio* the phrase meant "general philosophical" study, in *Paradiso* the significance is "clearly theological," a matter of "religious truth," and is restricted to "only revealed truth." Dante, *Paradiso*, trans. Robert Hollander and Jean Hollander (New York: Doubleday, 2007), 46. But has Dante really changed his mind, such that the phrase once used to signify philosophy is now used to signify theology? To understand why the answer to this question must be no, one needs to acknowledge that, in the Aristotelian tradition, theology is one of the parts of philosophy. Beatrice *is* a theologian, which is to say that she is a *philosopher* directing her attention to the highest of existing things. If it is true that in the *Commedia* knowledge of these things can only be attained through a kind of revelation, this is in keeping with Avicenna's view that the philosopher can only know the highest metaphysical entities through an illumination that comes from above, from the Active Intellect.

7. The "Conjunction with the Active Intellect" is the philosophers' version of beatitude, ultimate felicity, and salvation. For an excellent advanced introduction to Albertus Magnus's extremely influential understanding of "the Conjunction," see Alain de Libera, *Métaphysique*

et noétique: Albert le Grand (Paris: Librairie Philosophique J. Vrin, 2005), esp. chap. 6.

8. The notion that with the *Commedia* Dante renounces philosophy in favor of religious revelation has become such a commonplace—indeed, a dominant—paradigm that it hardly seems necessary to mention specific critics. But, for an influential example, see John Freccero, *Dante: The Poetics of Conversion* (Cambridge, Mass.: Harvard University Press, 1986), esp. 1–28, 187–94. For a specific instance, see Hollander's treatment, mentioned in note 6, of the phrase "bread of angels." Freccero's exegesis is in part rooted in the works of the great Italian Dante scholar Bruno Nardi. See, for example, Nardi's *Dal "Convivio" alla "Commedia"* (Rome: Istituto Storico Italiano per il Medio Evo, 1960) and his *Saggi di filosofia dantesca* (Milan: Società Editrice Dante Alighieri, 1930). Nardi, who more than anyone else has demonstrated that Dante draws freely from the Islamic philosophical tradition (often by showing that, on various delicate questions, Dante is closer to Albertus Magnus than to Aquinas), is also more than anyone else responsible for viewing the *Commedia* as Dante's act of repentance following the overly audacious formulations of the *Convivio* and, especially, the *Monarchia*. Nardi is firmly of the opinion that the *Commedia*'s basic allegory is meant to subordinate Vergil (reason, philosophy) to Beatrice (faith, theology). Nardi and his followers fail to consider that the distinction between Vergil and Beatrice is a distinction between two kinds of philosophy—i.e., the practical and the theoretical. Beatrice's association with revelation does not mean that she surpasses philosophy, for there is a philosophical version of "revelation"—illumination by and conjunction with the Active Intellect. For philosophical readers, *Paradiso* tells the story of this philosophical revelation. For a compelling interpretation of Beatrice as the Active Intellect, see Francesco Perez, *La Beatrice svelata: Preparazione alla intelligenza di tutte le opera di Dante Alighieri* (Palermo: Reber, 1897). Perez's often maligned and more often neglected work has recently been reprinted (Palermo: Flaccovio, 2001). For more on the significance of the distinction between Vergil and Beatrice, see my "Dante's *Commedia*, Islamic Rationalism, and the Enumeration of the Sciences," *Doctor Virtualis* 12: 135–167.

9. Lawrence V. Berman, "Maimonides the Disciple of Alfarabi," *Israel Oriental Studies* 4 (1974): 154–78.

10. As Howard Kreisel remarks, Gersonides's mastery of *falsafa* testifies to the fact that "a large circle from the intellectual elite within Provençal Jewry were brought into the orbit of Arabic culture despite the fact that few of them knew Arabic. . . . The situation by Gersonides's

time allowed him to feel at home in the world of Islamic Aristotelian thought simply on the basis of the extent of the Hebrew translations and other works. There was no longer any need to know Arabic in order to enter into this world of thought." Kreisel, *Prophecy: The History of an Idea in Medieval Jewish Philosophy* (Dordrecht: Kluwer Academic Publishers, 2001), 319.

11. For a detailed study of the question of the intellect in the Islamic Aristotelian tradition, see Herbert A. Davidson, *Alfarabi, Avicenna, and Averroes on Intellect* (New York: Oxford University Press, 1992). In a series of important works, Antonio Gagliardi has amply demonstrated that the Averroist notion of the philosopher's ultimate felicity as "conjunction with the intellect" posed a challenge to the tenets of Christianity and was a perspective that had to be reckoned with, pro or con, by intellectuals and literary artists of Dante's time. See Antonio Gagliardi, *La donna mia: Filosofia araba e poesia medievale* (Soveria Mannelli: Rubbettino, 2007); *Tomasso d'Aquino e Averroè: La visione di Dio* (Soveria Mannelli: Rubbettino, 2002); *Guido Cavalcanti: Poesia e filosofia* (Alessandria: Edizioni dell'Orso, 2001); *Guido Cavalcanti e Dante: Una questione d'amore* (Catanzaro: Pullano, 1997); *La tragedia intellettuale di Dante: Il Convivio* (Catanzaro: Pullano, 1994); and *Ulisse e Sigieri di Brabante: Ricerche su Dante* (Catanzaro: Pullano, 1991).

12. Jean de Jandun, who, as Jean-Baptiste Brenet shows, was the best informed and most devoted Averroist of his age (see J.-B. Brenet, *Transferts du sujet: la noétique d'Averroès selon Jean de Jandun* [Paris: Librairie Philosophique J. Vrin, 2003]), was a colleague of Marsilius of Padua and, according to some, may have lent a hand to the composition of the latter's *Defensor pacis*. Due to the scandal caused by this pro-imperial treatise, Jean and Marsilius fled Paris together in 1326 to take refuge in Nuremberg, at the imperial court of Louis of Bavaria. In 1327 Jean was excommunicated and proclaimed a heretic—a fact that did not prevent Louis's appointing him bishop of Ferrara in 1328. On the possibility that Marsilius was personally acquainted with Dante, see my *Dante's Pluralism*, p. 13.

13. "Fiducia philosophantis est non coniungi tantum agenti ut efficienti, sed etiam sicut formae" ("The philosopher's firm hope is not to be conjoined with the Agent [i.e., Active Intellect] only as efficient [cause], but also as form"). Albertus Magnus, *De anima* 3.3.11, cited in de Libera, *Métaphysique et noétique*, 302. In other words, the philosopher's ultimate goal is to *become* the Active Intellect, not merely to have his human intellect activated by the Active Intellect. As de Libera remarks (p. 302), this formulation by Albert is "the Charter of Latin Averroism,

or, more precisely, of Radical Aristotelianism." Cavalcanti longs for such a conjunction but is also convinced of its impossibility—hence the tragic pessimism that pervades his poetry.

14. As de Libera quips (ibid., 308–9), "L'Aristote d'Albert est un Aristote (f)arabisé" ("Albert's Aristotle is an Aristotle who has been [al-F] ārābized"). De Libera, with magisterial command of his material, shows that Albert's philosophy is fundamentally al-Fārābian even though Albert's al-Fārābi is secondhand, mediated through Averroës.

15. In one of his letters to Boccaccio, Petrarch reports on an angry exchange that he had with an Averroist, "one of these philosophers of modern stamp": see Petrarch, *Seniles* 5.3, in *Petrarch: The First Modern Scholar and Man of Letters*, trans. James Harvey Robinson (New York: G. P. Putnam, 1898), 211–12.

16. Antonio Gagliardi, *Giovanni Boccaccio: poeta filosofo averroista* (Soveria Mannelli: Rubbettino, 1999).

17. The Venetian humanist Lauro Quirini, who studied at the University of Padua from 1440 to 1448, advised an apprentice in philosophy to read Averroës "continuously without stopping" and to study Aquinas only as a quick introduction to Averroës: see Marwan Rashed, "L'averroïsme de Lauro Quirini," in *Averroès et l'averroïsme: Un itinéraire historique du Haut Atlas à Paris et à Padoue*, ed. André Bazzana, Nicole Bériou, and Pierre Guichard (Lyon: Presses Universitaire de Lyon, 2005), 309.

18. In brief, Avicenna maintains (in *Metaphysics of "The Healing"* 9.7) that only philosophers—and, of these, only those who have attained a certain required degree of intellection—have an immortal afterlife; Averroës, in his esoteric works meant only for other philosophers, suggests that the afterlife is not the immortality of the soul but is speculative felicity attained, by a happy few, *after* a life of study in *this* life. See Averroës, *The Epistle on the Possibility of Conjunction with the Active Intellect*, ed. Kalman P. Bland (New York: Jewish Theological Seminary of America, 1982).

19. The notion of agreement with *both* Aristotle and Plato may sound odd to us, since we are accustomed to emphasizing their differences. But al-Fārābī, in *The Philosophy of Plato and Aristotle*, argues that—rightly interpreted—the two great Greek philosophers are in accord. The Aristotle of the *falasifa* was always to some degree a Platonized one.

20. Richard Walzer, ed., *Al-Farabi on the Perfect State* (Oxford: Oxford University Press, 1985), 479, 441.

21. "È adunque da sapere primamente che li movitori di quelli cieli sono sustanze separate da materia, cioè Intelligenze, le quali la volgare

gente chiamano Angeli" (*Conv.* 2.4.2 "And so it is first necessary to know that the movers of the heavens are substances separate from matter, namely Intelligences, which the common people call Angels"). Compare Avicenna: "Now it is a widely spread notion in the disciplines based on religious Laws that angels are living beings and that, unlike man who perishes, they never perish. Once it is said that the spheres are rational living beings and the rational living being that does not perish is called an angel, the spheres are then called angels. . . . It is customary in the religious Law to call the subtle powers that are not perceived by the senses 'angels.' " *On the Proof of Prophecies and the Interpretation of the Prophets' Symbols and Metaphors*, trans. Michael E. Marmura, in *Medieval Political Philosophy*, ed. Ralph Lerner and Muhsin Mahdi (Ithaca, N.Y.: Cornell University Press, 1972), 118, 120. Albertus Magnus likewise notes that "has intelligentias secundum vulgus Angelos vocant" ("following the common people, these intelligences they call Angels"). *Metaphysics* 11.2.10, cited in *Convivio*, ed. Ageno, 79.

22. In *Convivio* 4.22.14–18 Dante says that Christ, our *Salvatore*, is another name for our felicity and beatitude, which is theoretical speculation. He formulates clearly the equation *lo speculativo* = *la beatitudine* = *lo Salvatore* (the speculative = beatitude = the Savior). Averroës, in *The Epistle on the Possibility of Conjunction with the Active Intellect*, similarly allegorizes scripture as if it refers to the speculative (i.e., theoretical) felicity of the philosopher.

23. As Peter Heath says, commenting on a passage in which Avicenna does not hesitate to use the term *Cherubim* (when what he means, in philosophical vocabulary, is "Intelligences"): "In such passages, the philosopher does not just align religious and philosophical terms on a superficial level, or allegorize the former in terms of the latter; here religious and philosophical terminology are equivalent, interchangeable. For Avicenna the Intelligences are not *like* Cherubim; they *are* Cherubim, and one of their members *is* the Holy Spirit. . . . For sophisticated theologians, mystics, and poets in the centuries after Avicenna, the Necessary Existent, the First Cause, and God are synonymous terms; the Cherubim do not symbolize the Neoplatonic Separate Intelligences, they directly signify them, and Ptolemy's spheres and orbs have become the Seven Heavens of the Qur'an." *Allegory and Philosophy in Avicenna (Ibn Sînâ)* (Philadephia: University of Pennsylvania Press, 1992), 182. Beatrice is precisely that—a "sophisticated [i.e., philosophical] theologian."

24. Averroës, *Decisive Treatise and Epistle Dedicatory*, trans. Butterworth, 8–9.

25. "But he [i.e., the philosopher, in his role as prophet-lawgiver] ought not to involve them [i.e., the masses of ordinary believers] in anything doctrinal pertaining to the knowledge of God, exalted be He, beyond the knowledge that He is One, the Truth, and has nothing similar to Him. . . . For it is only with great strain that they can conceive the true states of such matters in their true aspects; it is only the very few among them that can understand the truth of divine 'unity' and divine 'transcendence.' The rest would come to deny the truth of such existence, fall into dissensions, and indulge in disputations and analogical arguments that stand in the way of their performing their civil duties. This might even lead them to adopt views contrary to the city's welfare, opposed to the imperatives of truth. . . . Nor is it proper for any human to reveal that he possesses knowledge he is hiding from the commonality. Indeed, he must never permit any reference to this. . . . [H]e must instill in them the belief in the resurrection in a manner that they can conceive and in which their souls find rest. He must tell them about eternal bliss and misery in parables derived from what they can comprehend and conceive. Of the true nature of the afterlife he should indicate only something in general, that it is something that 'no eye has seen and no ear heard' and that there are pleasures that are great possessions and miseries that are perpetual torture. . . . But there is no harm if the legislator's words contain symbols and signs that might call forth those naturally disposed toward theoretical reflection to pursue philosophic investigations." Avicenna, *The Metaphysics of "The Healing,"* trans. Michael E. Marmura (Provo, UT: Brigham Young University Press, 2005), 365–66 (10.2).

26. "The truest of all propositions is that every prophet is a wise man, but not every wise man a prophet." Averroës, *The Incoherence of the Incoherence*; this translation is from Averroës, *Decisive Treatise and Epistle Dedicatory*, trans. Butterworth, 45.

27. "Every Law comes about from revelation and has intellect mixed with it. For anyone who holds that it is possible for a Law to come about from intellect alone, it necessarily follows that it is more deficient than the Laws inferred from intellect and revelation. And everyone agrees that the principles of practice must be taken on authority, for there is no way to demonstrate what practice demands except through the existence of virtues acquired through practical moral actions" (ibid.).

28. "A necessity of the virtue of such a one [i.e., the philosopher] is not to make light of [the religion] he has grown up with. . . . And if he explicitly declares a doubt about the Law-based principles in which he has grown up or an interpretation contradicting the prophets (God's

prayers be upon them) and turning away from their path, then he is the person who most deserves to have the name of unbelief applied to him and to be judged with the penalty of unbelief in the religion in which he has grown up" (ibid., 44).

29. As Averroës says in his treatise *Exposition of Religious Arguments*, "If the Precious Book [i.e., the Qur'an] is contemplated with all the laws, which are useful both for knowledge and actions conducive to happiness it contains, and then compared with what all other religions and scriptures contain, they [i.e., the laws of Islam] would be found to infinitely surpass them all in this respect." *Faith and Reason in Islam*, trans. Ibrahim Najjar (Oxford: Oneworld, 2001), 103.

30. Trans. Butterworth, 44.

31. Lenn E. Goodman, *Ibn Tufayl's* Hayy Ibn Yaqzan, 4th ed. (Los Angeles: Gee Tee Bee, 1996), 103. For further information on Ibn Ṭufayl and Ḥayy Ibn Yaqẓān, see in this volume Giorgio Battistoni, "Dante and the Three Religions." See also Avner Ben-Zaken, *Reading* Ḥayy Ibn Yaqẓān: *A Cross-Cultural History of Autodidacticism* (Baltimore: The Johns Hopkins University Press, 2011).

32. Goodman, *Ibn Tufayl's* Hayy Ibn Yaqzan, xii.

33. Ibid., 156.

34. Ibid.

35. Ibid., 160.

36. Ibid., 163.

37. Ibid., 164.

38. The issue of Dante's debt to Islamic philosophy, particularly in the domain of cosmology, has been treated by Carmela Baffioni, "Aspetti delle cosmologie islamiche in Dante," in *Il pensiero filosofico e teologico di Dante Alighieri*, ed. Alessandro Ghisalberti (Milan: Vita e Pensiero, 2001), 103–22. For a brief but excellent treatment of the question, see Paul A. Cantor, "The Uncanonical Dante: *The Divine Comedy* and Islamic Philosophy," *Philosophy and Literature* 20.1 (1996): 138–53.

39. Averroës, *Epitome of Parva Naturalia*, trans. Harry Blumberg (Cambridge, MA: Medieval Academy of America, 1961), 41.

40. Although the sources from which the exempla of virtues and vices on the seven terraces of Purgatory vary, normally the exempla of virtues are drawn from a pagan (classical Greek or Roman) source, from an Old Testament story, and (always) from a Gospel narrative involving the Virgin Mary, while the exempla of vices are drawn from pagan sources and Old Testament stories. In every case there is, at minimum, a pagan and a biblical source—the point being that the imaginative representation of the principles of right practice is not confined to the

Bible, but is available to non-biblical communities through their own *scrittura*.

41. Al-Fārābī, *The Attainment of Happiness,* trans. Muhsin Mahdi, in *Medieval Political Philosophy,* 63.

42. Walzer, *Al-Farabi on the Perfect State,* 281.

43. Al-Fārābī, *The Political Regime,* trans. Fauzi M. Najjar, in *Medieval Political Philosophy,* 41.

44. Al-Fārābī, *The Political Regime,* 41.

45. Al-Fārābī, *The Attainment of Happiness,* 79–80.

46. *Book of Religion* 5, in *Alfarabi, The Political Writings: "Selected Aphorisms" and Other Texts,* trans. Charles E. Butterworth (Ithaca, NY: Cornell University Press, 2001), 97.

47. Avicenna, *The Metaphysics of "The Healing,"* 359 (10.1) (emphases added).

48. Avicenna, *On the Proof of Prophecies,* 115: "Revelation is the emanation and the angel is the received emanating power that descends on the prophets as if it were an emanation continuous with universal intellect. It is rendered particular, not essentially, but accidentally, by reason of the particularity of the recipient."

49. Kreisel, *Prophecy,* 129–30.

50. Avicenna: "It is thus the condition of prophets that they arrange every intelligible that they perceive as a sensible and put it into speech so that the community can follow that sensible. They perceive it as an intelligible, but make it sensed and concrete for the community. They thus increase (its usefulness) for threats and promises and foster good beliefs, so that its provisions become perfect, so that the basis and code of religious law and the foundation of religious devotion not be dissolved and disordered and that which is the intention of the prophet not remain concealed. When it reaches intellectuals, they perceive it with their intellects. They know that the prophet's words are all symbols, filled with intelligibles. When it reaches ignoramuses, however, they look at the external speech. Their hearts are satisfied with non-intelligible concrete forms and sensibles. They are enveloped by the imagination and do not pass beyond the doorway of estimation. They ask, unknowing, and listen, uncomprehending. 'And praise be to God, for indeed most of them do not know [Qur'an 31.25].'" Avicenna, *Mi'râj Nâma* [The Book of Ascent], trans. Heath, *Allegory and Philosophy in Avicenna,* 121–22.

51. As Roger Arnaldez says, for Averroës, the faculty of practical intellect is always bound up with imagination: "In humans, images are the moving force of the practical rational faculty. *Practical intelligibles are thus always linked with images,* which permits reasonable action to take

place in the world of perceptions and experience. Thus the 'practical intelligibles' are not to be thought of as eternal truths that can be the objects contemplated by speculative [theoretical] knowledge; rather, they can be 'generated' and are 'corruptible,' and they only appear to humans in concrete situations. . . . Averroes concludes: 'If these practical intelligibles existed without the imaginative soul, their existence would be vain and useless.' Thanks to this faculty [of practical intellect], humans love and hate, live in society and form bonds of friendship. It is the source of the moral virtues, '*because the existence of these virtues is nothing more than that of the images by which we are moved to practice virtuous deeds.*'" *Averroès, un rationaliste en Islam* (Paris: Editions Balland, 1998), 86–88 (my translation; emphases added).

52. *Monarchy* 1.2.5; ed. Prue Shaw (Cambridge: Cambridge University Press, 1996), 5.

53. Al-Fārābī, *Selected Aphorisms* 35, in *Alfarabi, The Political Writings: "Selected Aphorisms" and Other Texts*, trans. Charles E. Butterworth (Ithaca, NY: Cornell University Press, 2001), 29.

54. I have treated this issue at length in *Dante's Pluralism*, esp. 124–71.

55. Averroës, *Long Commentary on the* De anima *of Aristotle*, trans. Richard C. Taylor (New Haven, CT: Yale University Press, 2009), 295.

FALCONRY AS A TRANSMUTATIVE ART:
DANTE, FREDERICK II, AND ISLAM
Daniela Boccassini

1. The reference is of course to *Par.* 10.22–24, although there Dante does not dwell on any sufferings to come, musing instead over "ciò che si preliba" ("what you have already tasted").

2. Another instance of metamorphosis *in bono*, and thus especially relevant to the present discourse, is the one Dante evokes for himself by means of a reference to the Ovidian Glaucus at the moment of his "trasumanar" (*Par.* 1.67–72 "metamorphosis beyond what is human"). Needless to say, Dante is also a master in showing us how humans excel in the art of metamorphosis *in malo*, the very perversion of the principle of becoming. On this subject, though, Dante seems to imply that, in order to achieve such destructive feats, humans need no teachers or guides other than their own misguided will. In this essay I shall not consider the negative/destructive aspect of metamorphosis; I focus, rather, on its positive, redemptive potential.

3. At least within Western culture, and as far as we know today. I will not provide a list of references here, as the topic is of a general nature

and has been widely discussed. The basic reference is Jacques Le Goff, *La naissance du purgatoire* (Paris: Gallimard, 1981), but I will make some more specific comments on the issue of how Dante's invention has been and continues to be understood. The greatest paradox is quite possibly the fact that the Catholic Church has to a large extent espoused a vision of Purgatory derived from Dante's, albeit *purged* (*figura etymologica* by all means intended) of precisely those implications that, as we shall see, are of paramount importance to Dante's distinctive poetics of transmutation.

4. My inclusion of the Islamic world within the sphere of Western cultures may seem odd to today's readers, but, as has been discussed in the introduction to this volume, it certainly was not to a medieval mind. Not only was Islam part of the Mediterranean world at large, as Dante himself shows in the *Commedia*, but Islam was then typically understood as no less—but also no more—than a wicked deviation from a shared religious origin. In the same perspective, we find the souls of some of the most accomplished Islamic figures in limbo—on a par, that is, with the Latin and Greek heathens.

5. A number of classic studies deal with the origins and developments of these Mediterranean narratives of otherworldly travels. Among the most authoritative is I. P. Culianu, who points out that "le tradizioni arabe relative al 'viaggio notturno' e all''ascensione celeste' del profeta Muhammad sono direttamente derivate dall'apocalittica ebraica" (*Psychanodia* [Leiden: Brill, 1983], quoted in Carlo Saccone, *Il libro della scala di Maometto* [Milan: SE, 1997], 182).

6. If it is doubtful whether "a description of the world beyond is [per se] an act of heresy" (Frederick Goldin, as quoted Mark J. Mirsky, *Dante, Eros, Kabbalah* [Syracuse, NY: Syracuse University Press, 2003], 201); it seems, however, likely that Dante's decision to write a poem based on his personal vision of the beyond was at the very least veering on the unorthodox. Hence the need either to condemn it or, conversely, redeem it by declaring it a poetic fiction, as did most of the early commentators, from Pietro di Dante to Boccaccio. Ever since, the latter has been the most elegant (and escapist) solution to the problem. See Christian Moevs, *The Metaphysics of Dante's "Comedy"* (Oxford: Oxford University Press, 2005), 4, 10.

7. We owe one of the best syntheses of this thorny issue to Saccone, *Il libro della scala di Maometto*. For an earlier guide to it, see, in this volume, Vicente Cantarino, "Dante and Islam: History and Analysis of a Controversy." In summarizing Cerulli's multiple annotations, Saccone rightly points to the most valuable contribution that book made to the

field—the *one* contribution that scholars typically set aside in discussing Dante's supposed "borrowings" from Muḥammad's journey: the fact that "vari testi contenenti riassunti più o meno ampi della leggenda . . . testimoniavano la più ampia diffusione in Italia e in Europa di notizie riguardanti il *mi'râj* maomettano" (167).

Even in her most recent review of the issue, Maria Corti limits her references to the *Liber scale*. See "Dante e la cultura islamica," in*"Per correr miglior acque . . .": Bilanci e prospettive degli studi danteschi alle soglie del nuovo millennio*, ed. L. Battaglia Ricci et al. (Rome: Salerno, 2001), 1:183–202, translated in this volume as "Dante and Islamic Culture." See also the recent French edition of this text, *Le livre de l'échelle de Mahomet. Liber Scale Machometi*, trans. G. Besson et M. Brossard-Dandré, préface R. Arnaldez (Paris: Livre de Poche, 1991); and Giorgio Battistoni, "Dante, l'Islam e altre considerazioni," *Labyrinthos* 11 (1987): 26–49.

8. *Epistole* 13.10, par. 15–16: "omissa subtili investigatione, dicendum est breviter quod finis totius et partis est removere viventes in hac vita de statu miserie et perducere ad statum felicitatis. Genus vero phylosophie sub quo hic in toto et in parte proceditur, est morale negotium, sive ethica; quia non ad speculandum, sed ad opus inventum est totum et pars" (Dante Alighieri, *Opere minori* 2 [Milan: Ricciardi, 1979], 624). "Leaving aside any minute examination of this question, it may be stated briefly that the aim of the whole and of the part is to remove those living in this life from a state of misery, and to bring them to a state of happiness. The branch of philosophy to which the work is subject, in the whole as in the part, is that of morals or ethics; inasmuch as the whole as well as the part was conceived, not for speculation, but with a practical object" (*Dantis Alagherii epistolae: The Letters of Dante*, ed. P. Toynbee [Oxford: Clarendon Press, 1920], 202).

9. Compare Peter Armour, *The Door of Purgatory: A Study of Multiple Symbolism in Dante's Purgatorio* (Oxford: Clarendon Press, 1983), 137, quoted in extenso below.

10. As we shall see, this is of course where the heart of the issue lies. Francis Fergusson set it in a classical framework: "The classical conception of the learning process may be put in the formula *poiema, pathema, mathema*; making, suffering, knowledge. . . . The rhythm of Purgatory is tragic in this sense; in many analogous figures, wisdom is acquired through effort and suffering" (*Dante's Drama of the Mind. A Modern Reading of the "Purgatorio"* [Princeton, NJ: Princeton University Press, 1953], 56–57). Others, however, take a rather different interpretive stand. See, for example, Adriano Lanza: "Le tappe del viaggio che viene narrato

corrispondono agli stadi attraverso i quali si opera la trasformazione del protagonista, il quale si viene spogliando della caligine corporea e si trasforma in essere di luce," *Dante all'inferno* (Rome: Tre Editori, 1999), 19. One of the most obvious textual references is *Purg.* 13.1–3 ("Noi eravamo al sommo de la scala / dove secondamente si risega / lo monte che salendo altrui *dismala*" [emphasis added]), which in and of itself is both clear and vague enough to warrant widely different readings of the purging process enacted on the slopes of the mountain.

11. *Purg.* 4.25–30, 4.88–96, 4.27.121–25. Of course, Dante is the one who faces the challenge, allegedly because of his body, and of course the intervention of Saint Lucy will prove decisive (the climb can be considered ineffectual because her intervention is required for Dante and Vergil to move from Antepurgatory to Purgatory proper)—but even so, Dante will have to ascend the mountain in its entirety so as to free himself of all of the seven letter *P*'s marked on his forehead, in order to experience the lightness he acquires by virtue of his purgative ascent.

12. And certainly not the kind of fraudulent art by which Ulysses had imagined he could deceive God as he had his shipmates—the art, that is of "making wings of our oars" (or "turning our wings into oars" if we want to accentuate the metamorphic implications of the Italian "de' remi *facemmo* ali"), for a *volo* that from the depths of Hell the Homeric hero finally acknowledges as intrinsically "folle," hence bound to failure and ultimate death (*Inf.* 26.125).

13. For a more detailed analysis of this and other falconry references in Dante's writings, and more in general on the subject at hand, see "La falconeria nell'opera di Dante" in Daniela Boccassini, *Il volo della mente: Falconeria e sofia nel mondo mediterraneo: Islam, Federico II, Dante* (Ravenna: Longo, 2003), 335–88.

14. In *Il volo della mente* I have shown how images of falconry are present in the *Inferno*—the most glaring cases being Ulysses's and Ugolino's—to designate precisely those procedures which might have led the souls to salvation but were refused by them (ibid., 359–61). Yet at the very outset of the poem the souls of the damned respond with desire to the call of Charon: a fearful proof of the laws that govern the universe and impose upon the souls the exacting urge to respond to their karmic stance even against their own inclination (ibid., 353–55).

15. See Maria Corti, "Dante and Islamic Culture," in this volume.

16. I quote from Corti, "Dante e la cultura islamica," 184; "Dante and Islamic Culture," in this volume (emphasis added). An earlier version of the same article was published as "La *Commedia* di Dante e l'oltretomba islamico," *Belfagor* 50 (1995): 301–14.

17. To my knowledge, Roberto Mercuri is the only scholar aside from myself who has established a connection between the emergence of falconry imagery in Dante's poetry and his exile. See "Dante, Petrarca e Boccaccio," in *Letteratura italiana: Storia e geografia*, vol. 1, *L'età medievale*, ed. Alberto Asor Rosa (Turin: Einaudi, 1987): 238–39. For a more detailed reading of these *canzoni dell'esilio* from the perspective of falconry, see Boccassini, *Il volo della mente*, 341–47.

18. The *canzoni dell'esilio* cannot be dated any more closely than between mid-1303 to mid- or late 1304. Mercuri, for example, argues that "è probabile che la canzone ["Doglia mi reca"] sia composta nel 1304 quando Dante si trova nella provincia di Arezzo, subito dopo il soggiorno a Forlì presso Scarpetta Ordelaffi e la missione a Verona e il conseguente soggiorno presso Bartolomeo della Scala (forse come ambasciatore dei Bianchi presso gli Scaligeri), soggiorno databile dalla metà del 1303 alla fine del marzo 1304." "Dante, Petrarca e Boccaccio," 238–39. In contrast, Stephen Bemrose states that "it is highly probable that Dante's literary output increased markedly in Verona. . . . Certainly two very important post-exilic *canzoni* can be dated to the years 1302–04, and may well have been written in Verona" (*A New Life of Dante* [Exeter: University of Exeter Press, 2000], 67).

19. However, even this "ideological" distinction no longer seems to hold by the mid-1300s, if we are to judge from Lorenzetti's fresco of the "Good Government" made for the staunchly Guelph city of Siena.

20. Giorgio Petrocchi, *Vita di Dante* (Bari: Laterza, 1993), 96–97.

21. Compare Baudouin van den Abeele's authoritative opinion on this matter: "D'après le *De arte venandi*, on passe une aiguille pourvue d'un fil à travers la paupière [*scil.* inférieure], en ayant soin de procéder de l'intérieur vers l'extérieur, et l'on mène le fil au-dessus de la tête, pour faire la même chose de l'autre côté; en tirant ensuite délicatement le fil, les deux paupières se lèvent, et le fil est alors noué au-dessus de la tête." This procedure, minutely described by Frederick II, is absent from all other Western treatises. Hence, Van den Abeele argues, this must be "une technique qui a sans doute été importée d'Orient. Le cillage était effectivement d'un usage courant chez les Arabes, ce qui est encore le cas. La seule autre allusion dans un texte latin figure par ailleurs dans le *Moamin*" (*La fauconnerie au moyen âge: Connaissance, affaitage et médecine des oiseaux de chasse d'après les traités latins* [Paris: Klincksieck, 1994], 126–27).

22. For other techniques on whose Arabic (or Persian) origins the emperor is more explicit in his treatise, most notably the hood (*capellum*, to which Dante once again makes specific reference in *Par.* 19.34), see Boccassini, *Il volo della mente*, 206–7.

23. We do know that Frederick II's autograph copy of the *De arte venandi* was stolen from his encampment during the siege of the city of Parma (1248), while the emperor was out in the countryside hunting with birds (ibid., 104 n. 56). Years later, a Milanese merchant approached Charles of Anjou offering him a manuscript that may have been a copy of Frederick's autograph (ibid., 113 n. 88). As for the other few extant copies of the treatise, none of them can be traced to any of the Ghibelline courts of northern Italy (ibid., 107–10), despite the fact that Frederick II's illegitimate daughter, Selvaggia, for example, was married to Ezzelino da Romano in 1236.

24. The registers of Frederick's correspondence report that in the years 1239–40 there were more than fifty falconers at his court (ibid., 104). The emperor also took in young children of noble families, so as to educate them to future administrative tasks by teaching them the art of falconry in the first place (ibid., 113–14 and n. 91).

25. I use here the term Islamic to indicate the Persian cultural tradition, the Arabic tradition, and their later synthesis.

26. Both Bartolomeo and Cangrande's wives were Frederick's grandchildren. On the Della Scala brothers, their court, and leadership see Gian Lorenzo Mellini, "Verona, la Corte sveva, l'Oriente e le origini del Gotico," *Labyrinthos* 9 (1986): 3–49; and *Gli Scaligeri, 1277–1387: Saggi e schede raccolti in occasione della mostra storico-documentaria*, ed. G. M. Varanini (Verona: Museo di Castelvecchio, 1988).

27. We owe the most recent investigations on the controversial issue of Immanuel Romano in relation to Dante to Giorgio Battistoni, "Tramiti ebraici e fonti medievali accessibili a Dante, 3: Dante nel *Paradiso* di Manoello Giudeo," *Labyrinthos* 18 (1999): 41–80; and Battistoni, *Dante e la cultura ebraica* (Florence: Giuntina, 2003).

28. Here and below I quote from Vincenzo De Bartholomaeis, *Rime giullaresche e popolari d'Italia* (Bologna: Forni, 1977).

29. Various references to Cangrande's palace as organized to shelter those persecuted by Fortuna can be found in *Gli Scaligeri, 1277–1387*. We should not forget that Cangrande himself had been condemned as heretic by the papacy. See Battistoni, *Dante e la cultura ebraica*, 132 n. 55: "In uno scritto papale del giugno 1320 si legge: 'Ut Canem de Lascala, qui . . . de pravitatis hereticae labe nec indigne suspectus habetur,' (*Vatikanische Akten* n. 199, p. 107)." From this point of view, Dante's choice of Cangrande as patron, and Cangrande's status among the blessed announced in the poem before his death, are issues loaded with ideological and political implications that Danatists often seem—or prefer—to ignore.

30. It may be useful to quote *in extenso* Umberto Bosco and Giovanni Reggio's insightful comments in their introduction to *Paradiso* 17: "I Della Scala furono sempre favorevoli a Ezzelino da Romano; alla morte di lui (1259) ne raccolse l'eredità Mastino, fondatore della fortuna della famiglia, continuandone la politica filo-imperiale; dal canto suo Cangrande fu fedele a Enrico VII sino alla morte di questo e oltre, unico, tra i signori d'Italia, a tener fede alla sua idealità imperiale al disopra dei partiti, dei particolarismi comunali e familiari (Manselli). Sono le idealità stesse di Dante, quali saranno da lì a poco ribadite e fissate nella *Monarchia*. Dato che Cangrande era il capo del ghibellinismo italiano, e che l'accusa fatta dalla Chiesa e dai Neri a Dante esule era appunto di ghibellinismo, la lode a Cangrande qui, e indirettamente nel canto IX, e la dedica del *Paradiso* sono ulteriore testimonianza del coraggio di Dante: mentre era sempre vivissimo in lui il desiderio di tornare a Firenze, e lo confermerà in uno degli ultimi canti del *Paradiso* (XXV 1–9), con questa devozione a Cangrande non esitava a tagliarsi la strada del ritorno. Ha pienamente ragione il Sansone: ben oltre che un semplice atto di grazie, l'esaltazione delle future imprese di Cangrande è 'l'atto stesso di fede di Dante nella salvezza dell'Italia, dell'Impero, del genere umano'. Ancora una volta, insomma, le considerazioni private, i personali sentimenti s'inverano nelle grandi concezioni politico-religiose" (Dante Alighieri, *La Divina Commedia*, ed. Umberto Bosco and Giovanni Reggio, 3 vols. [Florence: Le Monnier, 1979], 3:280).

31. Although the Solomonic theme may be found among Guelph rulers as well, Dante's openly pro-imperial political position obviously colors his homage to Cangrande with that imperial, Frederician, and Ghibelline hue. For further contextualization of this issue, see Boccassini, *Il volo della mente*, 427–40; and Battistoni, "Dante, l'Islam e altre considerazioni," 45.

32. For further details on this subject see Boccassini, *Il volo della mente*, 56–80.

33. On these Islamic treatises, their translation at Frederick's court, and their circulation in the West, see ibid., 96–119, with further bibliographical references.

34. Ibid., 206–7 and passim.

35. On the importance of falconry in Frederick II's understanding of the art of ruling, see ibid., 181–220.

36. Frederick II's condemnation (which, for lack of an actual encounter, effectively amounts to silencing the emperor's very voice) appears all the more harsh when we consider that Frederick's son Manfred will tell Dante the story of his providentially guided last-minute

repentance (*Purg.* 3.118–20) and that Piccarda Donati will name Frederick's mother Costanza among the blessed souls in the sphere of the Moon (*Par.* 3.118–20). A few cantos later, Dante gives Pier della Vigna a chance to spell out the earthly view of the imperial power promoted by the emperor. The limitations of that secular worldview will be the cause for the death by suicide—and, most importantly, for the lack of faith in a transcendental horizon—on the part of the emperor's most faithful secretary (*Inf.* 13.58–72). This kind of distortion in the understanding of one's own process of self-taming was critiqued by Dante's alternative soteriological reading throughout *Purgatorio*.

37. Remarkably, 'Aṭṭār dwells in particular on the importance of the seeling phase. *The Conference of the Birds*, ll. 636–45, trans. Afkham Darbandi and Dick Davis (Penguin Books, 1984), 29–30, with the following note for the cave: "A reference to the Companion of the Cave. During a period of danger the Prophet Muhammad and a close companion, Abou Bakr, hid for a while in a cave on Mount Thaur. In mystical poetry this episode became a symbol of withdrawal from the world." For a more extensive analysis of 'Aṭṭār's use of falconry in his poetry, see Boccassini, *Il volo della mente*, 290–300.

38. See http://www.ibnarabisociety.org/index.html (last accessed on January 24, 2009) for a brief introduction to Ibn al-'Arabī, sizable selections from his writings, and a large sample of critical studies on his works.

39. See Miguel Asín Palacios, *Dante e l'Islam: L'escatologia islamica nella Divina Commedia* (Parma: Pratiche, 1997), esp. 389–410, as well as Saccone's comments in *Il libro della scala di Maometto* and *Storia tematica della letteratura persiana classica*, vol. 1, *Viaggi e visioni di re, sufi, profeti* (Milan: Luni, 1999). These topics are also covered in this volume in the essays by Cantarino and Corti.

40. See Henry Corbin, *Creative Imagination in the Sufism of Ibn 'Arabi* (Princeton, NJ: Princeton University Press, 1969); and my more ample remarks in Boccassini, *Il volo della mente*, 309–19 and 372.

41. For my discussion of this episode and further bibliographical references see ibid., 372–74.

42. Ibn al-'Arabī, *L'interprète des désirs: Tarjumān al-ashwāq*, trans. M. Gloton (Paris: Albin Michel, 1996), 377. On this passage and more in general on Ibn al-'Arabī's use of falconry imagery, see Boccassini, *Il volo della mente*, 309–19.

43. For example: "How many words the world contains! But all have one meaning. When you smash the jugs, the water is one," or "The window determines how much light enters the house, even if the moon's

radiance fills the east and west," in William Chittick, *The Sufi Path of Love: The Spiritual Teachings of Rumi* (Albany: State University of New York Press. 1983), 8 and 10. It should be noted that this same perspective was cultivated by Ibn al-ʿArabī, some of whose thoughts and images run parallel to these: "If the believer understood the meaning of the saying 'the color of the water is the color of the receptacle,' he would admit the validity of all beliefs and he would recognize God in every form and in every object of faith" (*Fuṣūṣ al-ḥikam*). See Chittick's helpful remarks and further quotations in *The Sufi Path of Knowledge: Ibn al-Arabi's Metaphysics of Imagination* (Albany: State University of New York Press, 1989), 352–54.

44. The theme of the soul's return to its lost home is, of course, a Platonic and Neoplatonic one, which the writings of Avicenna had contributed to revive throughout the Mediterranean. But see one passage from the highly influential *Liber de causis* that thoroughly captures the essence of Rūmī's image of the returning falcon: "Omnis sciens qui scit essentiam suam est rediens ad essentiam suam reditione completa" ("Every knowing being which knows its own essence returns to it by way of a complete return"). Latin text cited from Pierre Magnard et al., *La demeure de l'être: Autour d'un anonyme; Étude et traduction du Liber de causis* (Paris: Vrin, 1990), 62–63, no. 124.

45. *Dīwān* 1394/14785. For this quotation and a remarkable survey of the topic, with many more examples, see Annemarie Schimmel, *The Triumphal Sun: A Study of the Works of Jalaloddin Rumi* (London: Fine Books, 1978), 117–18. See also Boccassini, *Il volo della mente*, 303–9.

46. Jalāl ad-Dīn ar-Rūmī, *Discourses of Rumi (or Fihi ma Fihi)*, based on the original translation of A. J. Arberry, ed. Doug Marman (Ames, Iowa: Omphaloskepsis, 2000), 47–49, http://www.omphaloskepsis.com /collection/descriptions/discour.html.

47. As defined by Corbin in *Corpo spirituale e terra celeste: Dall'Iran mazdeo all'Iran sciita* (Milan: Adelphi, 1986), which was originally published in French, without introduction, as *Corps spirituel et terre celeste* (Paris: Editions Buchet-Chastel, 1979). In its role as *nexus* between the intellective and the sensory worlds, the imaginal proves to be the realm most proper to the fulfillment of the human being's potential; as such it plays a crucial role in the development of a number of Islamic authors, Ibn al-ʿArabī in particular. See Chittick, *The Sufi Path of Knowledge*, esp. 112–24.

48. Moevs, *The Metaphysics of Dante's "Comedy,"* 9.

49. As Dante makes clear in his letter to Cangrande. See note 9, above.

50. Dante does not tell us how the souls who have completed their process of purgation access Paradise; there is no evidence that they need to enter earthly Paradise so as to be washed in the waters of Lethe and Eunoe, as Dante did (Statius simply helps with the ritual for the benefit of Dante, not of himself). Thanks to Statius's example and Dante's reference to his own case, it seems possible to infer that the souls must go through all terraces, although the length of their stay in each varies depending on each soul's actual predicament.

51. Dante Alighieri, *The Divine Comedy*, ed. Robert M. Durling and Ronald R. Martinez, vol. 2, *Purgatorio* (Oxford: Oxford University Press, 2003), 10.

52. "The souls who arrive on the shores of the mountain have repented their sins and have been forgiven—and they are actually now incapable of sinning, their state of grace is permanent. But most of them are still suffering from the effects of sin. In classical terms, they have brought their vices with them, and these must be corrected before they can rise to beatitude. The process of moral discipline that they must undergo is conceived partly in Aristotelian terms and is repeatedly compared to the training of falcons (see 14.143–51) or of horses (see the terminology of "spurs" and "reins" for instance, in 13.37–42)—an analogy that goes back at least as far as Plato's myth of the chariot of the soul in the *Phaedrus*." Ibid., 9–10.

53. That process of taming culminates in Vergil's famous last words to his pupil, *Purg.* 27.139–42. On Vergil's role as falconer for the hand of God, see Boccassini, *Il volo della mente*, 361–77.

54. Peter Armour, *The Door of Purgatory: A Study of Multiple Symbolism in Dante's Purgatorio* (Oxford: Clarendon Press, 1983), 137 (emphasis added).

55. Robin Kirkpatrick, *Dante: The Divine Comedy* (Cambridge: Cambridge University Press, 2004), 78–79 (emphasis added).

56. Moevs, *The Metaphysics of Dante's "Comedy,"* 8 and 9. Moevs, however, does not address the issue of how this happens; he does not discuss the nature of the purgatorial process. If, as he states, "to achieve salvation or eternal life" means "to know oneself not only as a thing in space-time, but also as one with the source of space-time. It is to awaken to oneself Christically as the *subject*, and not only the object, of experience, by voluntarily sacrificing the attachment to, or obsessive identification with, the finite," we are not told how this can be, literally, "achieved." This, I believe, is the focus of Dante's *Purgatorio* and of the transmutative process therein enacted.

57. This is the fitting word chosen by Mandelbaum, 9, to translate Dante's "la materia è sorda" (*Par.* 1.129).

DANTE'S MUḤAMMAD: PARALLELS BETWEEN ISLAM
AND ARIANISM
Maria Esposito Frank

Research for this essay was supported by a Richard Cardin Grant. An abridged version was presented at the 42nd International Congress on Medieval Studies, Kalamazoo, Michigan, May 10–13, 2007. I am grateful to Jane McAuliffe for her bibliographic suggestions and to David Burrell and John O'Malley for their comments on earlier versions of this work. I am also indebted to the anonymous readers of *Dante Studies*. Last but not least, I wish to thank Ms. Christy Bird (Interlibrary Loan Office of the University of Hartford) and Ms. Karen Lesiak (Library Director of Archbishop O'Brien Library, St. Thomas Seminary, Bloomfield, Connecticut) who made my access to many necessary texts possible and expeditious.

　　1. I base my discussion on this *locus* in the *Commedia*, where Muḥammad is unequivocally and directly presented. I do not take into account passages such as *Purgatorio* 32.130–36, where the dragon that emerges from the ground to plant his poisonous tail in the chariot was by some commentators read as an allusion to, or allegory of, Muḥammad. Allegories in the *Commedia* are numerous, central, and crucial to the poeticity/poeticness of the text, and they cannot be disregarded or downplayed; nevertheless, it is equally important to acknowledge that, in a *historical* approach to the issue, precise identifications derived from allegorical interpretations of this kind are not feasible unless they are corroborated by other, less obscure indications within the poem itself or elsewhere by its own author.

　　2. In this largely negative picture, an exceptional period followed the peak of the "Cordovan martyr movement," after the 860s, when the more extreme Christians moved north and the remaining Christians coexisted peacefully with their Muslim neighbors. In addition to works cited below, works dealing generally with Christian views of Islam or Christian responses to Islam during the Middle Ages include the following: Carl Heinrich Becker, "Christian Polemic and the Formation of Islamic Dogma," in *Muslims and Others in Early Islamic Society*, ed. Robert Hoyland (Burlington, Vt.: Ashgate, 2004); Benjamin Z. Kedar, *Crusade and Mission: European Approaches toward the Muslims* (Princeton, N.J.: Princeton University Press, 1984); Bernard Lewis, *Islam and the West* (New York: Oxford University Press, 1993); Marie Thérèse d'Alverny and Charles Burnett, *La connaissance de l'Islam dans l'Occident medieval* (Ashgate, UK: Variorum, 1994); Michael Frassetto and David R. Blanks, eds., *Western Views of Islam in Medieval and Early Modern Europe:*

Perception of Other (New York: St. Martin's Press, 1999); Sidney H. Griffith, *The Church in the Shadow of the Mosque: Christians and Muslims in the World of Islam* (Princeton, NJ: Princeton University Press, 2007).

3. María Rosa Menocal, *The Arabic Role in Medieval Literary History: A Forgotten Heritage* (Philadelphia: University of Pennsylvania Press, 1987), 115–35.

4. Sidney H. Griffith, "Comparative Religion in the Apologetics of the First Christian Arabic Theologians," in *Proceedings of the PMR Conference* 4 (1979): 63–87.

5. See, for example, John V. Tolan, *Saracens: Islam in the Medieval European Imagination* (New York: Columbia University Press, 2002).

6. Sophronios, Patriarch of Jerusalem, Christmas sermon of 634, in "Die Weihnachtspredigt des Sophronios," ed. Hermann Usener, *Rheinisches Museum* NF 41 (1886), 500–516, and *Epistola Synodica*, in *Patrologiae cursus completus, Series Graeca*, ed. J.-P. Migne, 87.3:3147–200 (hereafter *PG*). Salient passages from both texts are quoted in translation in John C. Lamoreaux, "Early Eastern Christian Responses to Islam," in *Medieval Christian Perceptions of Islam*, ed. John Victor Tolan (New York: Routledge, 1996), 3–31, esp. 14–15. For discussion, see Robert G. Hoyland, *Seeing Islam as Others Saw It* (1997; repr., Princeton, NJ: Darwin Press, 2007), 67–73; Rollin Armour Sr., *Islam, Christianity, and the West: A Troubled History* (Maryknoll, NY: Orbis Books, 2002), 40.

7. *PG* 91, 540, quoted in translation in Lamoreaux, "Early Eastern Christian Responses to Islam," 14.

8. Armour, *Islam, Christianity, and the West*, 40–41.

9. Tolan, *Saracens*, 43–44; J. C. Lamoreaux, "Early Eastern Christian Responses to Islam," 20–21.

10. Or the 101st, depending on the editions of the text. *The Disputation between a Saracen and a Christian* and *On the Heresies* are available in Greek with English translation in Daniel J. Sahas, *John of Damascus on Islam: The Heresy of the Ishmaelites* (Leiden: Brill, 1972). See also Hoyland, *Seeing Islam*, 480–90.

11. The pressure upon Heraclius by Monophysite Syrians to embrace the Monothelite heresy "rent the Church in two," as Theophanes eloquently put it: see Tolan, *Saracens*, 65.

12. Ibid., 61–63.

13. Richard William Southern, *Western Views of Islam in the Middle Ages* (Cambridge, Mass.: Harvard University Press, 1962), 17–18; Tolan, *Saracens*, 73, 130, 226; Armour, *Islam, Christianity, and the West*, 45–46.

14. Thomas E. Burman, *Religious Polemics and the Intellectual History of the Mozarabs, c. 1050–1200* (Leiden: Brill, 1994), 33–37; Tolan,

Saracens, 83–97; Armour, *Islam, Christianity, and the West*, 48–49. Paul Alvarus and Eulogius were pupils of Speraindeo, abbot of the Cordovan Basilica of St. Zoilus, who in the 820s to 830s wrote a polemical disputation against Islam, a treatise in defense of the Trinity and Incarnation, and also about two martyrs executed by Muslim authorities in the 820s.

15. Salient passages from Guibert's *Dei gesta per Francos* are discussed in Tolan, *Saracens*, 135–47, passim; Norman Daniel, *Islam and the West*, rev. ed. (Oxford: Oneworld Publications, 1993), 169; and *The Dante Encyclopedia*, s.v. "Islam and Islamic Culture." For detailed studies of the portrayals of the Prophet and Islam in popular (and learned) sources, see Sidney H. Griffith, "The Prophet Muhammad: His Scripture and His Message according to the Christian Apologies in Arabic and Syriac from the First Abbasid Century," in *La vie du Prophète Mahomet: Colloque de Strasbourg, Octobre 1980*, ed. Toufic Fahd (Paris, 1983), reprinted in *The Life of Muhammad*, ed. Uri Rubin (Aldershot: Ashgate Variorum, 1998), 345–92; and Robert G. Hoyland, "The Earliest Christian Writings on Muhammad: An Appraisal" in *The Biography of Muhammad: The Issues of the Sources*, ed. Harald Motzki, Islamic History and Civilization, Studies and Texts, vol. 32 (Leiden: Brill, 2000), 276–97. Hoyland's chapter contains a rich bibliography and includes in its discussion the controversial work by Patricia Crone and Michael Cook, *Hagarism: The Making of the Islamic World* (Cambridge, MA: Cambridge University Press, 1977).

16. Armour, *Islam, Christianity, and the West*, 80–85. All the mentioned texts concerning Islam written by Peter the Venerable are available, in the original Latin language, in James Kritzeck, *Peter the Venerable and Islam* (Princeton, NJ: Princeton University Press, 1964), which includes an analysis of all Peter's writings on Islam. With particular regard to Peter's Letter III to Bernard of Clairvaux, see Gillian R. Knight, *The Correspondence between Peter the Venerable and Bernard of Clairvaux. A Semantic and Structural Analysis* (Burlington, VT: Ashgate 2002), 144–53.

17. On William of Tripoli and his *Notitia de Machometo*, and on the *De statu Saracenorum* as well as on Riccoldo and his other writings (*Contra legem Saracenorum, Five letters on the Fall of Acre*), see Ovey N. Mohammed, *Muslim-Christian Relations: Past, Present, Future* (Maryknoll, N.Y.: Orbis Books, 1999), 47–49; Tolan, *Saracens*, 211, 245–55; Daniel, *Islam and the West*, 220–40, 291–96; and Armour, *Islam, Christianity, and the West*, 59–60, 89–92.

18. Tolan, *Saracens*, 42–43.

19. Ibid., 67.

20. Christian (Arab) texts that may not have been terribly influential but that were composed in the period Tolan singled out (the first two centuries) have been discussed in theological dissertations focusing on the main mysteries of the Christian faith (Trinity, Incarnation, Redemption through Christ), as we can see in the Arab Melkite writings recently studied by Mark Swanson, "Cross of Christ in the Earliest Arabic Melkite Apologies," and, most notably, in Samir Khalil Samir's presentation of the apology preserved in Mount Sinai, Library of the Monastery of St. Catherine, MS Sinai Arabic 154 (a late eighth- to early ninth-century manuscript), a text extremely interesting especially for its use of Qur'anic and biblical passages together. Both studies are in *Christian Arabic Apologetics during the Abbasid Period (750–1258)*, ed. Samir Khalil Samir and Jørgen S. Nielsen, Studies in the History of Religions 63 (Leiden: E. J. Brill, 1994).

21. The most relevant passage occurs in Peter's *Liber contra sectam sive haeresim Saracenorum*: "Sed utrum Mahumeticus error heresies dici debeat, et eius sectatores heretici uel aethnici uocari, non satis discerno. Video enim eos hinc hereticorum more de fide Christiana quaedam suscipere, quaedam abicere, hinc ritu pagano quod nulla unquam heresies fecisse scribitur, facere pariter et docere." (Kritzeck, *Peter the Venerable and Islam*, 227). This passage, however, is part of a complex dissertation on the definition, manifestations, and effects of heresy, which—interestingly for the specific point to be later made in my study—refers also to Arianism, although Peter does not equate the "Mohammedan error" to what he saw as the most devastating of the early heresies. For a discussion of Islam as a Christian heresy, see also Kritzeck, *Peter the Venerable and Islam*, 141–49, and *The Letters of Peter the Venerable*, ed. Giles Constable (Cambridge, Mass.: Harvard University Press, 1967), 1:274–99, esp. 294–299, and 2:275–84; and *The Correspondence between Peter the Venerable and Bernard of Clairvaux*, ed. Gillian R. Knight (Burlington, VT: Ashgate, 2002) 144–53, esp. 150. For a reading of Peter's understanding of, and response to, Islam within the larger context of Cluniac ideology, see Dominique Iogna-Prat, *Order and Exclusion: Cluny and Christendom Face Heresy, Judaism, and Islam (1000–1150)* (Ithaca, NY: Cornell University Press, 2002), esp. 343–47.

22. The explanation of the origin of a new religion as a reaction to unfulfilled expectations or ambitions had also been presented in the case of the fourth-century theologian Arius, with whom Muḥammad was linked, as discussed below.

23. For discussions of these legends, see Alessandro D'Ancona, "La leggenda di Maometto in Occidente," *Giornale storico della letteratura*

italiana 13 (1889): 199–281, later republished as A. D'Ancona, *La Leggenda di Maometto in Occidente*, ed. Andrea Borruso (Rome: Salerno, 1994); Enrico Cerulli, *Nuove ricerche sul Libro della scala e la conoscenza dell'Islam in Occidente* (Vatican: Biblioteca Apostolica Vaticana, 1972); and Paola Locatin, "Maometto negli antichi commenti alla *Commedia*," *L'Alighieri* 20 (2002): 41–75.

24. I do not include here any of the numerous denigrations of the Prophet as a lewd, lustful person (or other equally derogative character-izations and descriptions, especially concerning the death of the Prophet), because—although often included in the legend transmitted by Christian texts—these kinds of references are irrelevant to the present discussion. What is most pertinent for my argument has to do strictly and exclusively with Dante's perception of the meaning and impact of the religious message of Islam and of Muḥammad as its messenger.

25. Brenda Deen Schildgen, *Dante and the Orient* (Urbana: Univer-sity of Illinois Press, 2002), esp. chaps. 2 and 3. See also Philip F. Ken-nedy, "The Muslim Sources of Dante?" in *The Arab Influence in Medieval Europe*, ed. Dionisius Agius and Richard Hitchcock (Reading, UK: Ithaca Press, 1994), 63–82.

26. On falconry, see Daniela Boccassini, *Il volo della mente* (Ravenna: Longo, 2003), as well as her contribution to this volume. In both she considers the literary, artistic, philosophical, and spiritual implications of falconry, as cultivated in Italy thanks to the influence of Frederick II, which attracted Dante's attention. On Manfred, see Karla Mallette, "Dante e l'Islam: sul canto III del Purgatorio," *Rivista di storia e letteratura religiosa* 41, no. 1 (2006): 39–62, as well as her essay in the present collection, n. 4 and n. 42.

27. Jeffrey Burton Russell, *Dissent and Order in the Middle Ages: The Search for Legitimate Authority* (New York: Twayne Publishers, 1992), 2–3.

28. Alison Morgan, *Dante and the Medieval Other World* (Cam-bridge, MA: Cambridge University Press, 1990), esp. 108–43.

29. There is an explicit mention, by Dante the pilgrim, of Islamic architecture in the description of Dis (*Inf.* 8.68–75), which may not necessarily be understood as connected to the specific circle of the Heretics, because at that stage of the journey, Vergil and Dante are addressing the whole section of the so-called Lower Hell, which the gates enclose.

30. To the best of my knowledge, an association between Dante's Muḥammad and Arius has been unremarked in the scholarly literature. At an advanced stage of preparation of this work for publication, I

came across a lecture, published online, in which Dante's Muḥammad is indeed linked to the historical Arius in an intriguing argument that starts with references to the vegetative faculty of the soul according to the Aristotelian system, and ends with a typological interpretation of Luke 16:19–31 and other biblical passages. See Otfried Lieberknecht, "A Medieval Christian View of Islam: Dante's Encounter with Mohammed in *Inferno* XXVIII," http://www.lieberknecht.de/~diss/papers /p_moham.pdf.

31.   Iogna-Prat's reading of Peter the Venerable's treatment of Islam places Peter in the history of the demonization of the other in the West, especially referring to Peter's view of Muḥammad as an intermediate stage between Arius and the Antichrist: see *Order and Exclusion*, 356.

32.   Henry Melvill Gwatkin, *Studies of Arianism*, 2nd ed. (Eugene, OR: Wipf & Stock, 2005); Robert C. Gregg and Dennis E. Groh, *Early Arianism: a View of Salvation* (Philadelphia: Fortress Press, 1981); Rowan Williams, *Arius: Heresy and Tradition* (Grand Rapids, MI: Eerdmans, 2002); Maurice Wiles, *Archetypical Heresy: Arianism through the Centuries* (Oxford: Clarendon Press, 1996); Michel R. Barnes and Daniel H. Williams, eds., *Arianism after Arius: Essays on the Development of the Fourth Century Trinitarian Conflicts.* (Edinburgh: T&T Clark, 1993); and Daniel H. Williams, *Ambrose of Milan and the End of the Nicene-Arian Conflicts* (Oxford: Clarendon Press, 1995).

33.   Born in 298 CE in Egypt, Athanasius served as bishop of Alexandria from June 328 until his death in May 373. Despite the fact that he was driven out of his church and office five times by the powers of the Roman Empire, the people of Egypt always viewed him as their bishop.

34.   The circumstances of Arius's death are described not only in Macarius of Constantinople (*De morte Arii* 1.1.340), in a letter of Athanasius to Serapion, but also in a number of late fourth- and fifth-century *Ecclesiastical Histories* written by Rufinus of Aquileia, Socrates Scholasticus, Sozomen, and Theodoret of Cyrus.

35.   *The Panarion of Epiphanius of Salamis*, trans. Frank Williams (Leiden: Brill, 1994), 320, 331. See also *Church History of Rufinus of Aquileia*, (New York: Oxford University Press, 1997), 25 (Book 10.14), from which Sozomen's and Socrates' accounts derive. For Athanasius's account see *Athanasius: Selected Works and Letters*, ed. Philip Schaff (New York: Christian Literature Publishing Co., 1892), 565–66. One could add to the long list Ambrose, who simply repeated previous accounts. For a critical reading of the various accounts of the death of Arius, see Alice Leroy-Molinghen, "La Mort d'Arius," *Byzantion: Revue internationale des études Byzantines* 38 (1968): 105–11.

36. Thomas speaks a total of 287 lines—more than anyone but Dante, Vergil, Beatrice, and Cacciaguida. In *Paradiso* 12 Thomas lets Saint Bonaventure, a Franciscan, present the praise of the Dominican Order, to which Thomas belongs.

37. On *Paradiso* 13, see Mark Musa, *Dante's Paradise* (Bloomington: Indiana University Press, 1984), 166–67. Robert Hollander's notes on this passage provide detailed discussion of previous commentaries that include references to the sword/blade as instruments of heretics. See Dante Alighieri, *Paradiso*, trans. Robert Hollander and Jean Hollander (New York: Doubleday, 2007), 325–26.

38. Ernst Renan, Alain Le Boulluec, and Etan Kohlberg noted the demeaning, despicable circumstances that characterized the death of heretics in the Middle Ages and the fact that certain accounts of Muḥammad's death equal in fierceness those describing Arius's final hour: "Mahomet pour tout le moyen âge ecclésiastique, est un second Arius, pire que le premier," wrote Renan. Quoted in Lucien Bouvat, "Le prophète Mohammed en Europe, légende et literature," *Revue du monde musulman* 9 (1909): 264–72.

39. Among numerous works on the subject, I will limit my reference to the excellent article by Etan Kohlberg, "Western Accounts of the Death of the Prophet Muhammad," in *L'Orient dans l'histoire religieuse de l'Europe: L'invention des origins*, ed. Mohammad Ali Amir-Moezzi and John Scheid (Turnhout: Brepols, 2000), 165–95.

40. *De Consolatione* 2.4.

41. V. E. Watts, introduction to Boethius, *The Consolation of Philosophy* (1969; repr., New York: Penguin Books, 1978), 8. See also John Marenbon, *Boethius* (New York: Oxford University Press, 2003), 179–89.

42. Boethius's martyrdom is not universally accepted as such by scholars, but the issue is not relevant to the present discussion.

43. V. E. Watts, *The Consolation of Philosophy*, 15–18.

44. Williams, *Ambrose of Milan and the End of the Nicene-Arian Conflicts* (Oxford: Clarendon Press, 1995), 1.

45. Edward Said, *Orientalism* (London: Penguin Books, 1978), 68–70; Mallette, "Dante e l'Islam: sul canto III del Purgatorio," 41; Elizabeth A. Coggeshall, "Dante, Islam, and Edward Said," *Telos*, no. 139 (Summer 2007): 133–51.

46. Maria Corti, "La commedia di Dante e l'oltretomba islamico," *Belfagor* 50 (1995): 301–14, esp. 301–2, and in this volume "Dante and Islamic Culture," and Daniela Boccassini, "Falconry as a Transmutative Art: Dante, Frederick II, and Islam." In his introduction to the Italian translation (by R. Rossi Testa and Y. Tawfik) of Asín Palacios, *Dante e*

l'Islam (Parma: Pratiche, 1994), Carlo Ossola had already stressed that medieval civilizations did not draw sharp dividing lines between Mediterranean cultures.

47. Mallette, "Dante e l'Islam," 42–44.

48. *The Dante Encyclopedia*, s.v. "Islam and Islamic Culture."

49. It is a well-established fact that Manfred's contemporaries, the Pope and Charles of Anjou first among them, referred to Manfred with this epithet or called him "the Sultan of Lucera." Manfred's inclusion of Saracen troops in his army, and his tolerance of Saracen colonies in his own kingdom largely explain why he was labeled so.

50. Charles Singleton first saw "something of the martyr about [Dante's] Manfred" and his wounds, which had been inflicted by a crusading army! See Dante Alighieri, *Purgatorio*, translated with a Commentary by Charles Singleton (Princeton, NJ: Princeton University Press, 1977), 56.

MUḤAMMAD IN HELL
Karla Mallette

It is my pleasant duty to acknowledge two debts at the outset of this essay. Maria Subtelny first suggested to me the idea that Dante's Muḥammad mimed Islamic depictions of the opening of Muḥammad's chest; it is a profound pleasure to repay her insight with the philological labors reflected here. And Thomas Burman, my fellow contributor to this volume, shared with me the fruits of his own archival labors, providing the unpublished texts of the Latin translations of the Qur'an I have used herein. This paper owes a great deal both to his collegial generosity and to his exquisite research on medieval Latin translations of the Qur'an.

1. For commentaries that attribute Muḥammad's sectarianism to competition with the Pope, see, for example, Jacopo Alighieri, comment on *Inferno* 28.31–33 and Anonimo Selmiano, comment on *Inferno* 28.31–33. *L'ottimo commento* repeats the tale but denounces it as false, reporting that Muḥammad was an epileptic who claimed to communicate with an angel (also a commonplace in the commentary tradition; see comment on *Inf.* 28.22–31). The commentaries freely blend the myths reported here—that Muḥammad was a renegade Christian, motivated by lust for power (his own or Sergius's), and used doves to mimic communication with the divine. I limit myself to citation of typical examples of each in the fourteenth-century commentaries. All cited commentaries were accessed on the Dartmouth Dante Project website: http://dante.dartmouth.edu/search.php.

2. See, for example, Benvenuto da Imola, comment on *Inferno*
28.22–24; Guido da Pisa, comment on *Inferno* 28.25–27; and Francesco
da Buti, comment on *Inferno* 28.28–36. Guido da Pisa also reports in his
comment on *Inferno* 28.32–33 that 'Alī was the Saracens' name for
Sergius.

3. See, for example, Guido da Pisa, comment on *Inferno* 28.25–27;
Pietro Alighieri, comment (1340–42) on *Inferno* 28.30–31; and Codice
Cassinese, comment on *Inferno* 28.23.

4. Quoted in Longfellow's commentary on *Inferno* 28.31. Longfellow showed a remarkable sensitivity to the Muslim cultural backdrop
of the Christian Middle Ages. See, for instance, his commentary on
Purgatorio 3: he was the first since Benvenuto da Imola to point out
Manfredi's intimate knowledge of the Muslims of his kingdom, which
contributed significantly to his heterodox reputation during his lifetime
and Dante's.

5. The *lecturae* of *Inferno* 28 that I have consulted include the
following: Paola Allegretti, "Canto XXVIII," *Lectura Dantis Turicensis:
Inferno*, ed. Georges Güntert and Michelangelo Picone (Florence: Franco
Cesati, 2000), 393–406; Vincenzo Crescini, "Il canto XXVIII
dell'*Inferno*," *Letture dantesche*, ed. Giovanni Getto (Florence: Sansoni,
1971), 549–64; Enzo Esposito, *Canto XXVIII dell'Inferno* (Naples:
Loffredo, 1985); Mario Fubini, "Canto XXVIII," *Lectura Dantis Scaligera:
Inferno*, ed. Mario Marcazzan (Florence: Le Monnier, 1967), 999–1021;
Francesco Gabrieli, "Inferno XXVIII," *Letture e divagazioni dantesche*
(Bari: Edizioni del centro librario, 1965), 17–30; Anna Maria Chiavacchi
Leonardi, "Il canto XXVIII dell'*Inferno*," *L'Alighieri*, n.s., 1–2 (1993):
41–57; Giovanni Niccolai, "Il canto delle 'ombre triste smozzicate,'"
Letture dell' "Inferno," ed. Vittorio Vettori (Milan: Marzorati, 1963),
230–55; and Thomas Peterson, "Canto XXVIII: Scandal and Schism,"
Lectura Dantis: Inferno, ed. Allen Mandelbaum, Anthony Oldcorn, and
Charles Ross (Berkeley: University of California Press, 1998), 368–77.
Other works on Dante's Muḥammad and on Dante and the *Liber scale*
tradition that I have found useful—in addition to those cited below—
include Claudia Di Fonzo, "Dalla 'terza' redazione dell'*ottimo commento*
il canto di Maometto: una nuova fonte," *Studi danteschi* 46 (2001): 35–62;
Giorgio Levi della Vida, "Nuova luce sulle fonti islamiche della *Divine
Commedia*," *Al-Andalus* 14 (1949): 377–407; Paola Locatin, "Maometto
negli antichi commenti alla *Commedia*," *L'Alighieri* 20 (2002): 41–75;
Ronald L. Martinez, "Dante between Hope and Despair: The Tradition
of Lamentations in the *Divine Comedy*," *Logos* 5 (2002): 45–76; and James
Miller, "Anti-Dante: Bataille in the Ninth Bolgia," *Dante and the*

Unorthodox, ed. James Miller (Waterloo, Canada: Wilfrid Laurier University Press, 2005), 207–48.

6. Hollander, comment on *Inferno* 28.7–21.

7. In this volume, consider Maria Corti, "Dante and Islamic Culture," on interdiscursivity, and Daniela Boccassini, "Falconry as a Transmutative Art: Dante, Frederick II, and Islam," in her *recusatio* of philological technique.

8. See Vicente Cantarino, "Dante and Islam: History and Analysis of a Controversy," in this volume; Maria Corti, "La 'Commedia' di Dante e l'oltretomba islamico," *Belfagor* 50 (1995), 300–314; and Maria Corti, "Dante e la cultura islamica," *"Per correr miglior acque . . ."* *Bilanci e prospettive degli studi danteschi alle soglie del nuovo millennio* (Rome: Salerno, 2001), 183–202, translated in this volume as "Dante and Islamic Culture." For Enrico Cerulli's argument concerning Dante and the *mi'rāj* material, see the magisterial *Il "Libro della scala" e la questione delle fonti arabo-spagnole della Divina Commedia*, Studi e testi 150 (Vatican City: Biblioteca Apostolica Vaticana, 1949), and in particular the closing essay, "Dante e l'Islam: Conclusioni storiche," 503–50.

9. On all three of these figures, see in this volume José Martínez Gázquez, "Translations of the Qur'an and Other Islamic Texts before Dante (Twelfth and Thirteenth Centuries)."

10. On Riccoldo, see in this volume Thomas Burman, "How an Italian Friar Read His Arabic Qur'an."

11. *L'Ottimo commento* also mentions the Qur'an in commenting on the lustfulness of women, both Christian and Muslim (on *Purg.* 23.103–4).

12. *Surat al-Isra* (17), 1: "Glory to (Allah) Who did take His servant for a Journey by night from the Sacred Mosque to the farthest Mosque, whose precincts We did bless" (*The Holy Qur'an: Translation and Commentary*, trans. Yusuf Ali [n.p.: Islamic Propagation Centre International, 1946], 693).

13. For details on the legend in both its popular and learned incarnations, see Harris Birkeland, *The Legend of the Opening of Muhammad's Breast* (Oslo: I Kommisjon Hosjacob Dybwad, 1955). Birkeland's study considers a variety of historical sources: legends dating to the first century after the life of the Prophet, with roots in pagan belief; the Qur'an; and *tafsīr*, or Qur'anic exegesis. These distinctions, though important for understanding the evolution and variety of Islamic belief, are not directly relevant to the present discussion; thus I have not specified historical sources in my discussion or in the citations below.

14. For versions in which angels open Muḥammad's breast, see ibid., 14–18, 52–53; for versions in which birds open his breast, see 8 and 56–59.

15. For the notion that the Prophet's heart was cleansed of impurities see ibid., 10, 15–17, 53.

16. For references to the purification of Muḥammad's heart by washing it in the water of the Zamzam well, see ibid., 18–19, 24, 31, 34–37, 45–46; for a version of the legend in which Muḥammad's heart is washed in a golden bowl filled with snow, see 10.

17. This is true in particular in the case of the Qur'anic sura that refers to the opening of Muḥammad's breast, *al-Inshirah* (sura 94; see Birkeland, *The Legend of the Opening of* Muḥammad*'s Breast*, 40–47).

18. For Birkeland's discussion of the opening of the heart as a sign of or preparation for vocation, see ibid., 13–28.

19. For versions of the opening of Muḥammad's breast as preparations for the *mi'rāj* see ibid., 13–15, 19–21, 26–30.

20. For graphic physical descriptions of the opening of Muḥammad's breast, see ibid., 6–7, 55–56.

21. For Birkeland's summary of the distinctions between the popular legends of the opening of Muḥammad's breast and learned commentary on the episode, see ibid., 54–60.

22. The words *sharḥ* (opening or expansion) and *inshirah* (solace, consolation, relief) derive from the same etymological root (*sh-r-ḥ*); thus the intimate relation between the sura and the episode in the Prophet's life is immediately recognizable to a speaker of Arabic. The other Qur'anic reference to the opening of the prophet's heart is extremely fleeting. *Surat al-Zumar* ("crowds" or "throngs"; 39), 22 refers to the Prophet as "one whose heart God has opened (*sharaḥa*) to Islam." Here the presence of a single word—*sharaḥa*, the verbal form of the noun *sharḥ*—signals the reference to the *sharḥ* episode. This passage is discussed below (note 28).

23. For a discussion of the manuscript tradition, see Thomas Burman, "*Tafsir* and Translation: Traditional Arabic Qur'an Exegesis and the Latin Qur'ans of Robert of Ketton and Mark of Toledo," *Speculum* 73 (1998): 705–7.

24. Mark of Toledo, *Liber Alchorani*, Turin, Biblioteca Nazionale Universitaria, F. v. 35, fol. 83r–v: "1. Nonne adaperui cor tuum / 2. et removi a te peccatum tuum / 3. quod tibi disrupit dorsum? / 4. Et exaltavi memoriam tuam / 5. quoniam cum difficultate facultas, / 6. et difficultate facultas. / 7. Et cum adimpleveris / 8. contemplare oraque creatorem tuum[o]."

25. *Lex Mahumet* (*Machumetis Saracenorum principis, eiusque successorum vitae, doctrina, ac ipse Alcoran*, ed. Theodore Bibliander

[Basel: Ioannes Oporinus, 1550]), 1:143, ll. 41–49, with corrections from Paris, Bib. nat., MS lat. 1162, fol. 137ra.

26. The verb in this form, n-q-ḍ (*afʿala* form), means to make a creaking or cracking sound, like joints when they crack. Lane translates it thus: "The load made his back to sound by reason of its weight, or pressed heavily upon him, so that his back was heard to make a sound" (Edward William Lane, *Arabic-English Lexicon* [Beirut: Librairie du Liban], 1997, s.v. "n-q-ḍ"). It is not a common verb; Mark's somewhat exaggerated translation could result simply from the fact that he doesn't understand it, and is supplying a verb based on his own understanding of the *sharḥ* tradition and his assumption concerning what the text *should* say. Robert of Ketton, on the other hand, produces a less colorful but more accurate translation.

27. See in particular Burman, "*Tafsir* and Translation."

28. The *surat al-Zumar* (39) also makes reference to the *sharḥ* episode (see vv. 22–23). There too the Arabic verb *sharaḥa* appears (the same used in the opening verse of the *surat al-Inshirāḥ*). The basic physical meaning of *sharaḥa* is "to open or expand." The verb may also mean "to explicate," however. Mark may have chosen the verb that he uses in his translation— *explano*—with this doubled semantic range in mind (*Liber Alchorani*, cit., F. v. 35, fol. 62rb). Like the Arabic *sharaḥa*, the Latin *explano* can describe either an intellectual or a physical opening. However, the physical connotations of the Latin *explano* are a bit strong for the context. *Explano* means "to flatten, to spread flat." Again, Mark may have been attracted to a strong physical interpretation of the episode by his knowledge of the popular traditions surrounding the episode. (In contrast, Robert of Ketton used the Latin verb *aperio*, which simply means "to open," to render this verse; *Lex Mahumet*, trans. Theodore Bibliander, 1:143, ll. 41–49.)

29. See Jan M. Ziolkowski, "Introduction," in this volume.

30. "At ipse statim manum suam posuit super caput meum, ita quod ipsius manus frigiditatem in corde persensi. At mox omnem scientiam ita me docuit quod ego scivi omnes res, que fuerunt hactenus et que in posterum sunt future" (Cerulli, *Il "Libro della scala,"* 147).

31. On popular Islamic versions of the *miʿrāj* legend, see Frederick S. Colby, *Narrating Muhammad's Night Journey: Tracing the Development of the Ibn ʿAbbas Discourse* (Albany: SUNY University Press, 2008); Colby graciously answered my questions on popular *miʿrāj* narratives, and it is my pleasure to thank him here.

32. On Riccoldo's life, see Emilio Panella, "Ricerche su Riccoldo da Monte di Croce," *Archivum fratrum praedicatorum* 58 (1988): 5–85; and

Panella's introduction to the issue of *Memorie domenicane* dedicated to Riccoldo: "Presentazione," *Fede e controversia nel '300 e '500* (Pistoia: Centro riviste della provincia romana, 1986 [*Memorie domenicane*, n.s., 17 (1986)]), v–xl.

33. On the quality of Riccoldo's Arabic, see in this volume Thomas Burman, "How an Italian Friar Read His Arabic Qur'an."

34. "Tetigitque me Deus manu sua inter humeros usque adeo ut usque ad medullam spine dorsi mei manus eius frigiditas perveniret" (Cerulli, *Il "Libro della scala,"* 349).

35. The *Liber denudationis* version of the text in question reads: "Usque ad medullam spine dorsi mei manus eius frigiditas perveniret." Cited in *Contra legem Sarracenorum*, ed. J.-M. Mérigoux ("L'Ouvrage d'un frère prêcheur florentin en Orient à la fin du XIIIe siècle"), *Fede e controversia nel '300 e '500*, 66 n. 29.

36. For further information, see in this volume Brenda Deen Schildgen, "Philosophers, Theologians, and the Islamic Legacy in Dante," and Gregory B. Stone, "Dante and the *Falasifa*: Religion as Imagination."

37. See, in addition to the works by Maria Corti cited above (note 7), Julia Bolton Holloway on Dante's relations with Brunetto Latini, and in particular on Brunetto as reader of Aristotle, *Twice-Told Tales: Brunetto Latino and Dante Alighieri* (New York: Peter Lang, 1993), 217–57.

38. The only appearances of the word *risma* in Opera del Vocabolario Italiano—a database of 1849 vernacular texts of the thirteenth and fourteenth century—are this passage in the *Inferno* and the commentators' citations of the passage. See http://www.lib.uchicago.edu/efts/ARTFL/projects/OVI/, accessed February 13, 2009.

39. The early commentators refer to the meaning of the word we know today: a bundle of paper, or, in the words of Benvenuto da Imola, a rank or troop, "because one follows after the other, just like the sheets of paper in a ream" ("idest, istius ordinis, quia unus sequitur post alium, sicut folia cartarum in rismate" on *Inf.* 28.37–40). Only Guido da Pisa proposes a meaning similar to the one I am suggesting. He glosses the word *risma* with the Latin *acies* (a sharp end or point) and *cuneus* (wedge; *Inf.* 28.39). However, Dante seemed to have first-hand familiarity with the manufacture of paper. See *Convivio* 3.9, where he refers to the damp surface of a newly poured sheet of paper, before it has dried and solidified. Furthermore, earlier in the *Inferno* Dante has described a sheet of paper as it catches fire:

> come procede innanzi da l'ardore,
> per lo papiro suso, un color bruno
> che non è nero ancora e 'l bianco more.

> just as a brown color that is not yet
> black moves up before a flame
> through paper, and the white dies.
>
> (*Inf.* 25.64–66)

The early commentators disagree about the meaning of Dante's *papiro*. Some (Jacopo della Lana, Guido da Pisa, Anonimo Fiorentino, Johannes de Serravalle) interpret it to mean *carta bambagina*, or paper. Others (L'Ottimo Commento, Guglielmo Maramauro, Francesco da Buti) think it means a candle wick. And Benvenuto da Imola offers both interpretations. Paper at this time was in use in northern Italy, but its introduction was recent enough that some commentators might plausibly never have seen a piece of paper catch fire and burn. Indeed the novelty of paper makes it uniquely well-suited to Dante's poetic purposes here. *Inferno* 25 is the canto of the metamorphoses; later in the canto (94–102), he will command Lucan and Tacitus to stand down, as he will now write new, better, more *modern* metamorphoses. In sum, Dante seems to have known more than his commentators about—or taken a greater interest in—a technological innovation that had a direct impact on his life as a writer.

40. Elsewhere in the *Commedia*, of course, Dante makes fleeting references to Islam. See the Muslim celebrities in Limbo (*Inf.* 4) as well as a number of much briefer passages: Guido da Montefeltro's complaint against Pope Boniface VII for *not* crusading (*Inf.* 27.85–90); the citation of the schism of Islam in the description of the trials of the Church at the end of the *Purgatorio* (*Purg.* 32.130–135); the mention of Francis's audience with the Malik al-Kāmil (*Par.* 11.100–102); Cacciaguida's reference to his own participation in the second crusade (*Par.* 15.142–48); and, arguably, Beatrice's identification of Dante as a pilgrim on his way to Jerusalem in the context of his catechism (*Par.* 25.52–57). Brenda Deen Schildgen's description of these and other passages remains the most authoritative response to this admittedly meager bouquet (see "Dante and the Crusades," *Dante Studies* 116 [1998]: 95–125; and *Dante and the Orient* [Urbana: University of Illinois Press, 2002]).

41. "Dante's *Inferno*, Canto IV," in *Dante's Inferno: The Indiana Critical Edition*, ed. and trans. Mark Musa (Bloomington: Indiana University Press, 1995), 299–309; "Dante's Limbo: At the Margins of Orthodoxy," in *Dante and the Unorthodox: The Aesthetics of Transgression*, ed. James Miller (Waterloo [Ontario]: Wilfrid Laurier UP, 2005), 63–82; and "*Inferno* IV," *Lectura Dantis* 6 (1990): 42–53.

42. Guido da Pisa—whose account of Muḥammad is extraordinarily lengthy and detailed, and to a surprising extent accurate—reports

that Muḥammad and his armies "invaded the kingdom of Persia and the Oriental empire, all the way to Alexandria" (comment on *Inf.* 28. 25–27). (Guido is also impressed by the cleanliness of Muslims ["they often wash themselves, and especially when they are supposed to pray"] and reports on the fundaments of Islamic faith with accuracy: "praying, they confess that God is one, and that he has no equal or peer.") Echoes of Christian admiration for Arab military power can be found in Frederick II's extraordinary treatment of his Saracen warriors, whom he housed in his Muslim ghetto city, Lucera, and protected from the Pope's efforts to convert them to Christianity: see in this volume David Abulafia, "The Last Muslims in Italy." Sicilian reliance on the Saracens of Lucera as a military resource endured until the death of Manfredi; it is witnessed in the commentary tradition, which records that Manfredi rode out to the battle in which he died from Lucera (and his wife took refuge in Lucera following his death) when discussing Dante's reference to that battle in *Inferno* 28. On discussion of Lucera in the commentary tradition, see my "Insularity," in *A Faithful Sea: Religious Cultures and Identities in the Mediterranean, 1250–1750*, ed. Adnan A. Husain and Katherine E. Fleming (Oxford: Oneworld Publications, 2007), 27–46.

43. See not only *Contra legem Sarracenorum* but especially the astonishing emotional honesty of the letters on the fall of Acre: "Lettres de Ricoldo de Monte-Croce," ed. Reinhold Röhricht, *Archives de l'Orient latin* (Paris: Ernest Leroux, 1884; repr., 1978), 2:258–96. Riccoldo was an eyewitness to the Muslim defeat of the city. His letters seek the meaning of the event, and he returns obsessively, again and again, to the problem posed by the Muslim victory: does it signify that God favors the Muslims (they do not call themselves *Saracens*, Riccoldo reports, but *Muslims*, "which means *saved*" [266]) over the Christians? "They say that Lord Jesus Christ cannot help us against Muḥammad. . . . They say: 'Where is your God?' . . . And you, Lord, irreproachable in wisdom and wondrous in judgement, you gave strength to that infamous sinner, and to the most wicked Muḥammad you gave earthly sovereignty!" (266). Ricoldo's gloss on the meaning of the Muslim (it "means saved") is particularly striking. The Arabic word *muslim*, of course, means one who has *submitted* to the will of God; and Ricoldo knew this well. Why did he mistranslate the word for his (presumably non-arabophone) audience? Did he intend to gloss the subtext of the passage, rather than speak with lexical precision? Is he simply carried away with emotion (many passages in these letters give that impression); does the lapsus give voice to his rage and frustration that God has (apparently) *saved* the Muslims rather than the Christians? Ricoldo's letters on the fall of Acre, full of suggestive

language like this, demand a closer reading than they have received, particularly in light of recent scholarship on intellectual relations between Muslims and Christians in the Holy Land and in Europe.

44. Asín Palacios mentions this comment at the beginning of his notations for the year 1919 (*La escatología musulmana* [2nd edition, Madrid: Estanislao Maestre, 1943], 484) and repeats it later in a summary of the polemic (508).

MENDICANTS AND MUSLIMS IN DANTE'S FLORENCE
John Tolan

1. Nick Havely, *Dante and the Franciscans* (Cambridge: Cambridge University Press, 2004); Santa Casciani, ed., *Dante and the Franciscans* (Leiden: Brill, 2006).

2. On Dante and Arabic philosophy, see in this volume Brenda Deen Schildgen,"Philosophers, Theologians, and the Islamic Legacy in Dante," and Gregory B. Stone, "Dante and the *Falasifa*: Religion as Imagination"; on Dante and the *mi'rāj*, Vicente Cantarino, "Dante and Islam: History and Analysis of a Controversy," and Maria Corti, "Dante and Islamic Culture."

3. John Tolan, *Saint Francis and the Sultan: The Curious History of a Christian-Muslim Encounter* (Oxford: Oxford University Press, 2009).

4. On the presence of the two orders in thirteenth- and fourteenth-century Florence, see Daniel Lesnick, *Preaching in Medieval Florence: The Social World of Franciscan and Dominican Spirituality* (Athens: University of Georgia Press, 1989); and Anna Benvenuti Papi, "L'impianto mendicante in Firenze, un problema aperto," in *Les Ordres mendiants et la ville en Italie centrale (v. 1220–v. 1350): Actes de la Table Ronde (Rome, 27–28 avril)*, Mélanges de l'École française de Rome 89 (1977), 595–608.

5. Rona Goffen, *Spirituality in Conflict: Saint Francis and Giotto's Bardi Chapel* (University Park: Pennsylvania State University Press, 1988), 1. See also Alberto Busigani and Raffaello Bencini, *Le chiese di Firenze: Quartiere di Santa Croce* (Florence: Sansoni, 1982), 23–100.

6. Goffen, *Sprituality in Conflict*, 5; the text of the bull is reproduced by Busigani and Bencini, *Le chiese di Firenze*, 25.

7. For the examples of Padua and the Veneto, see Louise Bourdua, *The Franciscans and Art Patronage in Late Medieval Italy* (Cambridge: Cambridge University Press, 2004).

8. *Enciclopedia Dantesca*, s.v. "Ubertino da Casale"; Havely, *Dante and the Franciscans*, 34–37.

9. Goffen, *Sprituality in Conflict*, 6.

10. Lesnick, *Preaching in Medieval Florence*, 44–45.

11. "Ch'uno la fugge, e altro la coarta" (*Par.* 12.126). For most commentators, the conventual Matteo "flees" the rule, while the spiritual Ubertino "constricts" or "restricts" it. See Manselli, "Ubertino da Casale."

12. Havely, *Dante and the Franciscans*, chap. 3.

13. Lesnick, *Preaching in Medieval Florence*, 47–49.

14. Augustine Thompson, *Cities of God: The Religion of the Italian Communes, 1125–1325* (University Park: Pennsylvania State University Press, 2005), 421–22.

15. Lesnick, *Preaching in Medieval Florence*, 61; Havely, *Dante and the Franciscans*, 32–33; Charles Davis, "Education in Dante's Florence," *Speculum* 40 (1965): 415–35; and Davis, "The Early Collection of Books of Santa Croce in Florence," *Proceedings of the American Philosophical Society* 107 (1963): 399–414.

16. "De scientia autem est una questio: utrum scilicet scientia litterarum humanarum vel bonitas intellectus conferat ad sanctitatem anime." Silvain Piron, "Le poète et le théologien: Une rencontre dans le studium de Santa Croce," *Picenum Seraphicum: Rivista di studi storici e francescani* 19 (2000): 131.

17. "Ricoldus Penini de Monte Crucis (1267–1310), Sacerdos . . . lector in pluribus et magnis conventibus." *Necrologio di Santa Maria Novella*, ed. S. Orlandi (Florence, 1955), no. 222, as cited by Lesnick, *Preaching in Medieval Florence*, 198–207; Panella, "Ricerche su Riccoldo da Monte di Croce," *Archivum Fratrum Praedicatorum* 58 (1988): 5–85; and Tolan, *Saracens: Islam in the Medieval European Imagination* (New York: Columbia University Press, 2002), 245–54. See also Thomas Burman's article in this volume.

18. *Bullarium Franciscanum*, vol. 1 (Rome, 1759): 740; Lesnick, *Preaching in Medieval Florence*, 59–60.

19. Lesnick, *Preaching in Medieval Florence*, 59–61.

20. Thompson, *Cities of God*, 427–33.

21. Ibid., 421.

22. Ibid., 425.

23. Tolan, *Saint Francis and the Sultan*.

24. Thomas de Celano, *Vita prima*, in *Fontes Franciscani*, ed. Enrico Menstò and Stefano Brufani (Assisi: Edizioni Porziuncula, 1995); English translation in *Francis of Assisi: Early Documents*, ed. Regis Armstrong, Wayne Hellman, and William Short, vol. 1 (New York: New City Press, 2003), 231. See also Tolan, *Saint Francis and the Sultan*, chap. 3.

25. Ibid., chap. 4.

26. *Regula non bullata*, prologue 2. This principle is confirmed by Pope Nicolas III in 1279, in his bull *Exiit qui seminat*: "Hii sunt illius sancte regule professores, que evangelico fundatur eloquio, vite Christi roboratur exemplo, fondatorum militantis Ecclesie apostolorum ejus sermonibus actibusque firmatur" ("These are those professors of the holy rule, which is founded on the evangelical discourse, strengthened by the example of the life of Christ, and made firm by the sermons and deeds of His Apostles, the founders of the Church militant").

27. The passage is Matthew 10:9–10, as found in both 1C 22 and LM 3:1, but the artist indicates, in the open book that the priest holds, "Sequentia sancti evangeli secundum Lucam" (Passage of the Holy Gospel according to Luke) referring no doubt to the similar passage in Luke 10:4.

28. Thomas of Celano, *Vita prima*, 1:57.

29. Tolan, *Saint Francis and the Sultan*, chap. 1.

30. Bonaventure, *Legenda maior*, 9:9.

31. Tolan, *Saint Francis and the Sultan*, chap. 7.

32. For a discussion of the controversy around the date of the text, see the introduction to the English translation of the text in *Francis of Assisi: Early Documents*, 1:523–27.

33. For Davis, "Education," 421, Dante used Ubertino's text; Manselli, "Ubertino," says that he probably read Ubertino but notes that his narration of Francis's life is based essentially on Bonaventure.

34. On *Paradiso* 11, and in particular on Dante's portrait of Francis, see Mario Marti, "Storia e ideologia nel San Francesco di Dante," *Giornale storico della letteratura italiana* 182 (2005): 161–79; Ronald B. Herzman, "Dante and Francis," *Franciscan Studies* 42 (1982): 96–114; Kenelm Foster, "Dante and Two Friars: Paradiso XI–XII," *New Blackfriars* 66 (1985): 480–496; and Nicolò Mineo, "Il canto XI del *Paradiso*: La 'vita' di San Francesco nella 'festa di paradiso'," in Attilio Mellone, ed., *Lectura Dantis Metelliana: I primi undici canti del Paradiso* (Rome: Bulzoni, 1992), 221–320.

35. Mineo, "Il canto XI," 273–74, shows that Dante may well be here using Ubertino da Casale, *Arbor vitae cruxifixi Iesu*.

36. Erich Auerbach, "Franz von Assisi in der Komödie," in *Neue Dantestudien* (Istanbul: Ibrahim Horoz, 1944). See also Marguerite Mills Chiarenza, "Dante's Lady Poverty," *Dante Studies* 111 (1993): 153–75. The erotic nature of Francis's relation with Poverty is also present in Ubertino da Casale's *Arbor vitae cruxifixae Iesu* (see Mineo, "Il canto XI," 292–94).

37. "Solvit proinde calceamenta de pedibus." Bonaventure, *Legenda maior*, 3:4.

38. Giovanni Boccaccio, *Vita di Dante*, ed. Paolo Baldan (Bergamo: Moretti & Vitali, 2001), 93.

DANTE AND THE THREE RELIGIONS
Giorgio Battistoni

1. Miguel Asín Palacios, *La Escatología musulmana en la Divina Comedia* (Madrid: Maestre, 1919); Asín Palacios, *Islam and the Divine Comedy*, trans. and abridged by Harold Sutherland (1926; repr., London: Cass, 1968); Asín Palacios, *Dante e l'Islam*, trans. Roberto Rossi Testa and Younis Tawfik (Parma: Pratiche, 1994), 2 vols.

2. For detailed considerations of the reception or non-reception of Asín Palacios's work in Dante studies, see in this volume the essays of Vicente Cantarino, "Dante and Islam: History and Analysis of a Controversy," and Maria Corti, "Dante and Islamic Culture." The theme of Dante and Islam is also discussed in Giorgio Battistoni, "Dante, l'Islam, e altre considerazioni," *Labyrinthos* 11 (1987): 26–49.

3. See particularly Gian Lorenzo Mellini, "Verona e l'Oriente in epoca gotica," in *Le stoffe di Cangrande: Ritrovamenti e ricerche sul 300 veronese*, ed. Licisco Magagnato (Florence: Alinari, 1983), 47–71; and Francesco Arduini, "Il problema delle sete esotiche scaligere e il dato ornamentale," ibid., 197–235, as well as *Cangrande della Scala: La Morte e il corredo di un principe nel medioevo europeo*, ed. Paola Marini, Ettore Napione, and Gian Maria Varanini (Venice: Marsilio, 2004).

4. "La traduzione del versetto proposta alcuni anni or sono dal prof. M. Mazzaoui, suona pressappoco così: *gloria al nostro signore il sultano, che Allah possa perpetuare la sua fortuna*": cited in Arduini, "Il problema delle sete esotiche scaligere," 205. "Si tratta . . . di una semplice formula continuamente ripetuta che significa: *A Te (Allah) più alto onore e potere*": cited in E. J. Grube, "Il problema delle stoffe di Cangrande," in *Le stoffe di Cangrande*, 45.

5. Ugo Monneret De Villard, *Lo studio dell'Islam in Europa nel XII e nel XIII secolo*, Studi e testi 110 (Vatican: Biblioteca Apostolica Vaticana, 1944): 53–54.

6. Enrico Cerulli, *Il "Libro della scala" e la questione delle fonti arabo-spagnole della Divina Commedia*, Studi e testi 150 (Vatican: Biblioteca Apostolica Vaticana, 1949), 17 and 248.

7. *Il Libro della scala di Maometto*, trans. Roberto Rossi Testa, notes and preface by Carlo Saccone (Milan: Mondadori, 1991).

8. Fazio degli Uberti, *Il Dittamondo e le rime*, ed. Giuseppe Corsi (Bari: Laterza, 1952), 5.12.94–96.

9. Cerulli, *Il "Libro della scala,"* 355, 357.

10. For the heirs of Farinata degli Uberti—Lapo, Taddeo, and Fazio—see Battistoni, "Dante, l'Islam, e altre considerazioni," 35–36.

11. For "il bel giardino," see Jacopo da Bologna, "Nel bel zardino che l'Atice cenge," in *Poesie musicali del Trecento*, ed. Giuseppe Corsi (Bologna: Commissione per i testi di lingua, 1970), 38. For "il verziere," see Maestro Piero, "Sovra un fiume regale," in Enrico Paganuzzi, "Il 'perlaro' e l'acqua dell'Adige nei madrigali trecenteschi per le nozze di Francesco Bevilacqua e Anna Zavarise," *Atti e memorie della Accademia di Agricoltura Scienze e Lettere di Verona*, ser. 6, vol. 38 (June 6, 1987), 418. For the "fiume chiaro," see Giovanni da Firenze, "Appress'un fiume chiaro," in Paganuzzi, "Il 'perlaro,'" 418. For the idea that the Adige is the color of the "perla," see Jacopo da Bologna, "O dolce appress' un bel perlaro fiume," in Paganuzzi, "Il 'perlaro,'" 417. For "corrente," see Maestro Piero, "A l'ombra d'un perlaro," in Paganuzzi, "Il 'perlaro,'" 417.

12. Among the compositions of the Italian *Ars nova* that are recognized to have originated at Verona, there stands out a group of madrigals that sings of a most beautiful "Anna," who is associated gracefully with a "perlaro": see Paganuzzi, "Il 'perlaro,'" 413. These madrigals constitute the "Ciclo del Perlaro." The topic is treated in Battistoni, *Dante, l'Islam ed altre considerazioni*, 39–42.

13. In earlier forms of the Lombard-Venetian dialect, the "perlaro" was also called the "bagolaro," from "bagola," or berry. In Venetian dialect, however, "bagola" represents fable; further, "bagolone" is the storyteller that loiters about telling stories. Thus it seems to me that these three poet-musicians situated themselves well in the shade of this tree of *chiacchiere* (chit-chat, banter). See "Perlaro," *Grande dizionario della lingua italiana* (Turin: Unione, 1986).

14. Cited in "Perlaro," *Grande dizionario della lingua italiana*.

15. Cerulli, *Il "Libro della Scala,"* 143: "Cum ego, Machometus . . . viderim mirabilia ista magna, de quibus locutus sum vobis, . . . Gabriel et Ridohan, qui mecum erant, duxerunt me ad quemdam locum qui nominatur 'zaderat halmouta,' . . . et ostenderunt michi quamdam arborem ita magnam et tam pulcherrimam quod vix hoc possem aliquatenus enarrare. Erat enim arbor illa de unica solum perla, mirabiliter alba. Et ita eciam pulcra quod ipsius pulcritudo cunctas superabat alias, excepta pulcritudine Dei et suorum eciam angelorum. Et omnia quidem ipsius folia et flores similiter atque fructus erant maneriei ejusdem. Habebant eciam fructus sui omnes bonos sapores quos possit cor homi-

nis cogitare. Nam ad pedem ipsius arboris manabat fons quidam aque albioris et clarioris quam res ulla et super mel eciam dulcioris. Ego vero quesivi a Gabriele cujusmodi fons ille esset. At ipse respondens dixit quod erat fons qui nominatur 'Halkaufkar,' quod interpretatur: gracie fons perfecte."

16. Battistoni, *Dante, Verona e la cultura ebraica*, 79 n. 18.

17. "Hence if before one were tempted to reconcile the hypothesis of Asín Palacios with the ambassadorship of Brunetto Latini at the Castilian court of Alfonso X, now it would rather seem that with regards to the Vision of Muhammad one must look not a possible link with the Florentine Guelfs, but rather at that group of Tuscan Ghibellines who in fact had a direct interest in the possible failure of that ambassadorship." Enrico Cerulli, *Nuove ricerche sul Libro della scala e la conoscenza dell'Islam in Occidente* (Vatican: Biblioteca Vaticana Apostolica, 1972), 6. If Cerulli's statement privileges the Ghibellines, we cannot neglect to note that, whether Guelfs or Ghibellines, the Italian link with the *Liber scale Machometi* always seems to be given to the Tuscans: again, the Lombard link is ignored.

18. Asín Palacios, *Islam and the Divine Comedy*, trans. Sutherland, 255; *Dante e l'Islam*, 1:377 and 513 n. 49.

19. For the knowledge of elite Hebrew culture to which Dante would have had access, see Battistoni, *Dante, Verona e la cultura ebraica*, at 32–33, where the potential intellect is compared to the child and the active intellect to the powerful king (as described by Giuda Romano). This comparison reminds us of the hidden relationship between the "great Lombard" and the nine-year-old Cangrande in *Paradiso* 17.70–93 and verses 36–37; where the "astronomic tables" are discussed as they were developed by Ya'aqob ben Makihir Ibn Tibbon, which Dante uses in calculating the astronomical course of his journey; verses 67–68, where the *I* and the *El* spoken by Adam in *Paradiso* 26.134–38 recall the two divine attributes (*middoth*) of Mercy and Diligence (*Rigore*) that according to medieval rabbinical exegesis are inherent in the letters that comprise the name of God; and finally, verses 66–67, where one can read a declaration that Cino da Pistoia puts in the mouth of Dante, who confesses to be indebted to Manoello Giudeo for the "biting satire" (*satiro morso*) with which he punished Alessio Interminei in *Inferno* 18.112–32.

20. Henry Corbin, *L'Iran e la filosofia* (Naples: Guida, 1992), 125–26.

21. Muhammad ibn 'Abd al-Malik Ibn Ṭufayl, *Ibn Tufayl's Ḥayy Ibn Yaqzān: A Philosophical Tale Translated with Introduction and Notes*, trans. Lenn Evan Goodman (Los Angeles: Gee Tee Bee, 2003).

22. Romano, *L'Inferno e il Paradiso*, 16 n. 161.

23. Ancient traditions on the nocturnal ascensions of Isaac and the revelations shown to him by the Angels are cited in a study on the year of Redemption. See Gershom Gerhard Scholem, *Le origini della Kabbalà*, trans. Augusto Segre (Bologna: Il Mulino, 1973), 296 and 310; and Gershom Gerhard Scholem, *Le Grandi correnti della mistica ebraica*, trans. Guido Russo (Milan: Saggiatore, 1965), 129.

24. Moshe Idel, *L'esperienza mistica in Abraham Abulafia*, ed. Pierluigi Fiorini (Milan: Jaca, 1992). See also Battistoni, *Dante, Verona e la cultura ebraica*, 24–26.

25. See Dante's interesting treatment of this simoniacal pope in *Inferno* 19.31–78. On Nicholas III and Boniface VIII, see Battistoni, "Il Gran Lombardo dantesco: Corpo politico e questioni di identità," 61–64; and Battistoni, *Dante, Verona e la cultura ebraica*, 104–5.

26. For the "accademia romana," see Battistoni, *Dante, Verona e la cultura ebraica*, 39–41.

27. Ibid., 23–24.

28. Hillel Ben Shemu'el of Verona, *Sefer tagmule ha-nefesh* (Book of the Rewards of the Soul), ed. Giuseppe Sermoneta (Jerusalem: ha-Akademyah ha-le'umit ha-Yisre'elit le-mada'im, 1981), 37 and 272 (in Hebrew).

29. For the "donna cara," see Battistoni, *Dante, Verona e la cultura ebraica*, 54–57.

30. Manoello Giudeo (2000) 104–6. "Gli *hassidim* sostengono che il Messia sarebbe già nato fra noi, dopo essere comparso originaria- mente come Ciro imperatore di Persia, il Figlio dell'Uomo di cui parlano molti profeti e i Vangeli: fu lui a togliere da Babilonia gli Ebrei rinviandoli a Gerusalemme ad aspettarvi l'inizio dell'Impero." Elémire Zolla, "Le chiavi del Santo Sepolcro," *Il Sole–24 Ore*, Decem- ber 24, 2000, 29. For Roman and Florentine "novelli Babilonesi," see *Epistole* 6.8; for exiles who like Dante suffer in Babylonia, *Epistole* 7.8.

31. Romano, *L'Inferno e il Paradiso*, 3–5.

32. In this connection, see the figure of the "three rings" in Gioac- chino da Fiore, where is written, precisely, IEVE. Recall Dante, who had Adam (whose original language had been Hebrew) say: "*I* s'appellava in terra il sommo bene / onde vien la letizia che mi fascia / e *El* si chiamò poi" (*Par.* 26.134–36 "the Supreme Good from whom comes the joy that swathes me was named *I* on earth and later he was called *El*"). This theme is examined in Battistoni, *Dante, Verona e la cultura ebraica*, 67–68, 88–89 n. 52.

33. In addition, Daniel in Hebrew means "God has judged," and in the *Commedia*, Dante the poet acts as a divine judge, locating people in their temporary or permanent resting-places.

34. Regarding the analogy of "Dante-Daniel the prophet," the essay of André Pézard is helpful, "Daniel et Dante ou Les Vengeances de Dieu," *Studi danteschi* 50 (1973): 2–96. I also speak of this relationship in Battistoni, *Dante, Verona e la cultura ebraica*, 78–82.

35. Romano, *L'Inferno e il Paradiso*, 86–89.

36. Giuseppe Sermoneta, "L'incontro culturale tra ebrei e cristiani nel Medioevo e nel Rinascimento," in *Ebrei e cristiani nell'Italia medievale e moderna*, 200; Giuseppe Sermoneta, "La dottrina dell'intelletto e la "fede filosofica" di Jeudàh e Immanuel Romano," *Studi Medievali*, 3rd ser. 6.2 (1965): 21 n. 41, 22 n. 45.

37. Romano, *L'Inferno e il Paradiso*, 86.

38. Ibid., 87.

39. Ibid.

40. For Cino's lack of loyalty to the idea of the Empire, see Bruno Nardi, "Dante e il 'Buon Barbarossa,' ossia Introduzione alla 'Monarchia' di Dante," in Dante Alighieri, *Opere Minori*, ed. Domenico De Robertis and Gianfranco Contini, vol. 2 (Milan: Ricciardi, 1988), 265–69.

41. For the poems of Bosone and Manoello upon the death of Dante, see Battistoni, *Dante, Verona e la cultura ebraica*, 44–65.

42. Dante would have also been consigned to hell for Cecco d'Ascoli. See Francesco Stabili (Cecco d'Ascoli), *L'acerba*, book 1, chapter 2, lines 55–66, ed. Crespi.

43. Boccaccio, *Decameron*, Day 1, Story 3.

44. Ibid.

45. *Il Novellino*, ed. Alberto Conte (Rome: Salerno, 2001), Story 73. See also in the same edition "Fonti," 365–67.

46. Bosone da Gubbio, *L'avventuroso siciliano*, ed. Roberto Gigliucci (Rome: Bulzoni, 1989), 201–2.

47. Friedrich Niewöhner, *Veritas sive Varietas: Lessings Toleranzparabel und das Buch von den drei Bertrügern* (Heidelberg: Schneider, 1988); and Sivia Berti, ed., *Trattato dei tre impostori: La vita e lo spirito del signor Benedetto de Spinoza* (Turin: Einaudi, 1994).

48. Mario Penna, *La parabola dei tre anelli e la tolleranza nel medio evo* (Turin: Rosenberg, 1953).

49. Moshe Idel, *Cabbalà* (Florence: Giuntina, 1996), 109.

50. As to a unitary (transreligious!) vision shown by primary components of the three "laws" ("Fratelli della Purità," Ibn Paquda, San

Francesco, Ibn Arabi, Rumi, "Sufi," Dante, Manoello Giudeo), see Battistoni, *Dante, Verona e la cultura ebraica*, 17, 128–31.

51. For an encapsulation of the thought of Maimonides on the three monotheistic religions, see Friedrich Niewöhner, *Maimonides: Aufklärung und Toleranz in Mittelalter* (Heidelberg: Schneider, 1988), 34–36. Manoello Giudeo, a declared follower of Maimonides, wrote this of a single God: "A dargli un nome il nostro cuore trema e teme / poiché ogni popolo lo chiama con un nome diverso. / Noi [i Pii delle Nazioni del Mondo], dunque, diciamo sia il Suo nome quello che è. / Noi crediamo al Primo Increato e che fa vivere, / che fu, che è, che sarà" ("To give Him a name our heart trembles and fears / since every people calls Him by a different name. / We [the pious of the nations of the world], therefore, say His name is what it is. We believe in the First Uncreated and who gives life, / who was, who is, who will be"). See Romano, *L'Inferno e il Paradiso*, 85.

52. This theme is addressed in Battistoni, "Il contesto veronese e il paradigma dei 'tre anelli,'" 23–27; and in Battistoni, *Dante, Verona e la cultura ebraica*, 134–37. These "tre giri," which depart from the traditional symbology that saw the Holy Trinity as an "equilateral triangle," moreover depart from the edifying teachings of the Church Fathers as to the Holy Trinity; at any rate, they represent something quite different from a cathartically happy ending that, in closing the *Commedia*, Dante could have offered up on a silver platter, in a complete and mimetic doctrinal acquiescence, to his Christian readers.

53. Richard Kay, "L'Astrologia di Dante," in *Dante e la scienza*, ed. Patrick Boyde and Vittorio Russo (Ravenna: Longo, 1995), 132: "perché abbiamo sempre saputo che Dante cercava di riconciliare ragione e rivelazione e di dare a ciascuna ciò che ad essa era dovuto. Non è quindi per niente sorprendente accorgersi che Dante cerca di scoprire il volere di Dio attraverso le stelle mentre è guidato in questo sforzo razionale dalla rivelazione cristiana."

54. Christopher Ryan treats the theme of "Nature and/or Grace" in Dante, Saint Thomas, and Sigieri in "'Natura dividitur contro Gratiam': concetti diversi della Natura in Dante e nella cultura filosofico-teologica medievale," in *Dante e la scienza*, 363–73.

55. *Paradiso* 10.1–27.

56. Salvatore Battaglia, "*L'umano e il divino nell'ultimo canto del 'Paradiso,'*" in *Esemplarità e antagonismo nel Pensiero di Dante*, 2 vols. (Naples: Liguori, 1974–75), vol. 1, 213: "Dante continua a pensare l'essenza divina sul fondamento razionale. Il suo Dio può essere accettato non tanto dai credenti, quanto a più ragione dai filosofi, da chi si è educato al pensiero di Platone e di Aristotele e di Cicerone."

57. Cited in Georges C. Anawati, *Islam et christianisme: La rencontre de deux cultures en Occidente au moyen âge* (Ciaor: Institut Dominicain d'Études Orientales, 1991); trans. Eugenia Fera, *Islam e cristianesimo: L'incontro tra due culture nell'Occidente medievale* (Milan: Vita e Pensiero, 1994), 50–51. For the philosophical-scientific adherence to truths of faith, see Battistoni, *Dante, Verona e la cultura ebraica*, 135–37.

58. Gian Luca Podestà, *Il tempo dell'Apocalisse: Vita di Gioacchino da Fiore* (Rome: Laterza, 2004), 134–35, 225–26.

59. Regarding the astronomical sources used by Dante in *Paradiso* 1–22, Kay, "L'Astrologia di Dante," 126, specifies the following percentages: Michael Scot, 26 percent; Guido Bonatti, 15 percent; Alcabizio, 13 percent; Ibn Ezra, 13 percent; and so forth.

THE LAST MUSLIMS IN ITALY
David Abulafia

1. Taking advantage of my more recent research, this article reconsiders points about the status of the Luceran Muslims made in my earlier "Monarchs and Minorities in the Christian Western Mediterranean around 1300: Lucera and its Analogues," in *Christendom and its Discontents: Exclusion, Persecution and Rebellion, 1000–1500*, ed. Scott L. Waugh and Peter D. Diehl (Cambridge: Cambridge University Press, 1996), 234–63, reprinted in David Abulafia, *Mediterranean Encounters, Economic, Religious, Political, 1100–1550* (Aldershot: Ashgate, 2000), essay 13; also, more briefly, in Abulafia, "La Caduta di Lucera nel 1300," in *Per la storia del mezzogiorno medievale e moderno: Studi in memoria di Iole Mazzoleni*, Pubblicazioni degli Archivi di Stato 48 (1998), 1:171–86.

2. Jean-Marie Martin, "La Colonie sarrasine de Lucera et son environnement: Quelques réflexions," in *Mediterraneo medievale: Scritti in onore di Francesco Giunta* (Soveria Mannelli: Rubbettino, 1989), 2:795–811. See also Julie Taylor, *Muslims in Medieval Italy: The Colony at Lucera* (Lanham, MD: Lexington, 2003), which, however, fails to develop the concept of the Lucerans as *servi camere*. G. Staccioli and M. Caesar, *L'ultima città musulmana: Lucera* (Bari: Carattere Mobili, 2012) appeared after the completion of this article.

3. "A Letter Concerning the Sicilian Tragedy to Peter, Treasurer of the Church of Palermo," in *The History of the Tyrants of Sicily by "Hugo Falcandus," 1154–69*, ed. Graham A. Loud and Thomas Wiedemann (Manchester: Manchester University Press, 1998), 254–55.

4. David Abulafia, "The Kingdom of Sicily and the Origins of the Political Crusades," in *Società, Istituzioni, Spiritualità nell'Europa*

medievale: Studi in onore di Cinzio Violante (Spoleto: Centro italiano di studi sull'alto Medioevo, 1994), 69–70, reprinted in Abulafia, *Mediterranean Encounters*, essay 11.

5. Robert I. Burns, Paul Chevedden, and Míkel de Epalza, *Negotiating Cultures: Bilingual Surrender Treaties in Muslim-Christian Spain under James the Conqueror* (Leiden: Brill, 1999).

6. Charles Dalli, *Malta: The Medieval Millennium* (Malta: Midsea, 2006), 101–17.

7. Taylor, *Muslims in Medieval Italy*, 100–2.

8. David Abulafia, "Ethnic Variety and its Implications: Frederick II's Relations with Jews and Muslims," in *Intellectual Life at the Court of Frederick II Hohenstaufen*, ed. William Tronzo, Studies in the History of Art 44 (Washington, DC: Center for Advanced Study in the Visual Arts, National Gallery of Art, 1994), 218–20, reprinted in David Abulafia, *Mediterranean Encounters*, essay 12.

9. David Abulafia, "The Italian Other: Greeks, Muslims and Jews," in Abulafia, ed., *Italy in the Central Middle Ages, c. 1000–1300* (Oxford: Oxford University Press, 2004), 215–36.

10. Dalli, *Malta*, 102; Taylor, *Muslims in Medieval Italy*, 37–38.

11. Taylor, *Muslims in Medieval Italy*, 191.

12. Jean-Louis-Alphonse Huillard-Bréholles, *Historia diplomatica Friderici Secundi*, vol. 4 (Paris: Henricus Plon, 1855), 452. For additional information on Gregory IX and the Dominicans, see John Tolan, "Mendicants and Muslims in Dante's Florence" in this volume.

13. James M. Powell, "The Papacy and the Muslim Frontier," in *Muslims under Latin Rule, 1100–1300*, ed. Powell (Princeton, NJ: Princeton University Press, 1990), 195.

14. Pietro Egidi, ed., *Codice diplomatico dei saraceni di Lucera* (Naples: L. Pierro & figlio, 1917), nos. 98 and 100; Abulafia, "Monarchs and Minorities," 242.

15. Huillard-Bréholles, *Historia diplomatica Friderici Secundi*, 4:831. See also Powell, "The Papacy and the Muslim Frontier," 196.

16. Taylor, *Muslims in Medieval Italy*, 71, 206.

17. Abulafia, "The Kingdom of Sicily," 219.

18. Martin, "La Colonie sarrasine de Lucera," 797–810.

19. Taylor, *Muslims in Medieval Italy*, 42–43.

20. Ibid., 102–11.

21. Huillard-Bréholles, *Historia diplomatica Friderici Secundi*, vol. 5 (1857), 680–81; Christoph T. Maier, "Crusade and Rhetoric Against the Muslim Colony of Lucera: Eudes of Châteauroux's *Sermones de rebellione*

sarracenorum Lucerie in Apulia," *Journal of Medieval History* 21 (1995): 342–85; Norman Housley, *The Italian Crusades: The Papal-Angevin Alliance and the Crusades against Christian Lay Powers, 1254–1343* (Oxford: Oxford University Press, 1982), 65.

22. Taylor, *Muslims in Medieval Italy*, 154–57.

23. Raffaeli Castielli, "Saggio storico culturale," in *Storia e cultura dei francoprovenzali di Colle e Faeto*, ed. Armistizio Mateo Melilli (Manfredonia: Atlantica, 1978), 7–21; Dieter Kattenbusch, *Das Frankoprovenzalische in Süditalien: Studien zur synchronischen und diachronischen Dialektologie*, Tübinger Beiträge zur Linguistik 176 (Tübingen: Narr, 1982).

24. Taylor, *Muslims in Medieval Italy*.

25. David Abulafia, "The Servitude of Jews and Muslims in the Medieval Mediterranean," in *La Servitude dans les pays de la Méditerranée occidentale chrétienne au XIIe siècle et au-delà: Déclinante ou renouvelée?* Mélanges de l'École française de Rome: Moyen Âge, Temps Modernes, 112 (2000), 687–714.

26. David Abulafia, "*Nam iudei servi regis sunt et semper fisco regio deputati*: Los judios en el fuero de Teruel (1176–7)," *XVII Congreso de Historia de la Corona de Aragón* (Barcelona: Publicacions Universitat de Barcelona, 2003), 2:1–10.

27. Shlomo Simonsohn, *The Jews in Sicily* (Leiden: Brill, 1997), vol. 1, no. 214; Bartolomeo Lagumina and Giuseppe Lagumina, *Codice diplomatico dei giudei di Sicilia*, vol. 1 (Palermo: Amenta, 1884), 27–28; Giuseppe Silvestri, *De rebus regni Siciliae: Documenti inediti estratti dall'Archivio della Corona d'Aragona* (Palermo: Tipografia del giornale "Lo Statuto," 1882–92), 514–15; David Abulafia, "The First *servi camere regie* in Sicily," in Giancarlo Andenna and Hubert Houben, eds., *Mediterraneo, Mezzogiorno, Europa: Studi in onore di Cosimo Damiano Fonseca*, vol. 1 (Bari: Adda, 2004), 1–13.

28. David Abulafia, *Frederick II: A Medieval Emperor*, 3rd ed. (London: Pimlico, 2002), 336–37.

29. Simonsohn, *The Jews in Sicily*, no. 209 (cf. no. 206) (dating to 1215).

30. Ibid., no. 212.

31. Ibid., no. 213; J. Aronius, *Regesten zur Geschichte der Juden im fränkischen und deutschen Reiche bis zum Jahre 1273* (Berlin: Simion, 1902), no. 498; discussed in Abulafia, *Mediterranean Encounters*, 695: "Judeos autem, etsi tam in imperio quam in regno nobis communi iure immediate subiaceant, a nulla tamen ecclesia abstulimus que super eis ius speciale pretenderet."

32. Gaetano Carcani, ed., "Registrum Friderici II," in *Constitutiones regni Siciliae* (Naples: Regia Typographia, 1786), reprinted, with introduction, in Andrea Romano, *Monumenta Juridica Siciliana*, vol. 1 (Messina: Siciana, 1992), 416a: "De mandato domini Iohannis Mauri scripsit Iohannes de Idronto, Alexandro filio Enrici, ut Abdolla servo Camere qui mictitur ad discendum legere et scribere licteras saracenicas det expensas ad requisitionem Magistri Iohachim, ex quo pervenerit ad eum, et cum eo morabitur." Carcani's careful transcription of the register formerly in the Naples archives should always be used in preference to the edition in Huillard-Bréholles, *Historia diplomatica Friderici Secundi*.

33. Jeremy Johns, *Arabic Administration in Norman Sicily: The Royal Dīwān* (Cambridge: Cambridge University Press, 2003), 244–45, with the relevant texts, though I see no evidence that Joachim was a Jew—the name was found among Greek and Latin Christians.

34. A second reference in the register of Frederick II to a certain "Abdolla servo nostro Tarrasiatori" apparently concerns a different individual, one of a group of artisans performing *servitia nostra* in Apulia, craftsmen working with tiles or even mosaics. This Abdolla is described, however, as *servo nostro*, though without the additional word *camere*. Carcani, "Registrum Friderici II," 398a.

35. Dalli, *Malta*, 105–11.

36. Notarial act printed in the collection by Robert S. Lopez and Irving W. Raymond, *Medieval Trade in the Mediterranean World*, 2nd ed. (New York: Columbia University Press, 1990), 116.

37. Dalli, *Malta*, 112.

38. Of the massive bibliography for Iberia, see in particular John Boswell, *The Royal Treasure: Muslim Communities under the Crown of Aragon in the Fourteenth Century* (New Haven, Conn.: Yale University Press, 1977); and Elena Lourie, *Crusade and Colonisation: Muslims, Christians and Jews in Medieval Aragon* (Aldershot: Variorum, 1990).

39. Egidi, *Codice diplomatico dei saraceni di Lucera*, nos. 58 and 142; Abulafia, "Monarchs and Minorities," 238.

40. Abulafia, "Monarchs and Minorities," and also Abulafia, "La Caduta di Lucera nel 1300." The classic work is Pietro Egidi, "La Colonia saracena di Lucera e la sua distruzione," *Archivio storico per le provincie napoletane* 36 (1912): 597–694; 37 (1912): 71–89, 664–96; 38 (1913): 115–44, 681–707; 39 (1914), 132–71, 697–766; and his invaluable *Codice diplomatico dei saraceni di Lucera*, cited above.

41. Taylor, *Muslims in Medieval Italy*, 184.

42. Ibid., 67.

43. David Abulafia, *A Mediterranean Emporium: The Catalan Kingdom of Majorca* (Cambridge: Cambridge University Press, 1994), 59–64; Abulafi, "Monarchs and Minorities," 246–49; Henri Bresc, "L'Esclavage dans le monde méditerranéen des XIVe et XVe siècles: Problèmes politiques, réligieux et morales," *XIII Congrès d'Història de la Corona d'Aragó*, vol. 1 (Palma de Mallorca: Institut d'Estudis Baleàrics, 1989), 89–102; Elena Lourie, "La Colonización cristiana de Menorca durante el reinado de Alfonso III 'el Liberal,' rey de Aragón," *Analecta Sacra Tarraconensia* 53, no. 4 (1983): 135–86; Lourie, *Crusade and Colonisation*, essays 6 and 7.

44. Abulafia, "Monarchs and Minorities," 249–57. For Anjou, see Robert Chazan, *Medieval Jewry in Northern France: A Political and Social History* (Baltimore, Md.: Johns Hopkins University Press, 1973), 184–86; and William Chester Jordan, *The French Monarchy and the Jews from Philip Augustus to the Last Capetians* (Philadelphia: University of Pennsylvania Press, 1989), 181–82. For southern Italy, see Nicola Ferorelli, *Gli ebrei nell'Italia meridionale dall'età romana al secolo XVIII*, ed. Filena Patroni Griffi (Naples: Dick Peerson, 1990); Moshe David Cassuto, "Hurban ha-Yeshivot be-Italyah ha-deromit ba-Me'ah ha-13," in *Studies in Memory of Asher Gulak and Samuel Klein* (Jerusalem: Hebrew University Press, 1942), 139–52; and Joshua Starr, "The Mass Conversion of Jews in Southern Italy (1290–93)," *Speculum* 21 (1946): 203–11.

45. No credence should be given to the views of Ariel Toaff, *Pasque di sangue*, 1st ed. (Bologna: Mulino, 2007) on this. See David Abulafia, "Blood Libels are Back," *Times Literary Supplement*, February 28, 2007.

46. Abulafia, "Monarchs and Minorities," 254. See also Taylor, *Muslims in Medieval Italy*, 174–77, 179, and 184, though she makes virtually nothing of the Jewish dimension.

47. Egidi, *Codice diplomatico dei saraceni di Lucera*, nos. 323, 324, 325, 611, 654, 655 (my translation).

48. Egidi, "Colonia saracena," 697; Housley, *The Italian Crusades*, 243. See also Abulafia, "Monarchs and Minorities," 240; Taylor, *Muslims in Medieval Italy*, 183–87.

49. Riccardo Bevere, "Ancora sulla causa della distruzione della colonia saracena di Lucera," *Archivio storico per le provincie napoletane* 60, n.s., 21 (1935): 222–28.

50. Taylor, *Muslims in Medieval Italy*, 183; Egidi, *Codice diplomatico dei saraceni di Lucera*, nos. 475, 548.

51. Peter Spufford, *Handbook of Medieval Exchange* (London: Royal Historical Society, 1986), 66: price of a Sicilian ounce in Genoese *solidi*

(72s) in Sicily, 1287; however, these rates do not allow for hidden interest and exchange fees.

52. David Abulafia, "Le attività economiche degli ebrei siciliani attorno al 1300," *Italia judaica: Gli ebrei in Sicilia sino all'espulsione del 1492*, Atti del V Convegno internazionale, Palermo, 15–19 giugno 1992 (Rome: Ministero per i beni culturali e ambientali, Ufficio centrale per i beni archivistici, 1995), 91–92, reprinted in Abulafia, *Mediterranean Encounters*, essay 14.

53. Egidi, *Codice diplomatico dei saraceni di Lucera*, nos. 320–21; for 'Abd al-'Azīz, see no. 443 and nos. 206, 242, and 323; Taylor, *Muslims in Medieval Italy*, 181.

54. Egidi, *Codice diplomatico dei saraceni di Lucera*, 470.

Bibliography

Al Sabaileh, Amer. "Between Sanctity and Liberty." *Doctor Virtualis* 12 (2013): 75–87.

Baccaro, Sabina. "Dante e l'Islam: La ripresa del dibattito storiografico sugli studi di Asin Palacios." *Doctor Virtualis* 12 (2013): 13–22.

Celli, Andrea. *Dante e l'Oriente: le fonti islamiche nella storiografia novecentesca.* Biblioteca medievale: Saggi 30. Rome: Carocci, 2013.

———. "Gli studi di Enrico Cerulli su Dante." *Doctor Virtualis* 12 (2013): 35–73.

Colby, Frederick S. "A Thirteenth Century Composite Account of Muhammad's Visit to Paradise." *Doctor Virtualis* 12 (2013): 169–189.

Curatola, Giovanni, ed. *Dante e l'Islam: incontri di civiltà.* Milan: Biblioteca di via Senato, 2010.

Dar, Bilquees. "Influence of Islam on Dante's Divine Comedy." *International Journal of English and Literature* 3 (2013): 165–168.

Di Cesare, Michelina. *The Pseudo-historical Image of the Prophet Muhammad in Medieval Latin Literature: A Repertory.* Studien zur Geschichte und Kultur des islamischen Orients 2. Berlin and Boston: De Gruyter, 2011.

Forte, Francesca. "Introduzione." *Doctor Virtualis* 12 (2013): 5–11.

Hede, Jesper. "Jews and Muslims in Dante's Vision." *European Review* 16 (2008): 101–114.

Longoni, Anna, ed. *Il libro della scala de Maometto.* Milan: Rizzoli, 2013.

Marín Guzmán, Roberto. "Sobre Dante y el Islam." *Estudios de Asia y África* 45 (2010): 757–770.

Martelli, Anna Maria. "Il viaggio oltremondano del Profeta nell'iconografia musulmana." *Doctor Virtualis* 12 (2013): 89–115.

Ossola, Carlo. "Introduction" in *Dante e l'Islam: Escatología musulmana en la Divina comedia*, ed. Miguel Asín Palacios, trans. Roberto Rossi Testa and Younis Tawfik. Nuove edizioni tascabili 221. Milan: NET, 2005, pp. vii–xxvii.

Piccoli, Maria. "Le visiones occidentali anteriori alla Commedia e la tradizione dell'Isra' wa' l Mi'râj. Intertestualità o poligenesi?" *Doctor Virtualis* 12 (2013): 191–241.

Pucciarelli, Valeria. *Dante e l'Islam: la controversia sulle fonti escatologiche musulmane della Divina Commedia.* Al-Qantara 4. San Demetrio Corone (Cosenza, Italy): Irfan, 2012.

Resconi, Stefano. "Maometto personaggio nel contesto." *Doctor Virtualis* 12 (2013): 243–278.

Shalem, Avinoam, ed. *Constructing the Image of Muhammad in Europe.* Berlin and Boston: De Gruyter, 2013.

Stella, Federico. "La prigionia e la salvezza dell'anima da Avicenna a Suhrawardî: quali fonti?" *Doctor Virtualis* 12 (2013): 117–133.

Stone, Gregory B. "Dante's *Commedia*, Islamic Rationalism, and the Enumeration of the Sciences." *Doctor Virtualis* 12 (2013): 135–167.

Contributors

DAVID ABULAFIA is Professor of Mediterranean History at Cambridge University. His books include *The Two Italies* (1977); *Frederick II* (1988); *The Western Mediterranean Kingdoms* (1997); *The Discovery of Mankind* (2008); and most recently, *The Great Sea: A Human History of the Mediterranean* (2011), all of which have been translated into Italian. He is a Fellow of the British Academy, which awarded him the British Academy Medal in 2013 for *The Great Sea* and his work on Mediterranean history.

GIORGIO BATTISTONI has published extensively on Dante, particularly on Dante's debt to Jewish writers such as Immanuel of Rome—and theirs to him. His scholarship has made widely known the homage to Dante in Immanuel's Hebrew *Mahberet of Inferno and Paradise*. Battistoni sets the relationship between Dante and Immanuel within a Veronan context. More important, he emphasizes how Dante studies was retarded by the rise of Italian fascism, which impeded acknowledgment of Muslim (and Jewish) influences.

DANIELA BOCCASSINI is Professor of Italian at the University of British Columbia. Her research focuses on the human quest for understanding and the esoteric, heretic, exilic dimensions of existence through which such a quest demands to be carried out in order to survive normalization. Among her most recent publications are *Il volo della mente. Falconeria e Sofia nel mondo mediterraneo* (2003); *Dreams and Visions in the Indo-Mediterranean World* (2009); and *Transmutatio, the Hermetic Way to Happiness* (2012).

THOMAS E. BURMAN is Distinguished Professor of the Humanities at the University of Tennessee, and is the author of *Religious Polemic and the Intellectual History of the Mozarabs, 1050–1200* (1994) and *Reading the Qur'ān in Latin Christendom, 1040–1560* (2007), winner of the Jacques

Barzun Prize for Cultural History. He has been a fellow of the Rockefeller Foundation (1992–1993) and the National Endowment for the Humanities (2002–2003, 2013–2014).

VICENTE CANTARINO is professor emeritus of Iberian studies at the Ohio State University. His areas of expertise encompass primarily medieval Spanish literature, medieval philosophy, and Arabic thought. His scholarship includes analyses of both medieval Iberian Christian and Muslim literature, and relevant books by him include *Arabic Poetics in the Golden Ages: Selection of Texts Accompanied by a Preliminary Study* (1975), and *Entre monjes y musulmanes: El conflicto que fue Espania* (1978).

MARIA CORTI (1915–2002) taught in secondary schools for much of her career, until she attained belatedly a secure position at the University of Pavia in 1964, where she remained for more than twenty years. A philologist and historian of the Italian language by training, she ranged broadly in her subsequent intellectual interests and productions (including several novels). She deserves especial note for applying semiotics to literary interpretation, and for her sustained passion for Dante.

MARIA ESPOSITO FRANK is the author of a book on Renaissance Humanism, *Le insidie dell'allegoria: Ermolao Barbaro il Vecchio e la lezione degli Antichi* (1999), and various essays on L. B. Alberti's *Theogenius*, Dante's *Paradiso* 2, Dante's *Monarchia*, fifteenth-century demonology, and Machiavelli, as well as articles on contemporary Italian poetry. She also coedited *The Translator as Mediator of Cultures* (2010). Her current project is a book titled *Boccaccio's Jews*.

KARLA MALLETTE studies medieval Mediterranean literature, especially Italian and Arabic. She is author of *The Kingdom of Sicily, 1100–1250: A Literary History* (2005) and *European Modernity and the Arab Mediterranean* (2010) and co-editor with Suzanne Akbari of *A Sea of Languages: Rethinking the Arabic Role in Medieval Literary History* (2013). She is Professor of Italian and Near Eastern Studies at the University of Michigan.

JOSÉ MARTÍNEZ GÁZQUEZ is professor emeritus of Latin philology at the Universitat Autònoma de Barcelona, with special emphasis on Medieval Latin. He has produced countless contributions to our understanding of the reception and perception of Islam within Christian Europe. A particular focus of his has been the edition of Latin translations of Arabic texts, ranging from the Qur'an to scientific and technical literature.

BRENDA DEEN SCHILDGEN, Distinguished Professor of Comparative Literature, 2008 recipient of the UC Davis Prize for Undergraduate Teaching and Scholarly Achievement, is a recipient of NEH, PEW, and National Center for the Humanities fellowships. Among her books are *Divine Providence, A History: Bible, Virgil, Orosius, Augustine, and Dante* (2012); *Heritage or Heresy: Destruction and Preservation of Art and Architecture in Europe* (2008); *Dante and the Orient* (2002); *Power and Prejudice: The Reception of the Gospel of Mark* (1999).

GREGORY B. STONE is Joseph S. Yenni Memorial Professor of Italian Studies and Professor of French and Comparative Literature at Louisiana State University. His writings on Dante include *Dante's Pluralism and the Islamic Philosophy of Religion* (2006). He is currently completing a book-length study of Guido Cavalcanti's "Donna me prega," aiming to situate that canzone in the tradition of Arabo-Islamic philosophy and Radical Aristotelianism.

JOHN V. TOLAN works on the history of religious and cultural relations between Europe and the Arab world. He received a BA in Classics from Yale and an MA and a PhD in History from the University of Chicago. He has taught and lectured in universities in North America, Europe, Africa, and the Middle East, and is now Professor of History at the University of Nantes (France) and a member of the Academia Europaea. He is director of a major project funded by the European Research Council, "RELMIN: The legal status of religious minorities in the Euro-Mediterranean world (5th–15th centuries)" (www.relmin.eu). He is the author of many books and articles.

JAN M. ZIOLKOWSKI is Arthur Kingsley Porter Professor of Medieval Latin at Harvard University, and Director of Dumbarton Oaks Research Library and Collection. His research into the Latin Middle Ages has concentrated on the classical tradition, especially Virgil (*The Virgilian Tradition: The First Fifteen Hundred Years* and *The Virgil Encyclopedia*); the grammatical and rhetorical traditions; and the relationship of folktales and vernacular epics with Latin. In Dante scholarship an edited volume on *Dante and the Greeks* is in press.

Index of References to Dante's Major Works

General Index

9/11, 13

'Abbasids, 142, 160
'Abd al-'Azīz (Adelasisius), 245, 248
'Abd Allah (Abdolla; *servus*), 243–45
Abeele, Baudouin van den, 309n21
Abraham (biblical patriarch), 20, 60, 81,
    83, 285–86n15, 287n24
Abraham Abulafia, 222, 229
Abraham Alfaquím, 10, 39, 55, 216
Abū al-'Ala' al-Ma'arri, 9, 44
Abū Ḥāmīd Muḥammad ibn
    Muḥammad al-Ṭūsī al-Ghazālī.
    See al-Ghazālī, *under* G
Abū Ma'shar (Albumasar; Ja'far ibn
    Muḥammad al-Balkhī), 21–22
Abū Qurrah (Theodore of Carra), 162
Abū Ṭālib, 168
Abubacer (Ibn Ṭufayl), 104, 117, 122, 221
Abulafia, David, 3, 27, 235, 347
Acre, 17, 329–30n43
Active Intellect, 116, 119, 131,
    297–98nn6–8, 299n13, 335n19
Adelasisius ('Abd al-'Azīz), 245, 248
Aeneid (Vergil), 12, 48, 52
Aeschylus, *Agamemnon*, 48, 275n11
affaire Gouguenheim, 26
Albertus Magnus, 22, 25, 53, 103,
    109–12, 116, 118, 120, 298n8,
    299–300nn13–14, 301n21
Albumasar (Abū Ma'shar; Ja'far ibn
    Muḥammad al-Balkhī), 21–22

alchemy, 19, 27, 213
Alchoran, id est, collectio preceptorum, 68
Alchoranus Latinus (*Liber Alchorani*;
    Mark of Toledo), 73–77, 79, 84–85,
    89–91, 181–83, 186, 189, 285n12,
    326n26, 326n28
Alemparte, Jaime Ferreiro, "Hermann
    el Alemán," 276n24
Alessio Interminei, 228, 335n19
Alexandria, Synod of, 170
Alfarabio/Alfarabius (al-Fārābī).
    See al-Fārābī, *under* F
Alfonso III (king of Aragon), 246
Alfonso V the Magnanimous (king of
    Sicily and Naples), 240
Alfonso X the Wise (king of Castile),
    10–11, 26, 35, 39, 45, 77, 216, 335n17;
    General estoria, 51–52; *Setenario*, 53
Ali ('Alī), 19, 21, 22–23, 26, 67, 112,
    166–67, 169, 176, 213, 323n2
allegory: Albertus Magnus and, 110–11;
    Arabic-Latin cultural transmission
    and, 49, 50, 52; ascension stories,
    mystical-allegorical, 34, 221, 233–34,
    336n23; Asín Palacios's theorem and,
    34, 36, 37, 41, 269n37; Bonaventure's
    use of, 109–10, 111, 112; *Commedia*,
    basic allegory of, 298n8; Dante's use
    of, 95, 100–3, 111, 120, 173; door of
    Purgatory as allegory of sacrament
    of penance, 151; dragon in *Purgatorio*
    as allegory for Muḥammad, 315n1;